AF701985

Digital Witness

Digital Witness

Using Open Source Information for Human Rights Investigation, Documentation, and Accountability

Edited by

SAM DUBBERLEY

ALEXA KOENIG

DARAGH MURRAY

OXFORD
UNIVERSITY PRESS

OXFORD
UNIVERSITY PRESS

Great Clarendon Street, Oxford, OX2 6DP,
United Kingdom

Oxford University Press is a department of the University of Oxford.
It furthers the University's objective of excellence in research, scholarship,
and education by publishing worldwide. Oxford is a registered trade mark of
Oxford University Press in the UK and in certain other countries

© The Several Contributors 2020

The moral rights of the authors have been asserted

First Edition published in 2020
Impression: 1

All rights reserved. No part of this publication may be reproduced, stored in a retrieval system, or transmitted, in any form or by any means, without the prior permission in writing of Oxford University Press, or as expressly permitted by law, by licence or under terms agreed with the appropriate reprographics rights organization. Enquiries concerning reproduction outside the scope of the above should be sent to the Rights Department, Oxford University Press, at the address above

You must not circulate this work in any other form
and you must impose this same condition on any acquirer

Crown copyright material is reproduced under Class Licence
Number C01P0000148 with the permission of OPSI
and the Queen's Printer for Scotland

Published in the United States of America by Oxford University Press
198 Madison Avenue, New York, NY 10016, United States of America

British Library Cataloguing in Publication Data
Data available

Library of Congress Control Number: 2019947227

ISBN 978–0–19–883607–0 (pbk.)
ISBN 978–0–19–883606–3 (hbk.)

Printed and bound by
CPI Group (UK) Ltd, Croydon, CR0 4YY

Links to third party websites are provided by Oxford in good faith and
for information only. Oxford disclaims any responsibility for the materials
contained in any third party website referenced in this work.

This book is dedicated to all of those people who have had their rights violated, or have witnessed the rights of others being violated, and have picked up a mobile telephone or other recording device and taken photographs or videos of those events, often at great risk to themselves. This book is also dedicated to the international community that has rallied to help bring their stories to the world.

Foreword

On 24 May 1844, Samuel F B Morse sent his famous message, 'What hath God wrought?' by telegraph from Washington to Baltimore. Morse's invention had great consequences that were not foreseen. One of them was a profound impact on human rights.

The rapid transmission of information made possible by the telegraph permitted the newspapers of Morse's era to invent a new profession: war correspondent. Before the telegraph, information about what transpired in armed conflicts often consisted of self-serving accounts written long afterwards by military commanders extolling their own glorious deeds. These generally did not include such matters as the mistreatment of prisoners; the neglect of the wounded; the rape of women in occupied communities as part of the spoils of war; and indiscriminate attacks that victimized non-combatants. All that changed with the invention of war correspondents. Using the telegraph, they provided daily accounts of the follies and cruelties of war, often dealing with matters that previously went unreported.

The first armed conflict to be covered by war correspondents using the telegraph was the Crimean War of 1854–56. There, the correspondent for the *Times* of London, William Howard Russell, distinguished himself. He wrote about the foolhardy and disastrous charge of the Light Brigade 'into the valley of death'; and his reporting on the lack of care for wounded soldiers inspired Florence Nightingale and a party of nurses to set sail for Crimea. Russell's reporting helped to create public awareness of the crimes of war, which in turn enabled the Swiss businessman Henri Dunant to secure support a few years later, in 1864, for the adoption of the first of the Geneva Conventions.

The telegraph was instrumental again in war correspondent coverage of another bloody conflict around the same time, the Civil War in the United States. The Civil War was also the first armed conflict in which another technological innovation, photography, played a significant part. The newspapers of the era were not yet capable of publishing photographs, but the pictures taken by Matthew Brady and other photographers of the era were widely reproduced and exhibited, giving viewers a more realistic grasp of what happened in armed conflicts than had been possible previously. The photos, along with the extensive war correspondent reports, created the context in which Francis Lieber, a German-born professor of law at Columbia University with contacts in the administration of President Abraham Lincoln, prepared a code of conduct for Union forces. The Lieber Code of 1863, consisting of 157 articles, was the first comprehensive attempt to codify norms of war conduct. It became the basis for much of the body of law, now known as international humanitarian law, that the contemporary human rights movement relies on to try to protect human rights in the context of armed conflict.

My own first experience in taking advantage of communications technology to protect rights took place just over a half century ago.

In the latter half of the 1960s, when I worked for the American Civil Liberties Union (ACLU), much of our work involved efforts to protect the rights of opponents of the war in

Vietnam. In New York City, as in many other places, street demonstrations against the war were often accompanied by large numbers of arrests. The police would testify in court that the demonstrators had conducted themselves in a disorderly or violent manner and, based on that testimony, demonstrators were routinely convicted of misdemeanours. Many were sent to jail.

The only way we could defend the demonstrators successfully was to show that they had conducted themselves peaceably. When demonstrations took place, we sent observers to the scene wearing large badges identifying themselves as ACLU observers. As we expected, the police were arresting large numbers of opponents of the war who behaved in a wholly orderly and lawful manner.

Our observers noticed something else. When police made arrests and put the detainees into police wagons, the arresting officers immediately went off to make additional arrests. Later, when we went to court to defend the demonstrators, other police officers turned up claiming to be the arresting officers and testifying about the disorderly conduct of the detainees they claimed to have witnessed. It was apparent to us that the police testimony had nothing to do with the actual conduct of the detainees. It was made up so as to secure convictions.

We dealt with this by arranging to have a few observers with movie cameras placed in buildings overlooking sites where we knew demonstrations would take place. My colleague Paul Chevigny, the director of our Police Practices Project, acquired a device commonly used in film editing called a 'moviola' that he attached to his desk. It was not a very advanced piece of technology, but it served us well. The moviola allowed Paul to examine films of demonstrations frame by frame to see what was happening when a particular person was arrested; and, more importantly, to show which police officer had made an arrest. Our first major use of this technology took place in connection with a demonstration in New York in December 1967 when the police made more than 600 arrests at a peaceful protest against the war. After using the film footage in court in a couple of cases to demonstrate that the police officers who claimed to be the arresting officers were lying, we showed what we had to the assistant district attorneys prosecuting these cases. The result was the dismissal of the remaining cases. In a subsequent episode in Washington, DC in May 1971, when the police made about 13,000 arrests of anti-war demonstrators in a single day—probably the largest number of arrests in one day in American history—we used the same approach. In that instance, we even succeeded in getting damages paid to many of those who had been arrested.

Later, in 1981, as founding director of Human Rights Watch, one of the ways my colleagues and I established that organization's reputation was by producing speedy reports on human rights abuses in remote places. Our ability to do so was helped greatly by the development of satellite telephones. They were large, heavy devices at the time, and making calls on them was very expensive. Yet they enabled our field researchers to report their findings to us much more rapidly than had been possible previously. We could get help to victims of abuses and influence press accounts of episodes that were often reported in biased ways by forces that committed those abuses. Later on, satellite phones became far more portable, and the cost of calls declined sharply. Internet communications came a little later and, of course, greatly increased the ease, the speed, and the quantity of information that could be collected and disseminated.

Satellite technology also played an important role in war-related human rights developments of the 1990s in the former Yugoslavia. Television broadcasters used satellite television starting in 1992 to report from the besieged city of Sarajevo, creating awareness of the daily sniping and shelling that was killing thousands of civilians. This played an important part in creating support for the establishment of the International Criminal Tribunal for the Former Yugoslavia. And in 1995, satellite photos were used to verify reports that 8,000 Muslim men and boys were killed by Bosnian Serb forces at Srebrenica and to locate the grave sites. Satellite photos have also helped make it possible for Human Rights Watch to document abuses such as the burning of Rohingya villages in Myanmar in 2017 and 2018.

The internet has of course been the most significant development in communications technology in recent decades and has had a revolutionary impact on gathering and disseminating information on human rights abuses. Unfortunately, it can also be used to foment hatred and abuses of rights and no ready means has been devised to counter such misuse. Although some governments have devised means of limiting internet communications, those intent on obtaining or circulating information are often able to find ways to circumvent restrictions. Despite China's 'Great Firewall', for example, human rights monitors outside the country are generally able to secure almost instant reports on the Xi Jinping government's arrests of dissenters.

For the most part, governments and anti-government forces that engage in human rights violations try to shield their actions from public view. There are exceptions, of course. Groups such as ISIS or Boko Haram flaunt their abuses to show their contempt for the norms of the societies they are intent on destroying, while some public officials, such as President Rodrigo Duterte of the Philippines, occasionally boast of their abuse of rights, perhaps as a way of enhancing their macho credentials. Yet the prevailing practice worldwide is to give at least lip service to human rights and try to hide their violation from public view. This is what compels so many organizations intent on protecting human rights to devote so much of their effort to exposing such abuses. Communications technology has become of enormous assistance in those efforts.

The documentation of human rights abuses, whether by the use of advanced communications technology or by far less sophisticated means, tends to engage human rights advocates in disputes over the facts with the perpetrators of abuses and their defenders. It is crucial that human rights proponents be able to back up their findings by citing the supporting evidence. Accordingly, it is essential that they should master the effective use of the technologies available in open source investigations.

When this homework is done, human rights proponents often gain great advantage from the efforts of those they identify as the perpetrators of abuses, along with apologists for those perpetrators, to deny the evidence. Such denials often draw far more attention to abuses of rights than could be obtained in any other way. In the early days of Human Rights Watch in the 1980s, my colleagues and I often regarded officials of the Reagan administration such as US Ambassador to the United Nations Jeane Kirkpatrick and Assistant Secretary of State Elliott Abrams, who regularly denied abuses of rights that we attributed to US client states in Central America and elsewhere, as our unwitting allies. Their denial of abuses, and their attacks on journalists and human rights researchers who reported on those abuses, attracted far more media attention than we were capable of generating on our own. They often spurred journalists to conduct their own investigations of the abuse we had identified. By taking great care in our reporting, we were confident that our findings would stand up to scrutiny. It was an information struggle that we fought with the aid of the technology that was then available, and we were often successful.

Advances in communications technology have enhanced the capacity of human rights organizations that document violations, disseminate information about them, and ensure that the information they circulate is valid to prevail in debates over abuses. This book deals with innovations in gathering and disseminating information on violations of rights and addresses the challenges that confront human rights investigators making use of the new means that have come into use. It addresses the most important developments in contemporary efforts to document and punish abuses. It is, therefore, an immensely important contribution to the growing body of literature on the effective promotion of human rights.

Aryeh Neier
New York
13 December 2018

Acknowledgements

Any worthwhile effort often requires the input of a community. We are fortunate to be part of an extraordinary one.

This book would never have come together without the help of several people. We thank Jack McNichol, Iona Jacob and everyone else at Oxford University Press who has helped shepherd us through the publication process. We also thank Jonathan Cobb for his careful editing, and all of our contributors for their patience, partnership, and pioneering spirit. Kevin Reyes has been invaluable in ensuring consistency throughout, while Haley Willis, Desiree Moshayedi, and Catherine Chung helped with organizing the images, formatting the manuscript, and conducting background research.

Sam would like to thank his colleagues and the team at the Human Rights, Big Data, and Technology Project at the University of Essex—especially Lorna McGregor—who supported this project from its inception. Thanks also go to Sam's colleagues on the Crisis Response programme at Amnesty International, in particular (but in no particular order) to Elena Sergi, Tirana Hassan, Scott Edwards, Brian Castner, Micah Farfour, Milena Marin, and Conor Fortune for their daily support. Summer chats with Françoise Hampson over morning sade Türk kahvesi and afternoon gins and tonic pushed this project forward, while keeping it grounded and realistic. Every single student from Berkeley, Hong Kong, Pretoria, Toronto, Essex, and Cambridge who has volunteered for the Digital Verification Corps since its inception in 2016 has contributed directly to Amnesty's open source investigations—you have made a crazy concept actually work and I have learnt more from each and every one of you than you could ever know. Daragh and Alexa have made the seemingly enormous challenge of putting this book together both straightforward and a lot of fun. Thank you to you both. Finally, to Başak and Ara—you both make everything worthwhile.

Alexa thanks the staff of the Human Rights Center at the University of California, Berkeley for helping with everything from edits to insights, and for their constant support. This remarkable team included Eric Stover, Andrea Lampros, Alan Iijima, Alexey Berlind, Audrey Whiting, Faris Natour, Ethan Hampton, Jesse Nishinaga, Julie Freccero, Kat Madrigal, Kim Thuy Seelinger, Lindsay Freeman, Stephanie Croft, and all of the incredible students who have come through the Human Rights Investigations Lab. A huge thank you also to Kelly Matheson and Brad Samuels for their interviews, and to Alison Cole and Kelly Matheson for many late night conversations, as well as their exceptional leadership in the effort to strengthen digital evidence in atrocity cases (an effort now impressively joined by Lindsay Freeman). I am also so grateful to have had this opportunity to work with Sam and Daragh—I cannot imagine two better partners. Thank you for making this process so enjoyable! An extra thank you to Andrea Lampros and Sam, who have taught me so much and—back in 2016—helped launch something incredible in the form of our Human Rights Investigations Lab. I am also extremely grateful to Donna Childs for helping come up with the title for this book, and all of our colleagues at the Bellagio Residency who provided feedback on title and content—as well as Steven Livingston, Rebecca Wexler and Eric Stover for helping me end up there in the first place. Last but certainly not least, I thank my family for their support and the freedom to travel and write, even when they would have far preferred to have me at home.

Daragh would like to thank Sam and Alexa for being wonderful colleagues, inspiring human rights professionals, and for very kindly—and patiently—first introducing me into the world of open source investigations a few years ago. This has been a fantastic project to work on, and I look forward to more collaboration. Onwards! Thank you also to the team at the University of Essex Human Rights Centre, and the Human Rights, Big Data. & Technology Project, under the leadership of Professor Lorna McGregor. I am privileged to work at the Centre, and to call you all colleagues. Finally, a special thank you to all the students who have worked with me at the Digital Verification Unit in Essex, and all those who will follow in their footsteps, both in Essex and around the globe.

The authors thank the following for research and funding support for this project. Sam Dubberley and Daragh Murray's work was supported by the Economic and Social Research Council [grant number ES/M010236/1], Alexa Koenig's by the Miller Institute for Global Challenges and the Law, Mesa Refuge in Point Reyes, and the Rockefeller Foundation, which provided her with the space and time to write.

Table of Contents

PART III

PART IV

Table of Cases

INTERNATIONAL

European Court of Human Rights

Inter-American Court of Human Rights

International Criminal Court

International Criminal Tribunal for Former Yugoslavia

NATIONAL COURTS

Table of Legislation

TABLE OF STATUTES

OTHER LEGISLATION

United States

TABLE OF INTERNATIONAL INSTRUMENTS

List of Contributors

Fred Abrahams Associate Director for Program, Human Rights Watch

Adam Brown Associate Professor of Psychology, New School for Social Research

Jeff Deutch Lead researcher, Syrian Archive

Sam Dubberley Research Consultant, Human Rights, Big Data, and Technology Project, University of Essex; Special Adviser, Crisis Response, Amnesty International

Scott Edwards Senior Adviser, Crisis Response, Amnesty International; Professorial Lecturer, Elliot School of International Affairs, George Washington University

Micah Farfour Special Adviser, Remote Sensing, Amnesty International

Lindsay Freeman Senior Legal Researcher, Human Rights Center, University of California, Berkeley

Joseph Guay Founding Director, The Do No Digital Harm Initiative; Lead Research Consultant, Weaponization of Inforamtion Research Program, the International Committee of the Red Cross

Isabel Guenette Thornton Doctoral Candidate, Digital Sociology, University of Cambridge

Gabriela Ivens Independent Open Source Investigator

Sarah Knuckey Director, Human Rights Clinic, Columbia Law School

Alexa Koenig Executive Director, Human Rights Center; Co-Founder, Human Rights Investigations Lab; Lecturer-in-Residence, University of California, Berkeley

Christoph Koettl Senior Video Journalist, *The New York Times*

Matt Mahmoudi Doctoral Candidate, Development Studies, University of Cambridge

Ella McPherson Senior Lecturer in the Sociology of New Media and Digital Technology; Co-Director of the Centre of Governance and Human Rights; Anthony L. Lyster Fellow in Sociology, Queens' College, University of Cambridge

Daragh Murray Senior Lecturer, University of Essex School of Law & Human Rights Centre; Director, Digital Verification Unit, University of Essex Human Rights Centre

Paul Myers Internet Research Specialist, BBC

Aryeh Neier Co-Founder Human Rights Watch; former President, Open Society Foundations

Yvonne Ng Senior Archivist, WITNESS

Niko Para Former Director of Technology, Syrian Archive

Zara Rahman Deputy Director, The Engine Room

Lisa Rudnick Fellow, The Policy Lab

Margaret Satterthwaite Professor of Clinical Law, New York University

Aric Toler Lead Eurasia, Eastern Europe Team, Bellingcat

PART I

Introduction

The Emergence of Digital Witnesses

Sam Dubberley, Alexa Koenig, and Daragh Murray

> 'Ahead of you,' explains a disembodied male voice on the video, 'we have the Boko Haram members arriving, those we picked up during the assault.'

Nearly two dozen people—a group containing two women, two children, and several armed men wearing military fatigues—come into view. According to our narrator, the leader of the group is Master Corporal TchoTcho. It gets 'bloody' when he is around, we are told.

TchoTcho shouts at one of the women. 'You're going to die, Boko Haram!' He drags her by the hair as she clings to a young girl. The women and children are led to a clearing where they are forced to kneel and are then shot twenty-two times in the back.

This horrific video surfaced on Facebook in July 2018 and quickly went viral, spreading across social media platforms. The person who filmed it was unknown, as was how it was released, and by whom. At first viewing, it seemed impossible to determine the location. Apart from the individuals, all the video showed was a dusty path surrounded by low buildings, shrubs, and trees. Comments on social media suggested Cameroon as the locus, though the government of Cameroon's Minister of Communication quickly dismissed the video as 'fake news' and a 'gross misinformation whereby the facts have nothing to do with the work of [Cameroon's] defense and security forces'.[1]

Human rights advocacy organizations—ranging from large non-governmental organizations (NGOs) such as Amnesty International and Human Rights Watch to smaller groups like the Syrian Archive—have become increasingly familiar with videos such as this that appear to depict human rights violations. They now devote considerable resources to investigating such incidents and other evidence that appears on line and off. In the video clip described above, for example, the horror of the incident caught Amnesty International's attention and it dedicated a team to studying the video (including one of this book's editors and two chapter authors) and tracking down other leads to verify the video and determine whether Amnesty had enough evidence to argue that the video showed an extrajudicial execution carried out by members of the Cameroon military.

[1] Ministère de la Communication: Cameroun, *Press Briefing of Cameroon's Minister of Communication on a Fake News Targeting Cameroon's Army* (2018) https://www.youtube.com/watch?v=nePJOorjgKg accessed 29 December 2018.

Human rights researchers watched and rewatched the video, hunting for any clues that could help solve the mystery of where and when the executions took place, and who is depicted. The men's uniforms were compared to official photographs of the Cameroon military. The topography was analysed, the flora and fauna shown in the video cross-referenced with records of the northern part of the country. Cameroonian contacts were asked to listen to the speakers' accents. The weapons were identified. And here was the key detail: some of the weapons—which were simply labelled as AK-47s by the Cameroon government—were unusual. One of the group was carrying what turned out to be a Zastrava M-21, a weapon that most of Amnesty International's research team had not even heard of. This simple detail was crucial. Yes, the uniforms were from the Cameroon military (they could have been stolen, was the government's reply). Yes, the landscape was consistent with north-western Cameroon (but also with an adjacent area of Nigeria). Yes, the men were speaking French with a Cameroonian accent (but this did not mean they were military). But the Serbia-made Zastrava M-21 is rare, and Cameroon is one of the very few countries to which this weapon is exported.[2] It was only by conducting this in-depth analysis over several days that Amnesty International felt confident to issue a press release identifying the perpetrators as members of the Cameroon military. With a huge reputation at stake, and human rights abusers always looking for a way to discredit human rights defenders, this type of caution is critical. But here, after careful, systematic research was conducted, was a case that could not be ignored. After Amnesty issued its press release,[3] the video was picked up and reported on by major news organizations such as Reuters, the Associated Press, the BBC, and Al Jazeera. Meanwhile, the Cameroon government continued its strategy of denial.

The government of Cameroon could no longer avoid addressing the incident, and soon announced the arrest of members of the military believed to be linked to the events. Other organizations and volunteer collectives became involved. Collaboration among researchers yielded the exact location of the execution: outside a small village called Zelevet in north-western Cameroon, just a few kilometres from the country's border with Nigeria. This discovery led researchers to travel to the region to interview possible witnesses. Several corroborated the incident. The date of the filming was narrowed to 2015. Building on Amnesty's work and the collaborative research across the open source community, the BBC produced an in-depth exposition of the video bringing all these different elements together which itself went viral.[4] Without such painstaking analysis and rigorous verification, the type of which is outlined in this book, it is unlikely that this video would ever have garnered an international spotlight, or resulted in bringing perpetrators to account in any form.

This single video serves to illustrate what compelled the writing of this book. Finding and using open source information available online and piecing together corroborating information to challenge official narratives are crucial to human rights work today. With more

[2] Lawrence Marzouk and Gordana Andric, 'Serbia Urged to Stop Selling Arms to Cameroon' *BalkanInsight* (19 July 2018) http://www.balkaninsight.com/en/article/serbia-urged-to-stop-selling-arms-to-cameroon-07-18-2018 accessed 29 December 2018.

[3] Amnesty International, 'Cameroon: Credible Evidence that Army Personnel Responsible for Shocking Extrajudicial Executions Caught on Video' (12 July 2018) https://www.amnesty.org/en/latest/news/2018/07/cameroon-credible-evidence-that-army-personnel-responsible-for-shocking-extrajudicial-executions-caught-on-video/ accessed 2 September 2018.

[4] 'Cameroon Atrocity: Finding the Soldiers who Killed this Woman' *BBC News* (24 September 2018) https://www.bbc.com/news/av/world-africa-45599973/cameroon-atrocity-finding-the-soldiers-who-killed-this-woman accessed 29 December 2018.

photographs and videos taken every day, with high-speed internet connections crossing the globe, and with social media networks increasingly available at low cost, people are sharing their experiences online at a rate never before seen. When these experiences relate to human rights abuses or violations, they can constitute information crucial to both human rights documentation and legal accountability.

Who shot the video in Cameroon may never be known. The videographer may even have been a perpetrator. This is not unusual—perpetrators regularly capture their atrocities as trophies to show colleagues, or as a form of political protest. What is clear is that, irrespective of who films a human rights violation, if the content is to be used for documenting a crime and holding those responsible to account, it must be verified. As we saw with the Cameroonian Minister of Communication in our example above, officials are quick to dismiss authentic documentation of human rights abuses as 'fake news'. It is therefore essential that those monitoring human rights violations and abuses around the world are able to convincingly verify the content of the information in question. They must be convinced that they are on solid ground, and that a piece of information depicts what it claims to depict, including the when and where. This is especially true if monitors hope to secure justice through courts. Providing guidance on and insight into how this can be achieved is our objective in creating this book.

Digital Witness brings together leading experts on open source research, in order to share the methodologies used to discover and verify content, to highlight key factors to consider when undertaking this type of research, and to discuss how open source methods can contribute to documenting human rights abuses and bring perpetrators to justice. These methods are relevant to everyone with an interest in discovering the truth—from journalists, to lawyers, to human rights activists, and concerned citizens.

Open source information—publicly available information that anyone can obtain by request, purchase, or observation—has been a valuable resource for a long time. But it is the volume of content available and the speed of its transmission and relay that has radically changed human rights organizations' ability to use open source content for advocacy and accountability, ushering in a new era of human rights investigation.

1. The Rise of Open Source Information

The embrace of digital open source information by journalists, human rights activists, and lawyers has occurred in a largely ad hoc manner, as individuals and organizations became aware of the investigative possibilities inherent in modern communications, and began—often tentatively—to adapt their work practices accordingly.

The recent history of open source information is marked by a number of milestones. The Indian Ocean tsunami of 26 December 2004 was one of the first times that news organizations received large volumes of what we now call user-generated content—video and photographs captured by the public at large and shared on social media. At the time, 'smart' telephones with built-in multi-megapixel cameras did not exist, but hand-held video cameras were common. It was these cameras that tourists in Thailand, Sri Lanka, and Indonesia used to capture the tsunami's immediate impact and subsequent devastation as the giant waves hit the shores. Soon after, events of the 2007 Saffron Revolution in Myanmar and post-election protests and violence in Iran in 2009 were captured on grainy, low resolution cameras showing how governments were repressing protest on their streets—violently in many cases. In 2009, a group of journalists based in Ireland created Storyful, the world's first social media news agency, which developed new methods for effectively and efficiently monitoring social media to detect outbreaks of violence around the world and to get that original content into the hands of media. Then came the Arab Spring, which swept across several countries in northern Africa and the Middle East, starting in Tunisia in 2010 and spreading to Libya, Egypt, and the Syrian conflict. A landmark in the mainstream media's recognition of the utility of open source information came in 2015 when *The New York Times* used nine images sourced from Instagram for a front-page story on snow blizzards in New York City.[5] However, while the use of open source information was increasing, few knew how to verify such content. The field of practice was, at this time, a 'Wild West',[6] with verification often an uncomfortable afterthought.

In 2014, the European Journalism Centre published 'The Verification Handbook'.[7] The handbook was the first to set down a methodology to tackle a question that had been plaguing journalism since 2009: in a world in which the use of Facebook, YouTube, Twitter, and other platforms was exploding, how could news organizations leverage the power of content shared on these networks without making mistakes? The Verification Handbook was a first attempt to address this challenge, and it remains one of the 'go to' guides for verifying social media content.

Beyond the journalists who pioneered open source methods, two other communities increasingly began to draw on open source information: human rights activists and human rights lawyers. Like journalists, lawyers and activists are fundamentally concerned with telling people's stories[8] and rely on information shared by others to do so. It was almost inevitable that human rights lawyers and researchers would also turn their attention to how they could harness the power of social media, global internet connectivity, and the cheap image sensors being built into mobile telephones and other cameras to collect evidence for human rights advocacy and accountability.

A new challenge was also emerging in the field of international criminal law. In 2011, the International Criminal Court was about to mark its tenth anniversary, but with very few convictions to celebrate. Many of the Court's cases had fallen apart at relatively early stages of prosecution. As part of a study conducted by the Human Rights Center at the University of California, Berkeley, researchers reviewed hundreds of pages of court records and conducted interviews to find out what was going on. One of the major problems faced by the prosecution, it turned out, was a lack of corroborating information. Indeed, judges chastised the Office of the Prosecutor at the Court for over-reliance on NGO reports—claiming that such reports did not constitute evidence—and on witness testimony that had little or no supporting documentation. Following this study, the Human Rights Center at Berkeley started working with the Court to explore how to make better use of new and emerging

[5] Katie Hawkins-Gaar, 'Instagrammers Discover Front-Page NYT Placement by Chance' *Poynter* (29 January 2015) https://www.poynter.org/news/instagrammers-discover-front-page-nyt-placement-chance accessed 23 August 2018.

[6] Claire Wardle, Sam Dubberley, and Pete Brown, *Amateur Footage: A Global Study of User-Generated Content in TV and Online News Output* (Tow Center for Digital Journalism 2014).

[7] 'The Verification Handbook' (European Journalism Centre 2014).

[8] Sharon Sliwinski, *Human Rights in Camera* (University of Chicago Press 2011).

technologies in international investigations and prosecutions. In 2012, the Center hosted a workshop that brought together many of the organizations and individuals who had been pioneering the adoption and adaptation of digital technologies in amassing evidence for human rights legal cases. Human rights actors and organizations from around the world came together to discuss how user-generated content could be harnessed to strengthen human rights investigations for legal purposes, with a particular emphasis on gathering corroborating information from smartphones and social media. At that meeting were large human rights organizations, such as Human Rights Watch, Amnesty International, and Physicians for Human Rights; former investigators and prosecutors from the criminal tribunals established for Cambodia, Rwanda, and the former Yugoslavia; groups that worked with big data, such as researchers at Benetech (now at the Human Rights Data Analysis Group); forensic experts from the International Commission on Missing Persons and the Netherlands Forensic Institute; experts in remote sensing; and groups that relied on other forms of scientific information. Several NGOs present were at the forefront of efforts to train citizens around the world to collect information for legal cases. The NGO WITNESS, for example, launched its Video as Evidence programme soon after with the goal of strengthening the quality of citizen video for court purposes, and the Women's Institute for Gender Justice was arming women with cameras to document gendered crimes.

The meeting was followed by a series of others, hosted variously by the Human Rights Center at UC, Berkeley, the Center for Human Rights Science at Carnegie Mellon, and other academic institutions. In 2015, the Human Rights Centre at the University of Essex launched its Human Rights, Big Data, and Technology Project to consider the challenges and opportunities presented by big data and associated technology from a human rights perspective—including the opportunities and challenges of using open source information.

These efforts are intended to ensure that technology can be developed and used to advance human rights. Not only are projects such as these resulting in fuller evidentiary records for courts, but they are also contributing to an international protocol on open source investigations that aims to improve the use of open source investigations for legal practice. For example, in 2016 the International Criminal Court began to turn such academic discussions into action by using open source methods to support the investigation of the *Al-Mahdi* case, which concerned the destruction of cultural heritage property in Timbuktu, Mali. Another milestone was reached when, in 2017, the Court issued its first arrest warrant based primarily on evidence collected from social media posts. The warrant was issued for Mahmoud Mustafa Busayf al-Werfalli, a Libyan commander whose followers had posted videos appearing to show him carrying out or ordering extra-judicial executions in Benghazi. And then, in 2018, the United Nations Independent International Fact-Finding Mission on Myanmar cited Facebook posts and videos in its calls for Myanmar's military leaders to be investigated for genocide, and other crimes.

The human rights community's embrace of this new, wide range of open source information comes at a time when physical access to sites of interest is becoming increasingly difficult, whether due to security concerns or diplomatic constraints. To give just a few examples: the Syrian conflict has taken the lives of countless Syrian and international reporters and human rights workers since it started in 2011; two UN human rights investigators were murdered in the Kasai-Central province of the Democratic Republic of Congo in 2017; North Korea has refused to cooperate with any form of human rights investigation within its territory; and human rights defenders in the Philippines were labelled as 'terrorists' by the government of President Rodrigo Duterte in 2018. Governments frequently deny visas to outside journalists and human rights workers—or put those working locally in pre-trial detention for indeterminate durations. In light of its potential to circumvent the risk to life or the loss of physical access, the use of open source information has become increasingly enticing.

While journalists, lawyers, and human rights advocates often experience similar challenges in using open source information, those challenges—while overlapping—are not the same. Typically, journalists are interested in stories that will interest their audience; human rights researchers are interested in those that depict human rights abuses; and lawyers in those that violate the law. These do, of course, intersect—but not always. While a journalist needs to get a story out as quickly as possible, the human rights researcher's task is often slower, and the lawyer's slower still. Lawyers also need to verify content to the highest of standards, documenting chains of custody and preserving content that may need to be held for decades before being used in court. Human rights advocates operate somewhere in a middle ground, occasionally working with courts in mind, and at other times trying to bring urgent and immediate attention to a story in order to help combat ongoing abuse.

Addressing the broad need to discover, verify, and archive—and the disparate concerns of these three, overlapping communities—is why we brought this book into being. Most of the resources that are designed to teach people how to find and use open source content are aimed at journalists. Yet verification has become a critical skill for many other human rights-oriented communities. There has been no comprehensive source available to introduce students and practitioners to the broad array of skills that are required in this new world of investigations. While many universities teach how to conduct field-based human rights investigations, there is a gap in university coursework that this book—aimed at academic audiences, students, *and* practitioners—hopes to close. We want to arm the next generation of lawyers, journalists, sociologists, data scientists, activists, and researchers with the cutting-edge skills and insights needed to work in an increasingly digitized and information-saturated environment. With this work poised to explode in importance and prevalence over the next few years, human rights organizations need to ensure that their staff—and academic institutions need to ensure that their students—are equipped to tackle these modern-day challenges.

2. Definitions

As with any new field of study, a terminology for open source investigations is gradually emerging. The definitions below are drawn from the draft International Protocol on Open Source Investigations, which is being coordinated by the Human Rights Center at the University of California, Berkeley, in partnership with the Office of the High Commissioner for Human Right, and is being developed in cooperation with dozens of leaders in the open source 'space'—ranging from international investigators and prosecutors to non-governmental organizations and journalists [cite to website].

2.1 Open Source Information

Open source information is publicly available information that anyone can obtain by request, purchase, or observation[9]. Open source information may include (but is not limited to) information created, shared, or collated by journalists and news organizations; state agencies; political and military actors; commercial entities; international organizations; non-governmental and civil society organizations; academics and academic institutions; private individuals; and groups of individuals on the basis of their military, political, commercial, professional, and personal affiliations.

2.2 Online open source information

Online open source information is open source information found on the internet. Common types of online open source information include online news articles; information found on blogs and websites; PDF reports and digital documents; social media posts and user-generated content; digital imagery, video and audio recordings; satellite imagery, maps and geospatial data; user data and statistical information; and information contained in internet archives and databases.

2.3 Open source investigation

Open source investigation is the process of identifying, collecting, and/or analysing open source information as part of an investigative process.[10] This is distinct from 'cyber investigations', a term often used to refer to the investigation of computer crimes or, more generally, to forensic activity whereby crime is detected via computers and other digital devices.[11] Cyber investigation is not limited to open sources and may involve coercive measures such as legal hacking.

2.4 Open source intelligence

Open source intelligence (OSINT) is information that is collected, exploited, and disseminated in a timely manner to an appropriate audience for the purpose of addressing a specific intelligence requirement.[12] While intelligence operations are distinct from criminal

[9] United States Office of the Director of National Intelligence, Intelligence Community Directive No 301, National Open Source Enterprise (Effective: 11 July 2006).

[10] According to the United Nations, an investigation is 'a legally based and analytical process designed to gather information in order to determine whether wrongdoing occurred and, if so, the persons or entities responsible'. See United Nations Office of Internal Oversight Services, Investigations Manual, Provisional, pending promulgation of the revised ST/AI/371 (OIOS Manual). See also International Protocol on Open Source Investigations (forthcoming 2020).

[11] International Association of Chiefs of Police, 'Cybercrime Investigations,' at http://www.iacpcybercenter.org/chiefs/cyber-crime-investigations/.

[12] ibid. See also s 931 of Public Law 109–163, entitled 'National Defense Authorization Act for Fiscal Year 2006', and 'International Protocol on Open Source Investigations' (forthcoming 2020).

investigations, OSINT practices, such as real-time monitoring, may inform certain aspects of open source investigations.

2.5 Open source acquisition

Open source acquisition is the act of gaining possession of, or access to, open source information and is synonymous with 'open source collection'. The preferred term is acquisition because, by definition, open sources are collected and disseminated by others. Open source exploiters acquire previously collected and publicly available information second-hand.[13]

2.6 Open source evidence

The legal definition of evidence is 'proof of fact(s) presented at a judicial hearing such as a trial'.[14] Open source evidence is open source information that is admitted to prove facts in a judicial hearing.

2.7 Authentication

Authentication is a legal term for the process of proving that something is genuine and not forged—in other words, that it is what it purports to be.

2.8 Verification

Verification is a technical term for the process of establishing the reliability or veracity of information—in other words, establishing whether a claim or assertion is true.

3. A Guide to This Volume

This edited collection is written by distinguished practitioners and academics who are pioneers in the use of new technologies in human rights research and investigation. While each chapter is intended to stand alone, we have organized the text in several sections: First, the book situates open source investigations in an historical, social, and theoretical context. Next, it covers the logistics of discovery, verification, and archiving. It then discusses the possibilities and limitations of using open source information in human rights monitoring and documentation, and suggests how future developments in open source information technology may affect human rights work.

In Chapter 1, Christoph Koettl, Daragh Murray, and Sam Dubberley discuss the history of using open source information in human rights reporting, and then, in Chapter 2,

[13] Intelligence Community Directive No 301, *supranote* 8.

[14] Duhaime's Law Dictionary, 'Evidence', at http://www.duhaime.org/LegalDictionary/E/Evidence.aspx, and 'International Protocol on Open Source Investigations' (forthcoming 2020).

Alexa Koenig discusses the history of open source investigations for legal practice. Lindsay Freeman next analyses how to use open source digital content in prosecuting grave international crimes, discussing some of the lessons the Office of the Prosecutor at the International Criminal Court has learned in grappling with the new, digital information environment. In Chapter 4, Ella McPherson, Matthew Mahmoudi, and Isabelle Guenette Thornton discuss some of the big-picture social considerations that underlie this field of practice: whose stories does open source information privilege and whose does it obscure? Who are the information workers who have access to this kind of content, and whose labour is minimized or excluded? Scott Edwards then outlines some of the current and future challenges that underlie how to use open source investigations in human rights practice.

Part II focuses on using open source information in practice. Paul Myers provides an overview of methods for conducting discovery using open source techniques, including how to glean material from social media sites like Facebook and Twitter. How might a researcher construct an investigatory plan that would help ensure the systematic collection of relevant information? In Chapter 9, Aric Toler discusses how to verify that content, trust being the currency of all human rights researchers. How, for example, can we establish that a video or photograph shows what its originator or sharer claims to portray? Micah Farfour tackles the use and analysis of satellite imagery and other remote sensing data for verification and documentation. Yvonne Ng outlines how to archive open source information appropriately, while Jeff Deutsch and Niko Para build on her work to explain how information can be scraped from the internet and archived en masse.

In Part III, the book shifts from the pragmatic considerations underlying open source investigations to issues of ethics and security, whether physical, digital, or psychosocial. In Chapter 11, Zara Rahman and Gabi Ivens discuss the ethical questions that should be considered when using open source information in human rights research. Sam Dubberley, Meg Satterthwaite, Sarah Knuckey, and Adam Brown summarize their research into secondary trauma—the psychological or social stress that can emerge from experiencing the first-hand trauma experiences of another—which is a risk for all human rights practitioners but becomes especially acute when looking at large volumes of graphic footage, and provide practical suggestions for how to build resiliency. In Chapter 13, Joseph Guay and Lisa Rudnick discuss the digital and physical security concerns specific to this area of practice, pulling from their analysis of a unit that conducts open source investigations for both human rights reporting and case building.

In Part IV, we contemplate the future of open source investigation in the field of human rights. Fred Abrahams and Daragh Murray provide a forward-looking perspective on how open source information can be responsibly and effectively harnessed to strengthen advocacy and increase awareness of human rights abuses globally. And in Chapter 15, Alexa Koenig and Lindsay Freeman outline minimal standards and best practices for adapting open source methodologies when researchers or legal investigators hope to maximize the value of their work for courts.

When marching two women and two children down a dusty path in north-western Cameroon, TchoTcho and his followers probably never imagined that their crimes would be witnessed by the world. A video recorded by a simple camera built into a mobile phone and shared through the internet made this possible. The video inspired the human rights community to rise up and challenge the executioners' actions. But human rights researchers were only effective because they were trained to interrogate the video's veracity. Such methods must now become an essential part of every human rights researcher's toolkit. We hope this book helps to make that potential a reality.

1

Open Source Investigation for Human Rights Reporting

A Brief History

Christoph Koettl, Daragh Murray, and Sam Dubberley

1. Introduction

Research utilizing open source information, such as publicly available documents, statistics, data, news reports, or maps is nothing new. Indeed, it is a practice upon which human rights organizations, governments, and individual researchers have relied for decades, if not centuries. Antique examples of open source information individuals could make use of even include Yelp-like reviews of restaurants written on walls in Pompeii,[1] such as this one: 'Traveller, eat bread in Pompeii but go to Nuceria to drink. At Nuceria, the drinking is better.' Militaries and intelligence agencies in the 20th century also took advantage of the wealth of public information. For example, during the Second World War, Allied intelligence agencies recognized a link between railway efficiency and the price of oranges in Paris, and used information on the fluctuating price of the latter to gauge the success of overnight bombing campaigns.[2] Similarly, Allied forces obtained small town newspapers from around Germany and used the obituary sections to estimate total German troop losses.[3] In the 1960s, professor-turned-private-investigator Josiah Thompson built his research into the assassination of US President John F. Kennedy on open source content.[4] Thompson conducted a frame-by-frame analysis of the assassination captured on the 26.6-second film Abraham Zapruder recorded on his home-movie camera as Kennedy's motorcade passed down Elm Street in Dallas on 22 November 1963. The analysis Thompson conducted of the Zapruder film and other audiovisual and photographic materials is just the kind of work using open source methods that is carried out today, though often with more advanced technology at hand.

Open source research focusing specifically on human rights violations is also longstanding. Indeed, the founding of Amnesty International, the world's largest human rights organization, was triggered by open source information. In 1960, British lawyer Peter Benenson read a newspaper article about two prisoners, reportedly in Portugal, punished

[1] Patrick Meier, 'Social Media: The First 2,000 Years' *iRevolutions* (3 February 2014) https://irevolutions.org/2014/02/03/ancient-social-media/ accessed 18 May 2018.

[2] Michael Glassman and Min Ju Kang, 'Intelligence in the Internet Age: The Emergence and Evolution of Open Source Intelligence (OSINT)' (2012) 28 Computers in Human Behavior 673.

[3] William J Donovan, 'Intelligence' *LIFE* (30 September 1946).

[4] Josiah Thompson, *Six Seconds in Dallas: A Micro-Study of the Kennedy Assassination* (B Geis Associates 1967).

for political activities, and subsequently launched a worldwide 'Appeal for Amnesty' for what he called 'Prisoners of Conscience' around the world.[5] As the organization developed, it has continued to rely on open source information, as do other human rights organizations. Historical photographs from the 1980s, for example, clearly show Amnesty volunteers clipping newspaper articles to create research dossiers on individual cases.

Figure 1.1 Keystone Press/Alamy Stock Photo

More recently, investigators at the International Criminal Tribunal for the former Yugoslavia used videos journalist Zoran Petrovic recorded to reconstruct scenes and events near Srebrenica in 1995,[6] while historian Gerhard Botz spent decades reconstructing the excessive use of force by Austrian police against demonstrators in July 1927.[7] Interestingly, a key method Botz used was image and shadow analysis, a method to determine the time of day based on the angle of shadows. Today, these have become standard processes for human rights investigators to determine the exact time of day of a specific visual—as discussed in Chapter 9 of this book.

Although the history of open source research in human rights stretches back decades, we focus in this chapter on the period from the late 1990s to the present, the digital age, in which open source research capability has expanded enormously thanks to the advent of publicly available satellite imagery, digital social networks, camera-enabled smartphones,

[5] Antony Barnett, 'The Man Who Fought for the Forgotten' *The Observer* (27 February 2005) https://www.theguardian.com/uk/2005/feb/27/humanrights.world1 accessed 20 December 2018.

[6] United States Holocaust Memorial Museum, *Zoran Petrovic Video* (1995) https://www.youtube.com/watch?v=344e_D-Vc7g accessed 20 December 2018.

[7] Werner A Perger, 'Österreich: Der Schattenvermesser' *Die Zeit* (Hamburg, 28 June 2007) https://www.zeit.de/2007/27/Portrait-Botz/komplettansicht accessed 20 December 2018.

and globally cheap and fast network connectivity. If in the categorization of Philip Alston, the first generation of human rights fact-finding describes the work of intergovernmental bodies, and the second generation represents the methods developed by international non-governmental organizations (NGOs) such as Amnesty International and Human Rights Watch in the 1970s and 1980s, our chapter covers what Alston calls 'third-generation fact-finding',[8] which was largely brought about by significant developments in information and communication technologies (ICTs). As a 2018 UN investigative report on the situation of human rights in the civil war in Syria put it: 'The volume of videos and other images—as well as the role played by social media—is unprecedented in any other accountability process with respect to international crimes to date.'[9]

2. Human Rights Investigations in the Digital Age: Four Key Developments

Four key developments since the late 1990s have greatly increased the value of open source investigations in human rights work—satellite imagery, camera-enabled portable phones, digital social networks, and increase in publicly accessible data.

2.1 Satellite Imagery

Satellite imagery with a spatial resolution under 1 meter was traditionally the exclusive domain of national governments. Imagery collected by government owned satellites were and are not available to the public, and so the emergence of a commercial satellite imagery market on January 1, 2000 following the successful deployment of the Ikonos satellite[10] was thus a game-changer. A second satellite, Quickbird, was launched in 2001 and provided images at 61-centimetre resolution. This improvement in spatial resolution capacity to identify objects smaller than 1 metre allowed investigations to be undertaken of previously inaccessible areas, such as North Korea or Darfur, in Sudan. These are places with reported serious human rights violations, which were traditionally difficult to research owing to lack of access and information. Scientist Matthew McKinzie described the value of satellite imagery for the North Korea investigation:

> With meter and sub-meter resolution satellite imagery, objects such as buildings, forests, orchards, fields, fences, rivers, railways, trails, and roads are easily recognizable. Indeed, these [satellite] photographs were shown to former North Koreans who were imprisoned in these places, and who were able to identify specific features in the photographs and to

[8] Philip Alston, 'Introduction: Third Generation Human Rights Fact-Finding' (2013) 107 Proceedings of the Annual Meeting (American Society of International Law) 61.

[9] Stephanie Nebehey, 'War Crimes Evidence in Syria "Overwhelming", Not All Can Be ...' *Reuters* (26 March 2018) https://www.reuters.com/article/us-mideast-crisis-syria-warcrimes-idUSKBN1H22GN accessed 20 December 2018.

[10] European Space Agency, 'Ikonos-2: EoPortal Directory: Satellite Missions' https://directory.eoportal.org/web/eoportal/satellite-missions/i/ikonos-2 accessed 20 December 2018.

describe their purposes. Using the satellite imagery, interviews with former prisoners were conducted in Seoul, Washington, DC, and Los Angeles . . .[11]

Figure 1.2 Political prison camp in North Korea. Satellite image © Maxar Technologies. Source: U.S. Committee for Human Rights in North Korea. McKinzie 2003, 115.

Additionally, the libraries of precisely dated satellite imagery that have been developed allow researchers to go back in time through archived images. These spatio-temporal records are highly relevant for human rights reporting. They allow researchers to document

[11] David Hawk, *The Hidden Gulag: Exposing North Korea's Prison Camps* (US Committee for Human Rights in NK 2001).

Figure 1.3 Close-up of Vegetation Death Southwest of Bodo Town
False-Color Imagery of Waterways Southwest of Bodo between 4 December 2006 (TOP) and 26 January 2009 (Bottom) Appear Consistent with Reports of an Oil Spill. Red areas Reflect Healthy Vegetation; the Green/Black Color Reflects Dead Plants. Vegetation Death Concentrated Primarily near the River and its Tributaries, while areas Further Inland Appear Less Affected.
Satellite images © Maxar Technologies. Source: American Association for the Advancement of Science.

occurrences such as the destruction of civilian infrastructure during armed conflict, for example, or in some cases the establishment of official or secret places of detention.

One often overlooked advantage for the open source human rights researcher is the fact that satellite imagery, because of its multi-spectral characteristics, shows more than meets the human eye. For instance, so-called false-colour imagery can be used to highlight the impact of oil spills on vegetation.

The single most important satellite-imagery innovation of recent decades has been the development of virtual globes. These make high-resolution satellite imagery available for anyone to access from their personal computer. The release of Keyhole Earthviewer in 2001 was a milestone in this regard. Rising to prominence through CNN's coverage of the beginning of the 2003 Iraq War,[12] the tool—today known as Google Earth—is now indispensable for any open source investigator. The development of virtual globes also reveals a morally complex issue when looking at the history of open source research in human rights reporting: Open source researchers often rely on tools and resources originally developed by the military or the intelligence community, the very actors often at the centre of human rights investigations for their direct or indirect role in violations. Indeed, Keyhole was initially funded by the CIA-backed venture capital firm *In-Q-Tel*.[13] (The same firm also funded

[12] Kevin Maney, 'Tiny Tech Company Awes Viewers' https://usatoday30.usatoday.com/tech/news/techinnovations/2003-03-20-earthviewer_x.htm accessed 20 December 2018.

[13] IN-Q-TEL, 'IN-Q-TEL Announces Strategic Investment in Keyhole' (25 June 2003) https://www.iqt.org/in-q-tel-announces-strategic-investment-in-keyhole/ accessed 20 December 2018.

Palantir, the big data analysis software used by the Carter Center, the Enough Project, and others[14] to organize and analyse publicly available data related to the conflicts and violence in, for instance, Syria and central Africa.) The newest development in the satellite imagery field is the creation of fleets of commercial micro-satellites. While these tiny satellites have a lower spatial resolution than their larger cousins, for the first time in human history every single landmass on earth will be imaged once a day, allowing researchers to monitor and track areas or features of interest in near real time. The next frontier in using publicly available satellite images could well be the use of satellite video.

2.2 Camera-enabled Phones

The second significant digital development for digital open source research was the global proliferation of camera-enabled phones, starting in the early 2000s. Suddenly, individuals subject to abuse and those in their vicinity often had new opportunities to document specific violations in a digital format that could be easily shared. For example, while the 1991 police beating of Rodney King had to be distributed through traditional media outlets to reach an audience, videos of police misconduct could now be published directly by the witness. Multiple examples and case studies throughout this book highlight the importance of such content for human rights reporting. The main difference from previous audiovisual human-rights-relevant footage, such as the Zoran Petrovic footage from Srebrenica, is that it is not only trained journalists or activists anymore who record. Rather, bystanders or other witnesses can themselves capture and share content.[15]

In addition to smartphones, the proliferation of other audiovisual sensors have added to the ubiquity of digital content. CCTV cameras,[16] dash- or body cameras,[17] or simple audio recordings now also play an increasingly important role in open source investigations. Transparency laws and regulations help with bringing materials such as body camera recordings of officer involved shootings into the public domain.

2.3 Digital Social Networks

The third development that allowed human rights investigators to tap into a global network of monitors was the creation of digital social networks enabling almost real-time sharing of videos or photos recorded on smartphones. This in turn was made possible by the exponential growth in internet penetration. In 2000, only 6.7 per cent of the world population used the internet. This has grown to 49.7 per cent in 2017.[18] Online platforms or messaging apps

[14] Obi Anyadike, 'Spies sans Frontières?' *IRIN News* (3 July 2016) https://www.irinnews.org/investigations/2016/03/07/spies-sans-fronti%C3%A8res accessed 20 December 2018.

[15] Interview with Sam Gregory, May 2018.

[16] Amnesty International, 'Footage Appears to Show Deliberate Killing of Palestinian Children' *Amnesty International* (21 May 2014) https://www.amnesty.org/en/press-releases/2014/05/israelopt-footage-appears-show-deliberate-killing-palestinian-children-spok/ accessed 20 December 2018.

[17] Christoph Koettl, 'What We Learned from the Videos of Stephon Clark Being Killed by Police' *The New York Times* (7 June 2018) https://www.nytimes.com/2018/06/07/us/police-shooting-stephon-clark.html accessed 20 December 2018.

[18] International Telecommunication Union, 'Individuals Using the Internet (% of Population)' https://data.worldbank.org/indicator/IT.NET.USER.ZS accessed 29 September 2019.

have created new ways either passively to collect human rights relevant information, or actively to make contact with potential witnesses or, in some instances, people who themselves were the subject of abuse.

2.4 Increase in Publicly Accessible Data

Finally, a general trend towards making data more accessible and open also has had an impact on human rights investigations. Researchers now can take advantage of easy-to-access databases, such as historical weather data, active global fire data, census data, and many government records, amongst many others. While such single data sources rarely document specific violations alone, the combination of some or all of these datasets can allow trends or patterns to be identified.[19] Specific types of documents, such as classified government information or internal corporate documents, remain difficult to access, or are only publicly accessible after a significant delay.

3. A Brief History of Human Rights-related Digital Open Source Research

The combined impact of these developments has been enormous: they represent a clear shift in the extent of information control, providing easily accessible tools to circumvent, in many instances, government and other traditional information gatekeepers. In 1961, Peter Benenson had to rely on newspapers to receive information about political prisoners. In the 21st century information sphere, human rights researchers can directly access raw data in the form of social media postings or satellite imagery, often receiving information on potential violations in real time. The impact of this shift can be best seen in concrete incidents and projects starting in the early 2000s.

3.1 Commercial Satellite Imagery

The US Committee for Human Rights in North Korea was the first human rights NGO that took advantage of commercial high-resolution imagery for an extensive report on the state of human rights in a country. The 2003 report, 'Hidden Gulag',[20] made use of satellite imagery to provide, for the first time, visual proof of a vast network of political prison camps in North Korea, reported previously by people fleeing the country. The fact that North Korea remains inaccessible to independent observers up to this day makes this a textbook example of the value of using publicly available satellite imagery for human rights reporting. The

[19] Human Rights Watch, 'A Costly Move: Far and Frequent Transfers Impede Hearings for Immigrant Detainees in the United States' *Human Rights Watch* (14 June 2011) https://www.hrw.org/report/2011/06/14/costly-move/far-and-frequent-transfers-impede-hearings-immigrant-detainees-united accessed 20 December 2018; Brian Root, 'Data Analysis for Human Rights Advocacy' *School of Data* (22 November 2013) https://schoolofdata.org/2013/11/22/data-analysis-for-human-rights-advocacy/ accessed 20 December 2018; Human Rights Data Analysis Group, 'HRDAG' (*HRDAG*, no date) http://hrdag.org/hrdag-25-years/ accessed 20 December 2018.

[20] Hawk (n 11).

same report would not have been possible only even five years earlier, owing to the lack of commercially available imagery with the necessary image resolution quality.

Although Amnesty International started using satellite imagery in 2004,[21] particularly noteworthy is the organization's 2007 Eyes on Darfur project, as well as the US Holocaust Memorial Museum's Crisis in Darfur Google Earth Project.[22] Both projects used high-resolution satellite imagery to document burned villages in Sudan's Darfur region, another area that remains inaccessible to international human rights monitors. Additionally, the Eyes on Darfur project employed satellite imagery to monitor villages at risk of attack. This approach built on Amnesty International's established practice of protecting individuals at risk by drawing attention to them. Using satellite images, this could now be done with villages at risk in difficult to reach areas. The success of the Darfur project led, in 2008, to the creation of a dedicated team (Science for Human Rights) at the organization, whose priorities included the delivery of research based on open source information.[23]

3.2 Cameras Everywhere

The nascent importance of audiovisual open source content for human rights investigations can be seen in some high-profile cases of the early 2000s. In June 2004, a host of personal photographs emerged—taken on soldiers' private digital cameras—that showed US personnel torturing Iraqi prisoners in Baghdad's Abu Ghraib prison.[24] The photographs sparked a global outcry about US military practices overseas and generated calls for greater accountability. A claim at the time nicely summarizes the importance of this event: "We're functioning . . . in the Information Age, where people are running around with digital cameras and taking these unbelievable photographs and then passing them off, against the law, to the media, to our surprise, when they had not even arrived in the Pentagon.'

The fact that this 2004 quote does not stem from a human rights activist or investigator, but from then US Defense Secretary Donald Rumsfeld,[25] underscores the power shift in information control. Of course, we do not claim that restrictions on information flows and journalists completely disappeared.

The mass distribution of human-rights-relevant citizen video started unusually: with a zoo. On 23 April 2005, Jawed Karim published an 18-second video of himself at the San Diego zoo in the United States. It is not the slightly awkward video that he uploaded to the internet, in which he clearly feels uncomfortable and does not know what to say, that proved to be a game changer for human rights open source reporting. It is the fact that the video was the first to be uploaded to a new video sharing website he had co-founded called YouTube.

[21] Amnesty International, 'Sudan: At the Mercy of Killers' (7 January 2004) https://www.amnesty.org/en/documents/document/?indexNumber=AFR54%2f072%2f2004&language=en accessed 20 December 2018.

[22] Lisa Parks, 'Digging into Google Earth: An Analysis of "Crisis in Darfur"' (2009) 40 Geoforum 535.

[23] Amnesty International, 'Technology for Human Rights: Evaluation of the Science for Human Rights Project 2008-2011' (18 July 2011) https://www.amnesty.org/en/documents/document/?indexNumber=doc23%2f002%2f2011&language=en accessed 20 December 2018.

[24] Kari Andén-Papadopoulos, 'The Abu Ghraib Torture Photographs: News Frames, Visual Culture, and the Power of Images' (2008) 9 Journalism 5.

[25] Sam Gregory, 'The Participatory Panopticon and Human Rights: WITNESS's Experience Supporting Video Advocacy and Future Possibilities' in Meg McLagan and Yates McKee (eds), *Sensible Politics: The Visual Culture of Nongovernmental Activism* (Zone Books 2012) 517–49..

Less than a year after Jawed Karim's visit to the zoo, a very different sort of content could be found on the website. In January 2006, a video was published that showed Malaysian police forcing a young woman, stripped naked, to perform squats. The video of the incident from June 2005, filmed by a police officer, had gathered attention in the fall/autumn of 2005, and was broadcast on Malaysian state television. A contemporary news article describes its spreading and impact:

> The clip began circulating phone to phone, e-mail to e-mail. Eventually it was posted on YouTube and other internet sites, to be viewed by millions. What started as cheap voyeurism escalated into an unstoppable cyberspace phenomenon, which forced the prime minister to establish an official inquiry that led to changes in police practice.[26]

The video eventually led to the suspension of the police officer involved in the incident.[27] In addition to showing the powerful combination of audiovisual content with modern communications technologies, the Malaysian police incident also exposed new ethical issues, such as re-victimization and rights of privacy, that arise with audiovisual open source content. As the victim described her reaction to seeing her abuse broadcast on national TV: 'I was surprised and angry and embarrassed all over again. Our culture doesn't allow this.'[28]

Videos rose to further prominence in human rights fact-finding in 2009, when a leaked video, taken by one of the perpetrators to show his peers, showed an extrajudicial execution in Sri Lanka. The shaky and blurry video showed Sri Lankan security forces killing captured Tamil Tiger fighters. A UN investigation authenticated the footage and this led to calls for an international inquiry and arrest of those responsible for the executions.[29]

While the previous examples were records of single incidents, the combination of smartphone cameras and digital social media networks have also documented mass protests and movements. Among the first movements to receive extensive digital exposure were the so-called Saffron revolution in Burma/Myanmar in 2007 and what became known as the Green revolution in Iran in 2009.

The 2007 protests in Burma/Myanmar, sparked by rising fuel prices, spread across the country and became the largest public protests in that country in twenty years.[30] Some of the authorities' violent response was recorded on camera and shared with a global audience. '[E]fforts at censorship were only partially successful', Human Rights Watch noted that year, 'as some enterprising and brave individuals found ways to get mobile phone video footage of the demonstrations and crackdown out of the country and onto the world's television screens'.[31] The 2009 documentary 'Burma VJ: Reporting from a closed country' captured

[26] Mary Jordan, 'Amateur Videos Are Putting Official Abuse in New Light' (15 November 2006) http://www.washingtonpost.com/wp-dyn/content/article/2006/11/14/AR2006111401312.html accessed 20 December 2018.

[27] Malaysiakini, 'Squatgate: Voyeur Cop Suspended' (23 January 2006) https://www.malaysiakini.com/news/46076 accessed 20 December 2018.

[28] Jordan (n 26).

[29] UN Human Rights Council, 'UN Expert Concludes that Sri Lankan Video Is Authentic, Calls for an Independent War Crimes Investigation: Sri Lanka' *ReliefWeb* (1 July 2010) https://reliefweb.int/report/sri-lanka/un-expert-concludes-sri-lankan-video-authentic-calls-independent-war-crimes accessed 20 December 2018.

[30] Radio Free Asia, *Myanmar's Saffron Revolution: 10th Anniversary | Radio Free Asia (RFA)* (2017) https://www.youtube.com/watch?v=zEYDjE3yx2E accessed 20 December 2018.

[31] Human Rights Watch, 'Repression of the 2007 Popular Protests in Burma' (12 June 2007) https://www.hrw.org/report/2007/12/06/crackdown/repression-2007-popular-protests-burma accessed 20 December 2018.

both the impact and challenges of these circumvention efforts, and human rights groups were able to integrate some of this footage in their human rights reporting.

While the dramatic videos from the 'Green' revolution in Iran raised the profile of the protests,[32] they also documented human rights violations such as excessive use of force by security forces. At the same time, however, this situation highlighted the dangers posed to human rights defenders and activists by a repressive state's own use of technological developments. The Iranian regime published photographs and screenshots of videos online to 'crowd-source' the identification of activists. This showed the immense danger of visual records and the coming 'arms race' between investigators and repressive regimes.

The conflict in Syria, which began in 2011, was the next milestone in the use of open source information in human rights documentation. Satellite images were of very limited use during the initial protests (satellite images are not useful to document excessive use of force, enforced disappearances, torture, or deaths in custody), but the large volume of videos of the conflict was and remains unprecedented. The situation in Syria—claimed to be the first 'YouTube War' by one of the authors[33]—accordingly forced human rights organizations to develop new skills, methods, and resources to discover and verify digital content, which was suddenly required on an almost daily basis. The risks of using misattributed content in an investigation continues to be enormous, posing a serious threat to the reputation of any human rights monitoring group. The risk is real, as mistakes by journalists or individual human rights workers show. In May 2012, the BBC erroneously published a photo from Iraq in 2003 with an article of a massacre in Syria.[34] In a different instance, Kenneth Roth, the executive director of Human Rights Watch, published a drone video showing infrastructure destruction in Gaza, claiming that it is from Aleppo.[35]

3.3 The Institutionalization of Using Open Source Digital Information in Human Rights Documentation

What began as a small, Irish start-up specializing in social media verification, Storyful, played an important role in the initial capacity building of digital verification at human rights organizations. Not only did the team at Storyful provide some of the first, general case studies on verification, they also created, in 2013, the Open Newsroom,[36] an online, collaborative space to share specific verification requests and best practices. Together with the Verification Handbook, published in January 2014,[37] the Open Newsroom and Storyful's cases were the key training resources at the time.

[32] British Broadcasting Corporation, 'Internet Brings Events in Iran to Life' (15 June 2009) http://news.bbc.co.uk/2/hi/middle_east/8099579.stm accessed 20 December 2018.

[33] Christoph Koettl, '"The YouTube War": Citizen Videos Revolutionize Human Rights Monitoring in Syria' *MediaShift* (18 February 2014) http://mediashift.org/2014/02/the-youtube-war-citizen-videos-revolutionize-human-rights-monitoring-in-syria/ accessed 20 December 2018.

[34] Chris Hamilton, 'Houla Massacre Picture Mistake' *BBC: The Editors* (29 May 2012) http://www.bbc.co.uk/blogs/theeditors/2012/05/houla_massacre_picture_mistake.html accessed 20 December 2018.

[35] Kenneth Roth, 'It Really Is This Bad. A Drone's Eye Tour of What Assad's Barrel Bombs Have Done to Aleppo' *archive.fo* (8 May 2015) http://archive.fo/YQoAv accessed 20 December 2018.

[36] Mathew Ingram, 'Storyful and the Open Newsroom: Journalism Gets Better When More People Do It' *GigaOm* (9 January 2013) https://gigaom.com/2013/09/01/storyful-and-the-open-newsroom-journalism-gets-better-when-more-people-do-it/ accessed 20 December 2018.

[37] 'The Verification Handbook' (European Journalism Centre 2014).

In July 2014, one of this chapter's authors launched the Citizen Evidence Lab, the first resource dedicated to open source human rights investigations.[38] The site includes case studies of the use of open source research in human rights reporting, a resource list, and training exercises.

Meanwhile, Amnesty International attempted to tackle a second challenge related to open source investigations. The volume of digital content coming out of conflict zones such as Syria and Libya proved too overwhelming for any single researcher to review and process in order to conduct any meaningful analysis. The organization thus attempted to build on its long history of activism by bringing volunteers into the research process, in order to create a sort of triage process to sort through the at times overwhelming amount for open source digital information. It launched a pilot project called the *Citizen Evidence Media Project* in September 2013,[39] which eventually led to the authors of this chapter and the editors of this book working, with others, on the creation of the *Digital Verification Corps* (DVC) in the autumn of 2016.[40] This university-based network of trained student volunteers plays a crucial role in discovering and verifying open source digital content and, in many ways, is the successor to Amnesty volunteers researching and clipping newspaper articles from the 1960s to the 1980s.

This growing capacity and expertise of human rights groups is most clearly in evidence when open source video analysis is combined with satellite imagery analysis. A prime example in this vein of the new opportunities that open source content offers to the human rights community is an investigation into mass graves in Burundi in late 2015. A single video showing a mass grave that was created following political violence in December 2015 proved enough to pinpoint its exact location on Google Earth, in a rural area outside the capital Bujumbura. A time-series of satellite images confirmed that the burial site emerged in mid-December, which was consistent with eyewitness testimony of when the massacre occurred. The available data allowed researchers to create a spatio-temporal record of an atrocity crime independently, and to counter official government narratives downplaying reports of state sanctioned extra-judicial killings.[41] The location and timeline of this mass grave might never have been known were it not for the review and analysis of open source information.[42]

In the course of this work, open source human rights investigators extensively draw on the expertise from various professions, especially to analyse visual content. This includes medical-, ballistic-, or weapons experts, among others. Practices and techniques borrowed from architecture, for example, started to become part of the analysis process. Architects

[38] Olivia Solon, 'Amnesty Platform Validates Civilian Conflict Footage' *Wired UK* (11 July 2014) https://web.archive.org/web/20140711065437/http:/www.wired.co.uk/news/archive/2014-07/08/amnesty-verification-tool accessed 20 December 2018.

[39] Will Moore, 'Introducing the Citizen Media Evidence Partnership (C-MEP)' *Will Opines* (23 September 2013) https://willopines.wordpress.com/2013/09/23/introducing-the-citizen-media-evidence-partnership-c-mep/ accessed 20 December 2018.

[40] Aviva Rutkin, 'Human Rights Squad Detects Abuse in Warzone Social Media Images' *New Scientist* (11 November 2016) https://www.newscientist.com/article/2112483-human-rights-squad-detects-abuse-in-warzone-social-media-images/ accessed 20 December 2018.

[41] Siobhán O'Grady, 'Satellite Images Point Finger at Burundian Forces in Mass Killing' *Foreign Policy* (28 January 2016) https://foreignpolicy.com/2016/01/28/satellite-images-point-finger-at-burundian-forces-in-mass-killing/ accessed 20 December 2018; Christoph Koettl, 'A Convergence of Visuals: Geospatial and Open Source Analysis in Human Rights Documentation' in Sandra Ristovska (ed), *Visual Imagery and Human Rights Practice* (Palgrave Macmillan 2018).

[42] ibid.

provide immense added value by producing detailed event and scene reconstruction, using a wide variety of digital open source content. The term 'forensic architecture' emerged in the 1980s,[43] and the field started to contribute regularly to human rights investigations in 2009, for example in Gaza, Syria, and Mexico, among many other locations.

4. Case Studies

Several recent investigations—in Myanmar, Cameroon, Libya, Democratic Republic of Congo, and Nigeria—vividly illustrate the remarkable value of open source research for human rights reporting. Similar to the Burundi case above, none of these investigations would have been possible, or would have had the impact they had, were it not for open source research and analysis.

4.1 Rakhine State, Myanmar (2016 and 2017)

Reporting on the serious violations committed by Myanmar's security forces against the Rohingya minority in Rakhine state in 2016 and 2017 demonstrates the value of open source research and some of the modern methods being used to document occurrences. They also demonstrate well the changing methods of human rights reporting. Rakhine state in northwest Myanmar was completely sealed off by the Myanmar authorities to independent, outside observers such as journalists, human rights investigators, and the United Nations,[44] some of whom suffered severe consequences when attempting to investigate on the ground.[45] The situation has thus appropriately been described as an 'information black hole'.[46] However, using remote sensing and visual social media content—complementing interviews with refugees—allowed researchers to document human rights violations meticulously during the 2016 violence and the ethnic cleansing campaign of 2017. To investigate this inaccessible area, human rights organizations took advantage of multiple open data sets ranging from geo-data to remote sensing and data available on social media.

First, it was important to find proper geographic data for villages in northern Rakhine state to investigate specific reports filtering out of Myanmar of widespread human rights violations. Google and other standard online mapping platforms often have only sparse data from such remote areas. Luckily, in this case the Myanmar Information Management Unit (MIMU) provided detailed geo-data that allowed for populating GIS programmes, such as Google Earth, with every village in the region. This was the starting point to investigate reports of violations, which are connected to specific places.

[43] Eyal Weizman, *Forensic Architecture: Violence at the Threshold of Detectability* (Zone Books 2017).

[44] 'UN Rights Expert "Disappointed" by Myanmar's Decision to Refuse Visit' *UN News* (20 December 2017) https://news.un.org/en/story/2017/12/639982-un-rights-expert-disappointed-myanmars-decision-refuse-visit accessed 20 December 2018.

[45] Richard C Paddock, 'They Documented a Massacre. Their Prize Is a Prison Cell in Myanmar' *The New York Times* (15 October 2018) https://www.nytimes.com/2018/04/10/world/asia/myanmar-reuters-journalists-massacre.html accessed 20 December 2018.

[46] J Jacob, 'Rohingya Crisis: "Latest Violence Marks Predictable Escalation in Genocidal Process"' *International Business Times* (15 October 2016) http://www.ibtimes.sg/rohingya-crisis-latest-violence-marks-predictable-escalation-genocidal-process-3938 accessed 20 December 2018.

Satellite images and other remotely sensed data proved crucial to both investigate attacks on specific villages and to show the scale of the violations. For example, Amnesty International used satellite images to confirm attacks on the villages of Tula Toli[47] and Hpar Wat Chaung.[48] The satellite images proved especially powerful in the case of Hpar Wat Chaung, documenting the destruction of the village in mid-September 2017. These allowed Amnesty International to refute public claims by Myanmar's State Counsellor, Aung San Suu Kyi, that military operations had ended as of 5 September. Satellite detected active fire data from NASA[49] made it possible to corroborate further and narrow down the date of attacks, since the satellite sensors collect the exact minute of an active fire. Later, human rights organizations used satellite images to document the final step in Myanmar's ethnic cleansing campaign: the permanent razing of former Rohingya villages in the spring of 2018.[50]

Images and videos that recorded the burning of villages, and which were largely shared via social media, provided the most detailed look at systematic human rights violations in Rakhine state. Using the above-mentioned MIMU dataset of settlements, researchers were able first to find an attack's reported location on Google Earth. Then, matching features visible in the images and videos, such as hills, rivers, or remaining structures with satellite images on Google Earth made it possible to confirm the exact location of an attack. In the village of Kyet Yoe Pyin, for example, Amnesty International was able to match videos of a burned market and mosque with satellite images. These findings were consistent with testimonies that the village was burned in October 2016.

Additionally, researchers reviewed every single piece of visual content for its provenance to ensure that it indeed represented a new violation in Rakhine. This can be either done through reviewing metadata, where available, or conducting a simple reverse image search—finding the same photograph online using reverse image search engines such as Google Images or TinEye—to detect previously shared content.

All these steps were crucial considering the massive amount of mis-information shared online related to the persecution of Rohingyas. The standard misinformation promoted in the context of Rakhine were a set of images some individuals (falsely) described as Buddhist monks burning Rohingya victims, including children[51]—in fact, these images showed the cremation of victims of the 2010 China earthquake by Tibetan monks. It helps that in this case the original images came from official news agencies,[52] and were easy to find using the reverse image search techniques outlined later in this book.

[47] Oliver Holmes, 'Myanmar: Satellite Imagery Confirms Rohingya Village of Tula Toli Razed' *The Guardian* (19 September 2017) https://www.theguardian.com/world/2017/sep/19/myanmar-satellite-imagery-confirms-rohingya-village-of-tula-toli-razed accessed 20 December 2018.

[48] Amnesty International, 'Myanmar: "Damning" Video and Satellite Evidence Shows New Fires in Rohingya Villages' (22 September 2017) https://www.amnesty.org.uk/press-releases/myanmar-damning-video-and-satellite-evidence-shows-new-fires-rohingya-villages accessed 20 December 2018.

[49] NASA, 'Active Fire Data' https://earthdata.nasa.gov/earth-observation-data/near-real-time/firms/active-fire-data accessed 20 December 2018.

[50] Human Rights Watch, 'Burma: Scores of Rohingya Villages Bulldozed' (23 February 2018) https://www.hrw.org/news/2018/02/23/burma-scores-rohingya-villages-bulldozed accessed 20 December 2018.

[51] Armen Hajdari, 'What's Your Opinion about Muslim Children Being Burned by Buddhists in #burma Do Muslims Matter Anymore???' *@armenhajdari* (6 December 2016) https://twitter.com/armenhajdari/status/805976812597739520/photo/1 accessed 20 December 2018.

[52] Ni Yuxing, 'China Earthquake Aftermath Photos and Images' *european pressphoto agency* (19 April 2010) http://www.epa.eu/disasters-photos/earthquake-photos/china-earthquake-aftermath-photos-02123961 accessed 20 December 2018.

4.2 Torture in Cameroon (2017)

A shaky video that emerged in January 2017 showed apparent members of Cameroon's special forces beating detained men in the courtyard of a house.[53] The scene certainly seemed emblematic of the widespread human rights violations committed by Cameroon's armed forces in their fight against Boko Haram, an armed group active across north-east Nigeria, Cameroon, Niger, and Chad. However, to confirm this, the accuracy of the video had to be established first.

In 2017, Amnesty International's Digital Verification Corps, a global network of trained university students, assessed digital content from Cameroon as part of a larger Amnesty research report.[54] The report's conclusions proved highly sensitive, as they included the exposure of torture at Cameroonian military bases that were also used by US and other foreign troops. And the report's release showed the immediate impact open source human rights documentation can have: In addition to extensive media coverage of the report's conclusions, the US Africa Command (AFRICOM) launched an inquiry into any knowledge of Cameroonian torture by US troops within days of the report's publication.[55] The video was originally posted on Twitter in the evening of 13 January 2017, but to begin to verify its veracity, researchers had first to check that the video was not from a previous date or non-Cameroonian location. Social media research always begins with determining the relevance of the content, ensuring that, in this case, the video had not appeared online previously. A first step in doing this is to run key thumbnail images through online reverse image searches. Reverse image search of thumbnails suggested that this version was the earliest available online. In addition, the social media profiles of the person who posted the video suggested that he was based in Cameroon.

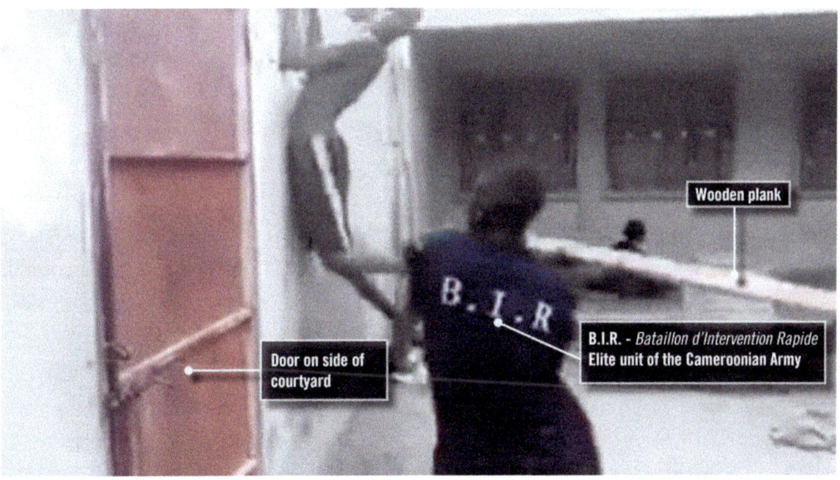

Figure 1.4 Graphic produced by Christoph Koettl

[53] Christoph Koettl and Haley Willis, 'Eyes on Cameroon: Videos Capture Human Rights Violations by the Security Forces in the Forces in the Fight against Boko Haram' *Lemming Cliff* (19 July 2017) https://medium.com/lemming-cliff/eyes-on-cameroon-videos-capture-human-rights-violations-by-the-security-forces-in-the-fight-ae537a5cdc4b accessed 20 December 2018.

[54] Amnesty International, 'Cameroon's Secret Torture Chambers: Human Rights Violations and War Crimes in the Fight against Boko Haram' (2017) https://www.amnesty.org/download/Documents/AFR1765362017ENGLISH.PDF accessed 5 May 2018.

[55] Paul McLeary, 'Pentagon Investigating if U.S. Troops Knew of Torture at Cameroonian Base' *Foreign Policy* (27 July 2017) https://foreignpolicy.com/2017/07/27/pentagon-investigating-if-u-s-troops-knew-of-torture-at-cameroonian-base/ accessed 20 December 2018.

The next step was to identify the primary actors. In the footage, the acronym 'BIR' is visible on the T-shirts of the perpetrators in several instances. BIR is an acronym for *Bataillon d'Intervention Rapide* [the rapid intervention battalion]—the elite unit of the Cameroonian Army tasked with fighting Boko Haram.

Descriptions of torture from a 2016 Amnesty International report are consistent with the crimes seen in the video, where victims are kicked and hit with wooden planks. According to the testimonies of former detainees quoted in the report, 'the men in plain clothes kicked them and slapped them violently, and hit them with wooden sticks'.[56] Reviews of previous reports of BIR misconduct suggested that the men in the video were being tortured based on the suspicion of being Boko Haram supporters. This information points to a very different motive for torture than that which was being circulated on social media at the time, namely, that the video was related to protests and a crackdown in the English-speaking regions of the country.[57]

One of the men being beaten in this video is speaking Fulani, a commonly spoken language in the Far North region of Cameroon. And the woman seen sitting in the background is wearing her clothes and hair in the traditional style of the Kanuri, an ethnic group living in the Far North region of Cameroon, and around the Lake Chad basin. This information points to events in the video occurring in the Far North rather than Cameroon's western Anglophone regions, as was claimed in multiple social media posts.

Further, investigators were able to match video evidence with a specific locale. BIR soldiers are stationed at several permanent and temporary fortified bases in the Far North, including the border town of Kolofata located 70 km from Maroua. Some of the bases even display BIR in large letters on the roofs of their barracks, which is easy to spot in publicly available satellite imagery.

Google Earth allowed researchers to identify a house that matched the features visible in the video within a fortified area in Kolofata. Using only a short, shaky video, the researchers were able to pinpoint the exact location of a torture site under the control of the BIR. Drawings and descriptions from a former detainee matched satellite imagery of the location, confirming the findings.

The conduct of torture in the country goes beyond the Cameroonian authorities. The United States and several other countries provide military assistance to Cameroon, and, as already noted, US military personnel are stationed in the country. This includes at the BIR headquarters and military base in Salak, one of the sites where incommunicado detention and torture of suspected Boko Haram members was routinely carried out between 2014 and 2017. US and French military personnel, as well as private Israeli contractors, were present in the BIR base in Salak to provide training and assistance. Research by Forensic Architecture, an independent research institute at Goldsmiths, University of London, uncovered multiple Facebook postings showing US soldiers in the immediate vicinity of locations of torture within Salak. It was this visual material and spatial proximity that prompted

[56] Amnesty International, 'Cameroon: More than 1,000 People Accused of Supporting Boko Haram Held in Horrific Conditions, Some Tortured to Death' (14 July 2016) https://www.amnesty.org/en/latest/news/2016/07/cameroun-conditions-de-detention-effroyables-voire-tortures-a-mort-pour-plus-de-1-000-personnes-accusees-de-soutenir-boko-haram/ accessed 6 October 2019.

[57] 'Eugene N Nforngwa on Twitter: "#SomeoneTellBiya: These Are Supposed to Be the Most Desciplined Soldiers in #cameroon #BIR ... "' https://twitter.com/en_nforngwa/status/819985183977963520 accessed 20 December 2018.

the AFRICOM investigation of what their own troops knew[58]—another instance of open source information complementing human rights investigations.

4.3 Libya (2017)

Human rights groups have also repeatedly used open source visual materials to document extrajudicial executions in Libya.[59] A string of executions from 2016 to 2018 featuring Mustafa Busyf Al-Werfalli, a commander of the Al-Saiqa Brigade (an elite forces unit of the Libyan National Army active in the city of Benghazi), were all captured on video. The videos provided the basis for both documentation by human rights and international organizations and, in August 2017, a first arrest warrant by the International Criminal Court (ICC) (a second was issued in 2018). The ICC warrant stated that Al-Werfalli 'appears to be directly responsible for the killing of, in total, thirty-three persons in Benghazi or surrounding areas, between on or before 3 June 2016 and on or around 17 July 2017, either by personally killing them or by ordering their Execution'.[60] The warrant alleged that the crimes happened during the Al-Saiqa Brigade's participation in Operation Dignity, a campaign launched in May 2014 by Field Marshal Khalifa Haftar to fight terrorist groups in Benghazi.

At first glance, there is nothing particularly remarkable in the warrant compared to other ICC warrants for arrest issued around the same time. What sets it apart, however, is the warrant's evidentiary basis: the warrant relies on both 'video material and transcripts of video material' and 'internal orders, and social media posts by the Media Centre of the Al-Saiqa Brigade' to come to its decision to prosecute Al-Werfalli. As Emma Irving notes, 'it is the first ICC arrest warrant to be based largely on evidence collected from social media'.[61]

To date, Al-Werfalli can be seen in eight execution videos posted to different social media accounts. Several of the posts come from persons with links to the Al-Saiqa Brigade—the brigade of which Al-Werfelli is believed to be a commander. The open source investigation collective Bellingcat set out to geolocate the incidents—including the execution of twenty people in July 2017.[62] Bellingcat not only located the video to Benghazi, but satellite imagery of 17 July 2017 appeared to show new bloodstains stemming from the bodies, thus also confirming the date. This perfect meshing of available evidence in open source information is rare—but when it does come together it strengthens the evidence base even more.

What is important in this case is that it is a first step to test if verified and geolocated open source video holds enough weight to be used in evidence in tribunals such as the International Criminal Court. To date, Al-Werfalli has not appeared in The Hague. But the fact that the Office of the Prosecutor was prepared to issue a warrant based predominantly on video evidence already shows the great strides that have been made towards open

58 Weizman (n 43).

59 Amnesty International, '"Public Execution" in Football Stadium Shows Libya's Descent into Lawlessness' (22 August 2014) https://www.amnesty.org/en/latest/news/2014/08/public-execution-football-stadium-shows-libya-s-descent-lawlessness/> accessed 20 December 2018.

60 Judge Joyce Aluoch, Judge Cuno Tarfusser, and Judge Péter Kovács, 'Situation in Libya in the Case of the Prosecutor v Mahmoud Mustafa Busayf Al-Werfalli' 17.

61 Emma Irving, 'And So It Begins ... Social Media Evidence in an ICC Arrest Warrant' *Opinio Juris* (17 August 2017) http://opiniojuris.org/2017/08/17/and-so-it-begins-social-media-evidence-in-an-icc-arrest-warrant/ accessed 20 December 2018.

62 Bellingcat, 'How a Werfalli Execution Site Was Geolocated' (10 March 2017) https://www.bellingcat.com/news/mena/2017/10/03/how-an-execution-site-was-geolocated/ accessed 20 December 2018.

source acceptance. As Emma Irving states: 'The approach taken to this type of evidence will prove crucial for any future proceedings in conflicts such as Syria and Yemen, where open source material abounds. The warrant for Mr. Al-Werfalli is just the beginning of what will be a long, and likely complex, relationship between open source evidence and international criminal justice.'[63]

4.4 Democratic Republic of Congo (2018)

In February 2018, witness reports emerged that villages in a remote region of the Democratic Republic of Congo were being burned amid a renewal of communal fighting.[64] The clashes between the Hema and Lendu communities—located on the eastern side of the Ituri province, bordering Uganda—started in December 2017 and escalated in early February 2018. Historically, such conflicts have been difficult to analyse because of lack of access to the affected area. But geospatial technologies and publicly available data allowed researchers and journalists to investigate this incident in close to real time and show that numerous villages were burned to the ground in February 2018.

The first step was to collect active-fire data from NASA—thermal anomalies, or hot spots, that are recorded daily.[65] It showed dozens of fires in the region on the densely forested mountain ridge and along the shoreline of Lake Albert, one of the African Great Lakes between the DRC and Uganda. Human rights groups previously used this type of data, in combination with other information, to document the military's scorched-earth campaign against the Rohingya in Myanmar, as was described above. Active-fire data does not provide the cause of a fire, so one must exercise caution in interpreting it, especially when researching violence. Further, the satellites that collect this information do not provide actual images; they only record the location of active fires, and very large ones at that.

Google and other online mapping platforms often show only blurry satellite images or have no location names for remote areas such as the small fishing villages around Lake Albert. This makes it difficult to pinpoint where people live. To deal with this challenge, the journalists used residential data from the online mapping site Openstreetmap, an editable online mapping site. Overlaying the NASA data with the Openstreetmap data in Google Earth allowed visual inspection of recorded fires that occurred in or near populated places—likely places that were affected by violence. This simple process produced a shortlist of ten locations to investigate.

Next, the satellite company DigitalGlobe provided high-resolution satellite imagery and analysis of these places. The results were disturbing: all the villages on the shortlist were at least partially burned, with hundreds of destroyed homes. This new visual proof provided a strong basis to report out the whole story. Taking advantage of open geospatial data resulted in reporting on very specific details from both sides of the lake, not just at the refugee landing site in Uganda, which had been the focus of reporting up to that point. Combining these findings with traditional reporting mainly interviews with humanitarian workers in

[63] Irving (n 61).

[64] Christoph Koettl, 'How We Identified Burned Villages in the Democratic Republic of Congo' *The New York Times* (25 September 2018) https://www.nytimes.com/2018/03/08/insider/burned-villages-democratic-republic-congo.html> accessed 20 December 2018.

[65] NASA (n 49).

Uganda—allowed the *New York Times* to present the findings in a very visual way to a large audience.[66]

4.5 Niger Delta, Nigeria (2018)

Amnesty International's 'Decoders' project is an innovative means of addressing one of the biggest problems associated with open source research, namely, sorting through exceptionally large volumes of information, typically contained in unstructured or 'messy' datasets, for pertinent information. Although invaluable information of potential human rights violations may be contained within the data, the resources—in terms of human hours—required to structure and prepare it for analysis are often prohibitive. In response, Amnesty developed a micro-tasking model, mobilizing 'digital volunteers' from across the world.

The micro-tasking model itself is relatively simple: the dataset is broken down into small, discrete packages, or 'tasks,' which are then made available to the digital volunteers. This allows for large amounts of information to be examined in parallel in a relatively small timeframe, opening up significant possibilities for future analysis and investigation. The Decode Darfur project, for example, involved 28,600 volunteers from 147 different countries, who submitted an average of 16.5 tasks every minute for seven weeks, contributing a total of 9,065 hours.[67] Had this task been approached in the traditional manner, by a desk-based researcher, it would have taken over four years of full-time work.

The digital volunteers involved with the decoder project do not undertake new forms of human rights work; instead they analyse satellite imagery to determine whether a village is present or whether it is damaged, examine documents, and so on. The key differences from traditional research are the scale and often transformative speed at which large datasets can be addressed. Whereas once a researcher could engage with only part of a dataset, owing to time and resource constraints, now the entire dataset can be examined, allowing for a comprehensive analysis of the situation and providing significantly greater evidentiary weight. In the 'Decode the Difference' project, for example, digital volunteers and Amnesty researchers were able to analyse every village in a 326,000 km^2 region of Darfur. As a result, the researchers were able to demonstrate convincingly that attacks against civilians were carried out in a systematic manner. Without the digital volunteers evidencing the systematic nature of the attacks—an essential element of a crime against humanity—would have been impossible.

The potential of the Decoders project can also be seen in a series of projects organized to respond to environmental harm caused by oil spills in the Niger Delta.[68] Through the destruction of livelihoods such as fish grounds, these oil spills have a significant impact on the local environment and thus on local communities. Environmental destruction caused by oil spills has have been the subject of Amnesty International campaigns for a number of years. One result of the campaigning has been that investigations are now jointly conducted by the company and the police once an oil spill is detected, with their handwritten investigative

66 Koettl, 'How We Identified Burned Villages in the Democratic Republic of Congo' (n 64).

67 Amnesty International, 'Decode Darfur' *Decode Darfur* (15 October 2016) https://decoders.amnesty.org accessed 20 December 2018.

68 Interview with Milena Marin, May 2018.

form then scanned and uploaded on to the company website. The thousands of approximately eight-page investigative reports indicate the claimed cause of the spill, its location, photographs of the pipeline, and so on. Amnesty International researchers simply did not have the time or staff resources required to transcribe these documents in order to prepare them for analysis.

Amnesty International engaged the digital volunteers to transcribe the documents in order to assist in the pursuit of accountability for the oil spills and compensation for the communities affected. In order to facilitate this task, Amnesty identified the key components to look for within the reports. The principal element of interest was information on the source of the spill, as this is relevant to compensation claims. However, this could be corroborated or contested based on other key information or hints in the document that could contradict the official cause. Key tasks therefore involved extracting information on the location and size of the spill and examining the photos. The photos of the spills were particularly relevant. If the documents claimed that a spill was the result of theft (a common occurrence in Nigeria), but the image showed significant corrosion, Amnesty could contest the reported cause and claim compensation for the community. Each document was sent to multiple volunteers, in order to facilitate accuracy of analysis. If the volunteers were split in the conclusions they reached, an Amnesty researcher might step in to conduct further investigation.

In total, 3,545 volunteers from 142 countries worked on the oil spill project over several weeks, analysing 2,985 documents. Eighty-nine suspicious reports were identified, allowing Amnesty to pursue compensation claims on behalf of local communities. The results of the data also provided a strong platform for advocacy and a means by which to engage the companies on their due diligence obligations. For example, if a large number of the spills were claimed to be a consequence of theft, Amnesty International could consult the data to identify the key locations along the pipeline where spills occurred, and then advocate that the companies establish focused patrols.

An added value of this crowdsourced model is that it mobilizes willing volunteers from around the world and provides a means whereby individuals can actively contribute to meaningful human rights work. This helps reduce the distinction between professional human rights workers and engaged citizens and provides a convenient means of engagement. Digital volunteers work on small tasks, meaning that they can contribute on a sporadic basis, and can work on a single task for a few minutes, or multiple tasks over a few hours, depending on their availability. The process itself is often 'gamified, in order to encourage volunteers to stay engaged, and to make the process as enjoyable as possible.

5. Conclusion

Human rights organizations have a long tradition of utilizing open source information in documenting abuse. As this chapter has shown, human rights organizations early on adopted, or led the development of, new research methods to integrate digital open source information into traditional reporting. Building on this body of work, some human rights groups have engaged volunteers to process the growing amount of digital open source information, which has given them a leg up in discovering and verifying human rights relevant digital content, as we saw in the Cameroon incident.

The need for integrating digital open source research into traditional human rights reporting was triggered by several structural changes in information and communication technologies in the 1990s and early 2000s. These changes offered opportunities for new data collection and circumvention of state information control. Human rights violations that governments had successfully concealed in the past were suddenly visible in plain sight owing to public access to high-resolution satellite imagery, for example in the analysis of images of North Korean detention camps. The global proliferation of smartphones and digital networks led to the next chapter in the use of digital open source information in human rights documentation. Single violations captured on video and shared to a global audience were followed by social media documentation of larger events such as protests in Burma, Iran, and, later, the war in Syria. This evolution has forced human rights researchers and organizations to develop new tools and methods of discovery, archiving and verification in order to take full advantage of the new information environment.

2

Open Source Evidence and Human Rights Cases

A Modern Social History

Alexa Koenig

It was late October 2012, and a characteristically damp morning in The Hague when roughly thirty-five people gathered in a white, windowless room at the International Criminal Court (ICC). Legal investigators from international and hybrid tribunals, geospatial analysts, and representatives from some of the world's largest human rights non-governmental organizations (NGOs) milled around the large rectangular table that dominated the room, some drifting into the hall to grab coffee and glance at the background papers for the workshop that was about to start.

Prosecutors at the ICC had recently seen four cases fall apart at relatively early stages of prosecution, and the question that had been laid out almost a year earlier on a very different table in Berkeley, California, was 'why?'[1] To answer that question, UC Berkeley's Human Rights Center had sent a young historian, Peggy O'Donnell, to the Office of the Prosecutor (OTP) for the summer. Her review of thousands of pages of court documents revealed a fairly straightforward answer: according to the judges, the OTP was relying too heavily on NGO reports and witness testimony. While NGO reports provided helpful background information, they did not meet the evidentiary threshold needed to convince the judges that the cases should proceed. And with time and trauma, and the terror tactics employed by the powerful people the Court was prosecuting, some witnesses' testimonies were falling apart from lack of corroborating information or witnesses so terrorized they did not show up at all. While the judges had been fairly lenient with the OTP during the Court's earliest years, they were starting to lose their patience.

Berkeley's Human Rights Center had organized the three-day workshop—'Beyond Reasonable Doubt: Using Scientific Evidence to Advance Prosecutions at the International Criminal Court'—to help the OTP overcome its evidentiary hurdles. The gold standard for proving any case is to triangulate physical, testimonial, and documentary evidence; this workshop would focus on what new scientific and technological methods could be used to shore up the heart-wrenching stories of survivors. The Center had invited prosecutors and investigators from numerous tribunals—including those investigating genocides in Rwanda, the former Yugoslavia, and Cambodia—to explain how they had overcome similar

[1] By 2011, the Human Rights Center already had a long history of engagement with the Court: its faculty director, Eric Stover, had been involved in establishment of the Rome Statute. Later, he consulted on a number of projects, including helping to establish surveys of witness experiences. The Center had also played a pivotal role in kickstarting the human rights and technology movement—and thinking through how emerging technologies could assist human rights documentation—by hosting the world's first global conference on the subject in 2009: the Soul of the New Machine (Piracés 2018).

challenges; invited representatives from NGOs to explain how they sourced their content; and asked a handful of scientists and technologists to showcase the relatively new tools and methods they were using for information collection. The diverse participants had been carefully curated to achieve two goals: (1) to 'promote an ongoing exchange of ideas, expertise and strategies for the application of new and emerging scientific methods and technologies to judicial investigations of serious international crimes'; and (2) 'to expand the range of strategic and technological resources for investigators and prosecutors to use in pursuing accountability for such crimes'.[2]

Each of the presenters had been asked to prepare six points that would help the OTP ascertain the feasibility of adopting their method or technology: (1) the cost and the apparent trajectory of that cost; (2) the likely time needed to collect, verify, and analyse that type of information; (3) how the method or tool complemented an overall case, including its potential to triangulate other documentary, physical, or testimonial evidence; (4) the potential to contribute 'linkage evidence'—evidence that would tie the crime to the accused who might be in command yet physically remote from the crime scene—one of the categories of information the OTP most desperately needed; (5) the security vulnerabilities and other concerns raised by the method or technology; and (6) strategies that could be used to overcome any cost or security challenges.[3]

As the meeting started, the mood was expectant, if a bit wary. Eric Stover, head of Berkeley's Human Rights Center, and Michel de Smedt, head of investigations at the OTP, welcomed everyone; others from the OTP introduced the participants to what constitutes court-admissible evidence. O'Donnell followed. The chambers, she explained, were no longer willing to accept the types of evidence the prosecutors were offering as sufficient at the preliminary investigations phase; investigators and prosecutors would need to have significant corroborating information even at very early stages of an investigation in order to be permitted to move to trial.

Next came the Office of the High Commissioner for Human Rights, followed closely by representatives from the biggest NGOs in the space: Human Rights Watch, Amnesty International, Physicians for Human Rights, and—to address the abundant investigatory challenges raised by sexual violence—Women's Initiatives for Gender Justice. The conversation with one NGO was particularly tense: investigators and prosecutors wanted that NGO to share more information about its sources; the NGO refused, chastising them to find their own evidence. Quite a bit of time was devoted to closing that gap, the NGO arguing that the OTP should get in country sooner, the OTP explaining the political, legal, and operational constraints that sometimes made that impossible.

The second day, as presenters began showcasing their techniques—remote sensing, video analysis, big data analytics, and new forensic techniques recently adopted by the Special Tribunal for Lebanon, the Institute for International Criminal Investigations, and the Netherlands Forensic Institute—the room began to fill: one by one and in small groups, ICC investigators crowded into the windowless, white space. An especially animated conversation focused on the recent global proliferation of smartphones and their potential use

[2] Peggy O'Donnell and others, 'Beyond Reasonable Doubt: Using Scientific Evidence to Advance Prosecutions at the International Criminal Court' (The Human Rights Center at the University of California, Berkeley, School of Law 2012).

[3] ibid.

by witnesses to document crimes, possibly overcoming many of the OTP's challenges over getting into countries quickly. What was needed was a way to communicate the needs of courts with those doing the documenting, the latter of whom increasingly captured significant quantities of information but not the kinds that were most helpful to legal processes. Many of the videos flowing out of conflict areas simply recorded the crime itself or its immediate aftermath, and not the contextual, lead, and linkage evidence for which the court was starved. Participants began to brainstorm how video and photographic content could be strengthened, reducing volume and increasing quality for court purposes, along with what was needed to disseminate that information to people who could help.

And with that, a new generation of human rights investigations had begun.

***

The OTP's strategic plan for 2012–2015, released almost a year after the workshop, underscored the need for more digital and scientific evidence. Over the next two years, the Court's Investigations Division would spend considerable time developing an infrastructure to make that possible, including establishing a Scientific Advisory Board and a Technology Advisory Board. The Human Rights Center would lead three more workshops, all focused on increasing the flow of digital evidence into human rights legal investigations:[4] the first concentrated on securing video, photographic, and other digital content from both closed and open sources; the second, on obtaining data from social media companies; and the third, on strengthening information sharing between international courts and first responders, whether those responders were atrocity survivors or representatives of NGOs.

In its 2014 workshop report on digital evidence, the Human Rights Center recommended that the OTP 'hire specialists trained in cyber investigation techniques and familiar with cutting-edge technologies', explaining that 'bringing on specialists in digital data mining and analysis will go a long way toward building a robust in-house capacity for vetting digital data and extracting quality evidence'.[5] For the second 2014 workshop, this time focused on social media, the Center invited the OTP to come to San Francisco, where—with Yahoo and the non-profit video documentation organization Videre est Credere—they brought together representatives from the world's largest social media companies to talk with the OTP about the data the companies held that had potential value for human rights and war crimes investigators. There, and at a public workshop at RightsCon the next day, the OTP explained its mandate: to serve as a court where survivors of human rights abuses that qualified as international crimes could secure justice against government and quasi-government actors.[6] The OTP also explained its need to identify and demonstrate relationships between

[4] The workshops were substantively and financially supported by Open Society Justice Initiative, with additional financial support from Humanity United, the John D. and Catherine T. MacArthur Foundation, Oak Foundation, and Open Society Foundations. The Salzburg workshops were also supported by Salzburg Global Seminars, and The New Forensics by the Rockefeller Foundation.

[5] Alexa Koenig, Stephen Cody, and Eric Stover, 'Digital Fingerprints: Using Electronic Evidence to Advance Prosecutions at the International Criminal Court' (The Human Rights Center at the University of California, Berkeley, School of Law 2014).

[6] Alexa Koenig, 'The International Criminal Court at RightsCon: Upping Its Cyber Game' *HuffPost* (5 November 2014) https://www.huffingtonpost.com/alexa-koenig-/the-international-crimina_1_b_4936346.html accessed 29 December 2018.

those who perpetrated the crimes and the higher ups who ordered or condoned them—what better way to identify those social networks than through social media?

Although the original goal of the Bay Area meeting was to see if a framework could be established for information sharing between the OTP and social media companies, still fresh on everyone's minds was the 2013 leak of documents by Edward Snowden establishing that the National Security Agency (NSA) was conducting global surveillance of everyday citizens in partnership with US government and foreign agencies.[7] The companies were concerned about sharing information about their users with anyone who might be perceived as law enforcement, such as the ICC. But, they explained, much of what the Court was saying it needed did not have to come through them, anyway: all the OTP needed was researchers who knew how to use the platforms' advanced search functionalities to comb for relevant content.

With that tip in hand, the next question for the OTP and its human rights supporters was, 'who are the people with those skills?'

1. Ethan Hampton, Kelly Matheson, Brad Samuels, and the *Al-Mahdi* Case

Ethan Hampton[8] had tried a couple of times to catch the ICC's attention. A journalist by background, he had started his career at a daily newspaper, one of a handful of young reporters who had a talent for poking around and digging up information online. By 2014, he was several years into a job at Storyful. Billed as the world's 'first social media news agency', the scrappy start-up—which had opened its doors in 2010 with an investment of US$100,000 and the innovative enthusiasm of a posse of young Irish reporters—had just been acquired by News Corp for a whopping US$25 million.[9] From the beginning, Storyful's team had effectively explored how social media could be creatively mined to detect breaking news and to scoop the major media outlets. By clustering tweets into streams, Storyful reporters could detect flurries of activity, for example, which could quickly be verified and shared with news outlets that paid for the original content the reporters harvested from social media.

Now, post-acquisition, Hampton had his heart set on putting his talents towards the law. He had recently finished a master's degree in international relations, completing a thesis on comparative genocide. The son of a military officer, he was nurturing a strong sense of justice and a relatively unique set of skills. What he did not know was that the OTP had been working hard to diversify its approach to evidence—and particularly its use of social media content—between his first application and his second, and that he would soon

[7] Scott Shane, 'No Morsel Too Minuscule for All-Consuming N.S.A.' *The New York Times* (11 March 2013) https://www.nytimes.com/2013/11/03/world/no-morsel-too-minuscule-for-all-consuming-nsa.html accessed 29 December 2018.

[8] A pseudonym.

[9] Stephen Smith, 'The End of the Beginning for Storyful' *Irish Central* (4 February 2014) http://www.irishcentral.com/business/startups/The-End-of-the-Beginning-for-Storyful.html accessed 29 December 2018; Ingrid Lunden, 'News Corp Pays $25M for Storyful, Which Digs Up and Verifies News from Social Sites Like Twitter and Instagram' *TechCrunch* (20 December 2013) http://social.techcrunch.com/2013/12/20/news-corp-buys-storyful-for-25m-to-dig-up-verified-news-from-social-media-sites-like-twitter-and-instagram/ accessed 29 December 2018.

become one of their first investigators focused on collecting, verifying, and triangulating open sources.

While some open source content had been used in earlier international criminal cases (see Chapter 3), the first big test of what could be achieved came with the *Ahmad Al-Faqi Al-Mahdi*[10] prosecution. The charges centred on Al-Mahdi's alleged destruction of cultural heritage property in Timbuktu, Mali. Investigators had obtained videos of the destruction—much of it filmed by the perpetrators themselves. Hampton and analysts from the prosecutors' Investigative Analysis section set to work analysing the open source videos and threading them together with evidence collected by OTP staff from external sources and through crime scene missions with support from investigators on the ground, who took original photographs to help verify the content. Geolocating the images, the team was able to identify multiple points of corroboration to confirm the likely dates and locations where the incidents had occurred. Their geolocation report—which pulled together both open source and original investigatory material—ultimately came to hundreds of pages.

***

One of the people who would soon eagerly await the judges' response to the *Al-Mahdi* geolocation report was Kelly Matheson. But for now—it was 2014—she was in San Francisco at RightsCon—the annual meeting of technologists and human rights activists—seeking out contacts who might advise her on a massive new project: developing a field guide that would help activists all over the world understand how videos captured on smartphones could potentially be used as evidence in courts. The guide would tell first responders what kind of information was most helpful—legal investigators were often drowning in crime-based evidence, for example, but sorely in need of linkage evidence, or a 360-degree shot of the crime scene—and how to document chain of custody and preserve that content for courts.

Matheson had worked with the non-profit WITNESS since 2007, having first run the organization's video advocacy institute and later launched its North America programme. While WITNESS had been working on video advocacy for years, in the wake of the *Beyond Reasonable Doubt* workshop and in light of feedback from its on-the-ground partners, the organization was shifting its strategy to train front-line activists how to capture evidence for courts. As Matheson explains it:

> [w]e had started doing work in Syria teaching activists and lawyers how to use video to tell the stories needed to compel human rights bodies—the U.N., the Security Council, etc.—to fight for accountability. But despite all of that [advocacy] information coming out of Syria, none of the officials were paying attention.[11]

The activists were determined to see justice done—and justice for them meant accountability in courts. Matheson continued:

[10] *Prosecutor v Ahmad Al-Faqi Al-Mahdi* (Warrant of Arrest) ICC-PIDS-CIS-MAL-01-08/16_Eng (18 September 2015).

[11] Interview with Kelly Matheson (13 October 2018).

> The Syrian activists came to us and said, 'can you help us document [war crimes and human rights abuses] for the long term? We know [any court cases] aren't going to happen next week, next month, or next year. But can you help us preserve this information so that someday, when there is a Syrian war crimes tribunal or when the ICC gets jurisdiction, we have the evidence to put these perpetrators behind bars?'

Although Matheson was a lawyer, she had never used video as evidence in legal proceedings; she had to adapt, and fast. She stated:

> CIJA [the Commission for International Justice and Accountability] basically mentored me in international human rights investigations. I had the honor of going to the border with their team and trying to teach media activists and lawyers to [film] to a legal evidentiary standard. This was new to WITNESS, it was new to me, it was new to the world, really. I mean new to the human rights world. People in criminal justice programs use video evidence all the time. But we weren't teaching these methods within the human rights community. At the same time, Alexa Koenig at the University of California, Berkeley and Alison Cole at the Open Society Justice Initiative were working with the International Criminal Court on developing their first responders program to coordinate the sharing of information between those documenting crimes on the frontlines and investigators. The challenge for all of us was how to get people to collect high quality, actionable information to a trial-ready standard. This coordination was needed because court investigators often couldn't get in country until months, even years, after an event, when the evidence would likely be deteriorated or gone.[12]

After the training, the activists asked Matheson if she would leave her facilitator notes with them so they could train others. She added:

> I said, of course, but let me run my notes by a few people to see if they're accurate. So I ran them by Alexa Koenig and John Ralston and Beth Van Schaack. And I'm just like, 'can you guys please tell me that I'm not lying to everybody, that this is at least accurate information?' That's all I cared about. The [activists] were desperate for information ... So we handed over our facilitator notes, and brought in peers to help us make sure that everything was on point. It just made sense that we [eventually] write the information down in a way that was accessible to the public.

Matheson became increasingly convinced about the potential utility of visual content to strengthen international cases, adding that:

> You know how you have your buckets of evidence, you have your documents, your witness testimonies, your physical evidence, your forensics, your imagery and your open source? Well, of course video fits into imagery and open source. And in the imagery bucket, video can work together with different kinds of information: If you have satellite imagery, drone

[12] ibid.

> footage, and video, you have your wide shots, your medium shots, and your close up shots. And they work just beautifully together to paint the big picture of what's happening on the ground. Your open source bucket is the same thing—you have your Twitter, you have your Facebook, you have your bank records, or whatever it is. And it's all used to corroborate each other.

By the time Al-Mahdi was surrendered to the Court in September 2015, Matheson was deep into drafting the 'Video as Evidence' Field Guide. Hungry for examples where video content had impact as evidence in human rights cases, she waited eagerly to see how the *Al-Mahdi* case would unfold, especially how the video content would be presented in court and how it would be received by both the judges and the defence.

***

Meanwhile, back at the ICC, Hampton had started working with another individual who had come to human rights investigations via a non-traditional route. Introduced to the ICC at a workshop hosted by Carnegie Mellon, Brad Samuels of Situ had studied art history as an undergraduate, later securing a second degree in architecture. Like Forensic Architecture, Situ was a research agency that used multiple forms of digital content (auditory, visual, analytical) to develop interactive multimedia reconstructions to help tell the story of what had happened in high-profile human rights cases. As Samuels explains about why he founded Situ,

> [f]rom the time I was a student I had been interested in the relationship between design, social, and political impact and felt that architecture as it's normally practiced wasn't as impactful as I'd hoped. So I was looking for other ways to leverage some of my expertise, education, and methodologies to those ends, and realized that when utilized as an analytical tool architecture can be thought about more broadly: as an aid to spatial analysis and visualization [around] fact-finding and reporting human rights violations.[13]

After the introduction at Carnegie Mellon, Samuels travelled to The Hague and 'had one of those meetings where we just try to show some of what we can do'. He began discussing the possibility of developing a tool that would help the ICC judges visualize the case, given all of the content that had been pulled from digital sources. At first, legal investigators and prosecutors were unclear how the non-traditional approach could help with cases. Samuels said:

> We [finally] arrived at something that made sense for us to collaborate on together, this idea for a presentation that could provide context. Presentation was something everyone agreed could be useful. So that's how [the *Al-Mahdi*] project came to be . . . Once we started, we were talking continually with the Office of the Prosecutor. At the end, [the *Al-Mahdi* project] became a prototype for future applications.

[13] Interview with Brad Samuels (11 August 2018).

Situ's work on the *Al-Mahdi* case was interactive and iterative, pulling together the open and closed source materials gathered by the investigators, including videos, photographs, geospatial information, panoramic imagery, and other content. Samuels added:

> The way we work is we partner with subject matter experts. We ask for assets that we think might be valuable or useful, and then the attorneys or the advocates see if they can find it. Or sometimes we can find it ourselves but ... we rely on our partners to have that deep knowledge about the subject at hand and then we work with them to figure out the best way to present or analyze a specific legal question.

After six or seven months of intermittent work, the multi-disciplinary team at Situ delivered a file 'that was a platform that basically organized various assets into an interactive tool that could be used in court'. One of the challenges the team faced was admissibility, however: 'Because of best practices around chain of custody, most courts don't allow online files to be admitted in the chain of evidence. So we [sometimes end up] delivering files on small computers, things that can live comfortably offline so that we can close that question around chain of custody.'

The potential hurdles to introducing such material can be significant. Samuels explained that:

> The first thing that we have to make sure [in any case] is whether [our file] will be admitted, that there's an openness to something like that. Almost in every case there's not been something done like it before ... [That] usually results in a dual deliverable: the digital content or the more experimental assets, and then something which checks the boxes of traditional expert testimony. Usually it's a PDF, something that is formalized in a static format ... as opposed to something which is dynamic or leveraging different media. Then there's also just understanding, quite literally, the [technological] capabilities of each court. At the ICC they had just moved into a new building and it was ideal because everyone had a monitor in front of them and you expected that everyone that was participating would be able to look at [the file] as if it were their own laptop and keyboard. Versus [at a later case] in Kiev there was one screen in the courtroom and some people were closer to it and some people were farther away, so that influenced how we designed the tool. Dealing with different browsers, mobile formats, bandwidth, all of these things are considerations as we're designing. Often the cases we're working on are focused on places that don't have super high bandwidth so you have to negotiate the goal of leveraging video evidence, which is pretty bandwidth-intensive, with the reality of the constituents and people being in a place that doesn't have good connectivity.[14]

Another challenge is who will be accepted as an expert witness and attest to the rigour of the underlying methodologies. To address this issue, Situ partners with those who have more traditional scientific credentials. Samuels continued:

> And you know, that might be a ballistics expert or it might be an oceanographer or somebody with a background in fluid dynamics. These are scientists doing ... research, they're

[14] ibid.

> often not in the field of human rights or, even, forensics. And so we frequently do a large portion of the work and they review it, provide feedback, and if they are comfortable with the analysis can then sign off that it is valid and it's accurate. [T]hey're often very happy to be part of these teams, and it ensures that the defense cannot get this work dismissed out of hand.

If concerns emerge, Samuels can provide all of the underlying data: '[h]ard drives full of photographs and laser scans and other assets for example ... People [think of] this work as, you know, a set of disparate data that all comes together in some crystalline moment, where we understand everything. It's way more banal than that.'

The ICC file Situ ultimately produced for the *Al-Mahdi* case was designed to walk the judges and other court actors through the various events in Timbuktu. Ultimately, working on the *Al-Mahdi* case 'was just like taking things that exist discreetly and putting them together into coherent, unified, deliverable [packages] and then allowing people to look at [the information] in different ways'.

***

In August 2016, at the start of the trial, Al-Mahdi admitted guilt, and he was sentenced to nine years. It was a win for the prosecution, but the OTP's geolocation report would never be challenged by the defence or publicly critiqued by the judges. Despite this, the hundreds of hours spent weaving together digital content was far from worthless, as it contributed to the volume of evidence presented in court. The project also helped civil society understand how open and closed digital data could be sourced, verified, analysed, and presented in ways that could advance legal accountability, as Matheson incorporated critical insights from the case into the 'Video as Evidence' Field Guide.[15] As for the interactive presentation, Samuels explains that: 'in terms of [the file's] impact, it's impossible to know exactly but [one of the prosecutors has told us] he thinks it was a big part of [getting a guilty plea]. And he also said recently that he can't imagine doing a case without a platform now.'

By the close of trial, the potential utility of open source information was clear. The OTP had begun to integrate social media and other online information into its investigation plans, especially during the preliminary examination phase of its cases,[16] and was becoming increasingly committed to its use. Its investment in developing an open source strategy would pay off just a few months later in a second watershed case: *Prosecutor v Mahmoud Mustafa Busayf Al-Werfalli*.[17]

[15] Kelly Matheson, 'Video as Evidence Field Guide' *WITNESS* (2016) https://vae.witness.org/video-as-evidence-field-guide/ accessed 29 December 2018.

[16] Alexa Koenig, 'The New Forensics: Using Open Source Information to Investigate Grave Crimes' (The Human Rights Center at the University of California, Berkeley, School of Law 2018) https://www.law.berkeley.edu/research/human-rights-center/publications/reports/new-forensics-using-open-source-information-investigate-grave-crimes/ accessed 29 December 2018.

[17] *Prosecutor v Mahmoud Mustafa Busayf Al-Werfalli* (Warrant of Arrest) ICC-01/11-01/17 (15 August 2017).

2. The *Al-Werfalli* Case

In August 2017, as explained in the introduction to this book, the ICC issued an arrest warrant for Mahmoud Al-Werfalli of Libya, the commander of al-Saiqa, an elite unit within the Libyan National Army. Werfalli was accused of executing thirty-three people in a series of acts captured on video and posted to social media. Legal and human rights communities hailed the warrant as a milestone, marking the first time the ICC had cited abundant open source information—including critical videos pulled from Facebook—as a basis for a warrant. It was also the first time that the OTP put open source information at the heart of an investigation: without the video content, there would have been no case. The OTP released a second warrant for Al-Werfalli in July 2018 based on the deaths of another eight people, which also incorporated significant quantities of open source content, including a public statement from Al-Werfalli's unit (which took credit for the killings), as well as a United Nations report and yet another video.

From the outset, Libya had been recognized as a particularly rich conflict for gathering open source content. One of the pioneers in thinking through how social media content can be helpful as evidence is Alison Cole, a former ICC investigator who helped direct the evolution of the use of digital evidence while a legal researcher at the Open Society Justice Initiative. Two years before the first warrant was even issued, she noted that the legal challenges to using social media content had become

> most apparent during the opening of the ICC investigations in Libya. The extent of citizen engagement in fact-finding [has been] unprecedented, with an overwhelming deluge of potential evidence uploaded on YouTube, Twitter and Facebook documenting the conflict in real time. The complexities of social media verification reached crisis mode as high-stake ICC allegations of mass rape, allegedly captured on video and then removed from YouTube, were questioned by the chairman of the UN Commission of Inquiry. It became obvious that it is essential to build new ways of managing technology-generated digital evidence and to join the ICC in preparing for the tidal wave of new technology before it hit the ICC and flooded the courtroom with untested evidence.[18]

Now, with the *Al-Werfalli* case, social media evidence could finally be tested in court.

Ultimately, the *Al-Mahdi* open source report and the *Al-Werfalli* warrants represent milestones in the history of accountability for human rights violations. While, at one point, open source information was believed to be helpful only as a lead to traditional evidence or to corroborate other content, the ICC's more recent work suggests this limited perspective has changed. As Matheson stated:

> When I first started in this field, [many of] the silverbacks of the field (and I use that term with endearment) ... said that the core of our evidence base is [traditional] documents, witness testimonies. They would *say*, 'Kelly, these videos are great, you're having impact.' But I still felt like, especially in the beginning ... this is only five years ago ... that the videos

[18] Alison Cole, 'Technology for Truth: The Next Generation of Evidence' *International Justice Monitor* (18 March 2015) https://www.ijmonitor.org/2015/03/technology-for-truth-the-next-generation-of-evidence/ accessed 29 December 2018.

were a nice add-on, not critical, to human rights cases. And now I feel there's been a paradigm shift, just in that short period of time. [When international criminal investigators and human rights researchers met in Bellagio, Italy in October 2017] to start discussing the possibility of creating guidelines for using open source material for evidentiary purposes, Cristina [Ribeiro of the Investigations Division at the ICC] confirmed that practice had shifted. Whereas before, witness testimony had been at the core of everything, now, increasingly, the core is open source material—and then the witnesses and the documents come in at the edges. This shift has happened in a number of cases. And I think we're going to see that trend continue, as this new generation, who documents everything on smartphones, on cameras, on social media, moves forward. So that's not just video—we have everyone posting everything on Facebook, on Twitter, on every social media platform, and that content is just going to become more and more important. It's like going back to World War II and the Nazi Regime when perpetrators were writing everything down. Today, people are also writing everything down, but they're not writing it down on physical documents—they're writing it down on Facebook and Twitter and YouTube.'[19]

Brad Samuels agrees: a massive shift took place between 2012 and 2017 in the willingness of human rights lawyers to embrace emerging documentation methods. As he said: 'I've seen that change a lot in just five years.'[20]

3. Civil Cases and Human Rights Courts

While this very brief history reflects an extraordinary shift in legal practice, the use of social media and other open source information as evidence originated to address civil cases—not those at the ICC. The jurisprudence surrounding the use of social media-derived information is especially robust when it comes to personal injury cases. In one case, *Bagasbas v Atwal*, in Canada, for example, the plaintiff claimed that, owing to the defendant's negligence, which resulted in a car accident, she suffered injuries that prevented her from being able to engage in most forms of physical activity. However, the defendant grabbed pictures from the plaintiff's Facebook account that showed her kayaking, hiking, and cycling after the accident. Those images contributed to the court's determination that the plaintiff's injuries were less serious than alleged, resulting in reduced compensation.[21]

Open source content has also frequently been used to challenge sexual harassment and discrimination claims. In a case in the United States in which a woman claimed she had been sexually harassed over a four-year period by a former fellow manager, the defendant used content pulled from the plaintiff's Facebook page to show her comfort with sexual banter and thereby suggest that his conduct was not unwelcome, defeating an essential element of her case. The judge agreed with the defendant, writing that the plaintiff's Facebook page revealed 'that she is very comfortable with sexual humor and [her page] contains numerous comments and e-cards making sexual references and jokes'.[22] Since she

[19] Interview with Matheson (n 11).
[20] Interview with Samuels (n 13).
[21] *Bagasbas v Atwal* 2009 BCSC 512 (Supreme Court of British Columbia M081193).
[22] *Gelpi v Autozoners LLC*, [2014] United States District Court Northern District of Ohio Eastern Division 5:12CV0570.

was Facebook 'friends' with nearly all of her former co-workers, '[h]er Facebook posts and status updates are indicative of jokes her co-workers would reasonably believe she found funny'.[23] The judge explained that where 'the plaintiff was a frequent or welcome participant in the sexual hijinks or banter at issue', such information is 'fatal' to a claim of sexual harassment.[24] Cases that are not in the human rights field may in fact provide some of the richest guidance for ways to use social media and other open source content in a legal context.

In addition, human rights cases are primarily adjudicated *as* civil cases before regional human rights courts in Europe, the Americas, and Africa,[25] and before domestic constitutional and administrative courts. In the United States, the Alien Tort Claims Act of 1789[26] and the Torture Victim Protection Act[27] of 1992 empower complainants to bring civil suits in US courts for international human rights violations. Notably, civil cases require a lesser standard of proof than criminal ones, which is an important consideration for evidentiary purposes. Ultimately, however, while the different standard may impact the scope of evidence collected, given the overlap in the kinds of wrongs adjudicated in such civil and criminal cases (including torture, rape, etc), the same kinds of open source information helpful in international criminal cases (including lead, linkage, and contextual evidence) will be helpful in civil ones.

Around the world, human rights issues are often indirectly addressed through immigration law as well. Open source information may be particularly helpful in ascertaining country conditions (in asylum cases, where those filing asylum claims have to show a reasonable basis for their belief that they would be persecuted if returned to their home country) and demonstrating the networks that seek to do them harm if sent back.

And some national courts—as opposed to international tribunals—are among the most promising places for adjudicating human rights violations. Given that war and other social unrest can complicate the evidence-gathering process by increasing the political sensitivity and/or physical security of fact-finding, remote information gathering may meet a number of logistical needs. Sending photos, videos, and other documentation out of the region via cloud computing, social media sites, or encrypted instant messaging can help safeguard those on the ground, while facilitating access by remote investigators. Whether the alleged violations are local or brought into national courts on the basis of universal jurisdiction (as with recent cases brought in Sweden and Germany that involve atrocities that took place in Syria, where videos have provided significant information about what has been happening on the ground), such methods are promising.

Open source content will increasingly be used in human rights cases brought in places other than the ICC.[28] While the ICC, in the words of Alison Cole, 'may be the leading forum for testing the greatest advances in the use of technology for truth-seeking purposes',[29]

[23] ibid.

[24] ibid.

[25] Başak Çalı, Mikael Rask Madsen, and Frans Viljoen, 'Comparative Regional Human Rights Regimes: Defining a Research Agenda' (2018) 16 International Journal of Constitutional Law 128.

[26] Alien Tort Claims Act 1789 (28 USC § 1350; ATS).

[27] Torture Victim Protection Act 1991 (TVPA; Pub.L 102–256, HR 2092, 106 Stat 73, enacted 12 March 1992).

[28] The International Criminal Court is technically not a human rights court since it focuses on international criminal law, not international human rights law. However, many human rights researchers and advocates work with the International Criminal Court as a standard setter for securing accountability for crimes that can also be categorized as human rights abuses, especially when the accused is affiliated with or acts on behalf of a state. The open source methods that are being pioneered at the ICC have tremendous value for other venues, including the many human rights courts that have been established around the world.

[29] Cole (n 18).

now that new approaches are being tested, those methods can be adopted and adapted in other jurisdictions. Whether the venue is a domestic court (operating under an authority like an Alien Tort Claims Act (US)[30] or the Human Rights Act (UK)[31]), a regional human rights court (the European Court of Human Rights, the Inter-American Court of Human Rights, or the African Court on Human and Peoples' Rights), or an international tribunal, online open source materials can play an important role in righting wrongs. Indeed, the use of open source, social media-derived content to demonstrate people's attitudes seems particularly promising in any cases where a party's mental state is at issue. From receptivity to sexual banter (as with the sexual harassment case mentioned above) to attitudes about racial, ethnic, and other groups (as with genocide cases), online open sources can provide a rich resource for gathering information about people's expressed thoughts and experiences—contributing important facts to the who, what, when, where, and how of criminal and civil wrongs.

4. The Future of Open Source Evidence

Whether for criminal or civil cases, lawyers around the world are increasingly using online open sources to generate evidence of human rights abuses. While this practice is still relatively new, the use of online digital content as evidence is poised to explode. Given how much of contemporary communications now happens in digital space—and how important mining those communications can be for building evidentiary records related to atrocities—not knowing how to comb online platforms may (and probably should) soon be considered a form of malpractice.

National courts in the developing world will soon need to grapple with—where they don't already have to—the same challenges that lawyers and investigators at the ICC have been faced with. Smartphone and social media use continue to proliferate around the world, in many places resulting in abundant digital documentation. Legal actors in developing countries are increasingly considering the value of open source information, especially video content, as evidence: Matheson says: 'We're talking about jurisdictions like Guinea, like the Democratic Republic of Congo, Western Sahara. I feel like what we've been doing at the international level is now being seen as "we need this at a national level". Part of what we need to do is ask whether that's true.' When national courts start seriously considering the admissibility and use of open source content, she goes on: 'I think it's going to be incredibly important to take what we learned at the international level and drop it down to the national level so that more video can result in more justice … We have to start infusing the national systems with an understanding of how to use this information.'[32]

An ever-increasing number of stakeholders are being trained in how to locate, capture, preserve, verify, and present digital content with an eye to legal accountability in a broad array of jurisdictions. For example, WITNESS, Videre est Credere, and eyeWitness to Atrocities are training activists and investigators to generate video evidence, while groups like Bellingcat, the Institute for International Criminal Justice, and UC Berkeley's Human

30 Alien Tort Claims Act 1789 (n 26).
31 Human Rights Act 1998 (c 42).
32 Interview with Matheson (n 11).

Rights Center are leading workshops to train lay and professional investigators how to use it. NGO-academic partnerships—from Asia to Africa to Europe to the Americas—are also being formed to train a next generation of human rights workers in essential open source skills, including participants in Amnesty International's Digital Verification Corps and UC Berkeley's Human Rights Investigations Lab.

These verification skills will be especially needed to deal with the next generation of video content, namely misinformation and disinformation promulgated through the use of bots and other automated technologies, and manufactured videos, commonly known as 'deep fakes', that make it look like someone said or did something they did not. These fake videos were most notoriously used to create pornography in which famous actors' faces were morphed onto the bodies in adult films. Essentially, such films are created by pitting two neural networks against each other. The system is fed from an underlying dataset comprised of thousands of images of the target. One of the networks, the 'generator', produces a sample image based on the underlying data, which is then evaluated by the second network, the 'discriminator', which provides crucial feedback regarding the first network's success in creating an image that is consistent with the underlying data. The two iterate until the generator can produce imagery that is eerily reflective of the target.[33] Given the relative simplicity of the underlying technology and rapidly falling costs, the internet may soon be inundated with this manufactured content. As discussed in Chapter 5, just as legal investigators are beginning to recognize the potential value of open source content, one of the biggest challenges for the field of open source investigations will be finding both technical and methodological ways to detect and reject false imagery.

Technology companies, as well as computer science and electrical engineering programmes within universities, are rapidly creating programmes to help with documentation, preservation, analysis, verification, and presentation of open source information for courts. Numerous tools have been produced to detect deep fakes, from Hany Farid's PhotoDNA (which detects visual manipulation) to DARPA's MediFor programme, to Gyfcat's Project Maru.[34] As for more general verification needs, even technologies originally developed for journalists and human rights advocates are being tweaked to meet the needs of lawyers and courts, such as preserving chain of custody. Participating organizations range from Carnegie Mellon's Center for Human Rights Science, which has spent a great deal of time on the automation of visual and audio analysis of satellite images and video content, to tools developed by InVid, Hunch.ly, Situ, Meedan, Forensic Architecture, eyeWitness to Atrocities, the Whistle, and others.

New guidelines are also emerging to help professionalize this field of practice. For example, Berkeley's Human Rights Center is working closely with the United Nations Office of the High Commissioner for Human Rights and a broad array of current and former tribunal leaders, human rights NGO representatives, and others to develop an international protocol on conducting open source investigations for legal accountability purposes (see Chapter 15). The project's goal is to help human rights researchers and other professional investigators ensure that they are collecting, preserving, analysing, and presenting

[33] Tianxiang Shen and others, '"Deep Fakes" Using Generative Adversarial Networks (GAN)' *NoiseLab* (2017); Minsuk Kahng and others, 'GAN Lab: Understanding Complex Deep Generative Models Using Interactive Visual Experimentation' (2019) 25 IEEE Transactions on Visualization and Computer Graphics 310.

[34] Alexa Koenig, '"Half the Truth Is Often a Great Lie": Deep Fakes, Open Source Information, and International Criminal Law' (2019) 113 American Journal of International Law 250.

information in a manner that maximizes the utility of open source content for courts. Meanwhile, the OSR4Rights project at Swansea University is mapping the use of open source content, as well as identifying biases that may be embedded within affiliated technologies and processes. Essex University's Human Rights Big Data and Technology project is partnering with UC Berkeley's Human Rights Center to establish an ethical and human rights-based framework for open source investigations, as well as mapping and analysing opportunities for using big data and emerging technologies to advance human rights. Finally, the University of Essex's Human Rights Centre Clinic has produced an introductory guide to open source intelligence and digital verification as a resource for training a next generation in basic practices.[35]

Where are all of these efforts heading? I asked Kelly Matheson. She replied:

> My big hope? One of the problems with Video as Evidence is that we often capture a video that tells us the *truth* but doesn't result in justice. I think WITNESS and other organizations—all of us want more truth to result in more justice. [But] we're going to have to look at things from a systems level. No matter how damning your video is, it's not going to make a difference if the systems aren't designed to deal with [digital visual content].' 'If you have to go into the national courts of Morocco, you can have the most damning, compelling video as evidence, the most damning open source evidence, and it's not gonna make a difference because the [technological] system isn't working. But my goal is, where the systems *are* working, that everyone along the chain from capture to courtroom—activists on the ground, prosecutors, defense attorneys, analysts, judges, everyone—understands how video evidence works and how it relates to the case in front of them.[36]

In the meantime, for Matheson, the next challenge is to develop guidance for the filming and handling of videos related to specialized topics such as environmental and financial crimes, as well as sexual and gender-based violence. For Hampton, it is to ensure fairness of process: 'We need to make sure this progress doesn't come at the price of having fair trials.'[37] And for Samuels, it is to foster interdisciplinarity. According to him, the kinds of innovation we have been seeing in the open source space

> [r]equires people working across fields, and ... getting out of a siloed approach to whatever it is: ballistics, or forensic anthropology, or architecture or computer science. I think that's the big promise of [combining all these digital sources], the entirely new thing that I think none of us could do on our own. And then in [a] very practical sense I think [this is an issue with] the culture of human rights work. [Human rights practitioners] are somehow slower adopters of technology than the private sector, although I think there is a productive tension between people who are pushing technologies, and people who are experts in human rights working together to produce new contributions to the field. To put it a bit differently, the ethos of each is very different, right? In design, it's always iterate, fail, keep going, do it again, fail. And in human rights work failure is not always an option. And so this idea that

[35] Fred Aahsberg and others, 'Introductory Guide to Open Source Intelligence and Digital Verification' (University of Essex Human Rights Centre Clinic 2017).

[36] Interview with Matheson (n 11).

[37] Interview with Ethan Hampton (11 December 2018).

> [you can't fail but] that in order to do new stuff you gotta be able to break things, pretty much [merging] two worlds together, is creating important new ways of fact-finding and reporting.[38]

For Enrique Piracés of Carnegie Mellon's Center for Human Rights Science, which has also been helping to advance the use of open source content for courts, the challenge is an ethical one. Piracés has been spotlighting the problems that arise with the introduction of digital technologies into less resourced parts of the globe. Noting the critical role of foundations and governments in funding and otherwise helping to develop an infrastructure for this content, Piracés explains how the use of new technologies in human rights cases has continued the 'persistent problems that faced the broader human rights movement, [including] the tendency to consolidate power in the economic capitals of the twenty-first century, geographically removed from most human rights crises'.[39] Piracés rightfully points out that 'current models of technology transfer' reflect a unidirectional relationship, where 'technology is largely decided, designed and created far away from the majority of people who need it'.[40]

The challenge, then, is to make sure that any methodological and technical advances can be adapted in ways that are empowering and appropriate to local context. As legal practice takes its next baby steps towards more systematically integrating these methods into case building, how can we make the process as inclusive, responsive, and effective as possible?

5. Conclusion

The past several years have enabled an extraordinary period of innovation in the use of open sources to strengthen legal accountability for human rights violations. Organizations ranging from UC Berkeley's Human Rights Center to WITNESS to Situ to the ICC have been working together to engender a critical shift in legal practice: one that recognizes the importance of traditional means of information collection but also comprehends the tremendous potential of digital technologies to strengthen some of the most complicated and pragmatically challenging cases in the world. Changes in the ways human beings communicate—from using traditional means to digital resources—mean that legal investigators have an opportunity to find new ways to capture what people are doing and saying. While the use of digital open source methods is still in its infancy, its potential for strengthening human rights cases is profound.

[38] Interview with Samuels (n 13).

[39] Enrique Piracés, 'The Future of Human Rights Technology' in Molly Land and Jay Aronson (eds), *New Technologies for Human Rights Law and Practice* (Cambridge University Press 2018).

[40] ibid.

3

Prosecuting Atrocity Crimes with Open Source Evidence

Lessons from the International Criminal Court

Lindsay Freeman

1. Introduction

This chapter focuses on the use of open source information in international criminal investigations and prosecutions with a particular emphasis on cases before the International Criminal Court (ICC). By analysing case law which contemplates the admissibility, reliability, and probative value of evidence derived from open sources, this chapter highlights the primary opportunities and challenges that arise when using open source information for legal accountability purposes. The examination of specific ICC cases and judicial decisions over time illustrates the changing nature of the open source information available in war crimes, crimes against humanity, and genocide cases—from analogue newspapers, radio broadcasts, and government reports to social media postings and other digital content from the internet. Thus, this chapter explores how the attitude of international judges has shifted and evolved with the changing nature of the information environment in the twenty-first century. By understanding the specific factors that judges will weigh when evaluating open source evidence at trial, human rights and criminal investigators can better appreciate the ultimate use of their work and, accordingly, improve their investigative techniques and procedures to comply with the court's expectations and standards.

Although open source information gathering and its application to criminal investigations are not new, the advent and popularization of social media and smartphones has dramatically expanded the information landscape.[1] Pre-internet, the field of open sources was finite, primarily encompassing traditional broadcast and print media and public records that required a trip to the library, city hall, or another physical location for access. With the arrival of the internet and the proliferation of mobile communication technologies, the range of open sources available for mining information has exploded, creating new challenges owing to the sheer volume of data and the speed with which digital information can be shared. There are also far more avenues today for monitoring events as they unfold in real time. The exponentially growing number of open sources on the internet provides new opportunities for investigators, but it also raises novel legal questions for lawyers and judges. As the desire to and necessity of using online open source information as evidence in international criminal prosecutions grows, the law must develop to address the complexity of

[1] 'Central Intelligence Agency, INTelligence: Open Source Intelligence' https://www.cia.gov/news-information/featured-story-archive/2010-featured-story-archive/open-source-intelligence.html

authenticating and verifying digital content. This chapter demonstrates the value of using open sources in atrocity crime cases and draws attention to the potential pitfalls and necessary considerations investigators should keep in mind when collecting, preserving, and analysing open source information with an eye towards future litigation.

2. Open Source Investigations in the Digital Age

Before discussing specific cases, it is important first to develop a common understanding of the terminology and language used by lawyers and investigators working in the legal context, which may differ from the vocabulary of journalists and civil society actors engaged in advocacy work. Among these terms, 'open source intelligence' (OSINT), a label often associated with spy craft, is a sub-category of open source information. OSINT, in the words of the US Office of the Director of National Intelligence, is "produced from publicly available information that is collected, exploited, and disseminated in a timely manner to an appropriate audience for the purpose of addressing a specific intelligence requirement'.[2] Whereas 'information' and 'data' are broad labels, 'intelligence' refers to actionable information[3] with context and value that is provided to government and military officials, usually to assist immediate policy or strategic decisions.

Intelligence communities first developed methods for OSINT collection, processing and analysis during the Second World War, concentrating on foreign newspapers and radio broadcasts.[4] Over time, different groups—from journalists to human rights advocates to private investigators—have used OSINT techniques for a wide range of purposes, using a variety of different practices and methods. In more recent years, law enforcement has capitalized on OSINT for monitoring criminal activity, tracking fugitives, or providing lead information.[5] In the law enforcement setting, 'lead information', like 'intelligence', refers to actionable information that may lead to new evidence such as witnesses, documents, or physical objects. Both 'lead information' and 'intelligence' are distinguishable from 'evidence', which specifically refers to information that can be used to establish facts in an investigation or admitted in legal proceedings.

In addition to distinguishing between intelligence, information, and evidence, it is important to understand what is encompassed in the term 'open source information' and how it is changing in the expanding information environment. There is still dispute over what precisely constitutes open source information in the digital age, as there is a growing volume of data available through purchase from companies or accessible to those with the technical skills to access it, but not then entirely open, free, and available for all.[6] The digital world changes both the nature of traditional open sources as well as the types of material, of which 'user-generated content'[7] is a notable example. Social media and other Web 2.0

[2] *Prosecutor v Callixte Mbarushimana* (Decision on the confirmation of charges) ICC-01/04-01/10 (16 December 2011).

[3] Actionable information is meaningful information that is useful to decision-making or problem-solving.

[4] Anthony Olcott, *Open Source Intelligence in a Networked World* (Bloomsbury 2012) https://www.bloomsbury.com/us/open-source-intelligence-in-a-networked-world-9781441166081/ accessed 29 December 2018.

[5] Els De Busser, 'Open Source Data and Criminal Investigations: Anything You Publish Can and Will Be Used against You' (2014) 2 Groningen Journal of International Law 90.

[6] Olcott (n 4).

[7] Rebecca J Hamilton, 'User-Generated Evidence' (2018) Columbia Journal of Transnational Law.

platforms allow users to upload to the internet content, including text, video, audio, and images, and proscribe varying degrees of openness based on users' privacy settings. With millions of content-creators online, digital information and the number of sources have grown exponentially, while at the same time their reliability has become more tenuous.

Further, while non-governmental organization (NGO) reports documenting human rights violations are not new, their number and accessibility has increased substantially with the proliferation of UN agencies,[8] civil society groups, and other international organizations working in the human rights space and their increased online presence. In addition, the field of journalism has changed in ways that make its use for intelligence purposes more problematic than in the past. As a consequence of a decline in paid news consumption and increased demand for new information, there are fewer resources dedicated to long-form investigative journalism. The number of people who do this work and do it well has been cut significantly. Newspapers are kept afloat financially by putting out mainly relatively short stories and getting the scoop on other papers, practices which often mean less time fact-checking and conducting source evaluation. With print newspapers, the start-up cost and barriers to entry were high, which kept their numbers down. The internet obliterates many of those barriers, since a news website can be created with minimal start-up costs by anyone, again leading to more channels of potential information, but with no guarantee of reliability.[9]

Thus, while the concept of exploiting open source information for military intelligence, civilian intelligence, politics, journalism, advocacy or criminal investigation has been around for decades, the changing information environment compels open source investigators to develop new technical skills and for lawyers to rethink the rules of procedure that govern investigative activities. The following section shows this changing information environment in the context of actual cases before the ICC.

3. Open Source Evidence at the ICC

The rules of evidence in ICC proceedings are generally permissive, with the Statute and Rules of Procedure and Evidence (RPE) affording considerable discretion to the judges on evidentiary matters.[10] However, as case law at the ICC has evolved, there has been a notable trend towards a stricter approach regarding the use of second-hand reports containing anonymous hearsay and other open source materials. While the judges were initially lenient in allowing use of a wide range of NGO, UN, and media reports, the prosecutor's over-reliance on such material as direct evidence eventually led the judges to denounce this practice and clarify that open sources should primarily be used as lead information or to corroborate

[8] For example, the United Nations Charter initially established seven principal organs of the UN, but as the organization has matured, a multitude of funds, affiliated programmes, ad hoc missions, specialized agencies, and related organizations have added to a crowded field. Today, there are over thirty distinct entities within the 'UN family', each with its own methodologies and information output, and each with varying degrees of reputability.

[9] Hunt Allcott and Matthew Gentzkow, 'Social Media and Fake News in the 2016 Election' (2017) 31 Journal of Economic Perspectives 211.

[10] Karim AA Khan, Caroline Buisman, and Chris Gosnell, *Principles of Evidence in International Criminal Justice* (Oxford University Press 2010) https://global.oup.com/academic/product/principles-of-evidence-in-international-criminal-justice-9780199588923?cc=tr&lang=en& accessed 29 December 2018.

other items of evidence.[11] This shift in the Chamber's approach emerged around mid-2013, marked by a few exacting decisions, the most striking of which was the Pre-trial Chamber's decision to adjourn the confirmation of charges hearing against Laurent Gbagbo.[12] Since then, the Chambers have limited the weight and scope of open source materials considered admissible—on rare occasions, excluding certain documents and reports as lacking proper authentication or sufficient indicia of reliability. This section first provides an overview of the types of open source evidence that have been used in ICC trials to date and then analyses the case law as it has evolved over time.

3.1 The Changing Nature of ICC Evidence

Since its inception, the Office of the Prosecutor (OTP) of the ICC has relied heavily on information from publicly available materials to build its cases. Reports from NGOs and the UN, for example, as well as news articles and media reports, have played an integral role in the investigation of situations[13] and the prosecution of cases.[14] In addition to public reports, open source imagery and video footage have increasingly been used in international criminal cases.[15] While witnesses may have provided some of this material directly to the prosecutor, an increasing amount of this content can be found on the internet.

Social media has become a profoundly powerful tool for first responders, survivors, and other actors in armed conflicts to communicate quickly and effectively what is happening on the ground.[16] As a result, there is now a steady stream of videos uploaded to YouTube, Facebook, and Twitter documenting atrocities in places like Ukraine, Libya, Syria, and Myanmar. In addition, there is a growing body of content produced by perpetrators themselves, particularly terrorist actors, who broadcast their crimes for propaganda and recruiting purposes.[17] Consequently, open source information derived from social

[11] *Prosecutor v Jean-Pierre Bemba Gombo* (Decision on the admission into evidence of items deferred in the Chamber's 'Decision on the Prosecution's Application for Admission of Materials into Evidence Pursuant to Article 64(9) of the Rome Statute') ICC-01/05-01/08 (27 June 2013).

[12] *Prosecutor v Laurent Gbagbo* (Decision adjourning the hearing on the confirmation of charges pursuant to article 61(7)(c)(i) of the Rome Statute) ICC-02/11-01/11-432 (3 June 2013).

[13] 'Situation' is the term used to refer to the temporal and geographic focus of an investigation. For example, the situation in the Central African Republic focuses on alleged war crimes and crimes against humanity committed in the context of a conflict in CAR since 1 July 2002, with the peak of violence in 2002 and 2003. See https://www.icc-cpi.int/car.

[14] *Situation in the Democratic Republic of Congo* (Decision on the Applications for participation in the proceedings of VPRS 1–6) ICC-01/04-101 (29 June 2006) para 65, recognizing the distinction between '*situations*, which are generally defined in terms of temporal, territorial and in some cases personal parameters', and '*cases*, which comprise specific incidents during which one or more crimes within the jurisdiction of the Court seem to have been committed by one or more identified suspects, entail proceedings that take place after the issuance of a warrant of arrest or a summons to appear'.

[15] Lawrence Douglas, 'Film as Witness: Screening Nazi Concentration Camps before the Nuremberg Tribunal' (1995) 105 Yale Law Journal 449 https://digitalcommons.law.yale.edu/ylj/vol105/iss2/3; Susan Schuppli, 'Entering Evidence: Cross-Examining the Court Records of the ICTY' in Forensic Architecture (eds), *Forensis: The Architecture of Public Truth* (Sternberg Press 2014) http://susanschuppli.com/writing/entering-evidence/ accessed 29 December 2018.

[16] David Patrikarakos, *War in 140 Characters* (Basic Books 2017) 3.

[17] 'The Use of the Internet for Terrorist Purposes' (United Nations Office on Drugs and Crime 2012) https://www.unodc.org/documents/terrorism/Publications/Use_of_Internet_for_Terrorist_Purposes/ebook_use_of_the_internet_for_terrorist_purposes.pdf; James M Brachman, 'High-Tech Terror: Al-Qaeda's Use of New Technology' (2006) 30 The Fletcher Forum of World Affairs 149.

media is becoming more and more important in international criminal and human rights investigations.[18]

Since 2016, there has been an observable and significant increase in the use of 'social media evidence'[19] in international and domestic courts. At the ICC, internet-sourced satellite imagery, videos, and geolocation data helped lead to the guilty plea and conviction of Ahmad Al-Faqi Al-Mahdi for the war crime of destroying cultural property such as mosques and mausoleums in Timbuktu, Mali.[20] In the case against Jean-Pierre Bemba Gombo and members of his legal team for abuses against the administration of justice for witness tampering, the prosecution submitted Facebook photographs to show the relationship between the parties to an alleged bribery scheme.[21] The following year, the ICC issued an arrest warrant for Libyan Commander Mahmoud Al-Werfalli for thirty-three counts of the war crimes of murder based primarily on execution videos found on social media.[22]

In addition, there have been a number of national atrocity crime prosecutions based on open source evidence that have resulted in convictions for the war crime of outrages upon personal dignity[23] for taking trophy poses with human remains and other degrading acts.[24] In at least nine cases to date in Germany, Finland, and Sweden, the defendants were migrants, asylum-seekers, or returning foreign fighters who participated in hostilities in Iraq or Syria. In each case, the prosecution relied on electronically recorded images and videos disseminated through social media as evidence to secure a conviction.[25] The ICC Chambers may, if necessary, look to national laws in its application of the Rome Statute, Elements of Crimes, and RPE.[26] The reasoning in these national cases, while not binding in ICC cases, may nevertheless play an important role in shaping how ICC judges interpret the law and rule on the admissibility of and weight attributable to social media evidence in the future.

[18] Alexa Koenig, Keith Hiatt, and Khaled Alrabe, 'Access Denied? The International Criminal Court, Transnational Discovery, and The American Servicemembers Protection Act' (2018) 36(1) Berkeley Journal of International Law 1 http://www.berkeleyjournalofinternationallaw.com/vol-36-iss-1/access-denied-the-international-criminal-court-transnational-discovery-and-the-american-servicemembers-protection-act/ accessed 29 December 2018.

[19] José van Dijck, *The Culture of Connectivity: A Critical History of Social Media* (Oxford University Press 2013).

[20] *Prosecutor v Ahmad Al-Faqi Al-Mahdi* (Judgment and Sentence) ICC-01/12-01/15 (25 February 2016).

[21] *Prosecutor v Jean-Pierre Bemba Gombo* (n 11).

[22] *Prosecutor v Mahmoud Mustafa Busayf Al-Werfalli* (Warrant for Arrest) ICC-01/11-01/17 (15 August 2017).

[23] Rome Statute of the International Criminal Court 1998.

[24] 'Prosecuting War Crimes of Outrage upon Personal Dignity Based on Evidence from Open Sources: Legal Framework and Recent Developments in the Member States of the European Union' Eurojust Genocide Network (2018) http://www.eurojust.europa.eu/doclibrary/genocide-network/KnowledgeSharing/Prosecuting%20war%20crimes%20of%20outrage%20upon%20personal%20dignity%20based%20on%20evidence%20from%20open%20sources%20(February%202018)/2018-02_Prosecuting-war-crimes-based-on-evidence-from-open-sources_EN.pdf.

[25] ibid.

[26] The Court shall apply: (a) In the first place, this Statute, Elements of Crimes and its Rules of Procedure and Evidence; (b) In the second place, where appropriate, applicable treaties and the principles and rules of international law, including the established principles of the international law of armed conflict; (c) Failing that, general principles of law derived by the Court from national laws of legal systems of the world including, as appropriate, the national laws of States that would normally exercise jurisdiction over the crime, provided that those principles are not inconsistent with this Statute and with international law and internationally recognized norms and standards. Article 21(c) of the Rome Statute.

3.2 The Evolution of ICC Case Law

At the preliminary examination stage, the prosecutor depends almost entirely on open sources in making a determination as to whether there is a 'reasonable basis to believe' that crimes within the jurisdiction of the Court have been committed.[27] Information from open sources has also made up a significant share of the evidence submitted at the arrest warrant and confirmation of charges stages in cases where state cooperation is lacking. In recent years, open source information derived from the internet, including satellite imagery, digital videos, and photographs, and posts from social media have increasingly been relied upon as lead information or evidence. In the modern era, direct evidence of crimes may be found on social media and other online open sources, which begs the question: what procedure is required and what process is desirable to authenticate and verify this content for judges to be able to rely on it as evidence of guilt in criminal proceedings?

3.2.1 The Initial Cases

The ICC OTP began operations in July 2002 and announced its first investigation two years later, when the government of the Democratic Republic of the Congo (DRC) made a self-referral to the Court.[28] The focus of the DRC investigation was alleged war crimes and crimes against humanity committed in the context of an armed conflict in Eastern DRC, in the Ituri Region and the North and South Kivu Provinces. The security situation in the DRC was unstable, particularly in the critical Ituri region. The lack of safe access presented a problem for investigators, who were under tremendous pressure to deliver results and prove the ICC's worth to the international community.[29] The prosecutor therefore enlisted the assistance of intermediaries to locate witnesses and relied heavily on the reports of Human Rights Watch and MONUC, the UN peacekeeping mission that was already working in the area.[30] This initial investigation led to the OTP's first two convictions (in *Prosecutor v Lubanga*[31] and *Prosecutor v Katanga*[32]), an acquittal in *Prosecutor v Ngudjolo*,[33] and a dismissal of charges at the confirmation stage in *Prosecutor v Mbarushimana*.[34]

While the charges were confirmed with relative ease in *Lubanga, Katanga*, and *Ngudjolo*, Pre-Trial Chamber I declined to confirm the charges against Mbarushimana, in a decision highly critical of OTP investigative practices.[35] In addition to issues with the manner in which witnesses were questioned,[36] the Court also disregarded any alleged facts that were based solely on UN or Human Rights Watch reports.[37] At the hearing, the defence objected to the admissibility of documents emanating from Human Rights Watch.[38] While the

[27] Koenig, Hiatt, and Alrabe (n 18).

[28] Darryl Robinson, 'The Controversy over Territorial State Referrals and Reflections on ICL Discourse' (2011) 9 Journal of International Criminal Justice 355.

[29] Alex Whiting, 'Dynamic Investigative Practice at the International Criminal Court' (2014) 76 Law and Contemporary Problems 163.

[30] The United Nations Organization Stabilization Mission in the Democratic Republic of the Congo or MONUC is a UN peacekeeping force: https://peacekeeping.un.org/mission/past/monuc/.

[31] *Prosecutor v Thomas Lubanga Dyilo* ICC-01/04-01/06 (14 March 2012).

[32] *Prosecutor v Germain Katanga* (Judgment) ICC-01/04-01/07 (7 March 2014).

[33] *Prosecutor v Mathieu Ngudjolo Chui* (Judgment) ICC-01/04-02/12 (18 December 2012).

[34] *Prosecutor v Callixte Mbarushimana* (n 2).

[35] ibid.

[36] ibid para 51.

[37] ibid paras 117, 194, 232, and 238.

[38] ibid para 75.

Chamber rejected the defence's arguments on admissibility, it noted that such arguments might have an impact on the weight to be attributed to the documents, stating that: 'As a general principle, the Chamber finds that information based on anonymous hearsay must be given a low probative value in view of the inherent difficulties in ascertaining the truthfulness and authenticity of such information. Accordingly, such information will be used only for the purpose of corroborating other evidence.'[39] The following year, in the trial judgment acquitting Ngudjolo, the Chamber affirmed this statement and added that forensic findings were lacking in this case. In the absence of better evidence, the Court observed that it was 'forced to rely primarily on witness statements and reports by MONUC investigators or representatives of various NGOs'.[40] While the judges did not exclude any NGO, UN, or media reports, their critical commentary on this material in the *Mbarushimana* and *Ngudjolo* decisions, which were both confirmed on appeal, foreshadows their harsher stance in the cases to come.

3.2.2 The Turning Point

The Court's patience with the prosecutor's repeated submissions of NGO, UN, and media reports without taking further investigative steps to ascertain sources ran out in 2013, when the Pre-trial Chamber adjourned the confirmation of charges hearing in *Prosecutor v Gbagbo*.[41] The overarching message in this decision is summed up succinctly in paragraph 35:

> [T]he Chamber notes with serious concern that in this case the Prosecutor relied heavily on NGO reports and press articles with regard to key elements of the case, including the contextual elements of crimes against humanity. Such pieces of evidence cannot in any way be presented as the fruits of a full and proper investigation by the Prosecutor in accordance with article 54(1)(a) of the Statute. Even though NGO reports and press articles may be a useful introduction to the historical context of a conflict situation, they do not usually constitute a valid substitute for the type of evidence that is required to meet the evidentiary threshold for the confirmation of charges.[42]

Thus, the Court has been critical of both the reliability of the content in public reports, as well as the credibility of the sources themselves. In addition, the Chambers have warned the OTP to be wary of the interests of journalists and NGOs, who might have ulterior motives, such as the desire to make a profit, gain greater readership, or raise money from donors. As Patrick Kroker, an attorney at the European Centre for Constitutional and Human Rights, explains: 'Institutions who autonomously seek to collect evidence often have their own focus and agenda that rarely matches the evidentiary needs of courts. They sometimes operate under cognitive bias, pre-select information or prioritize certain events, in line with their own perspective and funding scheme, which can affect the reliability of the evidence they collect.'[43]

[39] ibid paras 77–78.

[40] *Prosecutor v Mathieu Ngudjolo Chui* (n 33) para 117.

[41] *Prosecutor v Laurent Gbagbo* (n 12), affirmed on appeal ICC-02/11-01/11-572. The decision cites to the Appeal Chamber's judgment affirming the decision to decline charges against *Mbarushimana*.

[42] ibid para 35.

[43] Patrick Kroker, 'Emerging Issues Facing the Use of Remote Sensing Evidence for International Criminal Justice' Harvard Humanitarian Initiative (2014).

That same year, the trial chamber in *Prosecutor v Bemba* made several interlocutory decisions regarding the admissibility of evidence during the trial, in which some open source material was excluded or limited in scope. The majority of the Chamber[44] set out its approach to the admissibility of press reports early on, explaining that press reports 'may be admitted for limited purposes to be determined on a case-by-case basis' such as to 'corroborate other pieces of evidence' or to assess the prosecution's allegation that the conduct described in the charges was widely broadcast, which 'may have implications with regard to the Accused's alleged knowledge of the crimes charged'.[45] The defence opposed the admission of several NGO, UN, media, and academic reports, arguing that such reports represented 'un-tested and often times anonymous allegations of crimes which neither the Chamber nor the Defense have had the opportunity to examine'.[46] Concerning NGO reports, the majority found that they can be considered reliable 'provided that they offer sufficient guarantees of impartiality' and are therefore admissible 'for the limited purpose that the information contained therein may serve to corroborate other pieces of evidence'.[47]

While the majority ruled that most of the reports were prima facie reliable, emphasizing that the admissibility determination did not predetermine the final assessment of the evidentiary weight to be given various reports, the third judge dissented. In disagreeing with the majority's admission of the reports from the International Federation of Human Rights, Amnesty International, and the BBC, Judge Ozaki stated:

> The sources of information relied on in the reports are not revealed with sufficient detail, and as a result it is not possible to fully investigate their reliability. Due to the lack of guarantees concerning the reliability of these reports' sources, in my judgment the probative value of the three reports is low.

Judge Ozaki's many dissenting opinions on evidence in the *Bemba* trial, which align with the prior decision in first *Gbagbo* confirmation, are emblematic of the move towards stricter assessment of open source information. Judge Ozaki suggested that the weight of such reports could be strengthened if introduced through a witness who could attest to the content, methodology, and authorship of the report. This advice was later heeded in the *Gbagbo* trial, during which the prosecution called witnesses from Human Rights Watch and other NGOs to testify to the methods they used in compiling and producing reports in Côte d'Ivoire.

Taking the ICC's jurisprudence to this point as a whole, a few suppositions and inferences can be made about how judges generally assess open source reports. The first is that the Court will be likely to be most indulgent of the prosecutor's use of such material in early stages of the proceedings, but far less permissive about extensive reliance on open source reports at the trial stage. The second is that, in the eyes of the judges, there is a clear hierarchy of open sources based on their perceived legitimacy: official UN reports, particularly from commissions of inquiry, are at the top, followed by UN agency reports, then reports of the well-established international NGOs like Human Rights Watch and Amnesty International,

[44] Two out of the three judges on the trial chamber.

[45] *Prosecutor v Jean-Pierre Bemba Gombo* (n 11) para 269.

[46] Wairagala Wakabi, 'Judges Admit NGO Reports into Evidence against Bemba' *International Justice Monitor* (8 July 2013) https://www.ijmonitor.org/2013/07/judges-admit-ngo-reports-into-evidence-against-bemba/ accessed 29 December 2018.

[47] *Prosecutor v Jean-Pierre Bemba Gombo* (n 11) para 270.

followed by lesser-known and local NGOs, followed by media reports from reputable news outlets like the BBC and *New York Times*, with other news outlets and local papers at the bottom of the value-chain. Finally, factors that make the judges more likely to consider the content of these reports include transparency of the methods used and identities of the authors, especially if the author responsible for compiling the report testifies in court.

3.2.3 The New Digital Era

With a well-established framework in place for evaluating open source reports, the Court has been faced more recently with a new challenge: how to assess these same qualities in open source digital content. In 2016, when the prosecutor brought a case for destruction of cultural property in Timbuktu against Ahmad Al-Faqi Al-Mahdi as a direct perpetrator, over 600 pieces of evidence were admitted at trial, including videos depicting the accused engaged in destroying mosques, overseeing and ordering others to destroy mosques, and explaining his intent to destroy mosques.[48] Al-Mahdi pleaded guilty, so this evidence was not tested in court, but it is important to note that this was the first ICC case to introduce new open source information directly extracted from the internet through screenshot or download.

A year later, in August 2017, the ICC issued an arrest warrant for Al-Werfalli alleging his criminal responsibility for murder as a war crime committed in the context of seven incidents against thirty-three persons in the non-international armed conflict in Libya. The warrant was based primarily on seven videos depicting each of the seven incidents found on social media.[49] The Chamber issued the warrant of arrest based on:

> (i) Recordings of witness interviews and summaries of witness interviews; (ii) video material and transcripts of video material; (iii) internal orders, and social media posts by the Media Centre of the Al-Saiqa Brigade; and (iv) reports of international organizations, non-governmental organizations, and research centres.[50]

The prosecution alleged that Al-Werfalli was directly responsible under Article 25(3)(a), (b), or (d) for the war crime of murder in violation of Article 8(2)(c)(i)[51] for the murder of thirty-three persons, either by personally killing them or by ordering their execution, across seven incidents depicted in seven separate videos. For each incident, the arrest warrant provided a brief description of the relevant content and then stated that the video was posted on social media on a particular date. In only the first incident did the warrant specify Facebook as the social media platform and in no instance did it provide the specific web address or username.[52] This lack of specificity may have been a conscious choice made for unknown reasons, but it is troubling that the judges or the OTP treat social media as if it is one consistent, overall source.

Together, the *Al-Mahdi* and *Al-Werfalli* cases demonstrate a movement towards cases in which the crimes themselves have been captured on film and where videos uploaded to and discovered on social media may be admitted as direct evidence at trial. The case against

[48] *Prosecutor v Ahmad Al-Faqi Al-Mahdi* (n 20).
[49] *Prosecutor v Mahmoud Mustafa Busayf Al-Werfalli* (n 22).
[50] ibid para 3.
[51] ibid para 2.
[52] ibid para 11.

Al-Werfalli is especially notable because there would have been no case if the videos had been excluded. What is unclear at the time of writing is whether this type of proffered information will be admitted as evidence at trial and given adequate weight in proving elements of the crimes. Therefore, we may only make educated guesses based on the Court's past decisions as to how future Chambers might evaluate the admissibility of and weigh 'new' open source evidence in impending cases.

It is thus helpful to consider not just how judges have evaluated open source evidence at various stages of the proceedings, but how the OTP has used open source information in its investigation or to support specific parts of its case. The following section explains how open sources can provide valuable leads and information to investigators at the ICC and other international judicial institutions.

4. The Value of Open Sources in Atrocity Crime Cases

In traditional criminal cases, state law enforcement officers have the authority to collect closed or privately held information through legally coercive measures such as subpoenas and search warrants. ICC investigators, however, do not have law enforcement powers. The OTP's ability to collect evidence is entirely reliant on the cooperation of state parties, which has been deficient or non-existent in many cases (Kenyans for Truth 2014)[53]. When it comes to digital content, the ICC is often prevented from acquiring data directly from the source if it is stored on servers owned by American companies that do not cooperate with OTP requests.[54] Similarly, national prosecutors of atrocity crimes face obstacles in gathering evidence across borders: it often requires a cumbersome bureaucratic process provided for by mutual legal assistance treaties (MLATs). Presently, the laws governing cross-border data acquisition are in flux and laws on data protection and data sharing differ greatly from one country to another. The current legal uncertainty surrounding digital evidence collection from privately held servers and the conflicts of law between countries over data protection regulations compound the existing challenges. For these reasons, atrocity crime investigators benefit greatly from the ability to exploit open source information and use it as evidence without having to acquire it directly from the internet service provider (ISP).

Another difficulty unique to international criminal investigations, particularly those at the ICC, is that investigators are often tasked with investigating crimes long after the actual events have occurred. The ICC is a court of last resort, and the principle of complementarity[55] requires that national courts have primary jurisdiction.[56] According to Article 17(1) (b), (2), and (3) of the Rome Statute, only when national courts are unwilling or unable

[53] Kenyans for Peace with Truth and Justice, 'All Bark, No Bite? State Cooperation and the International Criminal Court' (December 2014).

[54] Koenig, Hiatt, and Alrabe (n 18); Kiel Ireland and Julian Bava, 'The American Servicemembers' Protection Act: Pathways to, and Constraints on, U.S. Cooperation with the International Criminal Court' (Stanford Law School: Law and Policy Lab 2016) https://law.stanford.edu/publications/the-american-servicemembers-protection-act-pathways-to-and-constraints-on-u-s-cooperation-with-the-international-criminal-court/ accessed 29 December 2018.

[55] The principle of complementarity governs the exercise of the Court's jurisdiction. The ICC may only exercise jurisdiction where national legal systems fail to do so or do so in bad faith.

[56] Robert Cryer and others, *An Introduction to International Criminal Law and Procedure* (3rd edn, Cambridge University Press 2014).

to prosecute cases is the ICC permitted to become involved.[57] In some instances, such investigations may not commence for years or even decades after the relevant incidents. Therefore, first responders such as members of civil society, UN workers, and journalists have an advantage over ICC investigators in their ability to get on the ground early and collect evidence first-hand. ICC investigators are therefore inevitably and unavoidably reliant on the work of those who can deploy more quickly in response to humanitarian catastrophes. Reports produced by NGOs or UN agencies often provide essential context for understanding complex and protracted armed conflicts and political violence, as well as identify significant incidents and estimate numbers of casualties, which help ICC investigators focus their investigations.

The following sections highlight the five main ways traditional open sources, particularly NGO and UN reports and media articles, as well as new open sources, such as social media content, may be used to meet various evidentiary thresholds and to support specific aspects of the prosecution's case.

4.1 Understanding the Broader Context

International crimes differ from traditional criminal cases in that they are frequently linked to a protracted and geographically distributed armed conflict. One's understanding of such conflicts is of course greatly enhanced by knowledge of the historical, cultural and social background of the region, as well as by religious, political, economic, and even environmental factors. Compared to a national murder case involving a specific act by a specific individual, murder as a war crime or crime against humanity is far more complicated since the act occurs as part of a greater course of conduct and requires proof of contextual, as well as specific elements. Information that provides insight into the historical background and context of the conflict and the groups involved, most of which can be gleaned from publicly available materials, will thus assist judges in their final assessment. While such information is not evidence per se, it can be used to assist the fact-finder in better understanding the evidence and the case.

Atrocity crime prosecutions typically target high-level perpetrators—often high-ranking government or military officials—responsible for the most serious crimes of international concern.[58] Government documents, press releases, court records, and public statements made by government officials thus can all serve as important circumstantial or direct evidence to support criminal changes. Democratic governments generally have rules to ensure transparency and make a significant amount of information about the government's administration, officials, and finances publicly available. Alternatively, information may become public through Freedom of Information Act requests, litigation, or leaks by whistle-blowers. In an OTP request to open an investigation in Afghanistan, for example, the prosecutor relied on 'tens of thousands of pages of such documentary material [that had] been released to the public through Freedom of Information Act ('FOIA') litigation in US courts'.[59] In

[57] Rome Statute of the International Criminal Court.

[58] ibid.

[59] *Situation in the Islamic Republic of Afghanistan* (Public redacted version of 'Request for authorisation of an investigation pursuant to article 15' ICC-02/17-7-Conf-Exp) ICC-02/17-7-Red (20 November 2017) para 36.

addition, the prosecutor used documents disclosed as part of a civil action brought against two former CIA psychologists and on the public findings of two Congressional inquiries into the detention and interrogation practices of the US military.[60]

4.2 Establishing the Court's Jurisdiction

Before filing a request to initiate an investigation, the OTP must ensure that the potential cases fall within the Court's jurisdiction.[61] A primary consideration in determining whether certain events fall within the jurisdiction of the Court is whether they occurred within a designated temporal and geographic scope or whether there is personal jurisdiction[62] over the actors involved. Open source information can frequently answer the necessary 'when', 'where', and 'who' questions. For example, digital imagery such as photographs, videos, maps, and computer-generated visualizations can provide important geospatial data. Geolocation, the process by which videos and images are analysed for landmarks to identify the depicted location, was used in the *Al-Mahdi* case to confirm the location where certain events occurred. Many personal digital devices are now equipped with global positioning systems (GPS) and many mobile applications use geo-tagging functions to record the location of the phone when various actions are taken, such as sharing a photograph. Open sources often contain GPS and temporal metadata such as embedded timestamps, which can help establish a timeline. Using geospatial data to place events in space and time can also play an important role in corroborating or contradicting witness statements.[63]

For a case to be admissible before the ICC, it must also be of 'sufficient gravity to justify action before the court'.[64] In addition to being part of the case selection criteria, 'gravity' is also incorporated into decisions about responsibility and charging.[65] Both quantitative and qualitative considerations are taken into account when assessing gravity, including 'the scale, nature, manner of commission, and impact of the crimes'.[66] The quantity of news coverage and attention by NGOs do not necessarily reflect the gravity of a conflict, but they may be a helpful indicator. If a conflict and perceived human rights abuses are serious

[60] ibid; 'Inquiry into the Treatment of Detainees in US Custody' (The Senate Committee on Armed Services 2008).

[61] OTP Policy Paper on Case Selection and Prioritization, 9. As set out in art 17(1) of the Statute, admissibility requires an assessment of complementarity (sub-paragraphs (a)–(c)) and gravity (sub-paragraph (d)) in relation to a specific case.

[62] Personal jurisdiction refers to the power that a court has to make a decision regarding a party to the proceedings.

[63] In *Prosecutor v Katanga*, judges discovered on a site visit that claims made by witnesses could not have been possible owing to the distances between their location and the events they allegedly witnessed.

[64] Article 17 of the Rome Statute of the International Criminal Court. Page 13 policy paper: Gravity of crime(s) as a case selection criterion is assessed similarly to gravity as a factor for admissibility under art 17(1)(d). However, given that many cases might potentially be admissible under art 17, the Office may apply a stricter test when assessing gravity for the purposes of case selection than that which is legally required for the admissibility test under art 17.

[65] 'Policy Paper on Case Selection and Prioritisation' (Office of the Prosecutor, International Criminal Court 2016) para 6.

[66] ibid para 37, citing *Abu Garda* (Decision on the confirmation of charges) [] ICC-02/05- 02/09-243-Red (8 February 2010) para 31; *Situation in the Republic of Côte d'Ivoire* (Corrigendum to 'Decision Pursuant to Article 15 of the Rome Statute on the Authorisation of an Investigation into the Situation in the Republic of Côte d'Ivoire') ICC-02/11-14-Corr (3 October 2011) paras 203–204.

enough to garner global attention, then they will probably more easily meet the gravity threshold.

At this stage, the OTP also makes an assessment regarding complementarity to determine whether there are any national proceedings underway and, if so, whether they are being conducted in good faith. As the OTP explains: 'If the national authorities are conducting, or have conducted, investigations or prosecutions against the same person for substantially the same conduct, and such investigations or prosecutions have not been vitiated by an unwillingness or inability to genuinely carry them out, the case will not be selected.'[67] If a state is uncooperative, the OTP can consult open source information to help make such a determination. For example, in the Afghanistan preliminary examination, the admissibility assessment of the scope and progress of relevant national proceedings in Afghanistan and the United States, which is not party to the Statute, was conducted 'primarily on the basis of public sources, including information submitted to and reported by United Nations bodies as well as the publicly available results of Congressional and DOJ inquiries in the US'.[68]

4.3 Proving Contextual and Specific Elements

The ICC has jurisdiction over the most serious crimes of concern to the international community: genocide, crimes against humanity and war crimes.[69] For each crime group, the prosecutor must prove contextual or 'chapeau' elements as well as specific elements, which include both mental and physical components. The prosecutor must also prove additional elements to establish the alleged mode of liability.[70]

For crimes against humanity, the Statute enumerates acts that qualify as such crimes when committed as part of a 'widespread or systematic attack directed against any civilian population'.[71] According to the Rome Statute and Elements of Crimes, the 'course of conduct' involving the multiple commission of acts or a 'pattern' of behaviour must be carried out 'pursuant to or in furtherance of a State or organizational policy to commit such attack'.[72] While the Court has broken down the elements slightly differently from case to case, the Prosecution must prove: (1) the existence of an attack; (2) directed against a civilian population; (3) the widespread or systematic character of the attack; (4) the course of conduct pursuant to or in furtherance of a state or organizational policy; and (5) the accused's knowledge of the attack.[73] The term 'widespread', according to the established jurisprudence of the Court, 'connotes the large-scale nature of the attack and the number of targeted persons'.[74] 'Systematic' may be demonstrated by showing a similar modus operandi

[67] ibid 11.
[68] *Situation in the Islamic Republic of Afghanistan* (n 59) (Request for Authorization of Investigation) para 27.
[69] Rome Statute of the International Criminal Court, art 5.
[70] 'The substantive definitions of crimes ... provide only a part of the picture of criminal liability. The general principles of liability apply across the various different offences and provide for the doctrines by which a person may commit, participate in, or otherwise be found responsible for those crimes.' Cryer and others (n 56) 353.
[71] Rome Statute of the International Criminal Court, art 7.
[72] ibid art 7(1) and (2)(a).
[73] *Prosecutor v Jean-Pierre Bemba Gombo* (Judgment) ICC-01/05-01/08-3343 (21 March 2016) para 148.
[74] *Prosecutor v Laurent Gbagbo* (Decision on the confirmation of charges) ICC-02/11-01/11-656-Red (12 June 2014) para 222 fn 527.

in the attacks. For example, many of the attacks on villages in Darfur bear similarities, such as men on horseback entering a village at daybreak, followed by trucks of armed men, followed by air support, which, taken together, suggest coordinated planning. The Court has accepted the admission of NGO, UN, and media reports to establish the widespread or systematic nature of the alleged attacks when corroborated by other types of evidence.[75] The Chambers have reasoned that high levels of news coverage of multiple events can support the assertion that the commission of crimes was widespread. Similarly, NGO reports, which are often based on interviews with a large number of victims, can be used to demonstrate systematicity.

According to the Rome Statute,[76] to qualify as a war crime, a crime must be 'part of a large-scale commission of such crimes' or shown to be part of a plan or policy. The prosecution must also prove the existence of an armed conflict, although neither the Statute nor the Elements of Crimes defines the concept of 'armed conflict'.[77] In *Mbarushimana*, the Pre-trial Chamber found that there were substantial grounds to believe that an armed conflict took place in the DRC between certain groups during a specified period, basing its decision, in part, on a Human Rights Watch Report.[78] Further, the prosecutor must prove whether the armed conflict is of an international (according to Article 8(2)(c)) or non-international (according to Article 8(2)(e)) character.[79] If the crime takes place within a non-international armed conflict, then the prosecutor must show the 'intensity threshold and protracted character of the conflict'.[80] There is also a 'nexus' requirement, since to qualify as a war crime, the alleged crime must have been committed 'in the context of and ... associated with an armed conflict'.[81] In determining whether the crimes are sufficiently linked to an armed conflict, "the Trial Chamber may take into account factors including: the status of the perpetrator and victim; whether the act may be said to serve the ultimate goal of a military campaign; and whether the crime is committed as part of, or in the context of, the perpetrator's official duties'.[82] To demonstrate the existence of specific elements, open source satellite imagery, for example, can show population movements, troop locations, mass graves, or destroyed villages.[83] Information on population movements can be used to support a charge of forced transfer or deportation, while tracking troop locations and movements can help establish that the suspected group was in the area where the crimes were committed.

[75] ibid.

[76] Rome Statute of the International Criminal Court, art 8(1); *Prosecutor v Jean-Pierre Bemba Gombo* (n 73) para 126.

[77] *Prosecutor v Thomas Lubanga Dyilo* (Judgment) ICC-01/04-01/06-2842 (5 April 2012) para 531; *Prosecutor v Germain Katanga* (n 32) para 1172); *Prosecutor v Jean-Pierre Bemba Gombo* (n 73) para 128.

[78] *Prosecutor v Callixte Mbarushimana* (n 2) para 95.

[79] This distinction is important because there is a higher threshold of violence required for non-international armed conflicts, and the classification dictates which statutory provision applies.

[80] Rome Statute of the International Criminal Court. Article 8(2)(d) and 8(2)(f) requires the conflict to reach a level of intensity which exceeds 'situations of internal disturbances and tensions, such as riots, isolated and sporadic acts of violence or other acts of a similar nature'.

[81] 'Elements of Crimes', art 8(2)(c)(i), 8(2)(e)(v), and 8(2)(e)(vi) (International Criminal Court 2011).

[82] *Prosecutor v Jean-Pierre Bemba Gombo* (n 73) para 143; *Prosecutor v Kunarac and Others* (Appeal Judgment) ICTY IT-96-23 and 23/1 (12 June 2002) para 59; *Prosecutor v Georges Rutaganda* (Appeal Judgment and Sentence) ICTR-96-3 (6 December 1999) para 569.

[83] Satellite imagery has been used for these purposes in the *Srebrenica* cases at the International Criminal Tribunal for Yugoslavia and in the *Darfur* cases at the International Criminal Court.

4.4 Ascertaining the Accused's Mental State

Article 30 of the Statute provides in addition that an individual may only be found criminally responsible for a crime within the Court's jurisdiction if 'the material elements are committed with intent and knowledge'. The international criminally accused are often heads of state or military commanders–public figures whose statements and actions are well recorded in public speeches and interviews, often demonstrating their knowledge, views, and intent regarding the conflict and crimes in question. Since all of this public information may be relevant in building a case against that person and establishing what he or she knew or should have known, analysing public speeches and official propaganda is an increasingly important part of the investigative process. Even the accused's public reactions to the issuance of an ICC warrant can serve as a valuable part of the narrative. Dictators and despots may feel invulnerable, but what they post in fact may be used against them in a court of law. In *Bemba*, the Court admitted an Amnesty International report that the prosecution alleged showed Mr Bemba's awareness of his fighters' capacity to commit crimes.[84] Further, the judges determined that a UN Security Council report 'may be relevant to determining the accused's ability to impose disciplinary measures [on his subordinates] and his power to prevent and repress the commission of crimes'.[85] It also admitted an NGO report that was sent to Mr Bemba while the conflict was ongoing to prove that he was on notice about the conduct of his troops[86]—a further indication that Bemba had knowledge of what was occurring under his command.

4.5 Linking the Perpetrator to the Crime

'Linkage evidence [evidence connecting an alleged perpetrator to the crime in question] is relevant and reliable information that helps prove responsibility for the crime.'[87] In other words, it helps prove 'who' committed the crime and 'how' they did it (e.g. individual perpetration, conspiracy, aiding and abetting, command responsibility).[88] In international criminal cases, the persons most responsible for the crimes are not always the ones who physically committed the crimes, but rather the ones who ordered their commission or were aware of their commission, had the power to stop the crimes, and/or punish their subordinates for committing those crimes, and did not exercise that power. The most compelling linkage evidence is usually documents containing direct orders. Traditionally such materials have been closed source, but with the rise in Twitter usage by political leaders, it is not beyond the realm of possibility these days that a tweet from an individual could link him to crimes on the ground. Additionally, social media networks provide information about users and their relationships to one another. One of the defining features of social-media networks is the ability to 'follow', 'friend', 'connect', or 'link' with other users—a connection that creates a digital record of one's relationship to others or a profile

[84] Wakabi (n 46).
[85] ibid.
[86] *Prosecutor v Jean-Pierre Bemba Gombo* (n 73).
[87] Kelly Matheson, 'Video as Evidence Field Guide' *WITNESS* (2016) https://vae.witness.org/video-as-evidence-field-guide/ accessed 29 December 2018.
[88] ibid.

of interconnectivity. Part of proving linkage in cases where traditional militaries are involved is establishing the organizational hierarchy, chain of command, and relationships between actors.

An important aspect of determining individual responsibility for a crime is proper identification of the accused. The Court has considered various criteria in identifying accused persons and their subordinates, including, in the *Bemba* case,

> the position and role of the accused at the time of the charges, the presence in and control of an area by the perpetrators and commanders, the direction from which a perpetrator came, composition of the troops, a perpetrator's uniform—including insignia, footwear, headwear, arms, and clothing, his or her language, and the perpetrator's specific behavior. In addition, chambers at the ad hoc tribunals have considered other factors, including the timing and location of an identification, self-identification by the perpetrator, indications of rank, and a perpetrator's vehicle, origins, and level of discipline.[89]

Open source imagery can be used to show relevant structures, people, uniforms, vehicles, and weapons, any of which can be used as identification evidence to show the direct perpetrators belonged to a specific military group.

While this section illustrates how open source information can be used to assist and support the investigation and prosecution of international criminal cases, the next section address the other side of the coin—in particular, the obstacles that come with conducting online investigations and relying on digital open source information.

5. Challenges to Using Open Source Information as Evidence

While there are clear benefits to using open sources to support international criminal cases, there are also significant challenges associated with internet-based open sources, particularly because the original source can be difficult to ascertain, and the digital format makes manipulation and forgery relatively easy to accomplish and often hard to detect. First, it is important to understand why the methods and approaches towards open source collection and analysis that are generally acceptable in other fields may be inadequate for the legal context. Actors outside the legal realm, such as intelligence analysts, journalists, and NGOs pioneered the use of open sources. While it is crucial that criminal investigators and lawyers learn how to tap into this trove of potentially useful information, it is equally important that they recognize that working within the criminal justice system places upon them unique duties and responsibilities. International criminal investigators and prosecutors must be wary of how the methods used in other fields might be inadequate to meet the legal requirements stipulated by international agreements and treaties, statutes, rules of procedure and evidence, case law, customary international law, codes of professional conduct, and codes of ethics. Lawyers are bound by strict professional codes of ethics, the breach of which could lead to the suspension or revocation of their licences and possibly to civil or, in extreme circumstances, criminal liability.

[89] *Prosecutor v Jean-Pierre Bemba Gombo* (n 73) para 243.

Unlike journalists and human rights investigators, who are not legally bound by a standardized code of ethics, criminal investigators are held publicly accountable for the way in which they conduct their investigative activities. They can be forced to testify about their methods and activities under oath; they must disclose their sources to the defence; and the evidence they collect may be excluded if procedural rules are not strictly followed. For criminal investigators and prosecutors, the search for the truth must, at all times, be balanced with numerous other obligations such as protecting victims and witnesses, respecting the rights of suspects and the accused, and ensuring the fairness of proceedings.[90] Further, in criminal proceedings, the prosecution must meet a clearly defined and very high evidentiary threshold: beyond reasonable doubt. This sort of delineated evidentiary standard, which must be met by prosecutors to secure a conviction, does not exist for journalists to publish articles, for NGOs to issue reports, or even for armed forces to take military action. The price for getting the facts wrong in a legal setting can be severe—it can lead to wrongful convictions of the innocent, failure to convict the true perpetrators, and other injustices. If courts admit evidence that is later proven to be false or misleading, this failure can undermine the public's faith in the system and weaken the rule of law. With that extreme caution in mind, investigators and lawyers should nevertheless embrace this new information-gathering approach. If done correctly, open source investigations can be an effective legal means of information and evidence collection.

In order to optimize the potential use of open source information as evidence it is essential that it be collected in a systematic manner, with evidentiary and procedural issues considered from the start of the investigation and that investigators take the extra steps to ensure its reliability[91]. At the ICC, the judges apply a three-step test for determining the admissibility of a piece of evidence: the item must (1) be relevant to the case; (2) have probative value; and (3) be sufficiently relevant and probative as to outweigh any prejudicial effect its admission may cause.[92] For documentary evidence, the category in which most open source evidence will fall, the following criteria are used to assess its weight: 'provenance, source or author, as well as their role in the relevant events, the chain of custody from the time of the item's creation until its submission to the Chamber, and any other relevant information'.[93]

Based on these criteria, the prosecution makes its own assessment during the investigation stage

> by evaluating sources and their information following a consistent methodology based on criteria such as relevance (usefulness of the information to determine the commission of crimes within the jurisdiction of the Court), reliability (trustworthiness of the provider of the information as such), credibility (quality of the information in itself, to be evaluated by criteria of *immediacy*, *internal consistency* and *external verification*), and completeness (the extent of the source's knowledge or coverage vis-à-vis the whole scope of relevant facts)'.[94]

[90] Rome Statute of the International Criminal Court, arts 54–69.

[91] 'Preparing Open Source Intelligence (OSINT) for Litigation' *CROSStrax* (19 November 2016) https://www.crosstrax.co/investigation-best-practice/preparing-open-source-intelligence-osint-for-litigation/ accessed 29 December 2018.

[92] Rome Statute of the International Criminal Court, art 69.

[93] *Prosecutor v Jean-Pierre Bemba Gombo* (n 11).

[94] *Situation in the Islamic Republic of Afghanistan* (n 59) para 29.

Digital evidence, whether open or closed source, raises a number of issues regarding collection, processing, preservation, and forensic analysis. Instead, this section focuses on the main evaluation criteria ICC judges apply to open source information, including digital information: authentication, credibility, and reliability.

5.1 Authenticating Open Source Material

Authentication is the process by which documentary evidence is proven to be genuine and not forged or faked. The party presenting the evidence must prove that 'it is what it purports to be', in other words. In some cases, an item may be 'self-authenticating', for example a certified document or record with official business logo. In other cases, authentication can be achieved in a number of ways, usually involving identification of the origin of the material, its completeness, and evidence of an unbroken chain of custody. When it comes to digital evidence, the chain of custody from the time of collection to presentation in court can be safeguarded by assigning a hash value[95] that shows that the item is unique and has not been manipulated. However, that process does not account for the potential of manipulation between the time of creation and the time of collection by the investigator.

Digital images, text, and videos can all be easily forged, and social media has facilitated the widespread distribution of disinformation, misattributed information, fakes, and forgeries. Thus, investigators must understand how and why people communicate the way they do over the various platforms, the possibilities for forgery, bots, and manipulation, and how coverage might vary based on factors such as geography, social status, and age of user. Now more than ever, investigators must be deeply sceptical and cautious about what they rely on and the inferences they draw from publicly available material.

If the item is found to be authentic, the Court will assess the credibility of the source and the reliability of the information or claims therein. Thus, verification often involves a two-step process: first, evaluating the source of the information and then validating the content.

5.2 Evaluating Online Sources

Criminal investigations use a process for source evaluation that is only effective if there is an identifiable source. Some online communications come from identifiable users, of course, but many are anonymous or pseudonymous. Investigators must then take extra steps to try to track down the actual source. When it comes to social media and the internet, there is a dual-source consideration. If a user posts a video to a social media platform, for example, then the investigator must evaluate the reliability of both the platform and the individual user.

In evaluating the reliability of alleged classified documents that have been leaked, the credibility of the source or leaker is a pivotal factor. When such documents are anonymously dumped on the internet—through WikiLeaks, for example—and their source is unknown, their credibility is impossible to verify without a reliable witness. Each source of

[95] A hash is a numeric value of a fixed length that uniquely identifies data. Hash values are used with digital signatures.

leaked documents and each document itself must be assessed on a case-by-case basis with a sceptical eye, especially when the purported original source denies the document's authenticity, or the document only exists in digital format.

5.3 Verifying Digital Content

Reliability refers to the trustworthiness of the content of the information contained in the digital document, video or image, the evaluation of which may differ depending on the purpose for which the item is being introduced. Even reputable news sources have been known to make serious reporting errors due to time pressure and misinformation. That danger is even greater with less-known sources. While traditional media may be helpful in pointing investigators to specific events, the stories themselves are extremely limited in evidentiary value, and any numerical data they provide should always be sourced. Hearsay is an equally huge problem with user-generated content, which is why investigators must reach out to the user and take steps to find the original information source to provide direct evidence, if possible. To ensure the credibility of the information, investigators must identify objectively verifiable information and verify it, and look to other evidence for corroboration.

When it comes to open sources, hearsay is a major problem. The rules on the admissibility of hearsay differ among jurisdictions. In common law countries like the United States, hearsay is inadmissible unless it falls within certain proscribed exceptions.[96] In most international courts, hearsay is admissible but will be given less weight than other evidence. Thus, how international judges will assess and rely on hearsay tends to be unpredictable. Investigators should be properly trained to identify hearsay, so that they know when it might be necessary to take additional steps to corroborate that information with other sources or find direct support of the claims.

6. Conclusion

While the ICC judges have established through experience the criteria they believe necessary to weigh traditional open sources, these standards have not yet been fully developed for new open sources. Judges know what makes some NGO or media reports more credible than others, but that same thinking does not yet transfer to the digital context. On one hand, there is greater unreliability and uncertainty due to the ease with which digital evidence can be faked and manipulated. On the other hand, digital space is what many people occupy today and therefore it is often where the evidence that gets us to the truth lies. Because it is often integral to the facts, social media and other internet-based open source content cannot be ignored. Judges must develop contemporary criteria assessment with clear-cut guidelines for admissibility and weight.

In the meantime, international human rights and criminal investigators should approach open source information on the internet with a critical eye and employ systematic methods

[96] United States Federal Rules of Evidence, r 803.

of inquiry to ensure that it can be relied upon in legal proceedings. As wisely stated in a recent separate opinion by ICC Judges Morrison and Van den Wyngaert:

> Indeed, what distinguishes judgments from reports of special investigation commissions, NGOs and the media is precisely the strength and quality of the evidential foundations of judicial findings of fact. In times where it has become ever more difficult to distinguish facts from "fake news", it is crucial that the judiciary can be relied upon to uphold the highest standards of quality, precision and accuracy.[97]

In the era of disinformation, fake news, and alternative facts—which some refer to as the 'post-truth era'—the courts are the last resort for uncovering the truth. The current lack of faith in political and journalistic institutions cannot spread to include judicial institutions without a catastrophic breakdown in the rule of law. It is, therefore, imperative that all the parties to proceedings take the time 'to get it right' and find the truth, despite the many hurdles. The OTP must establish coherent tools and standardized methodologies for ferreting out manipulation of the truth in digital material and develop approaches for presenting digital evidence to judges in a way that helps them embrace twenty-first century fact-finding. It is the courts, finally, who must combat the current crisis of trust by diligently, vigorously, and consistently ensuring that courtrooms are never 'post-truth'.

[97] *Prosecutor v Jean-Pierre Bemba Gombo* (Judgment on Appeal, Separate Opinion of Judge Christine Van den Wyngaert and Judge Howard Morrison) ICC-01/05-01/08-3636-Anx2 (8 June 2018) para 5.

4

Open Source Investigations and the Technology-driven Knowledge Controversy in Human Rights Fact-finding*

Ella McPherson, Isabel Guenette Thornton, and Matt Mahmoudi

It is 2018. There has been yet another attack in the Syrian conflict—this time in Douma, Eastern Ghouta, where a bombing has left the marketplace devastated. A team of student investigators has been trying to identify the position of a local hospital after they located a video on Twitter showing dozens of heavily injured, hospitalized people. These students belong to the Digital Verification Corps (DVC), Amnesty International's global project to train the next generation of human rights investigators at several university campuses worldwide. DVC students discover and verify open source information to help Amnesty researchers find evidence of human rights abuses. The video in question has been tweeted by a number of different users, each time accompanied by written text claiming that it documents the victims of the marketplace bombing. Should the students be able to geolocate the hospital, they will be better able to assess the scale of the attack through an indication of the minimum number of victims—information they can pass on to Amnesty's investigators, who are trying to establish the facts of the event. The video gives little away; shot from inside the hospital, few geographical clues are revealed. 'What's that?', says one of the students, pointing at two or three frames in the video that reveal a child in polka-dot trousers being carried into the hospital. Scrolling back to another video the team had geolocated earlier that day, the students compare this child with a similar-looking child in similar-looking polka-dot trousers being carried away from the scene of the marketplace attack. The student investigators excitedly agree: they have found a match that helps them establish the location of the hospital.

This scenario—student investigators helping Amnesty's research by analysing civilian witness video posted publicly online—was unimaginable only a few years ago. Investigations based on the proliferation of open source information like the Twitter video mentioned above have transformed the established practices of human rights fact-finding. As we explain below, this transformation is in terms of who is involved (amateurs and technologists, as well as professional human rights fact-finders), the data under scrutiny (including social media content and publicly available databases such as Google Earth Pro), the methods used (such as cross-referencing the metadata of open source civilian witness content), and the norms about knowledge production that participants bring to the table (an emphasis on quantitative versus qualitative, for example).

* We gratefully acknowledge the funding for this chapter, European Commission Horizon 2020 (H2020) Industrial Leadership (IL), grant 687967, 'ChainReact: Making Supplier Networks Transparent, Understandable and Responsive.

One way to understand this sort of transformation is as a type of knowledge controversy. A knowledge controversy can occur when previously settled and taken-for-granted practices of knowledge production (like the human rights evidence produced through the practice of fact-finding) are unsettled and questioned because of the introduction of a novel element in the form of new participants, data, methods, and/or norms.[1] The rise of open source investigations is part of a knowledge controversy in human rights fact-finding. This particular knowledge controversy is driven by the adoption of new technologies in the production and evaluation of human rights information for evidence in advocacy and courts.

In this chapter, we first describe the settled practices of human rights fact-finding that open source investigations have disrupted. Although the authority to shape these practices is centralized largely with Western human rights institutions populated by professional experts, the more decentralized underpinnings of open source investigation—namely, the use of information produced by civilian witnesses and through diverse networks—have an equally long history. We go on to detail how the rise of new technologies in human rights fact-finding has allowed for the participation of new actors in the form of civilian witnesses and analysts and necessitated the participation of others in the form of technologists and machine processes. These new actors bring with them not only new data and new methods, but also new norms about what human rights knowledge should be. The clash of these new elements with established practices produces a knowledge controversy in which much is possible and much is at stake.

In the subsequent section, we take a closer look at what is at stake through examining the power relations within human rights fact-finding revealed and disturbed by this knowledge controversy. Namely, we look at the power to shape human rights methodology, because methodology rules in and rules out particular types of human rights information with respect to evidence. It thus rules in and rules out particular types of corresponding subjects and witnesses of violations with respect to access to human rights mechanisms that can help them, in turn, speak truth to power. Ultimately, we are concerned with the impact of these power relations on pluralism, or the variety and volume of voices that can speak and be heard, both in terms of shaping the practices of human rights fact-finding, and in terms of access to human rights mechanisms that help subjects and witnesses speak truth to power.

1. Established Human Rights Practices Disrupted by the Knowledge Controversy

The appearance of a knowledge controversy marks the shattering of a prior consensus about an established practice of knowledge production and thus the type of knowledge produced by that practice.[2] In this section, we provide an overview of the settled and established practices for producing human rights knowledge disrupted by the adoption of new technologies. These practices, circumscribed by a particular set of actors and a particular set of methods, emerged from a set of institutions that have come to dominate human rights fact-finding in the international arena.[3] At first glance, open source investigations seem a radical departure

[1] Sarah J Whatmore, 'Mapping Knowledge Controversies: Science, Democracy and the Redistribution of Expertise' (2009) 33(5) Progress in Human Geography 587; Andrew Barry, 'Political Situations: Knowledge Controversies in Transnational Governance' (2012) 6 Critical Policy Studies 324.

[2] Whatmore (n 1); Barry (n 1).

[3] Diane Orentlicher, 'International Norms in Human Rights Fact-Finding' in Philip Alston and Sarah Knuckey (eds), *The Transformation of Human Rights Fact-Finding* (Oxford University Press 2016); Dustin N Sharp,

from these established, orthodox practices, but a longer gaze sees this new development as an extension of two other long-established practices in human rights fact-finding: the use of civilian witness information for evidence, along with collaboration among a diverse array of networked individuals and institutions.

The dominant institutional framework drawing on human rights fact-finding has consolidated over time, growing increasingly bureaucratic and elite. Early fact-finding involved select diplomats and legal experts conducting field visits and reporting their findings to intergovernmental organizations like the United Nations.[4] Following high-level concerns critiquing human rights fact-finding for—in the words of a 1964 United Nations Special Committee debate—its 'scantiness and unclearness', a number of attempts were made to standardize fact-finding methodology.[5] Under the influence of prominent human rights non-governmental organizations (NGOs), fact-finding evolved to focus on witness interviewing, often with or through known sources with established credibility.[6] Upon returning from the field, these investigators wrote up their reports, which were made public in order to shame identified states and other actors into complying with human rights norms. Fact-finding in these international NGOs continues to be conducted largely by elite investigators with degrees from globally renowned, well-resourced universities, who usually have been trained in law. Even those from non-Western nations have often received their educations in the West.[7] They maintain close relationships with other elite members of the political and press sectors in order to lobby them behind closed doors.[8] At intergovernmental bodies, similar investigations are undertaken by sets of experts belonging to each of the ten UN human rights treaty bodies. These include, for example, fact-finding missions and investigations carried out by the UN Office of the High Commissioner of Human Rights on behalf of the UN Human Rights Council, the General Assembly, and the Security Council. The formal and bureaucratic nature of these institutions developed in part as a counterweight to the formal and bureaucratic targets of their reports: states.

In both intergovernmental and international NGO institutional contexts, an insistence on the prescriptive and legalistic—as experts seek to construct what appear to be objective and undeniable facts—has become the dominant modus operandi of human rights institutions.[9] This insistence, as Philip Alston describes it, 'risked producing a somewhat formulaic and relatively inflexible style and format'.[10] That said, these orthodox fact-finding practices, undertaken by dominant institutions, are not necessarily taken up by other actors working in human rights and more broadly in emancipatory projects.[11] For example, post-war anti-colonialists avoided the use of human rights discourse, despite decolonization emerging

'Human Rights Fact-Finding and the Reproduction of Hierarchies' in Philip Alston and Sarah Knuckey (eds), *The Transformation of Human Rights Fact-Finding* (Oxford University Press 2016).

4 Philip Alston, 'Introduction: Third Generation Human Rights Fact-Finding' *Proceedings of the Annual Meeting (American Society of International Law)* (2013).

5 BG Ramcharan, 'Introduction' in Bertrand G Ramcharan (ed), *International Law and Fact-Finding in the Field of Human Rights* (Martinus Nijhoff Publishers 2014) 1; Philip Alston and Sarah Knuckey, 'The Transformation of Human Rights Fact-Finding: Challenges and Opportunities' in Philip Alston and Sarah Knuckey (eds), *The Transformation of Human Rights Fact-Finding* (Oxford University Press 2016).

6 Alston (n 4).

7 Obiora Okafor, 'International Human Rights Fact-Finding Praxis: A TWAIL Perspective' in Philip Alston and Sarah Knuckey (eds), *The Transformation of Human Rights Fact-Finding* (Oxford University Press 2016).

8 Sharp (n 3).

9 ibid.

10 Alston (n 4) 61.

11 Alston and Knuckey (n 5); Orentlicher (n 3).

during and in the immediate aftermath of the establishment of the Universal Declaration of Human Rights in 1948. Instead, self-determination was the operative language, working towards a collective vision of liberation, rather than universal individual rights. This was, in part, because anti-colonialists remembered all too clearly that Western concepts of emancipation were the backbone of colonialism's justification.[12] Still, the dominant discourses, practices, and institutions of human rights tend to eclipse these alternative emancipatory ideas and movements, with the consequence not only of diverting attention and funds, but also of depreciating alternative actors, methods, and norms of knowledge production.[13]

The multiple actors, multiple methods, and diverse data of open source human rights investigations may seem at odds with these established practices. Even at the core of bureaucratic and standardized human rights fact-finding, however, we see that open source investigation is as much a continuation of as a break from these established practices, which have always featured the use of civilian witness information and networked collaboration. For example, in one of the earliest accounts of the mobilization of civilian witness information in advocacy and accountability, the British human rights campaigner Emily Hobhouse arduously documented the Second South African War of 1899–1902. This war was between Great Britain and the two Boer republics over the expansion of British forces in South Africa and control over the Transvaal gold mines. About her attempts to document the conditions of refugee camps run by the British that had deteriorated into concentration camps, Hobhouse said, 'It is hardly possible to draw up an ordinary conventional report'. Instead, she relied on a combination of fieldnotes, letters of correspondence, and statements by Boer women and children, along with her photography.[14]

As camera use became more common among the general public, spontaneous acts of civilian witnessing increased. A searing example is the 31-year-old plumber George Holliday's capture on his camcorder of the Los Angeles Police Department brutally beating Rodney King after stopping him for a traffic violation on 3 March 1991. Although the responsible officer was eventually acquitted, the electrifying images seen around the world made the power of citizen media to shed light on human rights struggles palpable. They presaged the new forms of data pulled into human rights fact-finding through open source investigations, brought especially by advancements in camera-phones and social media platforms.

Today, civilian witness data can be solicited and captured relatively securely and digitally through reporting mechanisms such as digital forms tailored to particular situations of human rights violations, like those created by The Whistle,[15] or through relatively secure, widely used messaging services, such as WhatsApp, Signal, and Telegram. As platforms such as Facebook, Twitter, Instagram, and YouTube encourage 'intimate storytelling' and 'voluntary self-disclosure',[16] open source investigators may also discover civilian witness information through using deep searches on these platforms. Like Emily Hobhouse,

[12] Samuel Moyn, *The Last Utopia: Human Rights in History* (Belknap Press 2012).

[13] David Kennedy, 'International Human Rights Movement: Part of the Problem?' (2002) 15 Harvard Human Rights Journal 101; Günter Frankenberg, 'Human Rights and the Belief in a Just World' (2014) 12 International Journal of Constitutional Law 35.

[14] Guardian Research Department, '19 June 1901: The South African Concentration Camps' *The Guardian* (19 May 2011) https://www.theguardian.com/theguardian/from-the-archive-blog/2011/may/19/guardian190-south-africa-concentration-camps accessed 31 December 2018.

[15] www.thewhistle.org.

[16] Cristina Miguel, 'Visual Intimacy on Social Media: From Selfies to the Co-Construction of Intimacies Through Shared Pictures' (2016) 2 Social Media + Society 1.

open source investigators draw on a multiplicity of data sources, and today have access to a plethora of new types of data and methods. Satellite imagery, for example, has advanced to an unprecedented extent, with remote-sensing satellites now able to capture images in up to 30 centimeters resolution, meaning that each image pixel captured by satellites is now representative of 30 square centimeters on the ground. This is enough to capture everything from infrastructure and missile sites down to troop units and vehicles. In another example, corporate information publicly available online enables researchers to analyse complex networks that may hide abusive practices such as modern slavery. Equally, data scraping techniques allow even the most inexperienced of investigators to download large chunks of data from across multiple sites in a matter of moments. Common to all of the new trends in technology-assisted investigations is that they make data more readily available.

Because of the variety and scale of data involved, open source investigations often require collaborations among a diverse network of actors, another practice with a long tradition in human rights fact-finding. For decades, transnational advocacy networks incorporating human rights investigators—but also including journalists, church leaders, grassroots activists, and politicians—have worked together on the basis of shared values.[17] Given that a significant portion of the work of transnational advocacy networks is oriented around communicating between institutions and across geographic locations, the global infrastructure of the internet has further enabled the spread and effectiveness of their work. A variety of technologists, human rights practitioners, architects, academics, and activists are increasingly coming together to form networks and tools for supporting and improving evidentiary and advocacy techniques, as in projects produced by Forensic Architecture or Bellingcat. Private actors from the technology sector provide the platforms and tools for data collection, analysis, and output, either indirectly or directly, for the purposes of these investigations. Civilian analysts, crowds of amateurs who receive training in order to help with labour-intensive analysis tasks, are another new addition to open source investigation networks. For example, the Amnesty Decoders project on Raqqa has relied on digital volunteers to look through satellite imagery over time to help identify periods and sites of airstrikes by tracking the condition of buildings.

Amnesty International's DVC is a pertinent illustration not only of the use of open source investigation methods that have emerged across transnational networks, but also of the many layers of individuals who have to interpret and process relevant data into some form of knowledge about the particular event. A researcher in the vicinity of a human rights related event, for example, might be alerted to its occurrence by a witness, or, on rarer occasions, through personally witnessing the event. In some cases, the researcher is unable either to reach the area in question or to cover enough relevant ground to fully scope the event. Instead, she contacts Amnesty to request support from the DVC. Having been briefed on the often limited information known about the event, the DVC—which at the time of writing has a presence in the universities of Pretoria, Berkeley, Toronto, Essex, Hong Kong, and Cambridge—proceeds to put together a multi-disciplinary team of investigators to conduct discovery surrounding said event. The discovery process includes deep searches on Twitter, Facebook, YouTube, and other media fora that may contain content on the event within the given territory and timeframe. Investigators collect and archive these videos and

[17] Margaret E Keck and Kathryn Sikkink, 'Transnational Advocacy Networks in International and Regional Politics' (1999) 51 International Social Science Journal 89.

images, and proceed, collaboratively (at times across campuses), to process the information using techniques such as reverse image searches to see if the content has appeared online previously; satellite imagery comparison to scan for landmarks, signs, buildings, roads, and landscapes that might indicate the geo-coordinates of the event; and weather data corroboration to help establish time and place. Investigators might then look for further videos that portray the same event posted by different accounts or from different angles. The researchers ask, can we find additional pieces of media that corroborate what we initially discovered? Have investigators from other campuses found something different or reached different conclusions? Finally, in conversation with the DVC manager housed at Amnesty International, the DVC students author a report that establishes the probable veracity of the event and documents the verification process. The report is then either sent to the researcher on the ground to aid in further fact-finding and/or used by Amnesty International, in combination with its in-house researcher's observations, to write a press statement or to advocate action by stakeholders. Though it has roots in established traditions, human rights fact-finding in such instances is still a significant departure from human rights professionals using conventional methods; the new actors involved bring new understandings of knowledge, as we explore next.

2. New Actors in Human Rights Fact-finding and the Struggle for Interpretive Authority

Today, data about human rights has become increasingly accessible and is no longer solely the province of traditional human rights actors and experts. Advances in digital communication have provided various platforms for the collective development of new techniques to gather, contextualize, and verify data. These changes allow new actors unassociated with traditional human rights organizations, like technologists, volunteer digital analysts, civilian witnesses, and even algorithms, to participate in the location, interpretation, verification, and promotion of human rights information and offer traditional actors new methods to apply to their work. Thus, both the 'who' and the 'how' of traditional expertise are shifting. Who, then, are human rights experts today, if human rights information is no longer restricted to experts with relatively exclusive access to sites of struggle? How is information properly contextualized and verified outside of traditional paradigms of known authorship and chains of custody—particularly when there is so much more information, and so much of it is anonymous or from unknown sources? Understanding the ways in which the 'who' and the 'how' of expertise are changing should ultimately lead us to the 'why'. Why is it that these experts who are using certain methods are endowed with authority, and what norms, values, and power dynamics does this authority uphold?

One of the consequences of a knowledge controversy is the questioning of traditional expertise and established authority figures.[18] A critical aspect of knowledge production, contested during a knowledge controversy, is *interpretive authority*: the authority to build information, which is inherently limited, into a coherent account or story and to ascribe it meaning. Location-specific experts, for example, provide context for and explain the

[18] Whatmore (n 1); Barry (n 1).

significance of information that may not seem meaningful to the lay person or even other human rights professionals without relevant geographic and socio-political background knowledge of the event. With open-source investigations, data may be made available to all—a video posted on YouTube or images tweeted out, for example—but the interpretation of this information is often challenging. Even putting aside instances of malicious fakery, original posters of information may provide vague, misleading, or no context with which to understand their posts; similarly, in advocacy, disparate instances must be tied into a bigger story that reflects their shared context. Multiple possible interpretations often exist when data is meagre, or when posters provide conflicting explanations of events. Therefore, this interpretative function is key in the transformation of human rights information into evidence for advocacy and courts. It is up to experts to gather additional information to fill in the blanks or to verify or challenge existing explanations. Spaces for negotiation are crucial in this interpretative work, where stakeholders with different types of expertise and knowledge collaborate to produce truth-claims, persuading others of their views, contesting alternate framings, and acknowledging potential ambiguity in the interpretation.

Traditionally, interpretive authority has been the province of human rights professionals, who may visit or work *in situ* where human rights violations are taking place and develop networks of local informants; the information from these networks is then transformed into evidence by the human rights expert according to the accepted methods of her organization and her own expertise. This province is unsettled during the knowledge controversy by new actors who bring new understandings of interpretive authority, which we consider in turn below. Relatively new human actors in human rights investigations include civilians, who enter the sector either as spontaneous civilian witnesses who share their digital documentation of events around them, or as analysts tapped to deal with the deluge of digital data, as in Amnesty's Digital Decoders project or the DVC. Technologists are also newcomers, and they volunteer or are invited by traditional experts to assist with developing methods for analysing and managing the deluge of digital data relevant to human rights research. In order to incorporate new civilian analysts, human rights professionals must teach them a relatively standardized, relatively straightforward set of methods. As a result, human rights professionals are collaborating with technologists in developing tools to assist both civilians and experts in verification and analysis, helping to clarify, systematize, and speed up the investigative process. As we return to below, increasingly automated tools, because they can make information analysis decisions autonomously, can almost themselves be considered new actors with technologists acting behind them. In addition to being invited to collaborate directly with human rights groups, technologists are becoming increasingly powerful new actors in these investigations in their own right, as large private sector companies that deal in digital information must grapple with data about human rights abuses that appear on their platforms. For example, YouTube, Facebook, and Twitter have all developed policies about how to treat content that violates the company's community standards but may provide important documentation of a human rights violation, and have created teams dedicated to investigating and addressing those violations. Start-ups from the technology-for-good sector seeking to support human rights fact-finding have also proliferated.

Challenges around interpretive authority are inevitable when claims to authority depend on different backgrounds. Human rights professionals have authority based on their experience, proximity to witnesses, understanding of socio-political contexts, methodological expertise, and deep institutional knowledge, including familiarity with advocacy values and practices. In contrast, civilian witnesses have the authority of authenticity and deep cultural, social, and historical knowledge. Technologists invent tools and have the necessary technical expertise to analyse larger bodies of data in new ways. Given that it is unlikely that any one actor will have access to all types of expertise, these different experts must collaborate. During these collaborations, it may be difficult to translate methods, implicit knowledge, and underlying systems of values across boundaries.

As mentioned above, civilian witnesses' use of digital technologies to document potential situations of human rights violations represents a welcome step-change in the amount of human rights information available. This information does not always translate so easily into evidence, however. In contrast with the scientifically based, truth-claims epistemology central to dominant human rights institutions' fact-finding methodology—where things have to be exactly what they say they are, as proven through the triangulation of data and methods—civilian witnesses may bring differing understandings of interpretive authority to their notions of how to produce human rights knowledge. For example, a witness may share a report on social media but, lacking photographs of this particular event (or wary of posting images of victims), she may choose instead to post a proxy photograph of a similar event. For these witnesses, this epistemology of illustration facilitates a meaningful testimonial and truth telling that highlights their subjective experience: what happened was (a lot like) this. Human rights practitioners may believe this witness and want to support her; social media shares by human rights organizations can endow civilian witnesses and their accounts with legitimacy and credibility. At the same time, however, human rights practitioners are vulnerable to accusations of misinformation if they (re)post or support testimonial that includes material, such as proxy images, that isn't consistent with a professional truth-claims epistemology. This can result in tension between would-be allies, as witnesses seek to uphold their report's legitimacy as authentic and original, and their interpretive authority in making reports in the way that is meaningful to them, despite the fact that it then cannot be situated within interpretive and epistemological norms of human rights organizations.

Excitement about the potential benefits of technologists engaging in human rights discovery and reporting processes has been well documented, and indeed it is difficult to imagine how human rights reporting in the age of digital communication can succeed without technical expertise. However, this expertise also comes laden with techno-culture norms that reframe interpretive authority, sometimes in ways that are misaligned with implicit goals and values of the human rights sector. For example, a tension exists between the techno-capitalist goal of efficiency and pluralist goals of negotiation and ambiguity.[19] Technologists working on behalf of human rights organizations to develop digital human rights reporting apps often advocate for the accumulation of a greater amount of data, specifically the kind of evidence that is easier to interpret using technical means (statistics; shorter stories with identifying details; certain types of photographs), despite the above-mentioned dominant practice of long-form testimonials developed between witnesses and human rights practitioners.

This continued emphasis from technologists on more data that can be technically quantified (often with the idea that machine learning can separate the 'good data' wheat from

[19] Luis Suarez-Villa, *Globalization and Technocapitalism: The Political Economy of Corporate Power and Technological Domination by Luis Suarez-Villa* (Routledge 2012).

the 'bad data' chaff—a tricky proposition when dealing with involved testimonials) offers a different interpretive paradigm and standard for fact-finding than in-depth testimonials informed by personal relationships and bolstered by the longevity of the area-knowledge of a human rights professional. This new paradigm, sometimes described pejoratively by practitioners as 'quantity over quality', represents an uncomfortable incursion of technologist conventions and values into this traditional human rights territory—even as some practitioners hope that it can provide information from sources that they might not receive otherwise.[20] A focus on data rather than narrative is also seen in the quantitative turn within human rights led by figures such as Patrick Ball, a statistician who analyses large-scale human rights abuses and who has often provided expert testimony on war crimes. However, an emphasis on the quantitative creates new problems; according to Sally Engle Merry, the 'seduction' of quantitative data, stemming from its ability to provide concrete, seemingly objective truths, often obscures the power relations and assumptions inherent in the development of quantitative systems of measurement.[21]

The latter is particularly of concern in the rise of machine learning and automated decision-making in human rights information analysis. Anxieties about digital tools in effect overstepping interpretive authority—that is, being used to achieve seemingly objective conclusions, that, nonetheless, are based on potentially flawed, biased, or limited assumptions—suggests that these tools may be considered new actors in their own right, with varying degrees of interpretive authority. These new machine 'actors' represent both processes and analytical 'judgments'. For example, programmes may analyse the shadows in an outdoor image to suggest the time of day and year; extract and analyse the metadata attached to images and video; judge if social media posts contain human rights-relevant content using discovery algorithms; or suggest to civilian analysts working on a set of data which methods to try in what order. In this last instance, such programmes suggest the use of methods both based on human judgment and machine judgment, with varying emphases. While the mechanized paradigm is not new, having clear antecedents in Fordian models of efficiency and mass production, which similarly envisioned the human and machine working together as a mechanized unit, it is newly expressed in human rights within the context of advances in both machine judgment and instantly mediated digital communication. This interaction between old paradigms and new advances, in which new methods help us to reflect on old structures, is typical of a knowledge controversy.

These machine actors are developed by human actors (technologists, sometimes working in collaboration with human rights professionals), and therefore inevitably reflect the biases and limits of their creators. However, a techno-romantic view of machines as omniscient—and machine judgment as transparent and uncontaminated by human bias—has often buried this authorship. Norms like the fetishization of empiricism (prizing the use of quantitative methods, outputs, and formats, regardless of their fit for the research question or context), concerns with objectivity, anxieties about the fallibility of experts in the context of the 'post-truth' phenomenon, and the anticipation that institutions such as courts require data that is gathered, verified, and framed in an empiricized way, have reinforced this

[20] Isabel Guenette Thornton, Ella McPherson, and Matthew Mahmoudi, 'No Tech, Low Tech, Slow Tech: Human Rights Practitioners' Resistance to ICT4D' (January 30, 2018). Available at SSRN: https://ssrn.com/abstract=3466138.

[21] Sally Engle Merry, *The Seductions of Quantification: Measuring Human Rights, Gender Violence, and Sex Trafficking* (University of Chicago Press 2016).

perception that machine judgment is relatively pristine. Implicitly, this perception assumes that human judgment is comparatively contaminated. This assumption and the resulting obfuscation of potential biases in machine judgment already has consequences for vulnerable people, as Rebecca Wexler reveals in her work on the use of algorithms to inform legal judgment within the criminal justice system, and Virginia Eubanks discusses in the context of the flawed algorithmic indicators that are used to separate children from impoverished parents in Allegheny County, Pennsylvania.[22]

Each interpretive paradigm or epistemology views the balance of authority in truth-claims differently—whether, for example, authority should reside in statistical analysis, big data patterns, qualitative accounts by experts, or testimonies direct from witnesses. As new actors bring different paradigms and epistemologies of interpretive authority, this diversity of perspectives increases the risk of errors from actors who might misunderstand information produced across boundaries. This may occur, for example, as a result of uncritically replicating information that is seemingly direct from witnesses or is the automatic product of analytical tools produced without an informed consideration of context. Actors may repost material that has not been properly verified, perhaps because the tweet in question has already been taken up widely by the press or other social media users, exacerbated by fast-moving visibility methods like hashtag activism. Actors may reproduce statistics based on definitions or categories that they would not agree with were those categories made transparent. They may mishandle the chain of custody when gathering information, particularly digital information, such that the data is no longer admissible in courts. With machine processes, analysis is limited by the tools and methods offered, which may falsely suggest that a series of positive results on each test is enough to produce confidence, when tests may have varying relevance to the questions at hand.[23] This can be contrasted with traditional human-centred processes that emphasize the understanding that methods must remain flexible, and sometimes be created anew, to be an appropriate fit for the context.

Furthermore, new civilian witness and technologist actors may underestimate the scope of interpretive work within analysis and verification and, indeed, may be sceptical of seemingly intuitive processes, used by experienced human rights practitioners, that they are unable to replicate or understand easily. Human rights professionals construct, in the words of Stephen Hopgood, 'an appearance of objectivity out of subjectivity' to define what constitutes a human rights violation—which, according to Richard Wilson, requires 'a suppression of the authorial voice and the deployment of a language purged of all tropes, metaphors, and figurative elements', as a way to empiricize and simplify complex interpretive processes.[24] The underlying interpretive work—such as resolving the question of how to deal with ambiguous or incomplete data, inferring broader meanings of social and political movements from individual stories, categorizing complex experiences, and attempting to convey suffering—is thus easily obscured and devalued. The inherent uncertainty of such interpretive work, which exists for all methods, may be further obfuscated

[22] Rebecca Wexler, 'Life, Liberty, and Trade Secrets: Intellectual Property in the Criminal Justice System' (2018) 70 Stanford Law Review 1343; Virginia Eubanks, *Automating Inequality: How High-Tech Tools Profile, Police, and Punish the Poor* (St Martin's Press 2017).

[23] Orentlicher (n 3).

[24] Stephen Hopgood, *Keepers of the Flame: Understanding Amnesty International* (Cornell University Press 2006) 5; Richard A Wilson, 'Representing Human Rights Violations: Social Contexts and Subjectivities' in Richard A Wilson (ed), *Human Rights, Culture and Context: Anthropological Perspectives* (Pluto Press 1997) 149, cited in Hopgood (n 23) 5.

by the use of digital analysis tools that seem to give an empirical result. In the next section, we go on to consider the implications of the rise of these new actors, with their contested understandings of interpretive authority, on the core human rights norm of pluralism.

3. The Knowledge Controversy around Open Source Investigations and Its Implications for Pluralism

Knowledge controversies are unsettling, but this very state of unsettlement is productive in terms of analysing power relations and working to make them more equal.[25]The appearance of a knowledge controversy marks the shattering of prior consensus about a topic of knowledge and the methods for creating that knowledge—a consensus that naturalizes the knowledge and makes it seem as if it just *is* rather than *is constructed* by social actors.[26] The clash of actors, methods, data, and norms in a knowledge controversy creates an opportunity to be reflexive about the current practices of knowledge production and how they came about—as well as to revisit and reimagine what knowledge production should ideally be. Part of the latter involves identifying the norms that we value in knowledge production, and assessing how directions in the knowledge controversy measure up to those norms. This may be an uncomfortable process, as it requires us momentarily to step away from our stake in the knowledge controversy, about which we may feel passionately, in part because it is wrapped up in our own power positioning.

The norm of knowledge production that concerns us here is one that is central to our academic disciplines, as well as to our work on The Whistle, an academic start-up focused on supporting the reporting and verification of digital human rights information. It is also a core norm for human rights fact-finding, given this practice's concern with speaking truth to power and giving voice to the voiceless. The norm in question is pluralism, which, as mentioned above, is the variety and volume of voices that can speak and be heard, both in terms of shaping the practices of human rights fact-finding, and in terms of access to human rights mechanisms that help subjects and witnesses speak truth to power. Pluralism of knowledge production is supported in at least two ways: the creation and maintenance of spaces for opportunity and the creation and maintenance of spaces for negotiation. *Spaces for opportunity* provide chances to participate in knowledge production. *Spaces for negotiation* provide chances to negotiate that participation into the ultimate decision of what knowledge is produced, how, by whom, and why. This distinction is important, as it tells us something about not only the quantity of pluralism (spaces for opportunity), but also its quality (spaces for negotiation). It has parallels to long-standing debates in development and citizenship studies and practices around what exactly participation should look like, with greater quality of participation seen as having greater benefits in terms of equalizing power relations.[27]

[25] Sarah Franklin, *Biological Relatives: IVF, Stem Cells, and the Future of Kinship* (Duke University Press 2013); Sarah Harding, 'Feminism, Science, and the Anti-Enlightenment Critiques' in Linda J Nicholson (ed), *Feminism/Postmodernism (Thinking Gender)* (Routledge 1990).

[26] Barry (n 1); Brian Martin and Evelleen Richards, 'Scientific Knowledge, Controversy, and Public Decision-Making' in Sheila Jasanoff and others (eds), *Handbook of Science and Technology Studies* (Sage 1995); Whatmore (n 1).

[27] Sherry R Arnstein, 'A Ladder of Citizen Participation' (1969) 35 Journal of the American Planning Association 216.

Our overview of the settled practices of human rights fact-finding disrupted by the current knowledge controversy indicates that these settled practices provided spaces for opportunity and spaces for negotiation, albeit limited. Human rights practitioners have long included civilian witness accounts, translating them into the standardized reports necessary for influence at the international, institutional level. The traditional, orthodox practice of face-to-face interviews allows not only spaces for opportunity for civilian witnesses to convey their knowledge to fact-finders, but also spaces for negotiation, as this knowledge transfer happens through a conversation that allows its participants to explain their respective versions of interpretive authority and their respective epistemologies so as to arrive at a mutual understanding of the events under discussion. For example, a civilian witness who remembers the violation largely through the emotional as well as physical trauma they experienced may meet a fact-finder who is interested in an account that emphasizes specific facts, such as the place, date, and time of the violation. In cases like this, the interlocutors can, through negotiation, build bridges between differing visions of what human rights knowledge is and how to construct it. In particular, through listening to the civilian witness, the fact-finder can honour their account while also translating it for consumption by human rights institutions and possible use as evidence admissible in court.[28]

The resource-intensive method of face-to-face interviews has, however, always meant a limit on spaces for opportunity for witnesses. These limits stem not only from the cap on the number of civilian witnesses who can cross paths with fact-finders during their research, but also from methodological limitations: Those who have experienced violations that are less documentable using the traditional methodology of shaming based on witness testimonies (for example, violations without survivors or violations involving social, economic, and cultural rights) have generally had greater difficulty in accessing institutional mechanisms of human rights accountability.[29] At the broader scale of institutional politics, we see limitations on spaces for negotiation arising from the power dynamics among the different sets of actors involved. Though civilian witnesses and collaborative networks are important to developing human rights information into evidence, orthodox human rights institutions—because of their resources, their credibility, and their proximity to the corridors of power—usually have the dominant interpretive authority. This power imbalance ultimately circumscribes the potential space for negotiation in the production of human rights knowledge. It is also a historical precedent that is illuminatory for the dynamics of the current knowledge controversy.

First of all, despite predictions that information and communication technologies would allow the pursuit of accountability to be conducted extra-institutionally through peer networks of citizens, societies show no signs yet of entering a post-institution age. The multilayered human rights architecture that is advocated by bodies and agencies of the United Nations (UN) is still very much at the centre of how human rights practice is executed in the international context. There are, for instance, still significant constraints to what can be considered a legitimate method for evidence capture, with a preference for established sources with whom institutions have built trust—a fact that is in tension with the

[28] Ella McPherson, 'Technologies for Human Rights Witnessing: Humans, Machines and Ethics' (Working Paper).

[29] Kenneth Roth, 'Defending Economic, Social and Cultural Rights: Practical Issues Faced by an International Human Rights Organization' (2004) 26 Human Rights Quarterly 63.

adoption of open source methods, a prime feature of which is a greater diversity of voices (the majority of whom will not have the credibility of long-term sources and informants). International NGOs, and the UN bodies in particular, are here to stay and have a great degree of state-power behind them in shaping dominant epistemologies and norms; traditional ways of 'doing' human rights have, in other words, become somewhat cemented at this level. This makes it difficult to open up space for negotiation on human rights methodologies. Participants in open source investigations are thus potentially subject to a dilemma vis-à-vis human rights pluralism. On the one hand, they must plug into existing institutional frameworks to be effective in delivering citizens access to the mechanisms of human rights accountability; on the other hand, to do so, they may not have the space to negotiate alternative interpretive frameworks and norms into the production of human rights knowledge, but rather have to shoehorn this diversity into the standardized, dominant methods of these institutions.

Secondly, these institutional dynamics have set a precedent for how struggles over spaces for opportunity and spaces for negotiation might play out. Human rights professionals are well aware of power dynamics, including the inequalities around pluralism, involved in orthodox human rights practices;[30] this explains some of the excitement that has emerged about the spaces for opportunity afforded by new communication technologies.[31] These technologies have been invaluable for the spontaneous civilian witnesses who, upon experiencing a human rights atrocity or crime, can take to any number of platforms to seek uptake of their information among publics and professionals—a particularly attractive (if risky) possibility in the absence of a domestic rule of law system to which victims can appeal for remedy. Though inaccessible in some parts of the world (e.g. owing to cost or authoritarian censorship) or differentially accessible within a community (e.g. owing to gender or age norms around technology ownership), a camera and access to the internet would seem enough to shed light on an unseen event, regardless of geographic context or the nature of the atrocity.[32] It is not, however, just digital divide issues in terms of access—which can map onto traditional issues of fact-finder access to dangerous or remote regions—that limit potential new spaces for opportunity. Divides in terms of technical and information literacy are a concern as well.[33] Abuses that are easier to capture and corroborate visually, such as those occurring in public places, may be more easily identified and analysed than harms like sexual violence, which are more likely to happen in private and are difficult to document with current tools like smartphones. In another limitation to spaces for opportunity, human rights organizations' long-standing central concern with credibility means this is still a metric by which potential civilian witnesses are assessed; exclusionary power dynamics persist around this, where greater credibility can be associated with greater social capital, such as the number and type of followers.[34] Algorithmic privilege, namely a user's

[30] Alston and Knuckey (n 5).

[31] Molly Land, 'Democratizing Human Rights Fact-Finding' in Philip Alston and Sarah Knuckey (eds), *The Transformation of Human Rights Fact-Finding* (Oxford University Press 2016).

[32] Christoph Koettl, 'Citizen Media Research and Verification: An Analytical Framework for Human Rights Practitioners' (University of Cambridge Centre of Governance and Human Rights 2016).

[33] Ella McPherson, 'Digital Human Rights Reporting by Civilian Witnesses: Surmounting the Verification Barrier' in Rebecca Ann Lind (ed), *Produsing Theory in a Digital World 2.0: The Intersection of Audiences and Production in Contemporary Theory*, vol 2 (Peter Lang Publishing 2015).

[34] Ella McPherson, 'Advocacy Organizations' Evaluation of Social Media Information for NGO Journalism: The Evidence and Engagement Models' (2015) 59 American Behavioral Scientist 124.

relatively prominent positioning in other users' social media timelines owing to the opaque workings of timeline algorithms, and content moderation, or the removal of user content from social media platforms due to its perceived violation of community standards, are other ways in which new spaces for opportunity are limited.

Still, it seems spaces for opportunity are growing with new technologies not only in terms of civilian witness information but also in terms of the evaluation of that information for evidence. New networks are coming together across diverse professions to improve digital analysis techniques, including through the development of new opportunities for civilian analysts. In these scenarios, expertise is established through using accepted, rigorous (and often reproducible) methods: this is akin to what Diane Orentlicher calls 'accountability-through-methodology', rather than the authority of experts as such.[35] Put another way, the 'how' of human rights investigations leads to the 'who' and the 'why' of accepted expertise, instead of the other way around. A focus on methods—particularly reproducible and empiricized methods that can, in theory, be deployed by anyone to verify or challenge human rights stories—can thus create new spaces for opportunity. At the same time, however, it can undermine the value of other forms of human judgment, thereby reducing pluralizing spaces for negotiation and ambiguity.

A focus on methods in the current knowledge controversy means a focus on technologies, and these technologies and their associated technologists bring new norms of knowledge construction into the mix—or their increasing prominence makes their associated norms more dominant. A significant proportion of the new actors and methods introduced with open source investigations hail from the technology sector. Think, for example, of the use of Facebook, Twitter, and WhatsApp as human rights information transmission mediums, or of the development of human rights-specific applications by programmers. The programmers building these technologies, whether mainstream or working in a human rights niche, typically receive their formative training in a cultural context increasingly shaped by Silicon Valley values. A cornerstone of these values is the norm of efficiency, with associated knowledge values of quantification and objectivity that allow for more efficient analysis. Prizing efficiency means prizing the ability to do the same with less resources or to do more with the same amount of resources. The latter is especially important in the informational sector, given the oft-cited statistic that 90 per cent of the world's data was produced in the past two years.[36] In other words, prizing efficiency prioritizes a technology solution to a technology problem—that of big data.

Like every other information-based profession, the human rights sector faces a big data problem. Often, open source investigations involve the discovery of a vast amount of data, much more than was previously possible, which is both the exciting and challenging potential of these new forms of information collection—particularly given the time and expertise needed to verify new forms of digital data.[37] Given the hours involved, the interest among many actors in the human rights world and beyond in the development

[35] Orentlicher (n 3) 509.

[36] Bernard Marr, 'How Much Data Do We Create Every Day? The Mind-Blowing Stats Everyone Should Read' *Forbes* (21 May 2018) https://www.forbes.com/sites/bernardmarr/2018/05/21/how-much-data-do-we-create-every-day-the-mind-blowing-stats-everyone-should-read/ accessed 3 September 2018.

[37] McPherson, 'Digital Human Rights Reporting by Civilian Witnesses: Surmounting the Verification Barrier' (n 33).

and adoption of new technologies for making the collection and analysis of this data more efficient is understandable. This emphasis on efficiency, however, not only squeezes out space for negotiation but also may make negotiation a less desirable norm of knowledge production.

Knowledge production achieved through spaces for negotiation flourishes within human relationships, over time, with effort and exchange—elements at odds with the norm of efficiency. The efficiency of technologies often derives from their replacement of human endeavour with machine work, which often reduces time constraints in part through eliminating interpersonal contact.[38] Think, for example, of a civilian witness reporting a human rights violation through a web-based form rather than face-to-face with a fact-finder. A different instance is the rise of satellite imagery to document human rights violations. This has created new opportunities for inclusion in human rights cases, but such a data source places a great distance between those affected on the ground and the human rights fact-finders picking up their cases. In another example, ICTs allow the DVC to work collaboratively across time and place, yet this separation does not always lend itself well to in-depth conversation. Negotiation is a human-to-human process; it is difficult to negotiate with a machine—despite advances in artificial intelligence—or even sometimes to negotiate with another human through a machine.

If the rise of technologists and their tools in this knowledge controversy casts doubt on human judgment and non-mechanized processes (as contaminated, and also as inefficient compared to machine processes), this introduces consequences for interpretive authority. Human actors may increasingly be encouraged to act as consistent and efficient machines through following protocols that resemble algorithms, while machines are allowed to act as humans by making evaluative suggestions or even decisions about information.[39] In terms of the former, programmes supporting civilian analysts to assist with verification often provide a series of methods and tools following an 'if-then' structured series of tasks—an algorithmic paradigm. Examples of the latter include programmes in computer vision, where machines automatically identify objects in pictures, or algorithmic identification engines, where machines make judgments about what material might be valuable in human rights investigations such as through identification of key words.[40] The interpretive authority of machine processes is ascendant; human actors' space for negotiation is compressed by the new pseudo-mechanized processes involved in human rights fact-finding as well as by algorithms' invisibilization of interpretive moments and bias that otherwise might be identified and interrogated. Even if unintentional, this obfuscation of the falsity of machine processes' implied certainty is always political, as removing space for ambiguity and negotiation removes interpretive agency and connotes that only a single epistemology is valid. As a result, the norm of negotiation in knowledge production is depreciated.

The reduced spaces for negotiation resulting from the rise of technology tools and norms has a further consequence of introducing new inequalities and exacerbating existing

[38] McPherson, 'Technologies for Human Rights Witnessing: Humans, Machines and Ethics' (n 28).

[39] ibid.

[40] Jay D Aronson, 'Computer Vision and Machine Learning for Human Rights Video Analysis: Case Studies, Possibilities, Concerns, and Limitations' (2018) 43 Law and Social Inquiry 1188; Alan Blackwell and others, 'Computer Says "Don't Know": Interacting Visually with Incomplete AI Models' (2018) https://digital.lib.washington.edu/researchworks/bitstream/handle/1773/42857/DTSHPS18-Proceedings-final%20v2.pdf?sequence=8&isAllowed=yaccessed 2 January 2019.

ones. In other words, some actors have access to more space than others. For example, regarding negotiation around the shape and transparency of tool design, the elite populations working at Western NGOs are more likely to have connections to technologists than those in the Global South.[41] This inequality maps onto the existing dominance of the West over the South in terms of the direction of human rights knowledge.[42] It also means that the design priorities in technology for human rights will be more likely to come from Western perceptions that may or may not fit with Southern realities—again, a wider, long-standing problematic for human rights ideas and methods.[43] In another example, while actors external to the dominant human rights institutions may have increasing opportunities for their information to be seen by these institutions, they may have less space to negotiate the interpretation of this information, as this visibility occurs mediated by machines rather than by humans. The consequence is that, as under the established practice of human rights fact-finding, information might come from the 'bottom', but, as Dustin Sharp puts it, 'Solutions generally come from the 'top'.[44] In sum, the rise of open source human rights investigations may mean that, though we see more actors engaged in human rights knowledge production, we hear them less.

4. Conclusion

In this chapter, and in the spirit of the knowledge controversy approach, we have raised more questions than answers and more possibilities than conclusions about the changes wrought by and around the rise of open source human rights investigation.[45] We pose these questions with the aim of creating spaces for reflection among practitioners and scholars, rather than stating answers that might shut out alternative perspectives. As we have explained, human rights fact-finding is in the midst of a knowledge controversy spurred on by the rise of new technologies and manifesting in expanding practices, like open source investigation, involving new actors, who bring new norms. Knowledge controversies are marked by a departure from the taken-for-granted, established order, which in turn provides insight into the normative, practical, and power-related dimensions of the previous status quo. They feature potential misalignments in norms and epistemologies between actors, and contested expectations around methodological practices—conflicts visible in public and professional anxieties about changing paradigms of expertise, interpretive authority and power in the production of human rights knowledge. We have focused here on the implications of this knowledge controversy and its contests for the pluralism of human rights knowledge production. We go beyond concerns with the quantity of pluralism, associated with spaces for opportunity for participation, to the under-examined quality of pluralism manifested in spaces for negotiation over the methodologies used to establish the knowledge, and the associated interpretive authority necessary to do so. This more nuanced understanding of pluralism ensures that we push analytically far beyond the mistaken

[41] Alston and Knuckey (n 5).
[42] Okafor (n 7).
[43] Sharp (n 3).
[44] ibid 76.
[45] Whatmore (n 1).

assumption that the wider availability of technologies for human rights is in and of itself a measure of greater pluralism.[46]

Open source human rights investigation surfaced in a field dominated by institutional players, but also featuring looser networks, including civilian witnesses. This new practice is an evolution of the latter, but must also fit into the orthodox institutional framework to produce evidence that will be taken seriously by these still-dominant mechanisms of accountability and justice. As such, despite the significant new, exciting capacities and expanded spaces for opportunity for new actors to participate in the human rights knowledge production that new technologies have afforded, these are arriving in a context where the precedent has been to provide a narrower space for negotiation over the interpretation of that knowledge. This precedent has dovetailed with a troubling trend, which is that spaces for negotiation may be narrowing in the relatively new practice of open source investigation as well. Norms that have arrived with new technologist and technology actors—such as efficiency, quantification, and objectivity—can clash with the norm of negotiation. Not only are new, efficiency-oriented practices edging out spaces for negotiation, including reflection on information interpretation, but they are also depreciating negotiation as a norm of knowledge production—despite its benefits for pluralism.

At the time of writing, we are still in the midst of the knowledge controversy in human rights fact-finding. It remains to be seen how competitions and collaborations will develop. Will heterogeneous norms, goals, and methods resolve over time, leading to flexible, hybrid practices? Will they solidify into rigid practices dominated by particular actors? Or will they continue to provoke anxieties and struggles around contested interpretive authority?

Along with the anxieties of knowledge controversies come the benefits of the openness they create. This openness, however, is short-lived. It only lasts as long as the knowledge controversy. The actors involved often rush to settle the controversies that arise because norms and practices of knowledge production are unstable and evolving, and work based on these norms and practices can be discomfiting, slow, and difficult to complete. Returning to a taken-for-granted and standardized state allows knowledge workers to work more efficiently, but it comes at the expense of a critical awareness of why and how we are producing knowledge that would otherwise allow us to question and adjust our norms and practices. As a result, just as the opening of a knowledge controversy is an important moment for the power dynamics of knowledge production, so is its closure. This is the moment when knowledge and methods settle and become widely accepted anew. One version in the controversy has won. Its proponents have earned the power to define how knowledge is produced and how much space for opportunity and for negotiation is built into the system.[47]

As a result, we encourage participants in this knowledge controversy not to rush to resolve it, but rather to dwell in the openness it creates.[48] This is the moment to reflect on existing and desired norms and practices of knowledge production, to retain or change them, and to evaluate new norms and practices against them. It is a time to ensure that flexibility exists to tailor the traditional and the new to best fit each fact-finding situation. It is now

[46] Tamy Guberek and Romesh Silva, 'Human Rights and Technology: Mapping the Landscape to Support Grantmaking' Partners for Human Rights Information, Methodology and Analysis (2014) https://www.fordfoundation.org/media/2541/prima-hr-tech-report.pdf accessed 3 January 2018.

[47] Martin and Richards (n 26).

[48] Whatmore (n 1).

that participants should continue to build on the reflexive turn in human rights fact-finding to think not only about implications of changes for spaces for opportunity and negotiation and how to protect and grow these spaces, but also about relative inequalities of access to these spaces among different populations. Questioning along the way, even as you read this book, *how* interpretive authority and expertise are developed through norms, practices, and methods, *why* these methods are emphasized over others, and *who* is endowed with expertise as a result will draw attention to the power dynamics and potential inequalities inherent in this knowledge controversy.

More specifically for human rights fact-finders, the idea of a knowledge controversy may be at once familiar and unsettling. Given the contested nature of human rights reports, controversy is the murky air practitioners breathe. That said, human rights practitioners are usually trying to clear the air, to settle the dust, and allow the facts to emerge. Where they see violations, they employ methods to make their evidence as incontrovertible as possible. Part of this process entails the meta-method of publicly communicating the rigour of their methods in their reports and on their websites. So while human rights practitioners might be comfortable with controversies on the level of evidence about what happened in specific instances of human rights violations, more disconcerting is a knowledge controversy in how we arrive at human rights evidence overall. Still, even though practitioners may breathe a sigh of relief when this technologically afforded knowledge controversy closes and methods naturalize again, we encourage their retention of some of its openness as they practice the production of human rights knowledge.

Settling a knowledge controversy prematurely not only risks sedimenting power dynamics *within* human rights investigations, it may also pose risks *to* human rights investigations as malicious actors may co-opt new tools, methods, and forms of interpretive authority in ways contrary to pluralism. We are reminded by the increase of digital fakery scandals that the positive developments leveraging digital technologies for open source investigations may also be overshadowed and further complicated by new techniques adopted by nefarious state and non-state actors, and developed against the backdrop of leaps in artificial intelligence and machine learning. Although sites of digital verification expertise such as the Atlantic Council's Digital Forensic Research Lab and Bellingcat have established techniques for exposing disinformation and digital fakery, deep fakes—digital scenarios, including the video and audio-based imitation of individuals, generated via artificial intelligence—pose perhaps one of the greatest information challenges on our horizon, as Scott Edwards describes in Chapter 5 of this book. Furthermore, as open source investigation develops against the backdrop of the fake news era, it has become ever more common for opponents to attempt to discredit human rights fact-finders' methods and findings, and such discrediting discourses may take hold among broader publics. The socio-technical changes introduced in information-sharing in the late digital age must therefore be approached with caution; there is much to be excited about in open source investigations and human rights, but also reason to tread carefully to avoid falling into noxious challenges to human rights documentation. With civilian witnesses of human rights violations already considered suspect because of their lack of established credentials, the above-mentioned developments risk further jeopardizing marginalized voices.

As the risks for human rights investigations are so high, open source human rights investigation is, in a sense, the canary in the new information coalmine. The perspective of human rights practitioners is incredibly valuable for other knowledge professions such as journalism and academia, as, being at the frontier, they can provide thought leadership in terms of how to navigate this terrain as equitably and inclusively as possible. This can be showcased in an ethical approach to open source investigation that supports spaces for opportunity and negotiation—thinking all the while about how to settle the knowledge controversy with the utmost consideration of pluralism and power relations, while also retaining its spirit of reflexivity and flexibility.

5

Open Source Investigations for Human Rights

Current and Future Challenges

Scott Edwards

1. Introduction

Today, human rights investigators are inundated by tremendous amounts of data and other information of potential relevance to their work. Just as in commerce, governance, and other areas of public interest, so in human rights investigations the modern information environment has forced considerable adaptation in practice, often to the immense benefit of human rights defence. Nevertheless, considerable challenges face the human rights investigator using open source methods. This chapter will address three broad procedural challenges in open source investigations: the discovery of information; coping effectively with the ephemeral nature of open source content; and assessing information authenticity. While these challenges have spurred many adaptations and new techniques discussed in other chapters, the fundamental challenges detailed here are likely to persist. The chapter closes with a discussion of future trends that are likely to influence the science and practice of open source investigations and the broader pursuit of human rights investigation.

2. Background

Human rights research is as varied as the Universal Declaration of Human Rights 1948 itself. For our purposes here, it can be differentiated into two coarse sets: human rights *events* and human rights *circumstances*. Human rights events are discrete violations of human rights or humanitarian law, and have discrete attributes pertaining to 'who, what, where, and when'. Examples may include excessive force against protestors, a military strike on a legally protected site, or torture.

Human rights circumstances are situations that also constitute a breach of law, but may not be discrete or involve an overt act. Examples may include racial or gender disparity as the result of discrimination; inadequate housing, water, or food; or inequitable education. Although current and future challenges to open source investigations apply to all human rights concerns, they are most acute with event reporting and investigation.

Open source information relevant for human rights can take virtually any form, including one or a mix of the following:

- Sensor data: such as photos, videos, audio recordings, weather station data, and satellite imagery. This category of information includes data that is often closed source, including medical or fitness device readings, road camera data and CCTV video, and mobile phone tower data.

- Machine log data: information generated by a sensing system or machine such as a server recording traffic on its site, computer system logs, search engine query records, mobile phone location data, transaction receipts, and call detail records.
- Narrative text information: spoken or written human language, overheard or recorded, relaying subjective experience, beliefs, or prompts.
- Archives and other highly structured or relational databases: collections of information about the world, both historical and contemporary. Examples include events or news databases (such as LexisNexis), open government initiatives, crime statistics, and census data.

Using open source methods may be complicated by immense time pressures, especially when responding to ongoing human rights events. The overwhelming majority of human rights investigations are carried out by international and national non-governmental organizations that have a dual mandate: fact-finding about human rights violations and policy intervention. As such, investigations carried out by such organizations tend to proceed in fits and bursts, with information gathering, analysis, and fact-finding punctuated with public statements, lobbying, and pulling on various levers to pressure those in power.[1]

The mandate to intervene in human rights abuse lends itself to seeking the earliest possible policy intervention. It is better to bring abuses to light as soon as possible, before further harm is done. This requires rapid fact-finding at the outset of human rights events, even within the context of longer-term investigative work. Along the way, human rights investigators may be maligned as biased partisans and tools of rival interests or powers. Any error in human rights reporting may be taken by antagonists as proof of the investigator's alleged bias, potentially undermining the credibility of investigation, or the investigating organization as a whole.

3. Challenges in the Process of Discovery

The pressure to investigate quickly and without error permeates all human rights investigations, regardless of method. However, as open source methods play increasing roles in human rights research, the pressure to provide rapid fact-finding exacerbates already significant challenges related to the discovery of relevant information.

3.1 Context

Each day, people worldwide generate at least 2.5 quintillion (2.5 million trillion) bytes of data, a number that defies comparison.[2]. Every *minute*, nearly 50,000 photos are uploaded to Instagram and some 400 *hours* of video are uploaded to YouTube. Every minute, over

[1] See ch 14: 'Using Open Source Information for Advocacy and Awareness'.

[2] Matthew Wall, 'Big Data: Are You Ready for Blast-Off?' *BBC* (4 March 2014) https://www.bbc.com/news/business-26383058 accessed 29 December.

2 million photos or videos are sent on Snapchat, and nearly half a million Tweets are sent on Twitter. Every minute, about 13 million text messages and 160 million emails are sent.[3] These figures are likely to continue to grow exponentially, as they have in the past.

In addition to the immense growth in the volume of information, people are more networked and connected electronically than ever. Over the decade from 2008 to 2018, for example, the number of Facebook users grew from 100 million to 2.2 billion.[4] The natural consequence of this interconnectivity is an increase in the reach of information transmission, with ever more of an individual's experience potentially communicable to an ever wider global audience. Especially important for human rights investigations, the places of most rapid growth in connectivity—Asia, the Middle East, and Africa—are also places that have weak institutions, face acute economic or social challenges, or have a history of weak human rights protections.

3.2 Discovery and Search Criteria

Whether human rights inquiry proceeds through traditional witness identification and interview, physical discovery, or open source methods, investigators face an initial and often persistent challenge: they may have little prior knowledge of exactly what information will be relevant to the investigation. Of course, no investigator, regardless of method, approaches a human rights investigation in complete ignorance. An investigation will only start when an abuse is assumed to have occurred, and all investigations will start with a question of fact or suspicion of the likely perpetrators.

For the investigator relying on interviews and testimony, the challenge is to elicit the 'who, what, where, and when' of an event and develop a theory of the event that then requires confirmatory evidence. The first step in addressing this challenge will be some version of a simple query to a human source: 'tell us what happened'. Despite the biases and weaknesses of memory and recall that often creep in, witnesses and victims do classify, structure, and catalogue experience in a narrative form, well-suited for iterative questioning and investigatory refinement.

Unlike an individual's experience and recollection, the universe of open source information relevant to an investigation will not be structured by a human brain in narrative form and ready for simple query by an investigator. In contrast to information organized by a person's narrative of experience, open source information is captured by many non-networked sensors—from a handful to thousands—with no interpretative executive to synthesize the information into a coherent story. The open source human rights investigator cannot prompt the internet to 'tell us what happened'.

With some lead information—information that offers an avenue for further inquiry or otherwise cues an investigator to potentially relevant information—about the 'who, what, where, or when' of some event, investigators will seek potential evidence by querying the open source universe based on one, some, or all of these four questions. This approach to an

[3] Domo, 'Data Never Sleeps 6.0' https://www.domo.com/blog/wp-content/uploads/2018/06/18_domo_data-never-sleeps-6verticals.pdf accessed 20 December.

[4] 'WhatsApp: Number of Users 2013-2017' *Statista* https://www.statista.com/statistics/260819/number-of-monthly-active-whatsapp-users/ accessed 29 December.

event, while a useful way to structure a discovery methodology, will often not present itself readily. Even if the investigators have been fortunate enough to find lead information to inform a search by one or some of these four avenues of inquiry, they will quickly encounter the challenge that most open source information is not structured to facilitate discovery for investigations.

3.2.1 Discovery by 'Who' or 'What'

The challenge in developing discovery criteria with respect to 'who' or 'what' is that any such search criteria would presuppose what someone might attribute to a piece of content that depicts an event or the people in it. For example, the same piece of video shared in the open by two people could be characterized by one as 'indigenous protestors massacred by military' and by another as 'police repel foreign terrorist attack'.

A dispassionate and objective characterization of 'who' and 'what' will rarely be supplied by the providers of the open materials from which the investigator draws. As such, an additional burden on the investigator is to recognize that the beliefs and attitudes of victims, perpetrators, and witnesses may be imbuing content with language that must be assumed in the course of search and discovery.

3.2.2 Discovery by 'Where'

When searching by geographic attributes to begin to address the question of 'where', investigators are similarly challenged in establishing discovery criteria by metadata. This data may simply be someone's captioning or tagging of a piece of material with place-information (e.g. 'I took this picture in in Dadaab'). The precision of that self-structured tagging can be highly variable (e.g. by comparison: 'I took this picture in Ethiopia'), risking that discovery criteria set by the research may be so precise as to exclude relevant content.

Potentially, the content will already have been 'geo-tagged' with precise coordinates by some system or service allowing for quick and pointed discovery. This is uncommon, however. Studies on the use of geo-tagging on Twitter, for instance, found that more than half of the users do not enable location services, and only about 3 per cent of all Tweets are geo-tagged.[5] Attempting to discover content from a place based on a service's geo-tagging will exclude most of the content, making it an unreliable discovery pathway.

3.2.3 Discovery by 'When'

When discovering materials relevant for the timespan under investigation, the investigator faces two challenges. The first is that materials that predate the event may become open and discoverable during or after the event, risking the possibility of discovering irrelevant information if it is not discernible that the material predates the investigatory focus.[6] Another challenge is that materials relevant to the investigation of some human rights event may

[5] Luke Sloan and Jeffrey Morgan, 'Who Tweets with Their Location? Understanding the Relationship between Demographic Characteristics and the Use of Geoservices and Geotagging on Twitter' (2015) 10(11) PLoS ONE: e0142209 https://journals.plos.org/plosone/article?id=10.1371/journal.pone.0142209 accessed 29 December.

[6] Often, a human rights investigator will encounter the sudden emergence of 'old' material that predates some new event. Sometimes, this may be intentional misattribution. But, given some new instance of human rights abuse, local civil society will naturally share instances of similar abuses as part of the broader societal reckoning about the violations at hand, and desire for accountability.

become accessible only months or even years after the event, meaning the discovery process can never really end for the life of an investigation.

3.3 The Tension of Discovery Breadth

As may already be evident, 'open source' cannot be equated with 'readily discoverable'. With the dramatic increase in the volume and velocity of data, a consistent challenge in open source human rights investigations is the tremendous amount of information one may need to process to discover a piece of relevant information. This so-called 'signal to noise' problem is as common in human rights investigations as it is many other domains of research and intelligence gathering.

Using a wide range of search tools, open source investigators will of course want to tailor a search to maximize the likelihood of finding materials of relevance to the investigation and minimize the likelihood of collecting irrelevant information.[7] Searching too narrowly—classifying too much as irrelevant—may lead to three outcomes, each harmful to the overall goal of the investigation.

First, there is the risk that the investigators simply get it wrong. Facing a large amount of data, an overly restrictive discovery process can lead to a form of investigatory cherry-picking: discovery becomes the act of gathering materials that fit a prior theory, to the detriment of exhaustive, objective fact-finding that could lead to fruitful discoveries. While traditional investigations entertain multiple theories (or should), the act of searching for open source content is deliberate, based on prior beliefs, and may require dramatically different discovery strategies to examine alternative theories. For many human rights fact-finders, the pressure to gather proof quickly of some human rights abuse—perhaps to mitigate harm through public pressure or direct advocacy—is in tension with a methodical, exhaustive discovery *schema*.

Secondly, too narrow a discovery process may leave materials undiscovered by the investigator that *could* fit another, potentially plausible theory of the event. Investigators and their colleagues may ultimately be obliged to exclude or explain contradictory materials, either as a matter of impartiality and independence, or as a matter of strategic anticipation in adversarial legal or policy settings. Failure to do so could undercut the credibility of their reporting and even the goal of mitigating ongoing abuse.

Finally, too narrow a discovery process risks leaving key pieces of evidence which could strengthen a case unexamined. Even the most seasoned human rights investigator—examining dozens or even thousands of pieces of material—could mistakenly exclude a piece of key material as irrelevant if it does not comport to assumptions about what relevant information will look like.

Human rights investigators would naturally prefer not to miss information that will strengthen their case, but failing to discriminate wisely among avenues to pursue at the outset of the discovery process leads to its own challenges. Chief among those are related to available investigatory resources: every piece of information flagged as potentially relevant must be examined further for veracity and probative value.

[7] See ch 6: 'How to Conduct Discovery Using Open Source Methods'.

Suppose, for example, an investigator is researching a massacre committed by a paramilitary unit in a place where such occurrences are assumed to be rare. The investigator will of course set out to discover materials that inform the 'who, what, where, and when' of that specific event. Given that such an event is rare, the investigator may confine the search to signals that depict the massacre itself (e.g. perpetrator video of the event, photos from bystanders, textual/narrative social media posts from survivors).

In the materials dismissed wholesale as irrelevant, noise may be a piece of evidence of potentially greater value than any forensic reconstruction of the massacre itself, such as a post to social media by the proud recipient of a photogenic meal that happens to capture a lunch meeting between the offending paramilitary commander and a political leader. Such a photograph could turn out to be a key piece of linkage evidence,[8] yet one could hardly fault a human rights investigator for using discovery *schema* that excludes all food-related materials as irrelevant. Indeed, failure to do so may well swamp the investigation's ability to verify and assess the materials they have gathered.

For a further example of the challenge of discovery breadth, assume an investigator developing spatial (i.e. 'where') search criteria. Given some human rights event at a specific geographic point, the investigator may want to search for open source materials captured around that point—within, say, a radius of 50 meters. If the way people ascribe 'where' metadata in that context would even allow such precision, the investigator will be gathering all materials over an area of 8 km^2. If the theory of the event is such that the investigator wants to look for materials within 1 km of that point, the area of interest balloons to over 1,500 km, guaranteeing that the discovery set now includes significantly more noise, and a significantly higher burden in evaluating those materials for relevance.

Similarly, expanding temporally—hours, days, or weeks before or after the event—yields the same paradox: the larger and more inclusive the discovery effort, the harder it becomes to identify materials in the discovery set relevant to an investigation.

3.4 Biases in Discovery

Regardless of the strength of the discovery effort, open source investigators are often hampered by a significant natural bias: that documentary or other material depicting overt acts will be easier to discover—all things being equal—than materials that are exculpatory, obliquely corroborative, or serve other key functions in an investigation, such as linkage evidence or lead information. The causes of this bias are both a function of the information ecosystem, as well as the result of cognitive biases of the investigator. People and systems will naturally put more effort into structuring and providing metadata to materials that depict extraordinary or kinetic events, making them more readily discoverable. And human rights investigators, under pressure to make rapid findings of fact, are prone narrowly to seek that very information.

[8] Linkage evidence is material that demonstrates relationships between individuals or groups, as well as between individuals and overt acts. In the context of human rights investigations, it most commonly refers to information that implicates authorities that have compelled or directed others to commit abusive acts.

3.4.1 Implications of Inequity in Digital Connectivity

A common challenge to the open source human rights investigator comes not from noise, but from lack of signal. Despite the impressive expansion of infrastructure and digital access to geographies traditionally excluded from connectivity, information relevant to human rights investigation may remain hidden from discovery. The most fragile states, and places of limited statehood especially, remain under-connected from the wider information environment, limiting the extent and variety of digital open source information that can be drawn on for human rights research and thus restricting in turn the likelihood that the investigator will discover relevant information in the open source environment.

In addition to these vertical inequities, inequalities across state boundaries create predictable pockets of information 'gravity wells'—places where information and evidence diffuse more slowly from primary sources and observers to the venues and platforms in which the investigator searches. Notably, rural geographies—regardless of the country—typically lag in connectivity relative to cities. Low connectivity may simply suggest latency in the opening of information from people's recollections or their hand-held devices. How such variation in connectivity manifests during an investigation is also variable, requiring the investigator not only to assess open information, but also to assess the manner and timing in which information may *become* open.

In some instances, inequity in digital connectivity is accompanied by other social or economic correlates, such as limited access to hand-held technology or low literacy, reducing the likelihood of finding documentary materials or textual narratives. The open source investigator much therefore consider how material or technical capacities of witnesses or others will affect what form eventual open information from a given place may take and adjust discovery efforts accordingly.

Finally, there is wide variance in how populations and communities share information and the type and specificity of the information they share, requiring investigators to draw from different information pools dependent on local behaviour and habits. This, in turn, impacts the methods of, and pressures on, the investigator. For instance, the significant increase in the use of live stream video globally affects how and when investigators must begin the search process, given some human rights event. Especially for streams that are not ultimately archived, a human rights investigator may need to begin the discovery (and preservation) process well before theories about a given human rights event have fully formed. Variation within a geography across demographic lines—notably age, class, and gender—also require careful attention as to what form and on what platforms relevant information may ultimately become open.

3.4.2 Semi-closed Networks and Social Messaging

The extent to which information is sequestered on semi-closed information networks also varies across places and peoples. Social messaging apps, such as WhatsApp, WeChat, and Messenger are the predominant social information transmission mechanisms for many. Just one of these tools, the WhatsApp messenger service, saw the number of global users grow from 200 million in 2013 to 1.5 billion by the end of 2017.[9] The extent to which material transmitted in social messaging could be considered part of the 'open-source' universe is

[9] 'WhatsApp: Number of Users 2013-2017' (n 4).

academic for purposes here, but it is a foregone conclusion that information of relevance for human rights research is shared on these networks.

Similarly, social media platforms such as Facebook can be a rich source of information about individuals, their associates, and their movements, as well as a source of documentary information itself. Because such information may be thinly segregated from the purely 'open' by a user's privacy setting that, for instance, requires the observer to be associated with a 'friend' network, however, the open source investigator may hit a wall that—though permeable—differentiates 'open source' from its complement.

Information on semi-closed platforms and services where there are the most information nodes—that is, where the participant population is largest—is more likely to diffuse out into the open than information from smaller networks.

Materials of relevance to a human rights investigation on semi-closed networks may find an echo in the open; one may encounter open reference to some sequestered material or learn of its existence through human contacts. Even having detected such echoes and armed with the suspicion of the existence of relevant material, investigators have little guarantee that the information will be made open, and even less when it might be. Whether or not investigators have reason to believe probative material exists on semi-closed networks, they must assume that the discovery process has not been exhausted without an attempt to access relevant information from those networks.

Here, the open source investigator faces a significant challenge, one for which the solution straddles the distinction between open source and more traditional methods of information gathering. The most straightforward approach to gain access to such information—and least risky depending on the context of the investigation—is to develop human contacts on semi-closed networks where relevant information may be circulating. In this scenario, the contact potentially becomes a human source like any other in traditional investigations, providing leads and corroboration, and serving as a conduit for the material itself.

A less straightforward approach, one that requires careful consideration of ethical, legal, and security implications, is to gain access to the networks directly. For human rights investigations without significant legal or sovereign authority, such access can only be gained through direct participation on the network. In some instances, this can be accomplished without any subterfuge or deception. In other instances, the creation of 'sockpuppets'—false digital identities—or other false fronts to circumvent sharing restrictions and gain access to a network can be deployed. If larger networks, all things being equal, are more likely to diffuse relevant information into the open, then smaller networks are more likely to contain information—perhaps particularly telling information—that has not, and may not, become public. Yet the challenge and risks of—in effect—infiltrating a small network is non-trivial relative to gaining access to a larger network with more available nodes—that is, participants—to probe.

The professional standards or protocol of human rights investigating organizations may or may not condone such subterfuge. Additionally, the terms of service of the platform or service used may explicitly prohibit the creation of false identities. While there currently is little consensus in the human rights context around the use of subterfuge to gain access to semi-open information, there is a general unease in established human rights organizations with deception. The professional standards in many human rights investigations are built around notions of fully informed consent: being clear and open with a source about how information imparted will be used, along with what risks that may entail, and securing clear and affirmative permission to use the information provided. How such standards should be employed—if at all—in the context of open source investigations is an outstanding question, with the answers to which perhaps leading to variation among organizations and investigations in their information gathering methods and rigour of discovery.

Another dynamic that may prevent the open availability of evidence to the investigator's discovery is that of censorship, wherein authorities seek to limit information spread through targeted service interruptions, or complete disruption of internet or telecommunications access. While still relatively rare, such information disruption appears to be increasing in frequency, with the governments most likely to be subject to human rights investigations those most willing to go to great lengths to prevent the disclosure of pertinent information.[10]

For all these various challenges, the burdens on the open source human rights investigator are the same: the need to develop reliable human sources of information, careful consideration of the social, political, and information environment, and flexibility in approaches to the discovery process.

4. The Impermanence of Material

While navigating the challenges of discovery, human rights investigators are typically faced with a more pressing challenge: the rush of those perpetrating and supporting the abuses investigated to cover their tracks and frustrate investigations. If shining a light on abuses is the core of defending human rights, the loss of information about abuse serves to extinguish the light.

4.1 Context

In response to human rights investigations datasets may be taken out of public access,[11] webpages altered,[12] and social media accounts closed. The reasons for such actions can be varied, from individuals second-guessing the decision to post information that threatens powerful interests, to a commercial entity seeking to minimize potential legal action. For every motivation to make a piece of information about abuse open to public view, there is a motivation to conceal it. This impermanence of access to bits and bytes—the fact that the digital open source universe is not necessarily an ever-accumulating thing, that today's open source can be tomorrow's closed source—is perhaps the most significant challenge facing open source human rights investigators.

Perhaps the greatest threat to the integrity of open source information relevant to human rights investigations today comes not from the sharers of content or perpetrators

[10] '#KeepItOn' *Access Now* https://www.accessnow.org/keepiton/ accessed 29 December.

[11] Francie Diep, 'Climate Information Is Disappearing from Federal Websites under Trump' *Pacific Standard* (10 January 2018) https://psmag.com/environment/climate-information-is-disappearing-from-federal-websites-under-trump accessed 29 December.

[12] Charles Clarke, 'How HHS Buried Information about the Affordable Care Act' *Government Executive* (17 May 2018) https://www.govexec.com/oversight/2018/05/report-how-hhs-buried-information-about-affordable-care-act/148283/ accessed 29 December.

implicated by it, but from the commercial hosts of information. Content hosts such as Google[13] and Facebook have come under increasing public and regulatory pressure to remove certain kinds of material, including content that glorifies violence, incites hate, recruits for violence, dehumanizes, exploits, and so on. While one could hardly bemoan the loss of such odious material from the public sphere, for the open source human rights investigator, this odious content is more likely than others to depict events or circumstances that form the basis for human rights fact-finding. For instance, the Syrian Archive—an organization dedicated to the collection of the immense amount of open source content relevant for accountability efforts for the crimes committed in the conflict—has seen hundreds of thousands of videos removed by YouTube, some likely to be lost forever. Content that depicts violence and overt human rights abuses from the conflict are at heightened risk for removal.

4.2 Risk to Evidence

From the outset of an investigation, investigators must assess the risk of loss of available evidence or information. Human rights investigators face pressures to secure evidence, given the high risk of tampering or degradation, and the political costs associated with human rights fact-finding.[14] In traditional investigations, evidence preservation may involve rapid collection of testimony before victims or witnesses are intimidated, their recollections become less reliable, they move, or there is some other threat to the integrity of or access to the information they impart. In open source investigations, the imperative to secure potential evidence is no less pressing.

The implications for human rights investigations are obvious: if the original materials or documentation used in an investigation are no longer accessible, the credibility of any fact-finding is contingent on the word of the investigator or some later or lesser version of, or testament to, the content in question.

While the risks to evidence are most acute for documentary or demonstrative materials—those that may depict overt acts of human rights abuse—the disappearance of narrative materials, which often provide important leads, can be equally disruptive to an investigation. As a result, investigators must prioritize their efforts in discovery and preservation of open source materials based on a mix of relevance to key questions of fact, the relative abundance (or paucity) of materials that address those questions, and some measure of the risk to the accessibility of the evidence.

Of these considerations, the risk to evidence is the hardest to assess. Based on assessments of the interests and capabilities of an adversary, the commercial actors involved, and the broader information environment, the choices require thoughtful calculation as to the point when rapid preservation is needed. Among the many tools of those attempting to derail an investigation or prevent access to key information are regulatory attacks (such as shutting down information services or connectivity in a given place), legal manoeuvres

[13] 'YouTube Community Guidelines Enforcement: Google Transparency Report' (Google) https://transparencyreport.google.com/youtube-policy/removals?hl=en accessed 29 December.

[14] See ch 7: 'How to Preserve Open Source Information for Human Rights Research and Accountability Effectively'.

(such as demanding content hosts remove certain information), or more traditional intimidation of witnesses and others to dissuade open sharing of such content.

Ultimately, human rights investigators only know of the disappearance of a piece of evidence if they or another have previously discovered it or heard it described. Under such a scenario, investigators can at a minimum attempt to gather additional information (which may not exist) with the same implication of fact or attempt to reach the source of the content, if known. Depending on where a piece of disappeared content was hosted, even should an open source human rights investigator know that a piece of material exists—invisible on the platform but residing on the host's servers—there may be little recourse. Without enforceable subpoena power—an authority that most human rights investigators do not have—there is little chance that material will be recoverable or become discoverable.

How much online material—some of it presumably probative—is lost before any investigator comes to know of its existence? It is obviously impossible to say for certain, though because of increased transparency reporting by content hosts, we are beginning to get a better idea. In YouTube's first transparency report, for example, the video platform reported that over 8 million videos were removed in the three-month period between October and December 2017.[15] As widely suspected, many of these removals were prompted by individual YouTube visitors flagging content as objectionable. Of the 8 million removed videos, over 6.5 million were flagged by machines based on algorithms in YouTube's enforcement programme, and of that amount, some 5 million were removed before they were viewed by a single user.

Where the loss of relevant information is likely to be initiated by human flagging, there are opportunities to secure such content before it disappears from view. Where the loss of information is precipitated by algorithms, however, it is unlikely that the material can be discovered and secured before it is removed from the open. Indeed, as suggested by the YouTube transparency report, most materials that are ultimately removed will never be seen by anyone on the platform.

Further, the risk to evidence is not static and may dramatically increase over time as the result of the actions of third parties, or even as a result of the investigation itself. For instance, news coverage or NGO reporting of some human rights event or situation may pose immediate risk to source materials and related evidence in an active investigation. Even materials that are reasonably deemed to be at low risk of disappearing could unexpectedly become at high risk of loss or tampering, based on unpredictable developments or activity by external parties.

Public statements of concern by human rights organizations, calls to cease abuse, and other cues visible to a perpetrator that an investigation is ongoing or imminent may risk the loss of uncollected evidence. Even without such public acknowledgement of an investigation, the simple act of querying a database or visiting a website could alert a party, increasing the risk of evidence loss. Given that most human rights investigators operate within the dual mandate to document abuses and prevent further abuses, the obligations to speak out against violations early and to secure evidence are in direct tension with one another.

[15] 'YouTube Community Guidelines Enforcement: Google Transparency Report' (n 13).

4.3 Preservation Methods and Management

Today, human rights investigators use tools to assist in preservation, all serving in one way or another to retain a copy of that content elsewhere than the original open source spot where it was initially discovered, with non-trivial implications related to security, privacy, and duty of care.

The fact that potential evidence may be lost in short order incentivizes securing content before one can possibly be fully aware of the weight or value of that material. Operationally, this poses a significant burden for the open source investigator. Each human rights event requires rapid response—not only for the normative goal of mitigating the harm of that event, but to prevent the loss of evidence from the historical record.

The risk of evidence loss dramatically compounds the challenge of open source investigations, and the tension of breadth in discovery. Whereas a mis-specified discovery *schema* can be corrected through a shift in strategy, those opportunities for refinement disappear along with the content that is lost from the universe of open source information. This incentivizes another hazard, that of over-collection of materials, for fear that evidence may be inaccessible in the future. This over-collection tendency—arguably a professional imperative—creates additional burdens for the investigator.

The abundance of tools and techniques that could be used to preserve open source information requires investigators to make choices in preservation that may have implications far beyond the immediate purpose and scope of the inquiry.

Although a particular tool used for preservation may be easy and sufficient for the immediate inquiry, it may not adhere to forensic or best practice standards that would allow the materials to be used, for instance, in legal proceedings[16]. A key challenge for an open source human rights investigation, then, centers on determining what immediate costs are appropriate to shoulder for an undefined or uncertain payoff of justice and accountability in the future.

Additionally, the practical consequence of extensive evidence preservation is a data management challenge. Especially where preserved materials are sensor-mediated (e.g. video), mundane challenges around storage emerge. While data storage costs have been on a geometric decline over the years, any solution involves challenges. The easiest option—cloud storage—obviates the need for a physical digital evidence locker but opens the risk of interference by authorities in the jurisdiction of the servers or the service's legal headquarters.

The extreme alternative—local digital storage—can be costly, may require IT maintenance, and is more likely to be beyond the capabilities or resources of small investigative organizations or independent investigators. Redundancy requirements to prevent data corruption or loss are as important data-security considerations as are concerns about unwanted access to remote or cloud storage.

Beyond simple storage of preserved content, investigators will be challenged by the requirement to catalogue the information. Depending on the authority or mandate of the investigators, they may be obligated to make the collection of materials searchable—effectively be required to structure their preserved information by 'who, what, where, and when'. For complex cases with large amounts of information, this intensive archiving

[16] As discussed in chs 3 and 15.

and structuring may be necessary in any case, to enable the analysis required to make findings of fact.

5. Verification

Having discovered and preserved information that may inform the 'who, what, where, and/or when' of some human rights abuse, investigators must next assess the authenticity of that material: is the information what it purports to be? There are no objective standards, no accepted rulebook, for determining authenticity—only an assemblage of tools, techniques, and best practices.[17] Attaining certainty and precision in all four elements of a human rights event—the 'who, what, where, and when'—is uncommon when relying on open source information. Yet, the adversarial nature of human rights investigations, whether in legal proceedings or traditional human rights advocacy, demands attempts at certainty.

5.1 Context

When faced with accusations of human rights violations, governments and other actors rely on a nearly standardized set of responses. These responses are designed to avoid accountability, allow space for human rights violations to persist, or undermine the credibility of those who would attempt to document abuses. Among them is to simply deny findings of some investigation—to claim that the evidence gathered does not support the overarching conclusion. Another response is that of minimization: to acknowledge publicly there is a problem, but either assert that the scope or severity is overstated, or that the perpetrators are incorrectly identified.

Almost without exception, this interplay between fact-finding, denial, and counter-response in human rights investigation takes place in the public sphere. To sow doubt about findings of human rights violations, the alleged responsible actor may seek to undermine the investigatory methods used, offer up counter-evidence, or attempt to malign the motivations of the investigator as biased. When the transition from investigation to public reception occurs, human rights investigators must be prepared to engage in a struggle to fend off counter-narratives and recriminations offered by the alleged perpetrator.

While the 2016 U.S. Presidential election catalyzed growing awareness of the prevalence of propaganda, misleading content, and general deceit across information channels, open source investigators have long faced a similar basic challenge: the open source environment can be hostile to the truth. Open source investigations require the highest standards of verification and corroboration if they are to be credible, whether in a court of law, or in public opinion. As general awareness of the prevalence of digital disinformation grows—and the denials and recriminations by those accused become more plausible to a wider audience—adherence to those best practices becomes ever more important. Yet, these best practices pose unique risks in the context of human rights work.

[17] Addressed in chs 8, 9, and 15.

5.2 Triangulation and Method Transparency

While certainty is a rare standard to achieve in assessing an individual piece of evidence, something approaching certainty is the goal of the corroboration of many pieces of information. Specifically, the use of 'triangulation'—the validation of information through cross-verification from multiple sources—allows the open source investigator to leverage confidence in the either the 'who, where, or when' of an event to gain confidence in the others. In laying out a case in the public arena, however, the investigator quickly faces a dilemma.

On the one hand, investigators are incentivized to detail all the information they have; to provide any analytic or forensic work, such as remote sensing analysis and expert evaluation of documentary materials. Investigators are incentivized as well to ensure the provenance, custody, and corroboration of materials is transparent. Anything short of that offers a soft spot in human rights fact finding that will be exploited by the accused. How can the public know that some investigator—characterized as biased and politically motivated—did not fabricate findings, misuse information, or misconstrue evidence?

State security and intelligences services have tools at their disposal that far exceed the intelligence gathering and triangulation capabilities of any human rights investigation. Although it is safe to assume that capabilities across the range of potential bad actors are not uniform, it would be reckless to disregard the risk this poses. In some contexts, the full disclosure of materials underlying a finding of human rights abuses may pose risks to the safety and security of individuals, just as it would to name a victim or witness that provided testimony.

In laying out a case, the human rights investigator cannot always know what piece of information poses what risk. In some cases, it is obvious. Open source or other materials that include personally identifiable information or otherwise allow for the identification of individuals or groups present clear risk, and rights organizations will take steps to obfuscate that information or choose to exclude it all together, even at the risk of weakened public credibility. As in the case of discovery, however, one cannot know what piece of information is relevant for a bad actor; which piece of material that—innocuous on its face—would allow a hostile agent to triangulate sources, witnesses, and others who may present a political or legal threat to a perpetrator. Though presumably taking steps to protect sources and witnesses, an investigator may unwittingly provide a hostile party with a piece of bland information that allows that actor to determine the 'who, where, or when' of sources and witnesses.

Such professional obligation challenges in the context of reporting and public disclosure are inseparable from the broader strategic or adversarial relationship between fact finder and human rights violator, and naturally diffuse into the investigatory process.

5.3 Misinformation and Adaptation

Cataloguing the means and types of misleading or somehow false information is analytically difficult, though some have created useful rubrics.[18] The types of false information span

[18] Claire Wardle, 'Fake News. It's Complicated' *First Draft News* (16 February 2017) https://firstdraftnews.org:443/fake-news-complicated/ accessed 29 December.

a continuum of misinforming intent, from sloppy and accidental, to deliberate attempts to deceive. Misinformation also spans a range of means and methods, from false or over-simplified framing of an issue in order to subtly affect beliefs and perceptions to outright staging or fabrication of materials.

To aid with discovery, open source human rights investigators must consider who would share what material, and where. When engaged in the verification of discovered content, however, the investigator should also consider hypothetical motivations for the creation of sharing misinformation. While it is natural to identify suspected perpetrators as having the greatest motivation to attempt to disrupt an investigation by sowing false information, the risks of misleading information are pervasive across the information environment.

The decision to make a piece of documentary content public or to share openly one's observations of a human right abuse can be ascribed to a limited set of motivations, but the reasons to attempt to share misleading information are far more varied. This includes motivations that, but for the deception, are compatible with human rights practice, including attempts to secure relief for a loved one, bringing attention to real-world abuses with misattributed material, or even satire.

While some consideration of the hypothetical motivations to deceive or mislead can help an investigator identify pieces of information that may require extra scrutiny, the actual means employed to deceive are dynamic, evolving, and increasingly sophisticated. Here, again, the transparency of an investigator's methods—key to establishing the finding of fact when facing a denying perpetrator—invites a dilemma. The openness of methods invites innovation and adaptation by parties seeking to derail or muddy an investigation, and even the co-opting of investigatory techniques to engage in denial[19]. The Russian government, for example, has in particular relied heavily on public exposition of satellite imagery as 'evidence' in public relations efforts to undermine criticism, including in Ukraine relating to the shooting down of the MH17 commercial jetliner, and in Syria, in an effort to deny claims that it bombed a hospital in Aleppo.

5.4 Precision and Uncertainty

There is a trade-off between the certainty of one's findings, and the precision of those findings in open source inquiry. Invariably, an investigator will have greater confidence in some elements of the event (e.g., what and when), and less confidence in others (e.g., who and where). And for any permutation of the elements of an event, an investigator may have more specific findings in some of those elements than others. At some point, informed by the larger role and context of the investigation, inquiry must end, and findings must be detailed. Depending on the extent of uncertainty or imprecision, there may be no reason to delay reporting. For instance, depending on the context, it may suffice to say with high

[19] The Russian government, for example, in particular has relied heavily on public exposition of satellite imagery as 'evidence' in public relations efforts to undermine criticism, including in Ukraine relating to the shooting down of the MH17 commercial jetliner, and in Syria, in an effort to deny claims that it bombed a hospital in Aleppo.

confidence that the perpetrator of some abuse is a member of a state's security forces, even if the investigator does not have strong evidence to suggest a specific unit, or individual.

Uncertainty is ever-present to one degree or another in an open-source investigator's process. Hitting a dead-end when attempting to verify a piece of material is all too common, a fate made all the worse by uncertainty as to whether it is truly a dead-end. For open materials where there is no means to track the original source, or it is too costly to do so, the process of detecting the earliest open instance can never truly be exhaustive. There is often no point at which one can be certain to have secured the earliest instance. Like much of the verification process, the effort committed is informed by triage—by assessing the relative importance of a piece of material, if true and genuine, to one or more theories of the case.

The uncertainty inherent in the verification process is also evident in investigators' concerns over whether they have truly identified all the available avenues for corroboration. Traditionally, human rights investigators tended to come disproportionately from legal or sociological backgrounds, well suited for the collection of testimony. Increasingly, and especially as it relates to sensor-mediated content, human rights investigators must have sufficient expertise across a wide range of disciplines to even recognize a possible path of verification or corroboration.

For instance, when engaged in content analysis of a series of videos related to some human rights event, a single researcher may need awareness of how a forensic anthropologist or pathologist would assess the content; or maybe a metallurgist or ballistics expert. From architects to zoologists, nearly any conceivable expertise could in some circumstances be brought usefully to bear on a verification challenge—corroborating the purported 'who, what, where, and when'.

Ultimately, without a human being to interview, attempts to verify or corroborate a piece of content are limited by the content itself. For a hypothetical video, every pixel can be examined, and every byte of data that forms that content can be examined. Each frame can be analyzed, ascribing content tags to anything and everything discernible that may inform answers to 'who, what, where, and when.' The history of the video can be traced back to its first identifiable appearance in the open source world, with every iteration, edit, and metadata ascription documented. At the end of that exhaustive process, there are no questions left to ask; no additional insight to be gained by querying the content, and no greater confidence in its veracity to be leveraged. The investigator is then left only to make the assessment as to whether a piece of material is consistent with some theory of a human rights event, or not. Strong cases can be built, but the result of much of the verification process in open source human rights investigations is that there is no 'smoking gun' evident.

6. The Future

Any non-trivial forecasting of the future is necessarily fraught and doing so for the future of open source investigations for human rights defence is no exception. Among the phenomena that will determine such a future are mass behaviour, commercial and corporate business development, government regulation, and technological evolution. The further one forecasts, the greater the likelihood of some unpredictable structural shift, trend, or event upending how people capture, share, and interact with information. Nonetheless, for the foreseeable future, several trends are evident, with implications for the challenges facing modern and future human rights investigators.

6.1 Discovery

First, the inexorable geometric growth in the volume, variety, and velocity of open source data will continue. The problems associated with remoteness and lack of communications infrastructure undoubtedly will decrease globally and most rapidly in the Global South. This trend will alleviate some of the current challenges to leveraging open source methods for human rights investigations in places where infrastructure and technology access are lagging.

This increase in information could threaten to further swamp open source investigations, exacerbating the signal to noise challenge, and the overall process of discovery. However, another important trend may offset these mounting discovery challenges: the future will also bring ever greater expansion of the information economy. In this economy, value is created through the structuring of data to maximize its utility. Looking to today's information industry leaders we see a clear trend toward the monetization of structured and relational data: the commercialization of making information discoverable. While there is little commercial value in making human rights investigations easier, the march toward the structuring of the immense data generated by sensors, devices, actions, and transactions will inevitably strengthen the ability of open source investigators to corroborate and cross-validate information.

Less clear, however, is how the future of the inherent conflict between this value-creation and individual privacy will resolve. Though human rights advocates are taking up the cause of privacy in the new digital world, human rights investigations benefit from the permissive information environment that has raised privacy concerns. The societal and regulatory debates around data ownership, data handling, and access will have significant impact on future open source investigations, arguably especially so in the human rights context.

Another set of future developments of consequence for open source investigations can be found in technical advancements already emerging in the intelligence and security fields. The inevitable accessibility of algorithmic tools to identify features of interest automatically —such as insignia, faces, or geographies—will yield greater returns in the specificity of discovery efforts. Advances in computer vision and other machine learning will invariably assist in human rights investigations, even as the same technology is used by state and other actors in abusive ways.

As with much technical advance, the least well-funded human rights watchdogs will lag behind their peers in access to new capacities.

6.2 Preservation

The impermanence of information in the open source environment is likely to remain a fundamental investigatory challenge in human rights work. Indeed, the very same artificial intelligences that will increasingly assist with discovery of human rights content will also increasingly be used to identify materials that immediately violate a content host's community standards or terms of service. As this content—depicting violence, incitement, and other human rights-related material—is flagged ever quicker, awareness of the existence of material key to human rights investigations will become more elusive.

The content hosts racing toward immediate removals of objectionable material are today's largest commercial entities, such as Facebook, Alphabet, and Twitter. Given these firms' outsized footprint in the digital world, they are the most frequent targets of public and regulatory pressure to remove objectionable content. As new and smaller services and content hosts emerge, they will serve as new discovery grounds for open source human rights investigations. As today, the future investigator will require clear awareness of how people from a given place share information, and through what channels. Further, a key competency for any type of human rights investigator in the future will be deep understanding of the technologies and information channels used in their geography of responsibility.

6.3 Verification

The future challenges of verification in open source human rights investigations will be dominated by the level of public trust in institutions and the degree to which cynical suspension of belief dominates public dialogue. While the step-by-step methods used to verify open source content will advance in the future, the threshold for verification may be pushed ever higher by a public increasingly willing to reject evidence and empirical truth. With a mandate to document and intercede in ongoing violations, human rights workers will face future perpetrators who may be more likely to persuade segments of the public that legitimate and sound inquiry is a manifestation of political bias, with corresponding decreases in pressure to end abuse.

Even as future investigators face increasing pressures to present the strongest possible case, they will be confronted with an open source environment with ever more sophisticated misleading or false information. Difficult or impossible to identify fabricated or synthetic video, perfectly human-like chatbots, and mutually corroborating false content is likely to permeate the open source space, to the extent it has not already done so. Demanded by the public, content hosts and digital platforms will engage in a spiralling arms race between ever more sophisticated misinformation techniques and content moderation, with investigators left behind. Journalists, public officials, and maybe even human rights investigators will occasionally be duped, seizing on material that will ultimately be demonstrated as false: public confirmation of their ascribed bias.

While not a ruddy view of the future, we should be hopeful. The future will bring ever greater numbers of people empowered to document their experiences, express their views, and to share with other members of the human family. Ever greater numbers will be empowered to hold authorities to account. The future wealth of information will lower the barriers to fact-finding, empowering citizen investigators—not just watchdog organizations—to document and uncover abuses by the powerful. And in part *because* of the pollution of the information environment with misinformation, propaganda, and denial, the role of open source investigation in human rights defence will only increase in importance.

PART II

6
How to Conduct Discovery Using Open Source Methods

Paul Myers

The challenges human rights researchers face in discovery using the web are faced by every professional chasing information on the internet: finding reliable, useful information on the subject of interest. In this chapter I will explore the techniques that are most useful for researchers working in the human rights arena.

I will first be looking at the basics of information research and how we can manipulate search engines to find the evidence we need. You can do this in popular search engines with a combination of special commands and careful selection of keywords.

Then I will move on to 'time travel'. This is not going to be a lesson in metaphysics, but merely an exploration of how we can find information that has been removed from a website, such as deleted Tweets. I will also show how you can make use of historical satellite and image evidence to get a view of the world from the recent past—essential for seeing when, for example, a shopfront changed hands or a building was demolished.

Next, I will discuss 'people research', which, as the phrase implies, involves finding information about an individual person. One of the hardest aspects is identifying the right person as there may be many people with the same name, so I will explore collecting and using unique identifiers for the individual in question.

A related area is social media research, for which many tools and techniques exist that can help you profile individuals, businesses, groups of interests, and relationships between these entities. I will also show how we can search for social media posts by location and use images in our investigations.

Finally, I will look at how specialist databases and tools can provide useful contact information and evidence.

Much of this work has traditionally been obscured in geek-speak but I will try to stick to plain English.

1. Searching for Relevant Webpages

Even seasoned journalists and investigators use Google in a way that turns their results page into a lucky dip. Some results are relevant, most are useless. From observing people's research techniques over the years, it strikes me that our natural impulse is to approach search engines as if there are human beings at the other end who can understand our requests. We type in the word 'golf' and expect Google to know if we are looking for the *sport* golf or the *Volkswagen* Golf. In this section, we will be looking at how our use of language and logic can determine the effectiveness of our search.

Pages containing information can be defined by their subject, but also by the words contained on the page. Similarly, reference books contain a contents section at the front that lists the subjects covered, but they typically also have an index at the back that lists the keywords and the page numbers they appear on.

Subjects can be easily assessed by human beings reading the page, though that is much more difficult for computers. Usually they do not even try. It is up to you to force more specific results by choosing various words that are likely to appear on the page you are after.

Google is like the back of the book. It indexes websites by keywords that appear on the webpages. You type in the word and Google looks through billions of webpages in its database for any containing the word you searched for.

2. Treasure Hunting

Better keywords ensure better search results. Sometimes you can get too many results, none of which seems to fit the bill. In such cases, your searching needs to become cunning, structured, and strategic. You can get brilliant search results by choosing the right keywords.

The best keywords are ones that (a) are unique to the subject and (b) almost certainly appear on the page you are looking for.

Sometimes we know the best keywords, sometimes we have to 'phone a friend', and sometimes we just learn them after ploughing through loads of articles. As we pick up better keywords and put them into the search box, our results become more refined. I call this 'treasure hunting'. Ultimately, a good choice of keywords will leave Google with few options other than to give us the pages we are looking for.

However, if our search terms are too obscure, we may lose some useful pages from the results. Trial and error goes hand in hand with quality control.

Let us say that you are looking for a list of Syrian army officers accused of participating in chemical weapons attacks. It would be tempting to type 'Syria' and 'chemical weapons' into Google. This might be a decent starting point. However, as search terms, the words are rather vague and might appear on thousands of pages that do not exactly fit the bill, such as general newspaper coverage. It would be better to hunt for more specific words that will almost definitely appear in articles you want to find, such as the names of anyone suspected of involvement. Army ranks such as 'colonel' or words like 'accused' sometimes help. Ideally, our treasure hunting will find us names of a couple of the Army personnel implicated in the attacks—names that would definitely appear together on the list, but would not be found on thousands of irrelevant pages. 'Definite keywords' like this help anchor your investigation to the subject.

3. Keywords Are Your Currency

The nature of our keywords can affect the nature of our results. Let us say we are searching for a list of famous people who have been murdered. The words 'famous' and 'murdered' would not necessarily be on such a page. However, the word 'Kennedy' would. It is not enough on its own, but if you add the names 'Versace' and 'Lennon', logic suggests we will get lists of famous assassinations. Why else would all three people be mentioned on the same webpage?

Some keywords can be chosen for the characteristics they imply. Choosing 'Kennedy' and 'Versace' ensures coverage of both political and non-political murders. Adding 'Julius Caesar' to the mix brings us historical assassinations and searching for 'Gandhi' would bring us lists covering Eastern as well as Western figures.

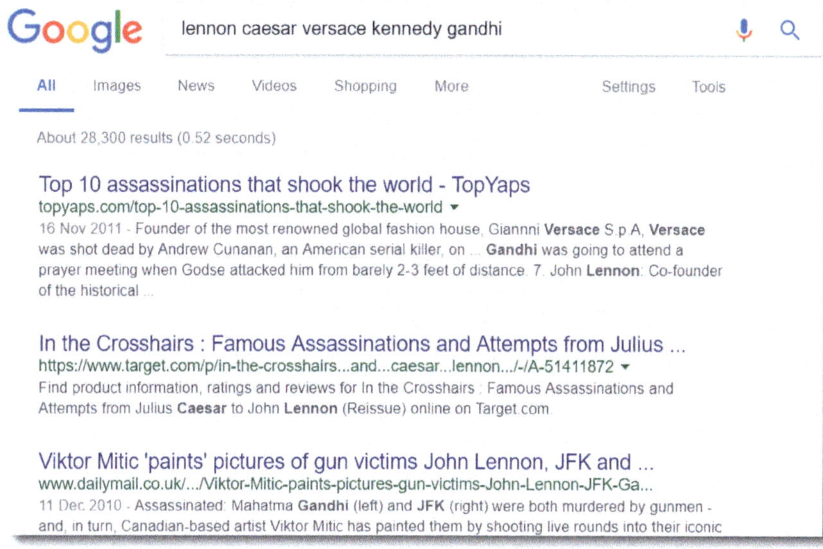

Figure 6.1

As you can see, the nature of our chosen keywords dictates the nature of our search results. A search with medical keywords related to torture and abuse will find articles written by doctors working in the field. Legal keywords will help to find specialist articles written by lawyers and local colloquialisms will focus your research on pages from targeted regions.

4. Search Syntax

Choosing the right keywords can go a long way towards ensuring great results, but that far from exhausts the versality of search engines. Search syntax and operators (special words and codes that have a unique function affecting the search) allow you to filter your results and define the nature of the websites you are looking for. In the following sections we will see how you can use these tricks to truly isolate the type of pages you are after.

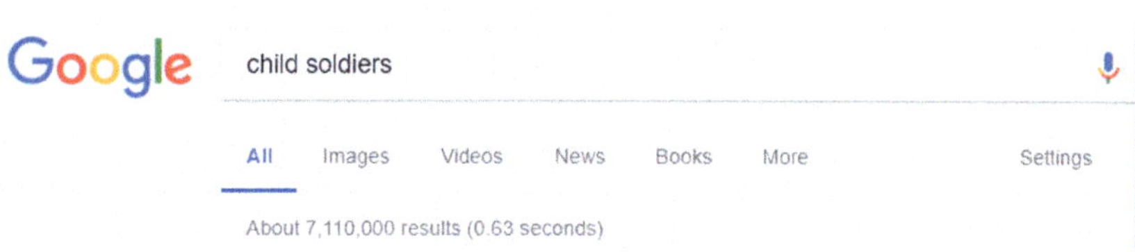

Figure 6.2

A search for the words *child* and *soldiers* brings over 7 million results; most of these are just pages mentioning both words but in an unrelated different context, however.

Figure 6.3

Using quotation marks around the pair of words brings the resulting count down to under half a million, by ensuring we find pages that contain the exact phrase *child soldiers*. We should use caution, however, as choosing a specific phrase might eliminate other suitable choices.

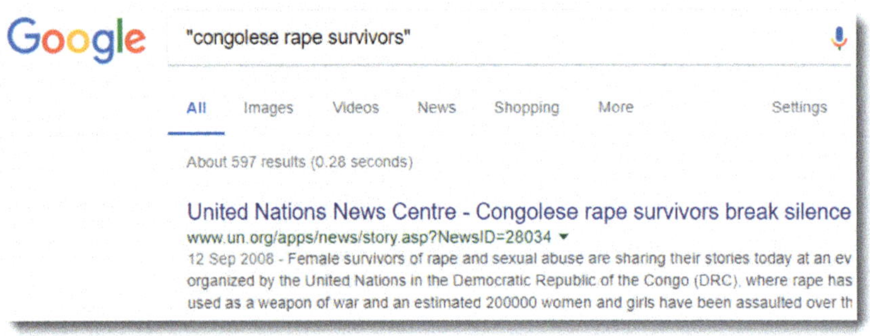

Figure 6.4

For example, there are many words you can pick to find survivors of rape in the Democratic Republic of the Congo. If you choose the exact phrase *Congolese rape survivors*, you limit yourself to just a few hundred results. It might be better to give your search more space by searching for *congo* and *rape survivors*, which brings nearly 28,000 results. A massive leap, yet still relevant.

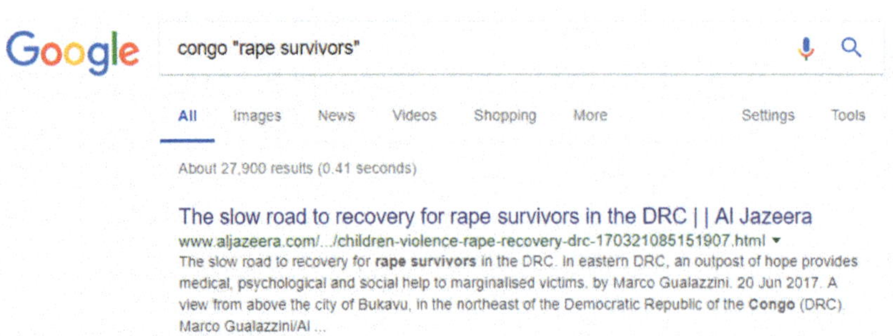

Figure 6.5

5. Specifying the Sites You Need in Your Search Results

With over 100 trillion pages to look through, filters can be a huge help in focusing on the right pages. One of the strongest tools we have is 'site:', which helps you specify the sort of website, the country code, or even part of the web address we want in our search results.

For example, the internet country code for Rwanda is '.rw', which therefore appears in many sites from that country. Whilst many pages have been written about Rwanda, using 'site:rw' alongside our keywords will force the search engine to return only those sites from a Rwandan domain.

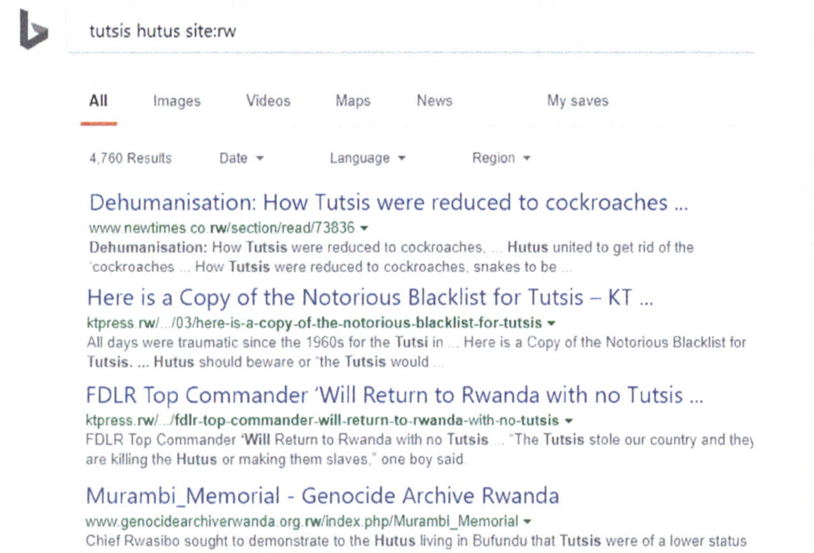

Figure 6.6

In many countries there is a further breakdown by domain type for government, military, academic and other specialist sites. Whilst it is easy to make a convincing sounding domain name for a fake news website, with a '.com' suffix, it is usually impossible for them to get a suffix '.gov', '.mil' or '.edu', unless they are a genuine government department, military body, or educational institution. For instance, companies offering fake degrees could never use '.edu' in their domain name.

When conducting discovery it is essential that we use authentic sources. If we do not, our entire case might be undermined. So-called 'fake news' is nothing new, even on the internet: hoax websites have been around for decades. It is easy for anyone to set up a site that looks and sounds authentic, but which is loaded with false information.

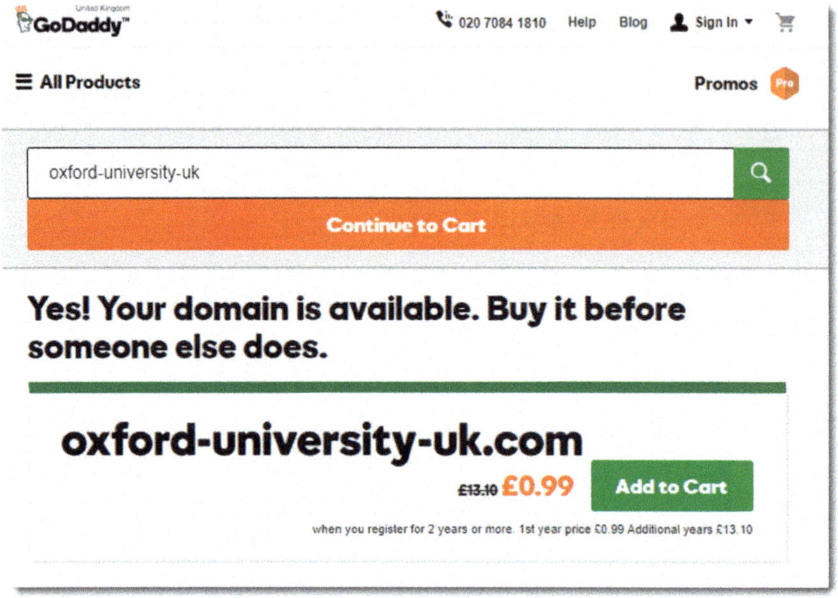

Figure 6.7

As I write this, anyone can buy the domain name 'oxford-university-uk.com' for a small amount of money; the real Oxford University uses instead the domain 'ox.ac.uk'. To focus your search purely on Oxford University, therefore, use 'site:ox.ac.uk' in the search box alongside your keywords.

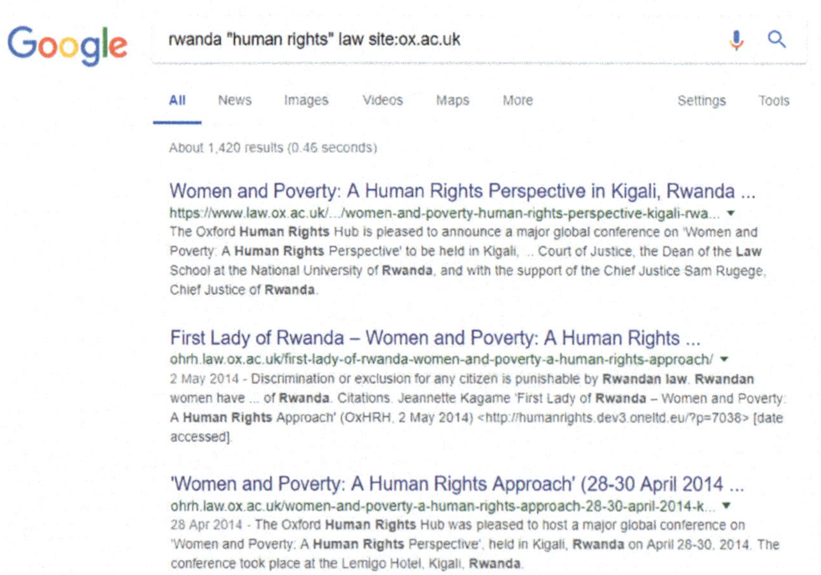

Figure 6.8

The 'site:' operator can also help us overcome the shortcomings of the search tools that are built into many websites. Perhaps the website's own search does not yield all of the possible results. Perhaps it does not have the flexible options given to us by Google. Some websites have an agenda and hide pages with out-of-date or embarrassing content. Google is not bound by the restrictions of a website's built-in search. It builds its own index of the site that you can search through. You can bypass a great deal of policy by simply searching a domain with 'site:' in a Google search.

6. Adding Flexibility with an OR

Occasionally, we might want to build a few options into our search. We might want to search for three possible spellings of someone's name or look for human rights abuses in any of ten possible locations. To go back to our first search, let us say we wanted to find pages mentioning chemical weapons and their use in Syria. We have a few options there. We could search pages mentioning either 'chlorine' or 'sarin'. We could also add towns like 'Kafr Zita' or 'Al-Lataminah'. However, just sticking those words into Google's search box will not give us the flexibility we are looking for. It will simply return pages that have all the words on them.

This was a mere 312 results the last time I looked.

Figure 6.9

We can bring that much needed flexibility to our search by simply adding the word 'OR' (in capital letters) between the optional keywords. So we search for 'chlorine OR sarin' and 'Kafr Zita' OR 'Al-Lataminah'. This brings us a staggering 61,000 results, and more if we add more towns or types of chemical weapon.

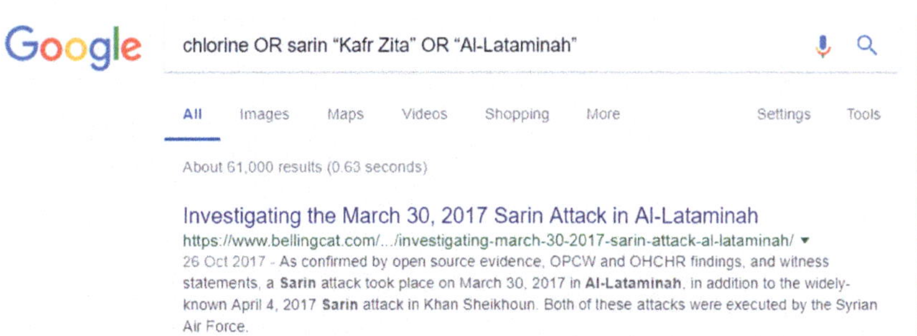

Figure 6.10

You can even use 'OR' in conjunction with other Google search types like 'site:' to search, say, five different government departments, eight Middle Eastern countries or three different social networks.

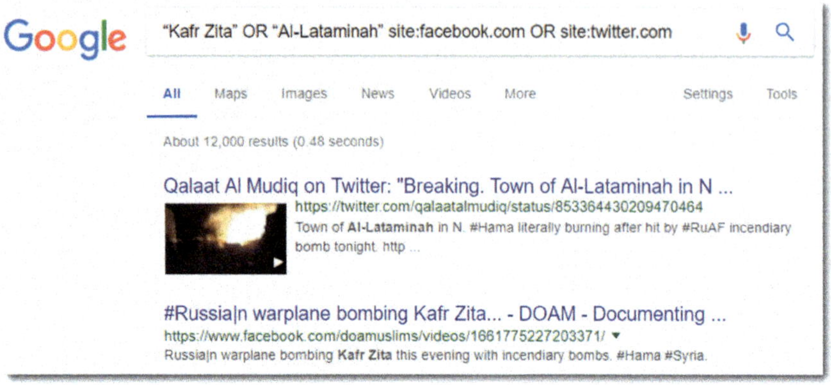

Figure 6.11

7. Advanced Searches

Search engines have many other tricks up their sleeves. You can easily use many of Google's extra search tools by visiting its 'Advanced Search' page, available at www.google.com/advanced_search, and using the search form.

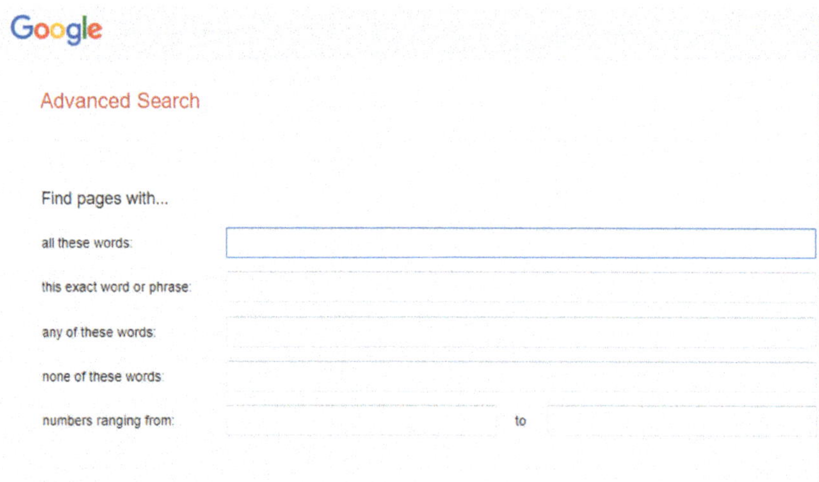

Figure 6.12

This lets you:

- specify phrases and linked words, as opposed to individual words anywhere on the page

- specify optional keywords (e.g. different possible towns or name spellings)
- target specified domain names, domain types or web addresses
- eliminate problematic pages by eliminating certain words that would appear on them. For example, eliminating 'swimming pool' from searches for 'chlorine'
- choose pages written in a certain language or from a certain country
- specify when the page was last updated (day, week, month, or year)
- choose where you want your keywords to appear
  - in the title of a web page
  - in the page's text
  - in the web address
  - in links that point to results pages
- you can choose a range of numbers that must appear on the page (for example, 1920..1930)
- you can choose a data file type (e.g. 'docx', '.xlsx', '.pdf', '.pptx').

8. Extra Tools

As you can see, Google allows you to search through its massive database, but also allows dedicated news, video, image, and other searches, which you can reach through the tabs that come up below the search box after entering your search terms.

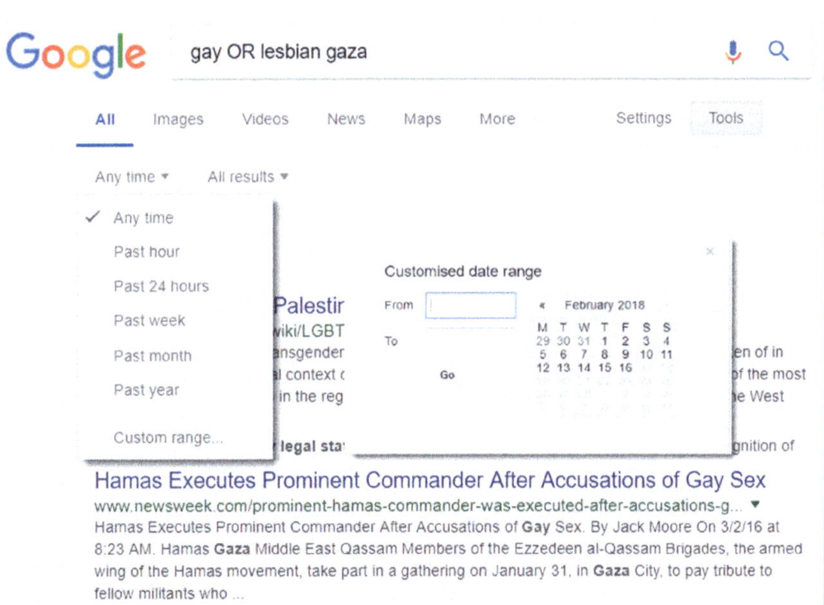

Figure 6.13

The button marked 'Tools' on the right-hand side allows you to specify extra search functionality.

- The tools in the 'All' tab allow you to specify a date range. This is really useful for eliminating recent coverage of an event or person and locating earlier coverage.
- The tools in the 'Images' tab allow you set a date range but also to specify image size, colour, and usage rights.
- The tools in the 'News' tab allow you to set a date range, choose a search within blogs, and order your results by date or relevance. You can also use the operator 'source:' in the news tab to specify the name of a newspaper. For example, 'source:times' will return stories from newspapers with Times in their name, whereas 'source:cnn' will only find results from CNN.
- The tools in the 'Videos' tab allow you choose a date range, video duration (short, medium, or long), and even the source of the video (CNN or YouTube for example). In some respects, it is better to search for YouTube videos via Google video search as Google gives you extra functionality; however, the results might not be as up-to-date as searching via the YouTube site itself (despite the fact that YouTube is owned by Google!)
- The 'Books' tab allows date ranges and also the ability to choose searches within books or magazines. As with the 'News' tab, you can sort the results by date or relevance.
- You can use some of the normal Google operators, such as 'OR' and 'site:' in these tabs to make your search more specific, for example, to find images just from the UN.

9. Getting what You Searched for

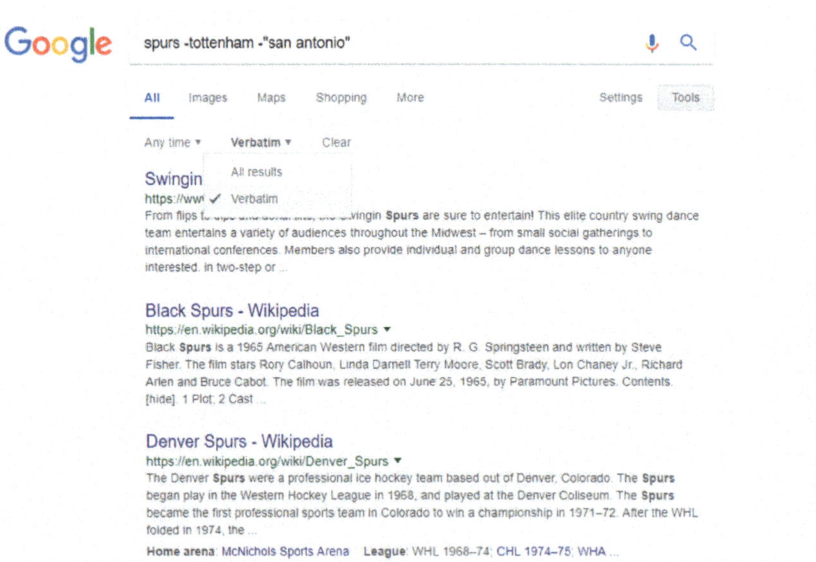

Figure 6.14

A search for the word 'spurs' will include the English football team Tottenham Hotspurs (whose nickname is Spurs) and a basketball team named San Antionio Spurs.

Google does have a habit of adding synonyms and popular alternative suggestions to our keyword search. This can be useful, but sometimes it can lead to words we do not want in the search box. For instance, I once used 'cardiac' in a search related to a comedian who had suffered a cardiac arrest. Google automatically added the word 'heart' to my search and gave me links to interviews he had given to a radio staion named Heart FM!

To overcome this problem, you can put quotation marks around a single word that must be searched for verbatim.

You can also use the minus sign '-' to filter out a problematic keyword. You must ensure there is no space between the sign and the word or phrase you wish to eliminate: for example '-tottenham'. Alternatively, you can help ensure you get what you searched for by clicking on 'Tools' and choosing 'Verbatim' from the 'All results' drop-down box.

Neither solution is 100 per cent effective, but they can help clean up your results.

9.1 Word Order

The way Google chooses its top results can depend on the order in which keywords appear in the search box. This is because it looks for word pairs (bigrams). A search for 'Hilton Paris' prioritizes results about the hotel, but you seem to get more than three times the results for 'Paris Hilton', which stresses the Reality TV star. For convenience, a summary of Google's main search opereators is provided below.

Table 6.1 Summary of Google's Main Search Operators

Operator	What it does	Example
' '	Links words together as a phrase or name.	'North Carolina' rather than North Carolina.
OR	Finds optional keywords, phrases or spellings.	Egypt 'Fattah el-Sisi' OR 'Fatah al-Sisi'
site:	Specifies a domain name or type.	site:lb OR site:sy OR site:jo OR site:ir.
AROUND(n)	Specifies proximity between two words or phrases, where ***n*** is the number of possible words between the search terms.	Trump AROUND(5) 'human rights'.
..	Allows you to set a number range. This is often used to search a range of years, but can be used for any numerical range.	Berlin 1939..1945
intitle: allintitle:	The operator 'intitle:' will find a single search term in the title of a webpage; the operator 'allintitle:' will find more than one search term in the title.	intitle:'human rights' site:cnn.com allintitle:'human rights' Israel site:cnn.com
inurl: allinurl:	'inurl:' finds a keyword or phrase in a site's address.	inurl:foi OR inurl:foia site:police.uk allinurl: request foi OR foia
filetype:	This specifies the format of the document required. It can be used to find Word, Powerpoint, Excel, MPEG videos, MP4 videos, Comma Separated Values files, log files, text files, and PDF documents, among others.	torture sudan filetype:xlsx

10. Time Travel Online

Sometimes the information that we need is no longer available. Life moves on. Buildings are demolished, people switch jobs, companies go out of business. This is also the case in the online world. Webpages are edited or removed, websites disappear, and Tweets and other social media posts are deleted. Unlike in real life, however, time travel is possible and easy on the internet. In this section I will detail how you can bring information back from the past.

Most websites concentrate on giving us new material; however, a few exist to give us information from the past. We can use archives to travel back in time and discover information that has been deleted from its original source.

This can be visual information in the form of photos, maps, and 'street views', or it can be text-based information such as web pages, newspapers, and other documents. Google Earth Pro and sites like Terraserver.com can also give us access to satellite images from many years back.

11. Visual Evidence Augments Text-based Evidence

We tend to focus our online research work on pages we find on the internet, but we should never underestimate the value that visual information can bring to the discovery process.

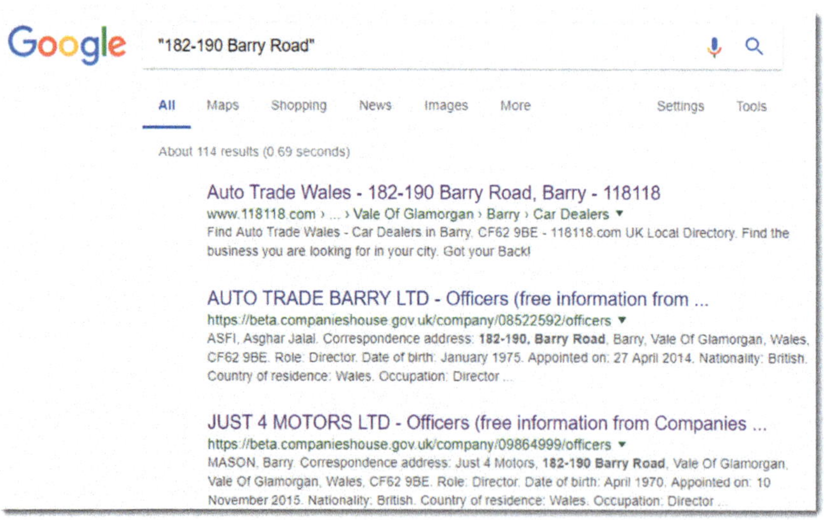

Figure 6.15

Let us say that we are interested in a former used car business located at the address 182–190 Barry Road, Barry, South Glamorgan, CF62 9BE in North Wales. If we want to see which businesses have occupied the same premises, it would be a clever move just to Google the address, as this will consistently reveal pages containing the names we are after. Indeed, a quick Google search for '182–190 Barry Road' shows Auto Trade Wales, Auto Trade Barry, Just 4 Motors, and Auto Solutions (Wales), previously listed at that address.

Figure 6.16

A Google Image search shows me photos from a property website taken when the property was previously up for sale. At that time, the business was called Cars R Us.

More information is available by viewing the property on Google Maps Street View. This shows navigable images of roads and their surrounding scenery taken by a special camera mounted on a Google car. Users just click on arrows to move up and down the road. They can scroll and zoom into the buildings on either side. For the investigator, this can be a useful part of the discovery process, as it reveals whether a business address is actually residential property, a shop, or an office. It reveals the state of repair and displays other information, such as the phone numbers and web addresses on signs outside the buildings of interest.

Figure 6.17

For example, a Google Street View of 182–190 Barry Road shows the company name *Cars For You* and its phone number. The sign is in poor repair and a missing panel shows the word 'cars' from a previous company at the address.

The box at the top left reveals the date this image was taken as July 2015. However, clicking on the little clock in this box allows you to travel back in time to previous Street Views, the earliest being October 2008, where we see that the original sign displayed the domain name tradepricecars.biz.

Figure 6.18

12. Website and Webpage Archives

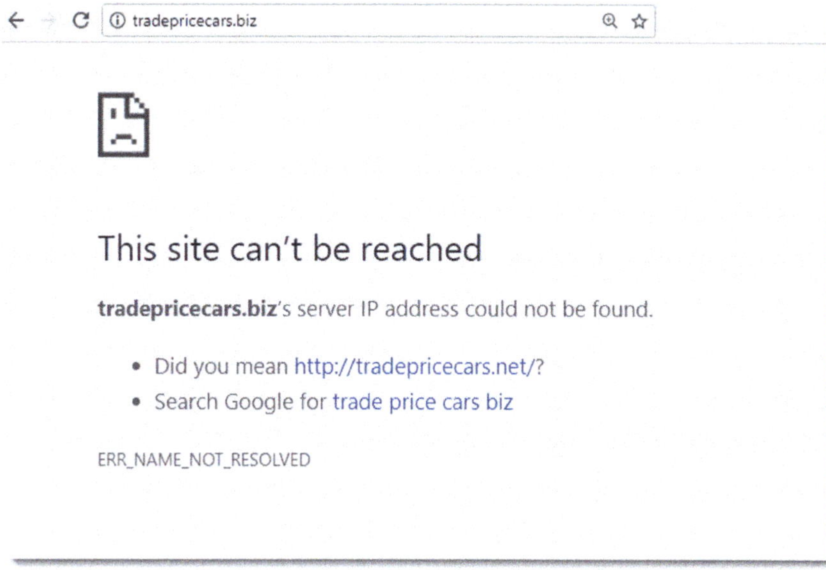

Figure 6.19

Grabbing an old web address like tradepricecars.biz, however, is no use if, as the Street View suggests, the company has gone out of business. The domain name might have expired or, confusingly, may have been sold to another company.

However, we can travel back to the October 2008 version of the website by using the WayBack machine (available at http://web.archive.org).

Figure 6.20

The Wayback Machine gives us a timeline for that IP address. We can scroll across to choose a year of interest and click on a blue circle to view how the site looked on that date.

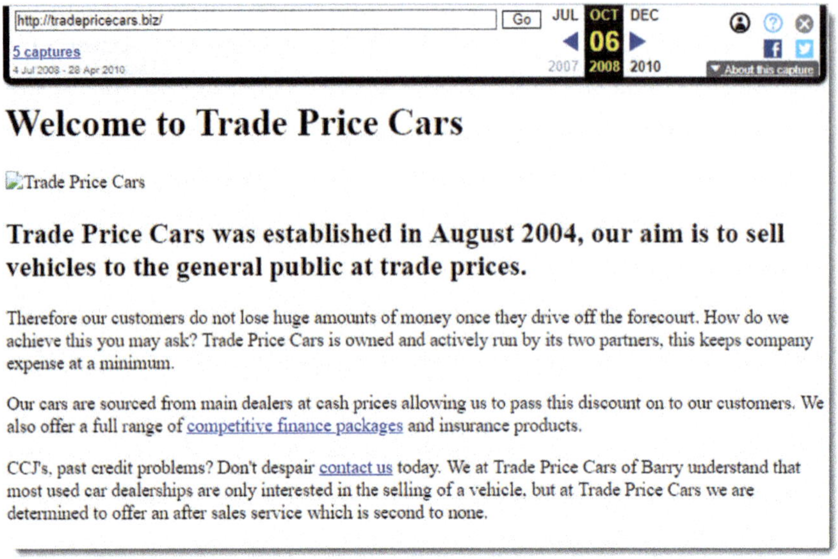

Figure 6.21

While the 6 October version of the site looks somewhat basic, it does give us useful and still-relevant contact information.

Time travel on the world wide web can be incredibly useful. It can confirm or refute whether someone was once involved in a company or organization. It can provide photographic as well as text-based evidence. It can provide email addresses and phone numbers that might still be in use today or searchable in diverse databases and search engines.

The WayBack machine is a hugely important site for researchers, but it does have some weaknesses. Whilst it grabs the contents of websites and their linked web pages, it cannot search the databases of sites that no longer exist. It cannot tune into live streams. Videos are often missing from archived YouTube pages. The system might not have captured more recent material and it misses a large number of social media posts. The Wayback Machine unfortunately cannot log into sites like Facebook in order to store copies of pages. However, another site, http://www.archive.is, can overcome this and is better for finding social media posts—even those embarrassing deleted tweets.

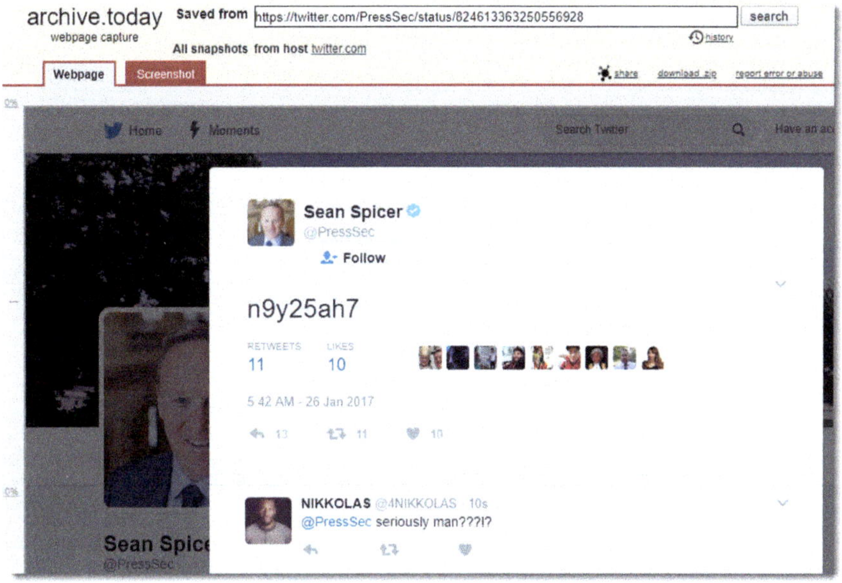

Figure 6.22

13. Search Engine Caches

If you have ever wondered how search engines like Bing, Google, and Yahoo! scan the web so quickly, well here is their secret: it is not a live search. You are actually searching their database of stored webpages. Google, for instance, has a program called Googlebot which surfs the web, following links and finding pages. When it finds a new page, it copies the text and images and stores them on the database alongside the page's web address. If it finds a page that has changed since the last visit of the Googlebot, it updates the database with new content.

Sadly, this is not done instantly; it can take weeks for the database to be updated. Thus, we can get false results and 'page not found' errors if the page's status and content have not yet been updated in their databases.

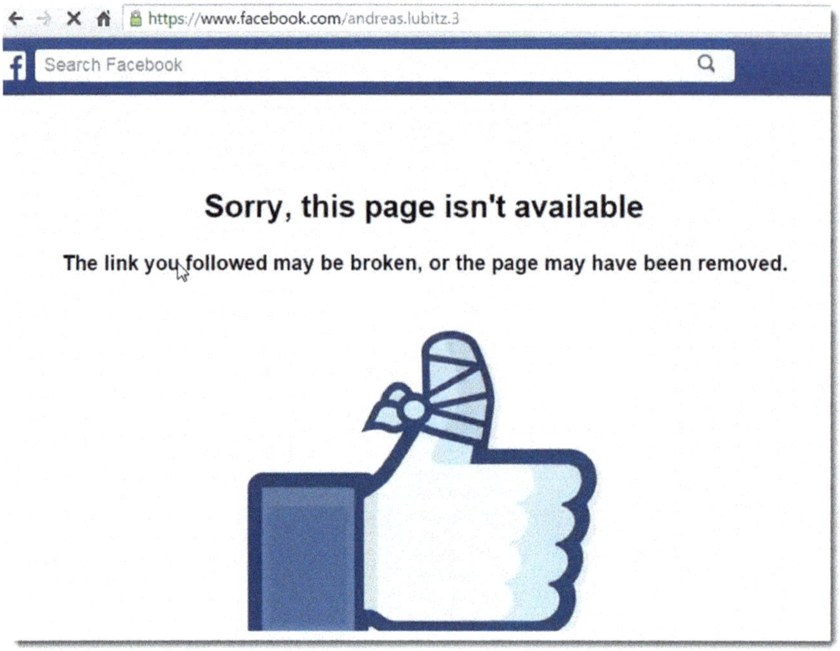

Figure 6.23

We can, however, gain access to the out-of-date version of the page that exists in the search engine database. It often has crucial information that is not available in other archives. To do this, click the word 'cache' next to the link on the search engine results page. For example, Andreas Lubitz was the pilot who deliberately crashed a passenger plane he was flying into the Alps, on 24 March 2015. When his name was announced, I could not find his profile on Facebook as it had been deleted.

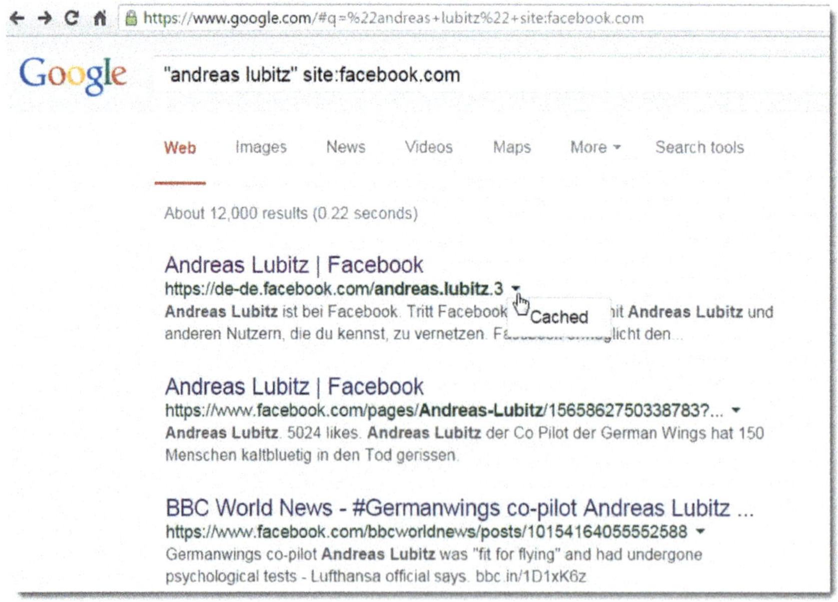

Figure 6.24

However, using 'site:facebook.com' with my search on Google brought me to the cached version of Lubitz's profile, which in turn gave me a photograph of the pilot and other useful information.

Figure 6.25

Interestingly, the cache date for this page was 25 March 2015, a day after the crash. This means the account must have been closed posthumously either by the police, a relative, or Facebook itself.

Sometimes a court might order a website to remove controversial comments, a company or institution might delete embarrassing content, or a user might delete a post or Tweet. Finding the original page might be possible in a search engine cache; the main search engines all have caches from different dates, so you stand a good chance of getting it. You will have to move quickly, however, as search engines do eventually delete out-of-date links.

14. People Research

When investigating people, it is vital that we exemplify the ethical standards expected of professional researchers. Of course, we also have to comply with the law. The General Data Protection Regulations, brought into force in May 2018, for example, protects the privacy and personal data of EU citizens, but it has implications for researchers working in countries around the world. It is highly recommended that, when researching people, you consult with legal and ethical experts.

In this section I will discuss approaches to researching people and the difficulties involved. We will see how best to collect information unique to our target.

In a world with over 7.6 billion people—with more than 3.6 billion online—how is it possible to find the person we are looking for? The key is to gather information that, taken together, is unique to that person. Given enough detail about the person we are investigating, we stand a good chance of finding them or their associates online. A great investigator will keep a keen eye open for any information that can help. They will pick out unique details from newspaper articles or ask their sources for personal information.

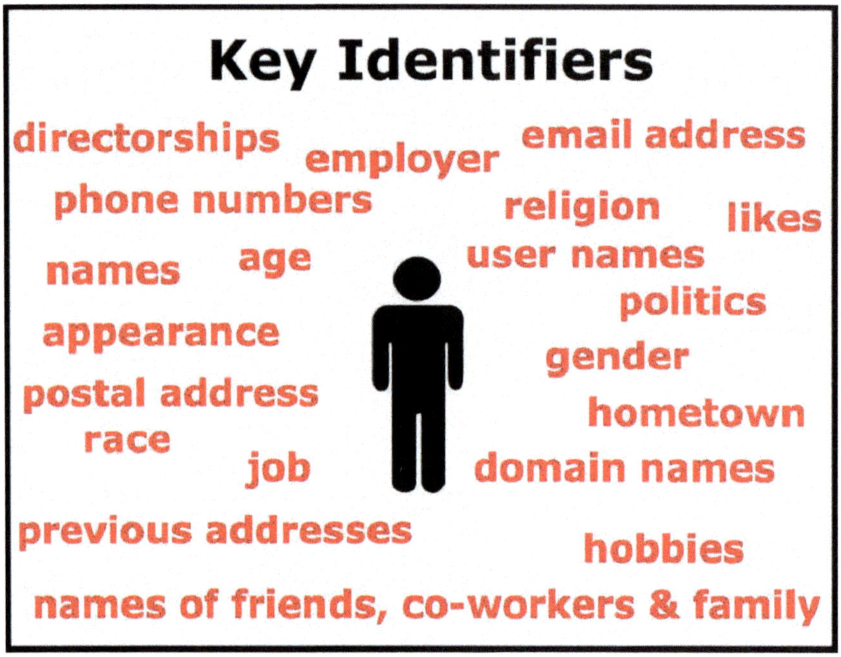

Figure 6.26

There is a cloud of personal information around each of us. While certain aspects such as age, gender, employment, and mother's name might not be unique to the person we are looking for, when searched together, they form a picture that can be used to identify and locate them online.

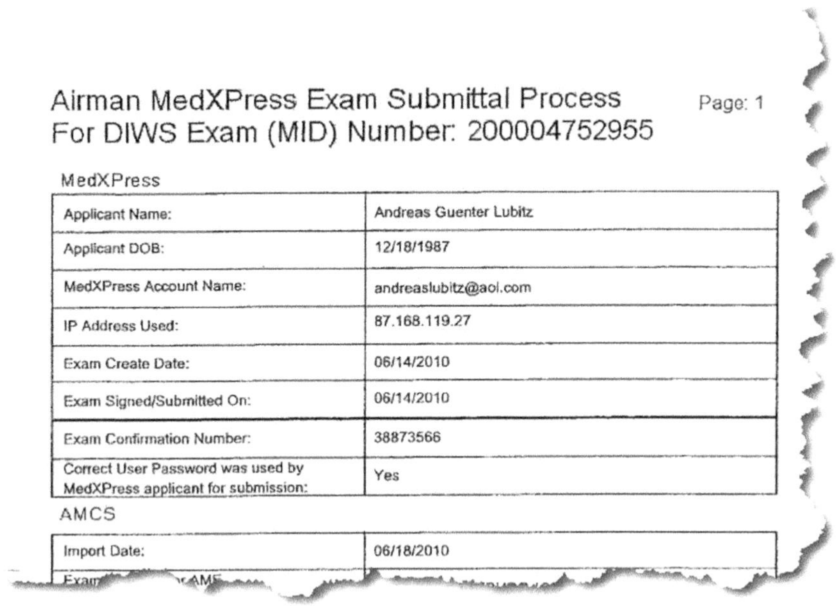

Airman MedXPress Exam Submittal Process
For DIWS Exam (MID) Number: 200004752955

Page: 1

MedXPress

Applicant Name:	Andreas Guenter Lubitz
Applicant DOB:	12/18/1987
MedXPress Account Name:	andreaslubitz@aol.com
IP Address Used:	87.168.119.27
Exam Create Date:	06/14/2010
Exam Signed/Submitted On:	06/14/2010
Exam Confirmation Number:	38873566
Correct User Password was used by MedXPress applicant for submission:	Yes

AMCS

Import Date:	06/18/2010

Figure 6.27

How many people are there named Andreas Lubitz? Maybe thousands. How many of them are 27-year-old pilots from Montabaur who work for a company named German Wings? Such details are not always immediately available but can be collected over the course of your search.

15. Key Identifiers

You will discover many clues to identity as your online journey progresses. A Google search, say, leads to a Facebook page, where you discover a user name, which leads to another site, where you discover a phone number in an advert that reveals someone's probable location or area code, and so on.

Let us take a look at some of these common identifiers.

16. Name

This seems straightforward but has hidden complications.

- A man named Alexander on official paperwork might have a social network presence under the name Alexander, Alex, Alec, Sasha, Xander, Zander, Lex, etc.
- A woman's name that is native to one alphabet may be spelled in many different ways when rendered in another, for example the Roman alphabet.
- A person could use either his parent's surname, his step-parent's surname, or even adopt a totally new surname.

- Many people change surname when they marry but their original may appear on relevant documents, websites, and in newspaper articles.
- Remember to hunt for a middle name or initial; some people prefer to use their middle name.

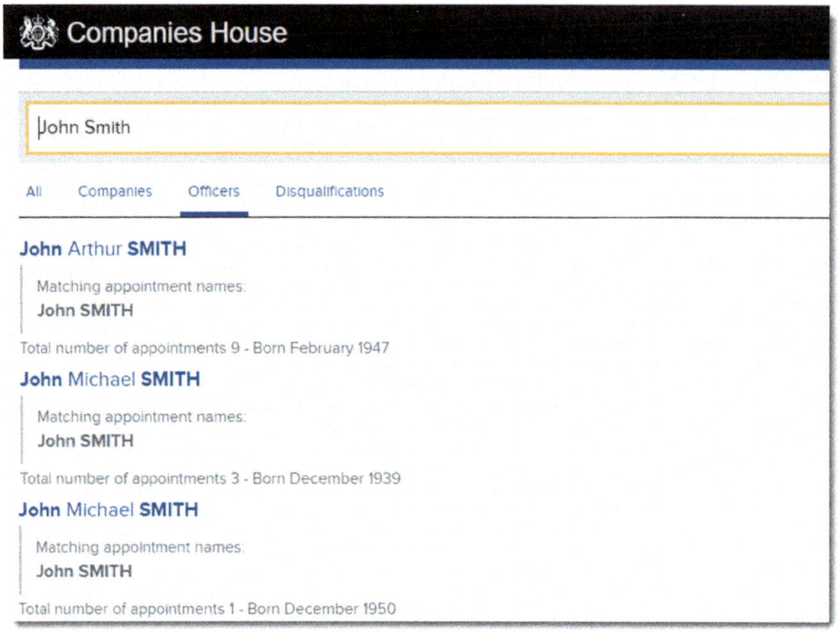

Figure 6.28

17. Date of Birth

This of course appears in many official documents, such as company registrations and licences to drive. It can not only help you find the right John Smith amidst many people with the same name, but it can also help with a visual search through profile pictures: a 79-year-old Susan Jones is going to look very different from a 15-year-old Susan Jones.

18. Gender

Confronted with gender neutral names like Jess, Lee, Toni, Nicky, Cameron, Les, or Robin, if we know the gender of our target we might be able to narrow down our field of possibilities. Sometimes this is implicit in the use of pronouns in documents and newspaper articles, but remembering to capture and record the subject's gender in your notes may save valuable time.

19. Friends, Family, Co-workers and Other Associates

When investigating people with common names, we often come across many possible candidates among social media sites. It can be reassuring to find known associates on our target's friend or follower list. How many John Smiths are there on Facebook? Maybe over a million. But how many have a father named Basil, a mother named Sybil, and a sister named Polly? Again, it is the triangulation of facts about someone's life that helps define the individual footprint found on their social media presence.

I often meet fellow investigators who, knowing the power of open source research, tell me they stay well away from having social media accounts themselves. I can understand why, but their absence will not assure their anonymity. However hard we try to keep a low profile, our efforts can be ruined by those around us. So, if I find no photographs or information about the person I am investigating, I look for tags and mentions in the social media posts of their known or suspected associates.

20. Connected Places

Someone's hometown, where they were born, grew up, are currently living, or lived in previously can form a huge part of the mosaic defining their uniqueness. Such information can help you locate the person you are interested in and it can be valuable intelligence in itself. As with all the constituent parts of one's online footprint, these details can be closely linked. An area code, for example, might reveal a location. If someone dresses in a fashion that is unique to an area, uses dialect from that region, or even supports a local football team, we might surmise (correctly or incorrectly) that they have a connection to that place. All of this can help us find and confirm their social media accounts.

21. Career and Employment Details

A subject's job will often motivate their social media activity, allowing you to identify them on the net. A soldier in the Syrian army will be likely to belong to groups related to their regiment and click 'like' on pictures and pages related to their mission.

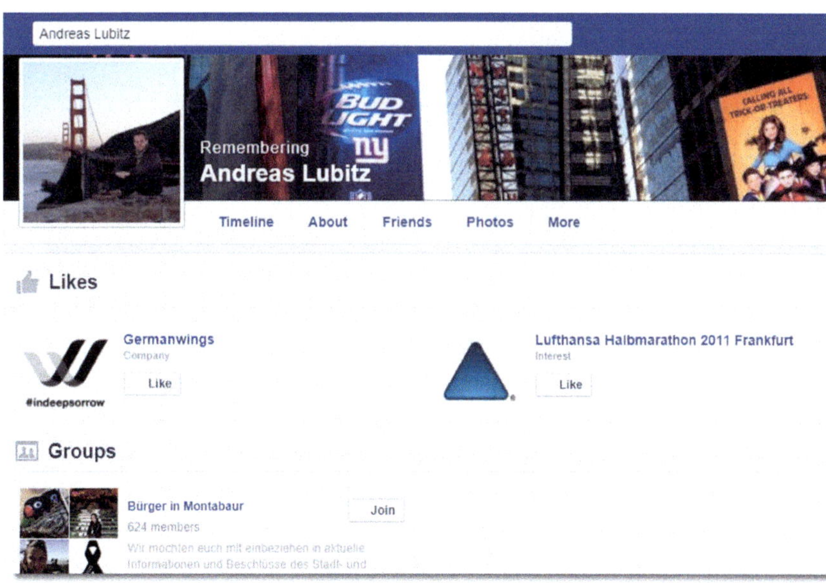

Figure 6.29

To return to our earlier example, the pilot Andreas Lubitz 'liked' pages related to the company he worked for, as well as aviation-related pages and that of his hometown, Montabaur.

Many social networks allow you to search by employer's name or by industry in addition to other factors, such as hometown and age.

If the person of interest is a director of a company, scrutinize company records for addresses, dates, colleagues, and so on. Remember to look further afield than you might expect for company information. A political figure in Zimbabwe might have registered companies in New York, London, Paris, and Munich. A company name found in a newspaper article could start a trail that begins in a business registry and finishes in Instagram!

22. Photographs

Photographs of the subject can also be a great resource. A photo can help establish that someone was in a certain location at a certain time, or suggest the person was spending way beyond what would be consistent with their reported income.

Also, photos—especially profile pictures—are primary identifying factors for any social media account. If you cannot obtain photos directly, try looking towards associates of the person you are investigating: your target may have been tagged in their photos. (For more details on how photographs can help your investigation, see the sections below on reverse image searching, graph searching, and geodata further on in this chapter.)

23. Hobbies, Interests, Political Views and Other Passions

You can even use a hobby or pastime to trace a person's social media account. Whilst their hobby might seem of little interest on its own, it could be the factor that brings down a list of search results to a manageable size and helps you trace an expert, witness, or other person of interest.

For example, at the time of writing, there are currently nearly fifty soldiers from Nairobi named David on Facebook. Only ten of them, however, have clicked 'like' on Manchester United.

Their support of Manchester United, fanatical love of the Beatles, passionate involvement in a political party, or attachment to a charity or cause will almost certainly be reflected in the posts or tweets they send, the pages they like, the people they follow and the groups they belong to. Their location may even be reflected in their choice of username.

24. Email Addresses

It is rare to have a unique name, but an email address is unique to its owner/s. To ensure messages go to the right people, no two email addresses are exactly the same.

Email addresses can tell us a great deal about their owners. They can reveal their regular username, their full name, their country, their company, and sometimes the year of their birth or their star sign.

As some social networks are searchable by email address, finding one can lead you directly to the profile you seek.

Figure 6.30

Email-format.com correctly guesses the commonly used corporate email address format of the BBC. If you do not know an email address, it might be guessable. This is especially true for work email addresses, as many companies use a certain format for all staff. If you know the name of the employer, you can use sites like email-format.com and hunter.io to find the format. Then it is just a matter of applying the format to the person of interest's name and, for example, entering the guessed email address into the Facebook search box to find a linked account.

25. Usernames

We are often asked to choose a username for a website, social network, or email account. People will often pick the same username for all their online identities. If a username is incredibly distinctive, it might be easy to find linked accounts and email addresses by just searching for it online. However, do not assume that a common username like 'gemini66' on Twitter is the same person as 'gemini66' on Facebook, eBay, or Hotmail.

In Facebook, the username usually—but not always—contains the name of the account holder with some numbers. In Twitter, Instagram, and Facebook, the username appears in the address bar directly after the domain name—for example 'facebook.com/john.smith9678536'. The username is not always the same as the account name, however. Facebook only allows you to change the username once, so if you think someone has picked a new pseudonym to hide their identity, check the address bar for their original username.

Both Facebook and Twitter also have numerical IDs for each account. It is worth recording these as they can be useful. If a Twitter account changes its username, the numerical ID will stay the same. You can find a Twitter numerical ID by looking up the username in sites like TwitterId.com or the excellent Tweetbeaver.com, which also offers a host of other useful tools. Facebook IDs can be found for both users and pages at sites like lookup-id.com and findmyfbid.com.

26. Phone numbers

Phone numbers are not only a valuable way of contacting someone; they can also be a valuable research tool. Phone numbers can reveal their owner's country, city, business, and social media accounts. Even old phone numbers from companies that went bankrupt years ago could still be in use by their owners today.

When searching Google for a phone number, bear in mind that you may need to try different formats. Experiment with spacing and including the country code. Always use quotation marks and consider using the operator 'OR' to get all the permutations. In the example above, I used four different possible renderings of the Oxford University number, as I could not predict how it would appear on the page I wanted. It is easy to find an identity behind a number when it is a famous institution like Oxford, but with a more obscure number, it is essential to try all options as you do not want to miss a page with a valuable clue.

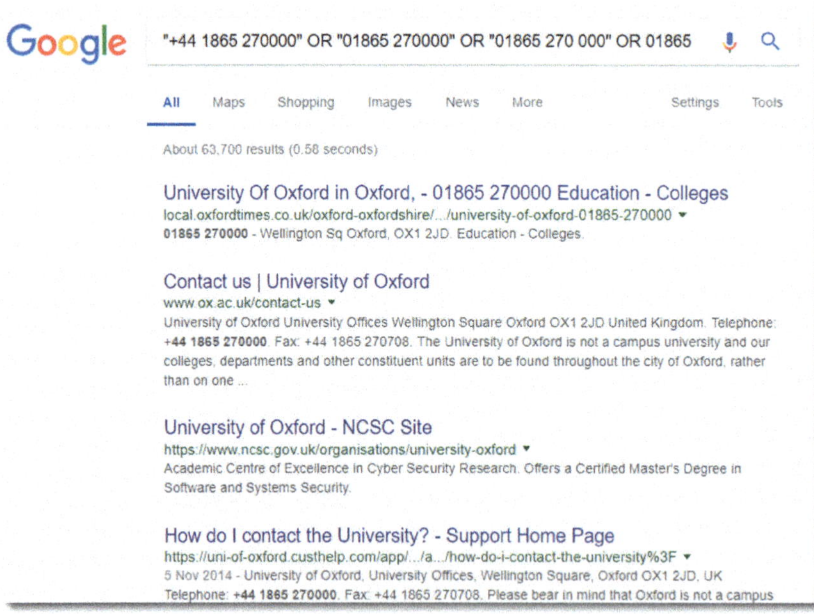

Figure 6.31

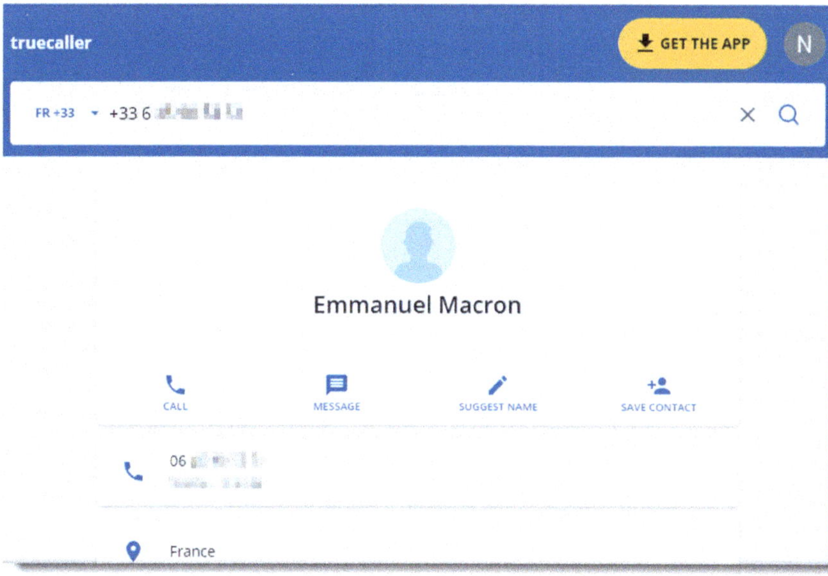

Figure 6.32

Truecaller.com traces a cell phone number to Emmanuel Macron. Sites like sync.me and truecaller.com have databases containing billions of phone numbers, many collected from the contact lists of those that install their app or use their webpages. They can provide a name for a phone number and are therefore a valuable part of the investigative process.

27. Searching Social Networks

Many social networks have a reputation among researchers for being a nightmare to search. To be fair, serving the needs of investigators is not the primary purpose of social networking sites, so we can hardly expect them to design their searches around us. That is not to say that we cannot use them for investigation; we just need to know how.

Some social networks present better investigation opportunities than others. Messaging apps like WhatsApp are largely private networks and therefore difficult to use for information gathering unless you are part of the network and in on the conversation. Others are very searchable. LinkedIn, for example, has a useful search facility thanks to its interest in facilitating job recruitment. You can search by first name, surname, location, current company, previous company, industry, and so on.

Hashtags can be used in the search box of many social networks. Unlike ordinary keywords, they act as subject labels for ongoing conversations on social media. They are easy to spot, as each hashtag is proceeded by a hash sign, for example #prayformanchester. Note that spaces are not used in hashtags. You may find that news events develop their own hashtags, as do individual online cultures and demographics. Websites like hashtagify.me and twxplorer.knightlab.com can help you find hashtags and lead to their affiliated conversations.

28. Searching Twitter

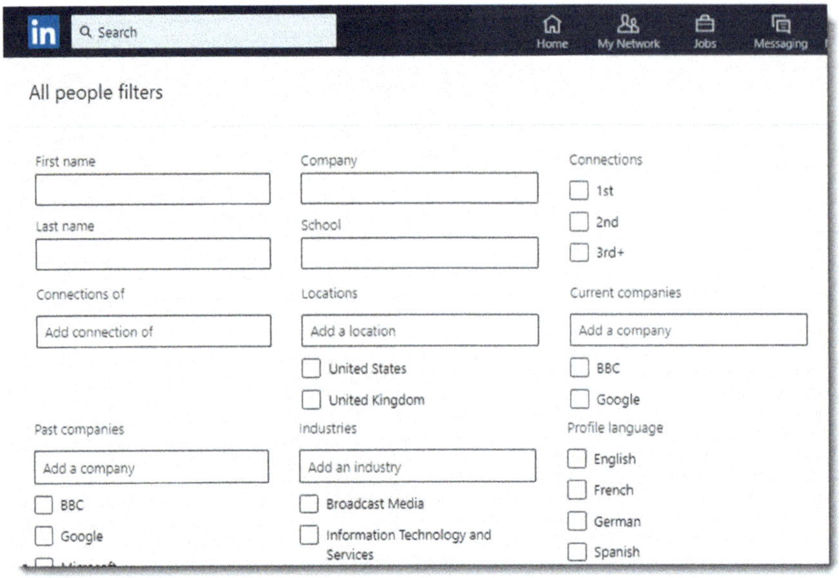

Figure 6.33

Like Google, Twitter uses search operators. This includes quotation marks for phrases, the minus sign to eliminate words and 'OR' to choose optional keywords. It also has its own unique operators and search functions. You can search by date range, language, and by the accounts in online conversations you wish to search for.

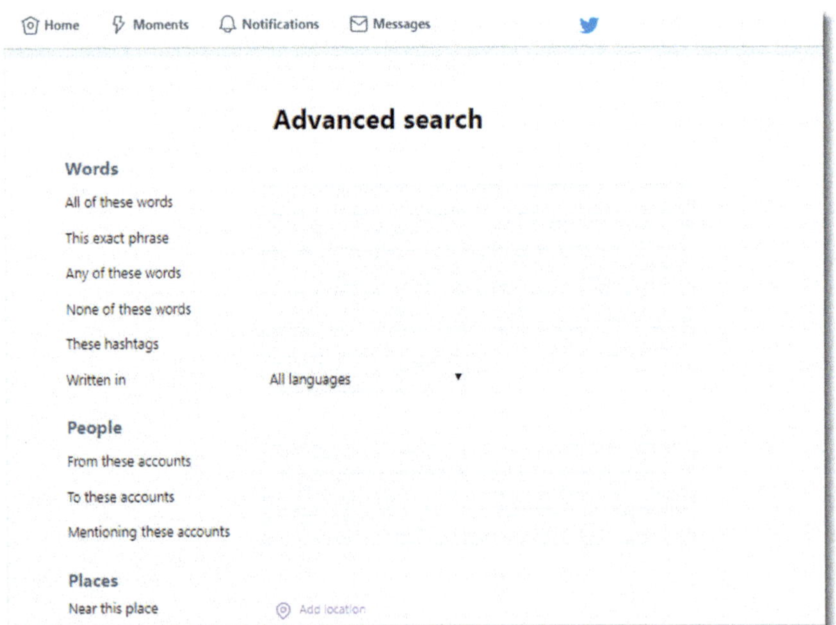

Figure 6.34

Websites like TweetBeaver.com, Allmytweets.net, and Followerwonk.com allow you to perform incredibly useful searches and sort through Twitter data to great effect. Their willingness to share data with third party developers makes Twitter one of the most flexible and searchable social networks.

Among Twitter operators, 'geocode': allows you to specify the area around a location of interest. To do this you will need to find the latitude and longitude. There are many sites that allow you to do this, for example mygeoposition.com; however, the latitude and longitude may also be found on Google Maps. The syntax for the search is:
keyword geocode:latitude,longitude,radius.

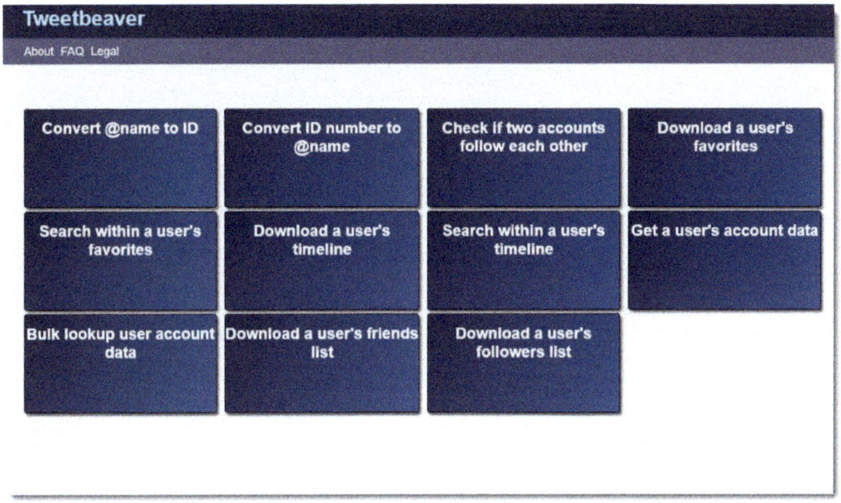

Figure 6.35

For example, the geographic coordinates of the Kremlin are 55.7520230 degrees latitude and 37.6174990 degrees longitude. To search for Tweets containing the word 'crimea' posted from within one kilometre around the Kremlin, our search would be:
crimea geocode:55.7520230,37.6174990,1km.

29. Searching Instagram

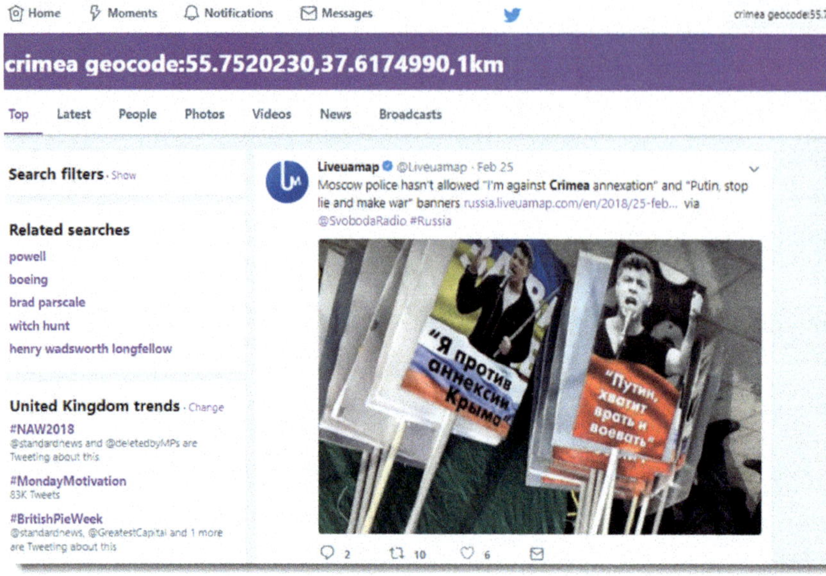

Figure 6.36

Fun sites and apps like Instagram may seem a little frivolous for the hard-bitten investigator, but if the people or organizations we are investigating are using them, they should not be overlooked. And whilst our target might just be posting pictures of his pizza, it may be useful to our investigation to know where he was eating the pizza, who he was eating it with, and who 'liked' his picture.

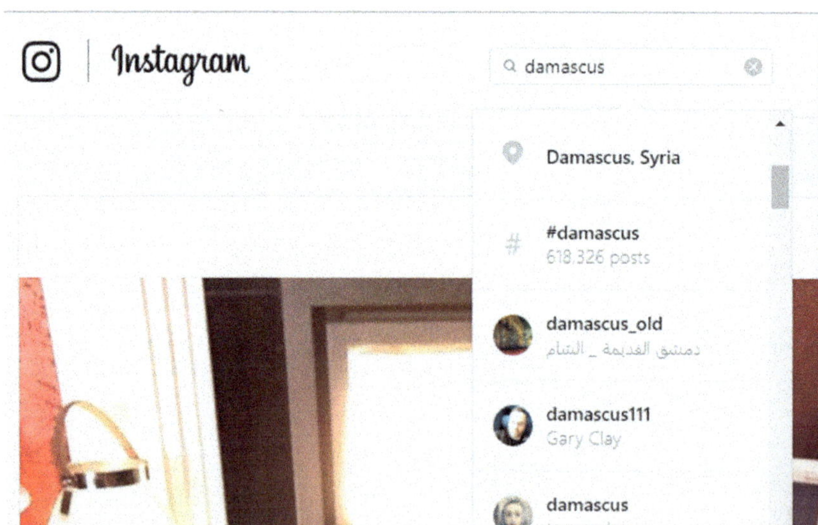

Figure 6.37

You can search Instagram by location, username, or hashtag with its mobile app, through its website, or via third party sites including websta.me/search, which provides great analytics.

30. Searching Facebook

Facebook's search box is reasonable enough for most users, but it can disappoint the serious investigator. Let us look at the positive aspects first.

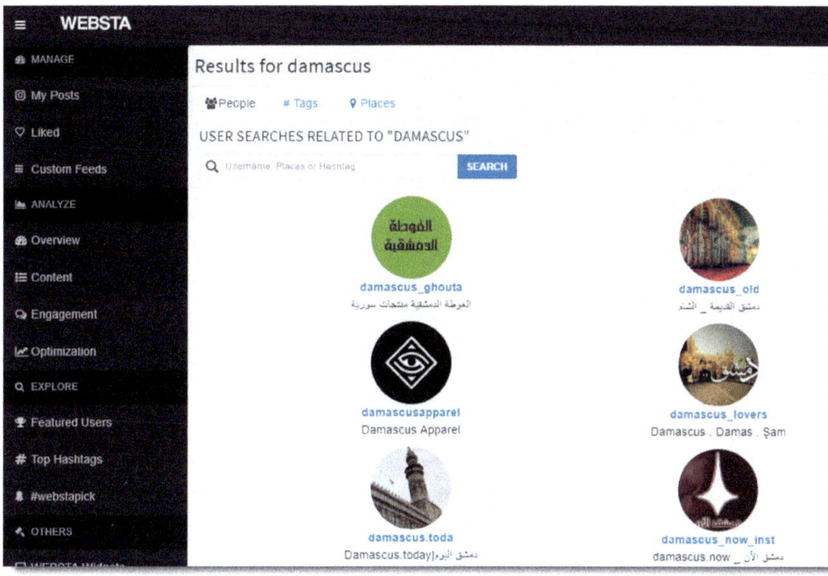

Figure 6.38

First, the interface. A search is divided into tabs providing various options. A search for 'Chelsea' will give you direct access to the following:

- *Posts* that contain the keyword 'Chelsea' in the account name or story text.
- *People* whose name is Chelsea, for example, Chelsea Clinton.
- *Photos* tagged with the name Chelsea or where 'Chelsea' appears in the text.
- *Videos* tagged with the name Chelsea or where 'Chelsea' appears in the text.
- *Pages* containing the name Chelsea, *for example* Chelsea Football Club.
- *Places* containing establishments with Chelsea in their name, like Chelsea Market.
- *Groups* with Chelsea in their name or description.
- *Events*, *apps*, and *links* involving Chelsea.

Each tab has its own search filters, found on the left-hand side, that help you specify source, location, date, and the like.

Groups and pages both offer discussion by users. Those on Facebook pages are centred on announcements posted by the page owner, whereas any Facebook member can start a discussion in a Facebook group as long as they are a member of the group. You can use extra keyword search boxes in both groups and pages.

31. Finding People in Facebook

You can use the search box to find Facebook members, and you can sometimes use the identifiers specified earlier to search. However, the system can only deal with simple searches. You can, for example, search for 'people named David that live in Oxford, United Kingdom' and get results. You can specify 'people named David who like The Beatles' and get results; however, you cannot use the search box to find 'people named David who live in Oxford and who like The Beatles'.

32. Relationship Analysis

When trying to prove somebody's involvement with other individuals, organizations, causes, and companies, it can often help to look at their online friendships and the people they follow.

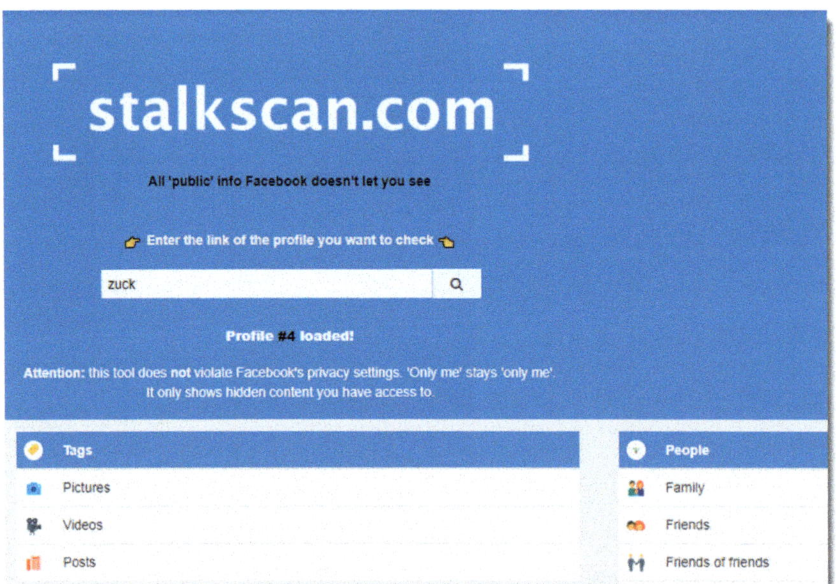

Figure 6.39

We can see someone's associations on each of the social network sites. We should, however, bear in mind that the nature of online relationships depends on a site's culture. A person's LinkedIn account might reveal their professional associates. YouTube accounts might be followed by people who simply have similar interests. Facebook friend lists often involve close relationships but might also include co-workers. People on Facebook friends lists are less likely to be complete strangers than, for example, followers on Twitter.

A Twitter account will include a list of people the persons of interest follow and who follow them. You are more likely to detect close associates by looking for people who follow each other. Sites like Tweepsect.com can organize Twitter followers into categories, while Followerwonk.com can find mutual friends of two or three different Twitter accounts. Careful sorting can help you find more potential associates and contacts. Deeper analysis may help you learn the nature of the underlying relationships; for example, how two apparent strangers might know each other.

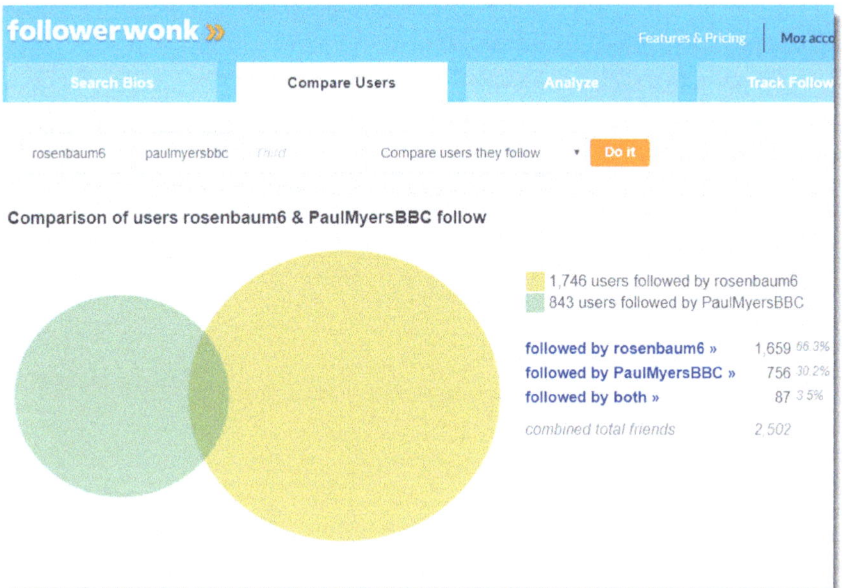

Figure 6.40

Figure 6.41

Relationship analysis on other social networks can be cumbersome and time-consuming. You might need to be a close part of a particular network to access private information, but at least some information is public. Try to see who has clicked 'like' on a post or picture as they may be friends of the author.

Friendship analysis in Facebook is easier if both parties have public friends lists.

33. Investigating with Images

All of the major search engines and social networks allow you to search for images. Bear in mind, however, that the search engine does not know the content or subject of images, simply the words that are associated with them on web pages.

Most allow advanced filtering and sorting, as well as the use of search engine syntax and operators. Google's image search, for instance, includes tools that allow you to specify you are looking for a face, or an image with a certain dominant colour (e.g. green for outdoor shots or black and white for old photographs).

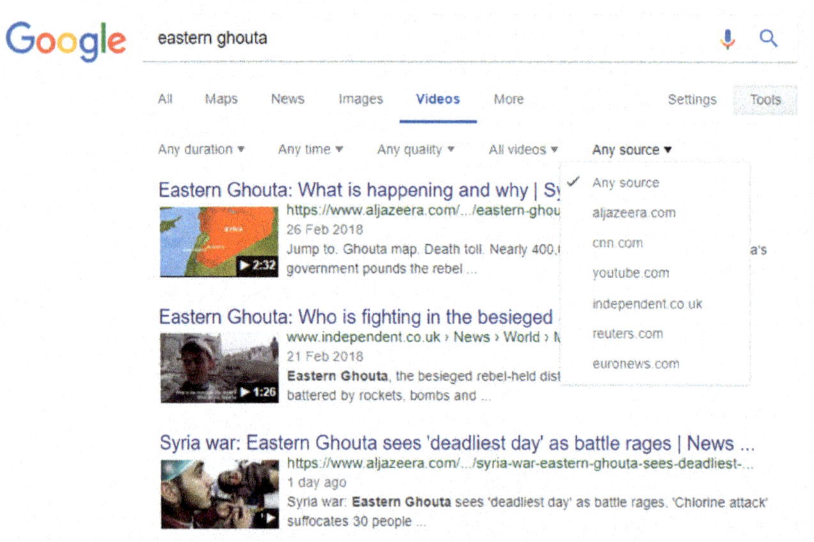

Figure 6.42

34. Reverse Image Searching

People post photos online that often betray clues to their location. We can use our deductive skills to identify this, if there are sufficient clues, from the names of shops, signs, car registration plates, even electrical sockets. Sometimes we need to locate different social media accounts that share the same profile picture or identify somebody in a photo, but we will not have much luck if we just type 'tall guy, mid-30s, curly hair and glasses' into Google's image search. At other times, we have to identify a logo that appears on a tee-shirt, building, or vehicle.

Google 'Search by Image' correctly determines the location of the uploaded photo (left) as Durbar Square in Kathmandu.

The answer to these problems might be found with Google's 'Search by Image' feature. This involves asking Google to analyse the colours and shapes in a photo so that it can point you to where the same photo appears elsewhere online.

To perform a reverse image search, simply visit the Google Images website and click on the little camera icon on the search box. This will let you upload the photo on your hard drive, or paste the web address of a photo that is online. (If you are using the Chrome browser, you can also right click on a photo and choose 'Search Google for image' to perform your reverse image search.)

There are other reverse image search engines apart from Google, and each may yield different results. Some people achieve good results by cropping the image so that you only search for a landmark, logo, or other prominent feature. Others have had great success by making an image black and white before searching in order to underscore shapes and patterns.

35. Searching for videos

All of the major video sharing sites offer some degree of searchability. YouTube, for example, allows you to search for your keywords in channels and movies, as well as in posted videos. You can also apply extra filters that specify duration and quality. You can even choose to exclude older videos.

You can get even more flexibility with Google's Videos tab. This allows you to use most of the normal Google operators, for example 'OR' for multiple keyword options, or 'site' to specify a domain as a source. The 'tools' button provides even more filters, allowing you to specify an exact date range or to choose a source from a drop-down menu.

Amnesty International has produced a useful tool to find information on YouTube videos. The YouTube Data Viewer is available at https://citizenevidence.amnestyusa.org/ and provides metadata, such as the upload date of any YouTube video and, perhaps most useful, the ability to do a reverse image search on an image from the video. Such images are often seen on pages that carry an embedded link to the video on YouTube and this can be useful for tracing the source of a video or those disseminating it.

36. Specialist Databases and Tools

Apart from search engines and social networks, there are many specialist databases, government websites, technical tools, and company research sites that can help our investigations.

37. Finding Domain Name Owners

There are many sites that let you investigate domain name ownership, although access to full details, such as domain owner names, phone numbers, and email addresses varies between countries.

Site like Domaintools.com, Whoisology.com, and Domainbigdata.com let you look up who currently owns a domain name, who owned it in the past, and even shows you other sites that are stored on the same computer as the website you are investigating.

38. Business and Government Databases

Most countries have official websites with useful databases. These can be used to trace company ownership, land ownership, patent holders, and other information. I particularly recommend OpenCorporates.com—a free tool that can look up company ownership information from international sources. See also https://investigativedashboard.org/databases/ for links to government and official databases from various countries.

39. Conclusion

In this chapter I have gone through the main online options for information and people research. There are many opportunities if you can see past the technology and jargon which usually clouds the simple techniques involved. There are other considerations as well, such as digital security, ethics, verification specialist technology, and legal compliance. One important area I have not touched on is how we save evidence; this is covered in the next chapter.

7

How to Preserve Open Source Information Effectively

Yvonne Ng

Audiovisual and other documentary evidence have long played an important role in human rights research and legal accountability, from the Nuremberg trials and the International Criminal Tribunal for the former Yugoslavia (ICTY) to the present-day International Criminal Court (ICC). During the trial of Congolese warlord Thomas Lubanga beginning in 2009 at the ICC, for example, prosecutors notably relied on open source video as prime evidence in their successful efforts to obtain a guilty verdict for war crimes.[1]

Until recently, the importance of properly preserving audiovisual and documentary information beyond its initial collection and registration has been mostly overlooked outside of the archives and preservation community. This lack of concern was somewhat understandable in an analogue world, when just neatly boxing materials and putting them in storage usually sufficed (at least in the short- to medium-term). However, in an online and digital world, attention to preservation has become critical.

The video used in the Lubanga trial, which showed that children visibly under the age of 15 were recruited as soldiers and bodyguards for the military wing of the Union des Patriotes Congolais (UPC), was recorded between 2002 and 2003. Given such dates, the videos would have certainly originated on a videotape recording format of the period, such as VHS, Hi8, or miniDV. For these original recordings to have remained accessible and usable by the start of the investigation in 2004, the start of the trial in 2009, and through to the verdict in 2012, care in handling and storage would have been required, but not much beyond the protocols for any other type of evidence. Content on videotape was, at the time, not a short-term preservation risk (although videotape does present significant long-term preservation risks).

Today, of course, audiovisual and other documentary information is rarely, if ever, recorded on tape or analogue media, but often exists as digital content stored on drives, phones, or platforms like Twitter and Facebook. The 2017 ICC arrest warrant for Al-Saiqa commander Al-Werfalli, for example, was based largely on video documentation of seven incidents posted on social media. With this evidence, the Court was able to charge Al-Werfalli with committing and ordering murder as a war crime in Libya.[2] The value of these videos, however, belies their permanence. Less than three months after the videos were

[1] 'Lubanga Judgment: The Prosecution's Investigation and Use of Intermediaries' *International Justice Monitor* (20 August 2012) https://www.ijmonitor.org/2012/08/lubanga-judgment-the-prosecutions-investigation-and-use-of-intermediaries/ accessed 29 December 2018.

[2] *Prosecutor v Mahmoud Mustafa Busayf Al-Werfalli* (Warrant of Arrest) ICC-01/11-01/17 (15 August 2017).

posted, the first video had already been deleted from Facebook. It would not exist today if it had not been downloaded and saved elsewhere.[3] This serves to illustrate how a passive approach to short-term preservation that may have been adequate in the past is no longer sufficient today. In the longer term, the downloaded digital copy will also require ongoing maintenance and preservation to remain accessible. We can no longer leave content in a box, or online, for any period of time and reliably expect it to be there later.

This chapter outlines the basic principles, components, and processes of digital preservation, aimed at human rights practitioners who collect and plan to retain digital information over time. The chapter begins by highlighting the particular vulnerabilities of online open source information and explains the meaning of 'preservation' in that context. It then delves into each of the functional areas involved in the process of digital preservation, drawing from standards established in the archives and preservation field and illustrated with real-life examples.

1. The Risks to Open Source Information

The permanence and availability of content posted on social media and, indeed, any content created by individuals, hosted by a third-party, and accessed on the internet, is precarious. Brewster Kahle, the founder of Internet Archive, has estimated that the average lifespan of a webpage is only ninety-two days.[4] Most web hosts and social media platforms make no commitment to keep uploaded content available over time, and in fact actively remove content that violates their terms of service, the rules by which a user agrees to abide as a condition of using the platform. Take-downs caused by terms of service violations can especially impact human rights media, which sometimes contain graphic or violent imagery, and are mistaken for extremist content by platforms' detection algorithms. This notably occurred in 2017 when YouTube's machine-learning-based algorithm removed hundreds of channels and thousands of videos documenting atrocities in Syria. It was only through advocacy by groups like Syrian Archive that many of the channels and videos were eventually restored.[5]

Platforms can also go out of business and shut down their services entirely. Blip.tv, Justin.tv, Yahoo! Video, and Orkut are just some examples of social media platforms that have shut down in recent years—but that fortunately have been archived by self-proclaimed 'rogue' archivists.[6] When services go out of business, they often give a timeframe during which users may download their media content before it is lost. Bambuser,[7] the mobile

[3] Bellingcat, 'How a Werfalli Execution Site Was Geolocated' (10 March 2017) https://www.bellingcat.com/news/mena/2017/10/03/how-an-execution-site-was-geolocated/ accessed 20 December 2018.

[4] 'Internet History Is Fragile. This Archive Is Making Sure It Doesn't Disappear' *PBS NewsHour* (1 February 2017) https://www.pbs.org/newshour/show/internet-history-fragile-archive-making-sure-doesnt-disappear accessed 29 December 2018.

[5] Dia Kayyali and Raja Althaibani, 'Vital Human Rights Evidence in Syria Is Disappearing from YouTube' *WITNESS* (30 August 2017) https://blog.witness.org/2017/08/vital-human-rights-evidence-syria-disappearing-youtube/ accessed 29 December 2018; Armin Rosen, 'Erasing History: YouTube's Deletion of Syria War Videos Concerns Human Rights Groups' *Fast Company* (7 March 2018) https://www.fastcompany.com/40540411/erasing-history-youtubes-deletion-of-syria-war-videos-concerns-human-rights-groups accessed 29 December 2018.

[6] Archive Team (https://www.archiveteam.org/) is a loose collective of 'archivists, programmers, writers, and loudmouths dedicated to saving our digital heritage'.

[7] 'Shutdown Announcement' *Bambuser* (2017) https://go.bambuser.com/shutdown-announcement accessed 29 December 2018.

live streaming service that was used widely by activists during conflicts in Syria, Ukraine, and Egypt, shut itself down in 2018, instructing users to download their videos within two months, after which they would be permanently removed. Unfortunately, not all platforms give their users adequate warning before they shut down, and not all users are prepared to take on the burden of preserving their own content and some may face security risks if they do so. While they are operational, many third-party platforms and web hosts often create barriers to downloading social media content and its accompanying metadata. Twitter, for example, places limits on its free Search API, its application programming interface for providing access to Twitter data; a full Search API is available but at a monthly cost, starting at US$99 per month and running up to US$1,899 per month as of February 2018.[8]

Even when open source information persists online, it remains susceptible to dislocation or so-called 'link rot'—a term that applies when websites are updated, reorganized, or deleted, and external links no longer point to the intended content. This makes information difficult to find over time, as links from webpages or documents are broken. In 2013, a Harvard Law School study[9] found that 50 per cent of URLs cited in US Supreme Court decisions since 1996 no longer linked to the originally cited information. Content shared on social media seems to fare even worse. In 2012, researchers analysing large datasets of social media related to culturally important events found that 27 per cent of the resources shared in those datasets had been lost after two-and-a-half years. Their modelling indicated that, within the first year of publishing, nearly 11 per cent of resources shared on social media are lost, and subsequently continue to be lost at a rate of 0.02 per cent per day.[10] Surprisingly, link rot is not just a problem for 'user-generated' content and webpages, but also occurs frequently on websites managed by governments and established institutions. The Chesapeake Digital Preservation Group,[11] made up of four law libraries in the United States, has studied a sample of online law- and policy-related materials annually since 2008. It found that 55 per cent of links on .gov domains, 56 per cent of links on .org domains, and 67 per cent of links on .edu domains in its sample were no longer active within just six years.

Online open source information also risks becoming unfindable when it lacks sufficient metadata or description to enable users to discover and retrieve it, or when users cannot adequately identify and disambiguate it from other content. With at least 400 hours of video uploaded to YouTube every minute,[12] users will have difficulty discovering the content they are seeking in the midst of this massive volume if it lacks an informative and relevant title, description, or tags. Even YouTube's own review teams are evidently challenged by the inadequacy of user-provided description properly to identify and disambiguate valid human

[8] Sarah Perez, 'Twitter Is Opening up Its Full Archive to the Broader Developer Community' *TechCrunch* (2 January 2018) https://techcrunch.com/2018/02/01/twitter-is-opening-up-its-full-archive-to-the-broader-developer-community/ accessed 29 December 2018.

[9] Jonathan L Zittrain, Kendra Albert, and Lawrence Lessig, 'Perma: Scoping and Addressing the Problem of Link and Reference Rot in Legal Citations' Social Science Research Network (2013) SSRN Scholarly Paper ID 2329161https://papers.ssrn.com/abstract=2329161 accessed 29 December 2018.

[10] Hany M SalahEldeen and Michael L Nelson, 'Losing My Revolution: How Many Resources Shared on Social Media Have Been Lost?' in P Zaphiris, G Buchanan, E Rasmussen, and F Loizides (eds), *Theory and Practice of Digital Libraries, vol 7489* (Springer 2012) http://arxiv.org/abs/1209.3026 accessed 29 December 2018.

[11] '"Link Rot" and Legal Resources on the Web: A 2014 Analysis' The Chesapeake Digital Preservation Group (2014) http://cdm16064.contentdm.oclc.org/cdm/linkrot2014 accessed 29 December 2018.

[12] 'An Update on Our Commitment to Fight Terror Content Online' *YouTube Official Blog* (8 January 2017) https://youtube.googleblog.com/2017/08/an-update-on-our-commitment-to-fight.html accessed 29 December 2018.

rights documentation from videos intended to incite violence or promote terrorism, which has resulted in flagged content being removed from the platform.[13]

Given the risks to open source information online, downloading or saving locally controlled copies of content (and metadata) is part of a good strategy for preservation. However, this is just the *first* step in digital preservation. Downloaded digital files require active stewardship throughout their lifespan. Once content is no longer stored by third-party platforms, the responsibility for storage and data management falls on the collector.

2. What Is Digital Preservation?

Digital preservation encompasses the policies, strategies, and ongoing actions involved in managing and maintaining digital information with enduring value over time, so that it is accessible and usable by its intended users. The work of digital preservation is typically done by archives. An archive is an organization—not necessarily a formal organization, but one in the sense of being a grouping of people and systems—that has accepted the responsibility to preserve information and make it available to identified potential user communities. Archives take all shapes and sizes, ranging from large national collecting institutions to those managed by a single person within a volunteer-run grassroots organization.

Several aspects of an information object, such as a video or an electronic document, need to be maintained for it to remain accessible and usable over time. The *Simple Property-Oriented Threat (SPOT) Model for Risk Assessment*[14] offers a useful categorization of digital information object properties that must be preserved and explains the threats to these properties that preservation actions must address. These properties are: availability, identity, persistence, renderability, understandability, and authenticity.

Availability of the digital object is a basic requirement that preservation must ensure. This may refer to availability, not only in the simple physical sense of existing and being retrievable, but also in the legal sense of securing the appropriate intellectual property rights to access and use the information. The deleted Al-Werfalli Facebook video discussed above, and the access restrictions imposed by the terms of service and tools provided by social media platforms exemplify the challenges to availability.

Identity, or the ability to be referenced, is another basic property of digital objects that needs to be preserved. A digital object must be identifiable and distinguishable from other digital objects so that it can be found and retrieved. Identity depends on basic metadata such as a name, title, or unique identification number, and can be threatened if this metadata is not created or maintained, becomes separated from the object, or itself becomes unavailable.

The third property, *persistence*, refers to the integrity and viability of the digital object in technical terms. To persist, the digital object's bit sequences must be intact, processible, and retrievable from its storage medium. Preservation therefore requires protecting the object from accidental damage or malicious alteration, and from file corruption or loss

[13] 'The Importance of Context: YouTube Help' https://support.google.com/youtube/answer/6345162?hl=en accessed 29 December 2018.

[14] Sally Vermaaten, Brian Lavoie, and Priscilla Caplan, 'Identifying Threats to Successful Digital Preservation: The SPOT Model for Risk Assessment' (2012) 18 D-Lib Magazine http://www.dlib.org/dlib/september12/vermaaten/09vermaaten.html accessed 29 December 2018.

from software or hardware failure. It also requires protecting the object from storage media obsolescence, through which stored content becomes irretrievable because the necessary storage hardware, such as the card readers, cables/ports, or tape/disk drives, is no longer available.

Next, *renderability* refers to the ability of humans or machines to use or interact with the digital object using appropriate hardware and software. Renderability becomes challenging when file formats become obsolete, and the hardware or software needed to read the file is no longer available or cannot be maintained. Consider, for example, once-popular software packages such as WordPerfect or FinalCutPro 7,[15] and the difficulty of working with the files these packages produced on modern systems. Preservation involves taking actions, like migrating to new formats, to keep objects renderable while retaining the essential characteristics of the original object that the archive's stakeholders deem important.

Fifthly, *understandability* refers to the ability of intended users to interpret and understand the digital object. Users may need to know, for example, where an object came from, why it was created, and what its relation is to other objects. They may need further supplemental information as well, such as a dictionary to understand the language of the object or instructions on how to open the file. Such information needs to be preserved along with the digital object itself. The requirements can vary widely, and the appropriate metadata depends on the archive's intended users, their existing knowledge base, and how they want to use the object, each of which may change over time.

Finally, *authenticity* is the property of the digital object being what it purports to be. Preserving authenticity requires that the digital object remains unaltered while in the archive's custody, or that any modifications to the original object be documented. A digital object's authenticity depends on metadata, which must accurately describe the object, its provenance, and any alterations that have been made to it.

3. The Basic Components of Digital Preservation

While an archive's preservation strategies must be customized to its circumstances, the nature of its collections, and the needs of its intended users, there are established guidelines that describe the basic components of digital preservation. The *Reference Model for an Open Archival Information System (OAIS)*[16] is an international standard and key foundational text. Broadly applicable and universally adopted, the OAIS reference model provides a conceptual framework for any organization, large or small, that is undertaking long-term digital preservation.

The OAIS reference model includes an information model that defines the key information objects that an archive manages, and a functional model that defines the sets of tasks that an archive performs. This chapter uses the OAIS information objects and concept of

[15] Charles Haine, 'Final Death Comes to Final Cut 7' *No Film School* (23 August 2017) https://nofilmschool.com/2017/08/death-comes-final-cut-7 accessed 29 December 2018.

[16] 'Reference Model for an Open Archival Information System (OAIS)' [2012] Consultative Committee for Space Data Systems 135.

'information packages' to explain the flow of content through the archive to its intended users, and the OAIS functional entities to structure the remainder of the discussion.

The OAIS information model defines an array of information objects that the archive manages in order to preserve and provide access to the content data it is entrusted with. This information includes, for example, reference, provenance, descriptive, and rights information. A detailed breakdown of OAIS information objects is beyond the scope of this chapter, but it suffices to say that this information exceeds the content data that is originally submitted to the archive for preservation. Preserving the availability, identity, persistence, renderability, understandability, and authenticity of a digital object requires much more than just saving its content; the archive must also maintain additional information.

In the OAIS information model (see Figure 7.1), the content data object and its associated information objects that the archive manages are contained within conceptual structures called 'information packages'. The OAIS model defines three types of information packages: *Submission information packages* (SIP) are used to transport information from the producer or creator to the archive; *archival information packages* (AIPs) are used to store information in the archive; and *dissemination information packages* (DIPs) are used to transport information from the archive to users.

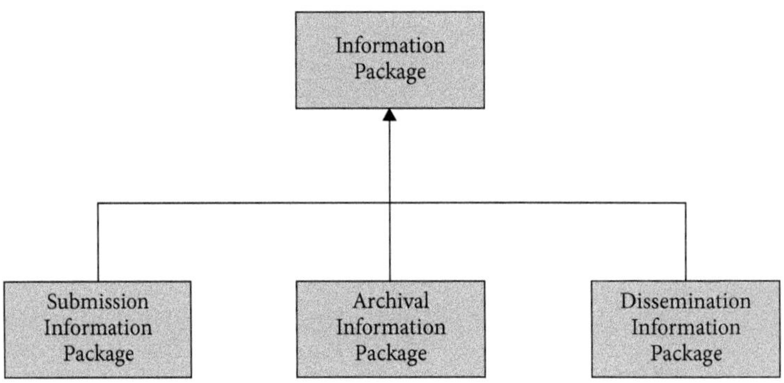

Figure 7.1. OAIS Functional Entities (CCSDS 2012)

The OAIS functional model (see Fiure 7.2) contains six functional entities: 'ingest', 'archival storage', 'data management', 'access', 'preservation planning', and 'administration'. Each entity contains a set of tasks or responsibilities to the data flow in the archive, and represents a conceptual area rather than how roles and systems should necessarily be implemented by an organization. This chapter explains each of these functional areas in more detail below, with the exception of 'administration', which oversees the overall operation of the archive.

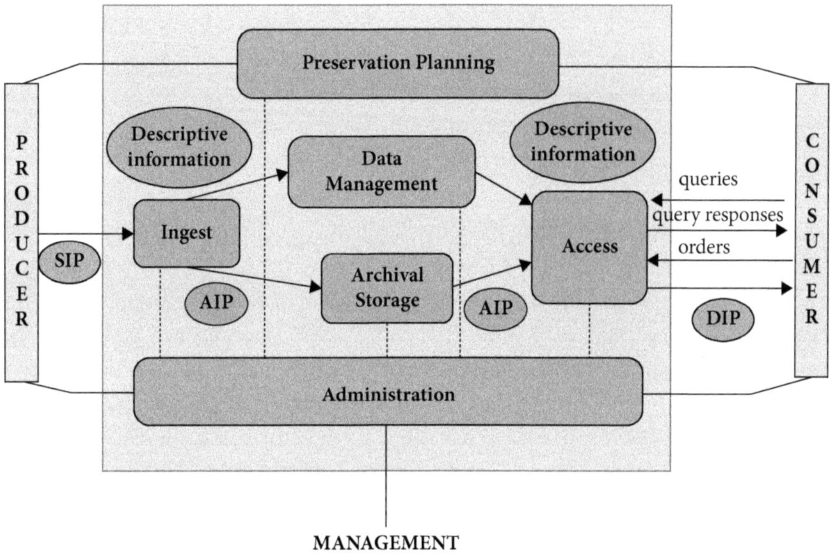

Figure 7.2. OAIS Information Package Taxonomy (CCSDS 2012)

It is important to stress that the OAIS reference model provides the terminology to describe the information that the archive manages and outlines *what* an archive should do, but does not dictate *how* its functions should be carried out, which can vary widely by archive or organization. The most appropriate preservation strategies for any given archive will depend on its circumstances, the nature of its collections, and its intended users. For this reason, this chapter gives examples of implementations across different types of organizations wherever possible. The key to any approach is that it is planned, consistently applied, and documented to ensure effective long-term preservation. Moreover, preservation activities can take place on a spectrum depending on available resources, and organizations can advance over time towards higher standards of care.

4. The Process of Digital Preservation: Ingest

Ingest refers to the function that receives or collects content (the submission information package, or SIP) from a content producer and prepares the content for storage and management in the archive. It is at 'ingest' where the most active work to transform the content is performed to create the archival information package, or AIP, for storage. The activities at this stage include obtaining custody of the content, collecting, and extracting metadata needed for preservation, checking for integrity and completeness, and packaging.

4.1 Understanding Intended Users and Uses

Organizations new to the archival process sometimes jump directly to thinking about tools and technologies for accomplishing ingest tasks. However, identifying the appropriate tools requires first making decisions about what to collect and how it will be collected and processed, and then codifying these decisions into policies so that they are enacted consistently. This decision-making is the most important, and often the most challenging, part of the ingest process. To make ingest decisions, the archive needs to have a clear idea of the intended users and uses of the information. The intended uses will determine what the archive needs to acquire (in terms of content, metadata, and rights), what properties of the digital object must be maintained, and what types of normalization (e.g. reformatting or re-organization of files) are acceptable or needed.

Issues with evidence in the ICC's *Bemba et al* case illustrate the value of intentional collecting and ingest processes. During the trial, the prosecution sought to introduce screenshots of a Facebook page as linkage evidence. The prosecution argued that the 'documents are open source materials from Facebook and, thus, *prima facie* authentic and reliable. The authenticity and reliability of these documents is further corroborated by their general appearance, which bears indicia that they originate from Facebook ...'[17]. The defence challenged this assertion, arguing that the screenshots could not be taken as prima facie evidence, since screenshots of a Facebook page are neither the Facebook page nor do they 'originate from' Facebook. The defence argued that the screenshots neither show whether the images are actually from Facebook, nor who actually created the profile page, nor when and how the screenshots were taken, nor who appears in the screenshots.[18]

Such a challenge could be mitigated if the evidence had been collected and preserved by an archive following appropriate ingest policies based on an understanding of the intended users' needs for evidence of authenticity. For example, instead of screenshots, the archive instead could have collected an interactive and digitally signed record of an interaction with the Facebook page on a given date (possibly using a web archiving tool like webrecorder.io),[19] saved it in Web ARChive (WARC) file format, and also obtained metadata directly from Facebook via its public API. It might have also required the person who captured the data to provide other contextual information corroborating its meaning and authenticity. This solution is only an example of one possible approach that would have captured more of the original properties of the Facebook page; the most appropriate approach would require an understanding of the needs of intended users in relation to the type of information being collected.

4.2 Significant Properties

'Significant properties' is a useful digital preservation concept for thinking about the needs of intended users and how objects should subsequently be captured and preserved. The term 'significant properties' refers to the technical, intellectual, structural, or aesthetic characteristics of an object that need to be preserved to ensure the object's accessibility, usability, interpretability, and authenticity to an archive's *designated community* (the OAIS term for an archive's defined set of intended users).[20] Importantly, significance is neither fixed nor inherent to the

[17] *Prosecutor v Jean-Pierre Bemba Gombo, Aimé Kilolo Musamba, Jean-Jacques Mangenda Kabongo, Fidèle Babala Wandu and Narcisse Arido* (Prosecution's Fifth Request for the Admission of Evidence from the Bar Table) ICC-01/05-01/13 (30 November 2015).

[18] ibid.

[19] Webrecorder (https://webrecorder.io/) is an open-source web archiving service developed by Rhizome that captures dynamic elements and preserves page performance.

[20] Gareth Knight, 'Framework for the Definition of Significant Properties' InSPECT Project (2008).

object. It is the designated community that determines which characteristics of an object are significant, and the properties of an object considered significant can vary according to different designated communities. For example, a pdf of a letter originally written in Microsoft Word (.doc) might be considered acceptable as an authentic preservation copy for a particular designated community, so long as the text and author's signature look the same to the naked eye. To this designated community then, the intellectual content and appearance of the document are seen as 'significant', while the file format and functionality are not. In another situation, to another designated community, file format and functionality might be considered highly significant. For example, a screenshot may be considered an unacceptable representation of a dynamic webpage for a particular designated community, because its members need to have content that reloads and hyperlinks that can be clicked and followed.

An archive needs to determine which significant properties of the objects it preserves are important to its designated community and shape its ingest and preservation policies around those properties. The InSPECT Project of the former UK Arts and Humanities Data Service usefully classifies significant properties into five general categories: *content* (e.g. the intellectual material, like words on a page), *context* (e.g. creator, creation date, and other metadata), *rendering* (the way the visual or audio elements look and sound), *structure* (the way pieces of content are related to each other, like pages or attachments), and *behavior* (the way the object functions or interacts).[21] This categorization can be used as a template for archives to analyse and identify the properties of the information it is responsible for preserving, to assess the relative importance of each property with its designated community, and to shape its policies with this evaluation in mind.

4.3 Ingest Policies

When working directly with known content producers or submitters, archives typically use *submission agreements*. These outline what content data and metadata the content producer will submit to the archive, how the submission should be structured, and a schedule for submissions. Submission agreements also transfer sufficient custody rights from the producer to the archive so that the archive can perform preservation duties and provide access. Finally, submission agreements outline what evidence of authenticity the archive needs from the producer, and if the content is particularly proprietary or difficult to interpret, what additional representation information needs to be submitted so that the content can be rendered and understood.

In the case of archives that collect open source information, content producers may often be difficult to reach. Archives might collect content indirectly, without the producer's knowledge, and without acquiring any rights. In such situations, the archive is in a sense submitting content to itself and can create an internal policy that covers the same elements as a submission agreement. In place of a transfer of rights, the archive in this instance can outline the risks associated with not obtaining rights and how it will manage them.

It is worth considering, in situations where an archive cannot reach or negotiate a submission agreement with a content producer, whether there is another archive better

[21] ibid.

positioned to collect and preserve that content and provide access to it. For example, a local archive with direct connections to a content producer may be able to acquire higher quality content with a shorter chain of custody, more complete metadata, and clearer rights than an archive simply scraping copies off the internet and with no connection to that producer. Cooperation among archives can reduce duplicated efforts and result in better preservation.

Following submission or collection, the archive needs to check the submitted objects, possibly normalize them into a pre-selected format or otherwise transform them, and package them for archival storage, following an *ingest policy*. Ingest policies define what aspects or properties of the content cannot be altered in the ingest process for the content to remain authentic. They define the make-up and structure of the AIP, such as its format and documentation requirements, and outline the procedures for generating the AIP.

4.4 Ingest Procedures

As an illustration of ingest procedures, here is a sample pre-packaging workflow for a small organization collecting video from field investigators, using primarily free and open-source tools:

1. Before starting, the archivist has anti-virus software and a firewall enabled on her computer.
2. In accordance with their submission agreement, the archivist downloads materials from a file sharing site and extracts a zipped folder containing video files and a document with specific descriptive information from the field investigator.
3. The archivist scans for viruses and quarantines files as necessary.
4. The archivist checks the hashes of downloaded files against hashes provided by the field investigator to confirm integrity and completeness of transfer, using a utility like md5deep.[22]
5. The archivist examines and validates the formats of the submitted content against the submission policy. She may employ a file identification tool like Siegfried,[23] a policy checker like MDQC[24] or MediaConch,[25] or spot-check the video files, using a video player like VLC.[26]
6. The archivist removes identified temporary cache files, like thumbs.db and ds_store files, which will not be archived, as per the ingest policy.
7. The archivist removes special and reserved characters from filenames that cause problems for the archives' operating system and software, as per the ingest policy.

[22] Md5deep and hashdeep (http://md5deep.sourceforge.net/) are open-source programs developed by Jesse Kornblum to compute and match hashes.

[23] Siegfried (https://www.itforarchivists.com/siegfried) is an open-source file format identification tool developed by Richard Lehane that implements various file format registries.

[24] MDQC (https://www.weareavp.com/products/mdqc/) is an open-source utility developed by AVP that reads metadata in a file and compares it against a set of user-defined rules.

[25] MediaConch (https://mediaarea.net/MediaConch) is an open-source project developed by MediaArea that incorporates an implementation checker, policy checker, reporter, and fixer that targets preservation-level audiovisual files (specifically Matroska, LPCM, FFV1 files).

[26] VLC Media Player (https://www.videolan.org/index.html) is an open-source multimedia player developed by VideoLAN.

8. The archivist does not alter the originally submitted files but creates transcoded copies of the videos in a web-streamable format, which will be used for access later on, using a tool like FFMPEG.[27]
9. The archivist exports technical metadata from the video files, using a tool like MediaInfo,[28] which is useful for preservation planning and data management functions.
10. The files are now ready for archival packaging.

The last task of the ingest function is to generate the AIP. An AIP must contain the content that is the target of preservation (e.g. the video, images, audio, or text) and information needed for its preservation. This includes reference, provenance, context, access rights, and *fixity*[29] information about the content. The archive also generates reference and descriptive information about the package so that it can be retrieved. The components of the package can, but do not have to be, stored in the same physical location so long as the package can point to the different locations where its various components are stored.

In practical terms, an AIP could be as simple as a set of related content files, stored in a folder with a unique identifying folder name, that is linked to a metadata record in a spreadsheet using its identifier (it is considered not ideal to store key information like identifiers solely in folder or directory names, as these can be lost during migrations). AIPs can be made much more complex, however, to facilitate more reliable identification, interpretation, validation, authentication, and use.

Archivematica, a well-supported, free, and open-source digital preservation system that enables users to perform ingest steps within a web-based application, implements a more elaborate standards-based AIP structure. The Archivematica AIP follows the BagIt specification,[30] a standardized hierarchical directory structure and set of documents used to package archival files (Artefactual n.d.). As an openly documented standard, tools have been created for BagIt that allow archives easily to validate, or check the integrity and completeness, of 'bagged' objects. The Archivematica AIP also contains a METS XML document,[31] which describes how the data objects (e.g. original files, transcoded copies, documentation, and metadata) within the package are related to each other, and what actions have been taken on the original files within the application.

5. The Process of Digital Preservation: Archival Storage

Once the AIP is generated, the package moves on to the archival storage function. In a preservation context, storage is an active function involving managed tasks and responsibilities. Storage encompasses all the mechanisms (local or remote) for storing, maintaining, and retrieving digital content. It includes permanent storage, in which storage media plays

[27] FFMPEG (https://www.ffmpeg.org/) is an open-source framework for encoding and decoding multimedia.

[28] MediaInfo (https://mediaarea.net/MediaInfo) is an open-source tool developed by MediaArea to display technical and tag metadata for video and audio files.

[29] Fixity information refers to information such as hashes or digital signatures that are used to determine whether content has been altered.

[30] BagIt (https://tools.ietf.org/html/draft-kunze-bagit-16) is a hierarchical file layout convention for storing and transferring of digital content published by the Network Working Group of the Internet Engineering Task Force (IETF).

[31] METS (http://www.loc.gov/standards/mets/) is a metadata standard for describing the structure and administration of digital objects, developed by the US Library of Congress.

a role, but also storage hierarchy management, media replacement, error checking, fixity checking, disaster recovery, and locating and returning stored objects. The archival storage function ensures the persistence of intact and authentic objects, and the ability to find and retrieve them over time, regardless of their physical location.

5.1 Storage Media Degradation

The challenge of archival storage is that media degrades over time. Archives can somewhat mitigate the risk of storage failure by choosing more durable types of media; however, any particular storage device will eventually have a defect, wear out, or randomly fail. A cloud storage provider, Backblaze, has provided annual statistics on hard drive failure based on the thousands of drives they employ in their services. It has determined that approximately 12 per cent of its drives fail after three years of use and estimated that, after six years, 50 per cent of its drives will have failed.[32] Although many hard drives may well exceed a six-year lifespan, many others will not. In the absence of a good storage strategy, storage media failure can lead to data becoming irretrievable.

Even without total failure, data errors or file corruption can occur as storage media decay. It is therefore important for the archive to continually monitor its storage infrastructure and the fixity of stored files, such as by checking their hashes on a regular basis. Hashes are calculations that can be run on any type of digital file to generate a fixed-length alphanumeric string. This string will remain the same every time the calculation is run as long as the file does not change. Errors and loss can also occur during data transfer, so it is also important to check file fixity whenever data is moved between storage media.

5.2 Back-up and Recovery

After discovering loss or errors, an archive must recover the original data from back-up copies. This requires that the archive has previously backed up or duplicated the data in a separate location. The back-up strategy often cited by information technology experts is to have at least three copies of data, stored on at least two different types of storage, with at least one copy geographically separated from the others. For example, an archive might have its primary copy stored on an in-house disk array, like a NAS (network-attached storage) or SAN (storage area network); its first back-up copy on LTO (linear tape-open) tape, also stored in-house; and its second back-up copy stored and managed offsite by a trusted partner organization or by a third-party cloud storage provider, like Amazon Glacier. As well as the data protection provided by using different types of media and an offsite location, developing a hierarchical storage arrangement also helps to balance cost and throughput. The most expensive storage is typically the highest-speed and most available storage, like a disk array, which makes it most appropriate for an archive's primary copy. Lower-cost storage like LTO tapes or low-access third-party storage services are slower and less available, so more appropriate for back-up copies that do not need to be accessed as frequently.

32 Brian Beach, 'How Long Do Disk Drives Last?' *Backblaze Blog* (12 November 2013) https://www.backblaze.com/blog/how-long-do-disk-drives-last/ accessed 29 December 2018.

5.3 Storage Media Obsolescence

Regardless of how durable any storage medium may be, the medium is at risk of becoming obsolete over time, which would make it difficult or impossible to retrieve stored data from it. Storage media becomes obsolete when the hardware needed to access the data is realistically no longer available or can no longer be maintained. Floppy disk, for example, was once a commonplace storage medium that is now obsolete. Meanwhile, CD-R and DVD-R discs used in many courtrooms are on their way to becoming obsolete. Even if a storage medium itself, like a hard drive, is not obsolete, the obsolescence of other hardware that it depends on may cause problems; for example, if a NAS device malfunctions and support or replacement parts are no longer available, it may be difficult to repair the unit and to access the data stored on the attached drives, especially if the data is distributed in a RAID (redundant array of independent disks) managed by the device.

Storage media obsolescence may be unavoidable, but it can be planned for and managed. The LTO Consortium, for example, provides a roadmap for planned releases of new generations of LTO drives and cartridges, a format designed for use by archives and for backup.[33] Archives can therefore better anticipate when their hardware and storage media will become obsolete, and plan to upgrade ahead of time. LTO further mitigates data irretrievability by being an open specification, meaning that hardware and media from different manufacturers should be compatible, and all LTO drives can read cartridges up to two generations prior to its own.

5.4 Storage Media Refreshment

To protect data from storage degradation and obsolescence, archives typically 'refresh' or copy content from old storage media to new storage media. Copying to storage media of the same type is usually a straightforward process, although the archive should anticipate the copying time and resources needed to perform and check the copy. Rsync is a commonly used open-source utility for copying and checking copies.[34] When an archive does not have the option to refresh to the same type of storage media, it may need to take additional steps to maintain retrievability. For example, if copying files from obsoleting DVD-R discs to a new hard disk array, an archive will need to update its pointers to where content is physically and logically located, and its methods for accessing the content.

More complicated are instances where it is not possible to copy the content bit-for-bit to a new storage medium, and some transformation of the content is required. For example, many broadcast and other archives store content on Digital Betacam (DigiBeta), a Sony digital videotape format once popular as a broadcast delivery format and used in archives as a preservation master format. Since the advent of file-based video formats, however, videotape has become largely obsolete. In 2016, Sony announced that it was ceasing production

[33] This roadmap, published by Hewlett Packard Enterprise, IBM and Quantum, can be found on the Ultrium LTO website (https://www.lto.org/technology/what-is-lto-technology/).

[34] Rsync (https://download.samba.org/pub/rsync/rsync.html) was originally written by Andrew Tridgell and Paul Mackerras, and is currently maintained by Wayne Davison.

of ½" videotape players and recorders, including DigiBeta.[35] Content stored on DigiBeta tapes therefore needs to be transferred to new media before there are no more viable playback machines. Complicating the process, however, is that DigiBeta uses a closed and proprietary compression algorithm that makes the content essentially unplayable if captured off the tape in its native encoding. The generally accepted preservation practice is thus to decompress DigiBeta video and save it in an uncompressed format. Preservation digitization and transcoding involves its own set of time-consuming workflows, and specialized hardware and software.

5.5 Cloud Storage

Because storage requires ongoing monitoring, management, and expense, some archives outsource their storage functions to third parties, such as commercial cloud storage services, non-profits like Internet Archive (whose mission is to provide free access to all knowledge), or to institutional repository networks. When outsourcing storage, an archive should consider various factors. First, the archive should ensure that the storage provider can accommodate the archive's requirements in terms of storage capacity, accessibility and retrieval, security, and reporting. Secondly, the archive must be able to trust the storage provider. This may involve qualitative considerations like the archive's relationship with the provider, or more quantifiable evidence of trustworthiness such as the metrics outlined in the *Audit and Certification of Trustworthy Digital Repositories*, an international standard that sets a high bar for assessing archives. Thirdly, the cost of services including upload, storage, and retrieval must be affordable in order to be sustainable. Finally, it is important for the archive to review the termination policies to understand how services may end; how the service provider will return the materials and metadata, and delete its copies; what termination costs are involved; and the timeline for termination.

5.6 Maintaining Authenticity

Transformations like digitization or media migration that are necessary for preservation can sometimes involve changing the digital object. The object's authenticity—its being what it purports to be—can be maintained as long as the transformation preserves the significant properties of the object, and the transformation is adequately documented. As discussed in the ingest section above, the bar for acceptable transformation and documentation is not fixed; the archive's designated community determines which properties are significant and what evidence of authenticity is sufficient. With an understanding of its intended users and uses, the archive must choose transformation techniques and workflows that preserve an object's significant properties. Considerations might include, for example, the audiovisual quality of the transformed object compared with the original object; the structure of the transformed object compared to the original object; and the transparency or reversibility

[35] 'Video Format Timeline' *Museum of Obsolete Media* (28 May 2014) https://obsoletemedia.org/digital-betacam/ accessed 29 December 2018.

of the transformation. The archive documents the transformation as *preservation metadata*, which is discussed in the next section.

6. The Process of Digital Preservation: Data Management

The data management function of an archive encompasses the activities to populate, maintain, and retrieve information that describes and identifies the objects in the archive, as well as administrative data needed for the day-to-day operation of the archive.[36] Data can therefore include not only descriptive catalogues for finding archived objects, but also user data, archive policies, and documentation, preservation process history, and security information. Data management activities include creating and administering databases, performing queries for access purposes, generating reports for the archive, and keeping the data accurate and up-to-date.

6.1 Types of Metadata

The information that describes and identifies the objects in the archive is especially important because it enables the archive's intended users to access the collection. The archive must therefore specify and provide at least a minimum set of information, or *metadata*. There are various types of metadata that an archive should consider. *Descriptive metadata* includes information like title, author, and subject that enables users to discover and understand the object. *Technical metadata* includes information like format and file size that enables machines to render the object for users. *Preservation metadata* includes information like hashes and actions taken on objects that enables archives to maintain the authenticity of the object for the user. *Rights metadata* includes information like copyright and terms of use that enables archives and users to understand how the content can be accessed and shared. *Structural metadata* includes information about the sequencing of objects or relationships between parts, like page numbers and a table of contents, that enables users to navigate the content.

6.2 Metadata Standards

While each archive needs to determine the appropriate set of metadata, or *metadata schema*, for providing access to its designated community, many communities have fortunately developed *metadata standards* and guidelines that can be shared among and be adapted by various archives. Well-designed community-supported metadata standards are useful not only for saving each archive from the task of developing its own scheme from scratch; they are also useful for ensuring a common semantic understanding of the metadata within a community, and for promoting technical interoperability and collaboration among archives. Archives using the same metadata standards can more easily integrate their metadata

[36] 'Reference Model for an Open Archival Information System (OAIS)' (n 16).

in shared technical systems or create federated discovery platforms that enable users to search multiple sources of information simultaneously. The European Union's e-justice portal, for example, uses a common European case law identifier (ECLI) to facilitate a 'correct and unequivocal citation of judgments' and the Dublin Core metadata schema to 'make it easier to understand and find case law' in the portal (European Commission 2017).

Some metadata standards define a *metadata structure* or data model, including metadata entities, elements, or attributes, and the relationships between them. Metadata structure standards may focus on particular metadata types, such as preservation metadata, or on the metadata needs of particular communities, such as television broadcasters. An archive might adopt multiple metadata structure standards to cover a range of metadata types and for the different kinds of materials it holds, such as audiovisual recordings or books.[37] Archives may also have additional data elements they wish to track that are not part of any metadata structure standard, although these elements may be less interoperable.

As well as specifying structure, metadata standards can also define *content rules*, such as controlled vocabularies, authority files (i.e. established forms for naming entities), classifications, and semantic rules. Using documented and shared content rules helps to ensure that terms are used consistently by cataloguers and that their meaning can be properly understood within the community. For example, if tagging human rights violations by a typology of acts, it is important to have a definition of each violation and know when a term should be applied. HURIDOCS, an organization that supports human rights organizations with information management and documentation, for example, shares forty-eight terminologies relevant to documenting human rights in its *Micro-thesauri*.[38] The United Nations similarly provides several terminology databases to facilitate subject analysis and document retrieval.[39] Archives may also point to glossaries or typologies that are not explicitly metadata content standards, but that nonetheless provide reliable and stable definitions of terms for a community.

6.3 Creating and Maintaining Data

Beyond implementing a metadata schema, there is much involved in the day-to-day data management work of administering, populating, updating, and querying databases, and ensuring that the associations between stored objects and their metadata are maintained over time. Cataloguing is one of the most time-consuming and skill-intensive parts of the archiving process. Many archives without dedicated cataloguing staff or volunteers find it challenging to keep up, resulting in backlogs of undescribed materials that remain difficult to access. In such situations, it may be preferable for an archive to use a simpler metadata

[37] Dublin Core, PREMIS, MODS, and PBCore are just a few examples of metadata structure standards. Dublin Core (http://dublincore.org/) is a deliberately simple general-purpose standard for digital objects. PREMIS (https://www.loc.gov/standards/premis/) is designed for preservation metadata. PBCore https://pbcore.org/) is designed for audiovisual materials in the broadcast community. MODS http://www.loc.gov/standards/mods/) is designed for library bibliographic metadata.

[38] Bert Verstappen, 'Micro-Thesauri: A Tool for Documenting Human Rights Violations' *HURIDOCS* (7 July 2010) /resource/micro-thesauri/ accessed 29 December 2018.

[39] Ariel Lebowitz, 'Research Guides: UN Resources: Terminology Databases' //research.un.org/en/un-resources/terminology accessed 29 December 2018.

schema, requiring only that a handful of fields be populated, and/or describing groupings of objects at a higher level, even if it provides less detailed description and fewer access points to individual items in the collection. The archive can also design workflows and negotiate with stakeholders to obtain metadata from external sources, especially content creators, or automate the creation of certain metadata.

Automatic metadata creation can be straightforward or complex. On the simple end, an archive might use built-in command-line tools like ls or stat (Mac), or dir (Windows) to output basic file system attributes, like time stamps. For scanned or photographed text, an archive might use an open-source optical character recognition (OCR) tool like Tesseract[40] to generate machine-readable and searchable text. For audiovisual media, an archive might use open-source tools like MediaInfo or Exiftool[41] to read and export technical and other metadata from files. On the more complex end, technologies that can infer information and that can recognize images and speech using artificial intelligence are quickly emerging. Outputting and generating metadata using simple or complex tools can be an indispensable time-saver for archives; however, at present, creating and assuring metadata that is meaningful, contextual, and accurate, and which takes into consideration potential ethical and security issues still requires significant human intervention.

Finally, the archive's choice of software tools for metadata storage and delivery will have an impact on workflows and costs. Some smaller archives manage with spreadsheets or off-the-shelf database applications. Archives with more resources and development support can implement databases using open-source solutions like Collective Access, ResourceSpace, or Access to Memory (AtoM).[42] Other larger archives may choose to build their own custom database solutions, or work with a vendor to implement a digital asset management system.

6.4 Developing and Documenting Metadata Schema

In the absence of existing metadata standards that meet the needs of an archive, an archive may decide to create and document its own schema. The International Organization for Standardization (ISO) Archives/records management committee provides some useful guidelines in its document, 'Building a metadata schema: where to start'.[43] In these guidelines, the committee strongly recommends that archives first ask themselves: 'Is it necessary to create a new metadata schema, or are there already existing metadata schemas which can be adapted for use?' Indeed, there is an enormous number of existing metadata schema, many for niche communities,[44] and it is sensible to consider first adapting what has already been painstakingly developed. Adaptations might include customized vocabularies or

[40] Tesseract (https://github.com/tesseract-ocr/tesseract) is an open-source optical character recognition engine developed by Google.

[41] Exiftool (https://www.sno.phy.queensu.ca/~phil/exiftool/) is an open-source tool developed by Phil Harvey to read and write metadata in multimedia files.

[42] Collective Access (https://www.collectiveaccess.org/), Resource Space (https://www.resourcespace.com/), and Access to Memory (https://www.accesstomemory.org/) are open-source applications for archival description, management, and access.

[43] 'Building a Metadata Schema: Where to Start' (National Information Standards Organization 2008) https://committee.iso.org/files/live/sites/tc46sc11/files/documents/N800R1%20Where%20to%20start-advice%20on%20creating%20a%20metadata%20schema.pdf.

[44] For an incomplete list see Digital Curation Center, 'List of Metadata Standards, http://www.dcc.ac.uk/resources/metadata-standards/list?page=1 accessed 4 September 2018.

syntax rules, or refinements of elements. The ISO committee recommends that new schema only be built when there are none that adequately serve the archive's sector, and preferably by leaders or authorities in that sector who can support it over time. Developing schema can be complicated, and if it is intended for wider adoption, the process should incorporate input from all relevant stakeholders, including archives, user communities, and content creators in the given sector.

Metadata schema need to be specified and documented to be of most value. This documentation is sometimes referred to as a 'data dictionary' or 'data element registry' and provides a unified view of all the concepts, terms, and values used to represent data. Ideally, the schema documentation is published in formats that it can be understood and interpreted by both humans and machines, such as XML. The ISO data management and interchange working group provides detailed guidance on the creation of data dictionaries and registries,[45] but in general they usually include:

- A general description of the schema, including its author and maintainer, version number, publication date, its intended users and uses, and what information or processes the schema describes.
- A glossary, if needed.
- A description and/or graphical representation of the overall schema structure, i.e. entities and their relationships, with a definition of each entity.
- A list of attributes or data elements, including for each:
  - The entity/class it belongs to.
  - Its name and definition.
  - Its information type, data type, format, and/or unit of measure.
  - Its permissible values (e.g. controlled vocabulary, range of numbers, etc).
  - Its syntax or other data entry rules.
  - Its obligation and occurrence constraints.
  - A sample valid entry.
  - Business rules, such as where the information should come from.

7. The Process of Digital Preservation: Access

The access function is the interface between the archive and its users, enabling them to discover the existence, description, location, and availability of the archive's holdings. Those serving the access function receive user queries, return responses, and coordinate with the archive's other functional areas to authorize, prepare, and deliver content in ways that are demonstrably authentic and usable. As discussed previously, the standards for what makes content authentic and usable can vary greatly, depending on the archive's designated community. For example, a local grassroots organization with first-hand knowledge of a situation may need different information to interpret and assess the authenticity of an archived document than a journalist or human rights investigator from outside the community.

[45] 'Home Page for ISO/IEC 11179 Information Technology—Metadata Registries' (*Metadata Standards*) http://metadata-standards.org/11179/ accessed 29 December 2018.

While access is a key function of the archive, the access interface of an archive is sometimes conflated with the archive as a whole in popular perception. This confusion is understandable, given that the interface is what users see, but it causes some fundamental misconceptions about archives that can affect decisions on data preservation. For example, many users think of a video sharing platform like YouTube as an 'archive' because it performs an access function, and they upload content with an expectation that their videos will be preserved over time. However, platforms like YouTube make no assertion or commitment to doing preservation, and videos can be lost—through take-downs, account termination, or other unforeseen events. The mistaken conflation of access portal with archive may also affect an organization's understanding of what resources are involved in building and maintaining an archive. For example, some organizations may embark on archive projects, only planning the front-facing website or access portal and without allocating adequate resources for collection and ingest, archival storage, metadata management, and ongoing preservation. This can result in unexpected costs and lost collections.

7.1 Access Copies

The ultimate purpose of the access function is to generate and deliver a dissemination information package (DIP) to the user. In some cases, the archive's DIP may be identical to its AIP, but in other situations—for reasons of security, say, or privacy protection—the archive may want to transform the content in some way before making it accessible to the user. The processing work to generate the DIP can be substantial. The UN International Criminal Tribunal for Rwanda (ICTR), for example, undertook a massive initiative spanning several years to redact selected audiovisual records of the tribunal's trial proceedings, which included testimony of protected witnesses and other confidential information, so those records could then be made public (Communication Cluster—ERSPS 2010). After the project digitized the original tapes for preservation, it selected and redacted a portion and produced high-quality access copies for news agencies, broadcasters, and film-makers, and lower-quality access copies for researchers, academics, legal professionals, and the general public. In the end, of the approximately 40,000 hours of audiovisual recordings generated from the trial proceedings, 3,000 hours of audio and 6,000 hours of video were selected and redacted for public access (President and the Prosecutor of the ICTR 2015). The work involved selection and prioritization, redaction using the Final Cut Pro video editing software package, quality checking, assembly of audio tracks in different languages into each video file, export of the redacted recordings into access formats, and verification of metadata.[46]

Most access projects will not have the scale of the ICTR archives, but may still require some processing to create DIPs that are distinct from the stored AIPs. For example, a small organization with its own video archive may partner with a larger collecting institution, such as a university library, to deposit its collection for long-term preservation and scholarly access. The DIP that the organization generates to send to the university library might contain the video files in their original format, unchanged from the AIP, but only a selection of the metadata that would be relevant to scholars, encoded in an exchangeable format like

[46] 'Report on the Completion Strategy of the International Criminal Tribunal for Rwanda as at 5 November 2014' (President and the Prosecutor of the International Criminal Tribunal for Rwanda 2014).

XML. The organization may also generate additional metadata for the DIP, such as access restrictions it expects the university library to place on the content, and contact information for the organization. Alternatively, an organization may want to upload a selection of their videos to a publicly accessible platform like YouTube. In this case, the processing to create the DIP may be done in part by the organization—for example, adding subtitles and blurring faces—and in part by YouTube, which automatically creates multiple web-streamable copies of uploaded videos in different formats.

8. The Process of Digital Preservation: Preservation Planning

The role of the preservation planning function in an archive is to monitor changes in technologies and in the needs of the archive's designated community, and to develop preservation strategies that respond to those shifts in order to keep content sustainable and accessible. While all archives can draw from established digital preservation models and standards as guides, each must develop its own plan of action appropriate to its structure, staffing, financial resources, and intended users and uses. There is no single correct approach to fit all situations, and approaches can and should evolve over time. Preservation activities can take place on a spectrum, and organizations can progress over time towards higher standards. The key is that the strategies are planned, documented, and consistently applied.

8.1 Monitoring Technology and the Designated Community

Good preservation planning is based on anticipating and understanding changes in the external environment. Technology change can affect the file formats, storage media, and software tools used in the archive and in the archive's computing environment. Technology monitoring is often done in an ad-hoc manner, by keeping up-to-date with emerging technologies and developments in the field of digital preservation. The Digital Preservation Coalition (DPC) in the UK, for example, publishes a series of useful Technology Watch Reports that identify developments in standards and tools relevant to digital preservation.[47] There are also numerous international conferences and associations within the digital preservation community, such as iPres and the Preservation and Archiving Special Interest Group (PASIG); and in the audiovisual archiving community, such as the Association of Moving Image Archivists (AMIA) and the International Association of Sound and Audiovisual Archives (IASA). In any case, a good strategy for strengthening an archive's 'immunity' from technological obsolescence is to use, whenever possible, well-documented and widely adopted open standards, formats, and tools with the fewest proprietary dependencies.[48]

[47] 'Technology Watch Reports: Digital Preservation Coalition' https://www.dpconline.org/knowledge-base/tech-watch-reports accessed 29 December 2018.

[48] 'Sustainability of Digital Formats: Planning for Library of Congress Collections' (*Library of Congress*) https://www.loc.gov/preservation/digital/formats/index.html accessed 29 December 2018.

The way that users in the designated community access information will also inevitably change over time, such as the shift from watching videos on DVD to web streaming. A designated community's criteria for evaluating the authenticity of information may also change over time. It is possible, for example, that as synthetic videos (anecdotally known as 'deepfakes')[49] become easier to produce with accessible consumer tools, a designated community may come to require more or different types of evidence to be satisfied of a video's authenticity. This may require the archive to renegotiate how content is submitted or what metadata it needs to obtain from content creators, and how the archive documents its own preservation actions. In the longer-term, a designated community's underlying knowledge base may also shift; for example, its awareness of particular historical events, its comprehension of a language, or its grasp of how certain objects function or what they are used for. At that point, the archive may need to provide additional information so that users can appropriately interpret and better understand the content on a basic level.

8.2 Making Progress over Time

Archives, no matter how large or small, work with finite resources. The ideal preservation strategies may not always be realistically achievable at a given time. This should not, however, deter archives from doing what they can and taking actions now that will allow them to take further action later on. This progressive approach to building and enhancing digital preservation strategies over time is expressed in the 'Levels of Digital Preservation' guidelines of the US National Digital Stewardship Alliance (NDSA). The first of the four levels, called 'Protect Your Data', defines the minimum preservation actions needed to ensure that objects remain intact; for example, storage, back-up, file fixity information, basic information security, and an inventory of objects and their locations.[50] Each subsequent level in the model builds on the previous one with more complex actions, with each level improving the ability of data to withstand threats to its availability, identity, persistence, renderability, understandability, and authenticity. This model can be applied to an organization's entire preservation approach, or to different classes of objects within an archive according to their relative value. It is also a useful tool for archives to assess their current level of preservation, and to think about their next steps.

The above-mentioned *Audit and Certification of Trustworthy Digital Repositories* (colloquially referred to as 'TDR' or ISO 16363) is a guideline on the high-end of the spectrum of measuring compliance with digital preservation best practice.[51] TDR is an international standard that provides criteria for measuring an organization's trustworthiness in providing reliable long-term access to managed digital resources. It includes a complex list of metrics within the categories of organizational infrastructure, digital object management, and

[49] Deepfakes are generated using a form of artificial intelligence called deep learning to synthesize audiovisual media that appears realistic. The 'Synthesizing Obama' project is one well-known example in which University of Washington researchers generated videos of Barack Obama and lip-synced them with pre-existing audio (http://grail.cs.washington.edu/projects/AudioToObama/).

[50] Megan Phillips and others, 'The NDSA Levels of Digital Preservation: An Explanation and Uses' [2013] National Digital Stewardship Alliance 7.

[51] 'Reference Model for an Open Archival Information System (OAIS)' (n 16).

infrastructure and security risk management. The TDR criteria sets a very high bar even for large collecting institutions, and few repositories actually go through the process of audit and certification. However, the metrics can serve as a useful checklist for any organization performing a self-assessment and they provide a detailed breakdown of an ideal environment for digital preservation.

9. Conclusion

Open source information, on digital media and online, exists in a precarious state. It is far too easily decontextualized, lost, deleted, corrupted, or put out of reach. If open source information is to remain accessible and usable for human rights research and legal accountability, it needs to be actively preserved. On the one hand, preservation requires significant dedicated resources and professionally trained archivists. On the other hand, concern for and knowledge about preservation needs to spread beyond its traditional confines to all the places where potential documentary evidence is being produced and collected and is at risk of slipping through the digital cracks. Increasingly, archiving and preservation are being practised within non-archival organizations, big and small, that understand the need, are appropriately situated, and want to play a role in preserving and ensuring access to information. This decentralized growth of archives can help ensure that evidence of human rights violations, especially in places that may be currently overlooked by the international community, does not disappear before those violations can be exposed and their perpetrators brought to justice.

8

Targeted Mass Archiving of Open Source Information

A Case Study

Jeff Deutch and Niko Para

In Chapter 7, Yvonne Ng covered some of the motivations behind why archiving in general is important for human rights purposes and discussed how a file and its metadata should be processed and treated. In this chapter, we build on that discussion and introduce various data strategies, concepts, and workflows utilized by Syrian Archive for mass archiving, explaining how to ingest as much potentially relevant digital content as possible, filter that content, and transform it into usable information. A Syrian-led and initiated collective of human rights activists (including the authors of this chapter), Syrian Archive is dedicated to preserving, verifying, and investigating open-source documentation related to human rights violations committed by any side since the start of the Syrian conflict in 2011 and to developing innovative open-source tools and methods to assist in these efforts. Since its founding in 2014, Syrian Archive has created an independent, publicly accessible, and interactive archive of verified data developed out of an ingested collection of over 1.5 million data points, over twenty terabytes of video and image data, and half a million additional units of user-generated content (e.g. Tweets, Facebook posts) from more than 3,000 diverse sources.

Syrian Archive uses this data to create publicly accessible datasets and conduct investigations into human rights violations. This offers a narrative based off of digital memory: ground-up accounts and content of Syrian citizens. Additionally, Syrian Archive's large archive is available for public use by human rights defenders, journalists, or lawyers for their own investigative or narrative purposes.

Human rights reporting and documentation groups that use open source information need easily accessed, persisted (preserved long-term with a platform independence),[1] verified, and topical user-generated content from a myriad of sources. This content is sometimes hidden in plain sight in the massive stream of information that flows across social media platforms. At other times, relevant human rights content might be solely in the possession of a particular media group that does not have the technical ability to make that content available.

When open source researchers do find, collect, and ingest user-generated content, that data is often provided in formats that are not machine readable, searchable, or clustered, as

[1] Michael Day, 'The Long-Term Preservation of Web Content' in Julien Masanès (ed), *Web Archiving* (2006 edn, Springer 2006).

we discuss later in this chapter. This lack of consistent structure in data makes it difficult for researchers to cross-reference, organize, or augment the findings, reducing its potential for analysis and other documentation efforts. The underlying challenges faced by documentation efforts when collecting and preserving such data are lack of coherent strategies for categorizing and storing disparate data formats and lack of understanding in structuring such data into usable collections.

This chapter takes the following form. First, the chapter discusses the concept of targeted mass archiving as applicable to human rights practice. This includes a brief discussion of alternate models of archiving, their relative disadvantages, and why we argue that targeted mass archiving, despite some drawbacks, is one of the most powerful archiving models available for human rights purposes. The chapter then explains *how* to use targeted mass archiving to meet numerous human rights objectives. Finally, we delve into how we developed an effective data model for targeted mass archiving.

1. Targeted Mass Archiving

Targeted mass archiving involves mass collection of the above-mentioned user generated content, targeted around topical umbrellas. Targeted mass archiving draws on lessons from science and technology studies, targeted surveillance, and mass surveillance in how it approaches, works with, and processes data. A 'collect everything, never delete' approach is used where a large amount of data is collected, securely preserved and stored for further investigation. States and institutions have historically used the concepts that construct targeted mass archiving. The following examples show how large collections of data on individuals and events can offer data owners tools to affect social change, for better or worse.

In the words of Norbert Wiener, 'The most profound technologies are those that disappear. They weave themselves into the fabric of everyday life until they are indistinguishable from it.'[2] Like physical infrastructures, informational infrastructures influence how people think, act, and behave. Susan Leigh Star uses Langdon Winner's critique of technologies to identify how informational systems give rise to implicit 'master narratives' that define a standard or an ideal data subject without accounting for those who fall outside of data norms.[3] Star uses the example of a medical history form for women that not only describes but also ascribes an individual as heterosexual, monogamous, and traditional by providing:

> Blanks for 'maiden name' and 'husband's name,' blanks for 'form of birth control,' but none for other sexual practices that may have medical consequences, and no place at all for partners other than husband to be called in a medical emergency.[4]

In *The Politics of Large Numbers*, Alain Desrosières similarly writes that the history of statistics is the history of the state; when data is collected it often takes the form of

[2] Norbert Wiener, *Cybernetics, or Control and Communication in the Animal and the Machine* (MIT Press 1961).

[3] SL Star, 'The Ethnography of Infrastructure' (1999) 43 American Behavioral Scientist 377; L Winner, 'Do Artifacts Have Politics' (1980) 109 Daedalus 121.

[4] Star (n 3).

reifying dominant power structures.[5] One need look no further than the case of women's medical history forms, highlighted above, and the ways they channel potential responses, which may reflect not only something of the background of individual women but also a larger patriarchal infrastructure in which women are expected to change their name at marriage.

At a larger scale, the concept of total information awareness (a United States programme based off the concept of predictive policing[6]) offers an example of how states view the running of a country as a simple question of having enough good data for effective decision-making. Take the case of the techno-utopian Project Cybersyn, a decision-making cybernetic infrastructure Stafford Beer constructed during the socialist regime of President Salvador Allende in Chile during the 1970s.[7] The project collected data from 500 nationalized factories that was sent in via telex machines to a central IBM mainframe computer in the country's capital, Santiago. Project Cybersyn was able to communicate to factories what they should make and in which quantities, based off its large cache of data and analysis. Project Cybersyn was most helpful in October 1972 when the government was able to keep the country running and deliver food and essential materials with only 200 trucks during a strike by 40,000 truck workers. Minimal truck workers were needed because the system was able to calculate the most efficient and minimum factory inputs required to maintain standards of production.

Yet during the time that Project Cybersyn was at its peak, the chief of the East German Ministry for State Security (Stasi) Erich Mielke dreamed of digitizing and cross-referencing the data contained on 2 billion sheets of paper in order to create a system that would supposedly know everything about everyone—although Mielke failed to realize fully the project before the fall of the Berlin Wall in 1989.[8]

More recently, leaks in 2013 by former US-intelligence agency contractor turned whistleblower Edward Snowden demonstrated to the world the extent to which major states have been indiscriminately collecting, parsing, and analysing billions of pieces of personal information about human populations in real-time. The Snowden documents revealed how current technologies allow for targeted mass surveillance: large sets of information defined by the new ability for data to be collected and parsed (mass) and then selectively traced back to individual persons, topics, or entities (targeted).[9]

But an interesting phenomenon is occurring: at a time when people are more concerned than ever about the collection, aggregation, and selling of their personal information by states and technology companies (largely for surveillance and advertising purposes), some groups within civil society are increasingly relying on and developing new data infrastructures. They are using statistics defined on their own terms and in their own language to highlight social injustices for the purpose of advancing their own social movement goals. This makes possible a counter narrative to state or corporate realities and shifts the focus to

[5] Alain Desrosières, *The Politics of Large Numbers: A History of Statistical Reasoning* (Camille Naish tr, Harvard University Press 2002).

[6] Sharon Weinberger, 'Defence Research: Still in the Lead?' (2008) 451 Nature 390.

[7] Eden Medina, *Cybernetic Revolutionaries: Technology and Politics in Allende's Chile* (The MIT Press 2011).

[8] S Konopatzky, 'Zentrale Personendatenbank' in R Engelmann (ed), *Das MfS-Lexikon. Begriffe, Personen und Strukturen der Staatssicherheit der DDR* (Ch. Links Verlag, 2011).

[9] Seda Gürses, Arun Kundnani, and Joris Van Hoboken, 'Crypto and Empire: The Contradictions of Counter-Surveillance Advocacy' (2016) 38 Media, Culture & Society 576.

recognition of marginalized voices and experiences as well.[10] In short, it allows for *counting the uncounted.*

The classic example of empirical sociology comes from W. E. B. Du Bois, the scholar-activist whose 1899 empirical study, *The Philadelphia Negro*, highlighted social issues faced by Philadelphia's seventh ward.[11] Almost a century later, Pierre Bourdieu's theory of cultural reproduction demonstrated empirically the existence of intergenerational class inequality in the French education system.[12]

As previous chapters have highlighted, collecting documentation from the field to support empirically driven human rights work in order to construct and challenge government narratives about what happens in conflict zones is not always possible. However, the Tunisian Revolution of 2010–2011 marked a significant shift in the way information about conflicts is documented and shared.[13] While once journalists, non-governmental organizations (NGOs), and governments were the main sources of conflict information and narrative construction, conflicts are now increasingly being documented through user-generated born-digital content that is primarily uploaded to large corporate social media platforms such as YouTube, Facebook, and Twitter.

This mass eruption of content presents challenges for the human rights sector, which has traditionally archived content from a relatively narrow perspective and at human scale, including only content deemed immediately relevant. That limited perspective has resulted in the loss of an unknown amount of critical content, whose relevance might only be recognized years or even decades after a conflict's end. The data models presented in this chapter outline how a targeted mass archival practice might overcome this and some other traditional limitations.

2. Approaches to Archiving

Previous chapters have discussed the importance of archiving in a human rights context. This section describes three distinct operating models human rights groups partaking in archiving utilize: *investigative* archiving, *platform* archiving, and *targeted mass* archiving.

2.1 Investigative Archiving

Investigative archiving involves archiving individual units of pertinent information soon after a researcher or documentation group has discovered it. This discovery, however, may occur a significant amount of time after the content was originally uploaded, and requires the researcher to have some knowledge of the archival process. Investigative archiving also introduces challenges of scale—namely, a manual discovery process will almost always

[10] I Bruno, E Didier, and T Vitale, 'Statactivism: Forms of Action between Disclosure and Affirmation: Partecipazione e Conflitto' (2014) 7(2) The Open Journal of Sociopolitical Studies 198.

[11] WEB Du Bois and Elijah Anderson, *The Philadelphia Negro: A Social Study* (Reprint edn, University of Pennsylvania Press 1995).

[12] P Bourdieu, 'Cultural Reproduction and Social Reproduction' in J Karabel and AH Halsey (eds), *Power and Ideology in Education* (Oxford University Press 1977) 487–511.

[13] Roberta Dougherty, 'Documenting Revolution in the Middle East' (2011) 31 FOCUS on Global Resources https://www.crl.edu/focus/article/7435.

proceed more slowly and less reliably than an automated one, such as when a machine preserves all content from pre-determined, relevant sources, with discovery of pertinent information carried out subsequently.

Manual collection has the disadvantages of only finding some content, potentially missing relevant content, and losing many fields of metadata. However, in preserving only some content, a more targeted or curated approach has the advantage of lowering storage costs and minimizing the requisite technical know-how, particularly in instances a high-level of expertise is needed to distinguish what is and what is not relevant and where the drawbacks of mass, or platform based, archiving outweigh their benefits. Groups who use this selective approach towards content preservation include Amnesty International, Human Rights Watch, and Bellingcat.

2.2 Platform Archiving

An alternate archiving model consists of documentation groups accepting direct submissions from networks of human rights defenders. The defenders' data is manually submitted directly to a collection platform. Such centralized platform-based collection strategies (which often take the form of mobile apps) may include metadata fields potentially useful for a legal or advocacy context, but they have the possible disadvantages of a relatively low usage rate and a need to train defenders on the use of these new tools—limiting the scale at which content can be acquired and potentially putting at greater risk those using such tools in conflict areas. Groups who take this approach include eyeWitness to Atrocities,[14] the American Civil Liberties Union (through their Mobile Justice app[15]), and Storymaker.[16]

As most digital tool development and training organizations do not have the capacity for continuous engagement with user-groups, the 'if you build it, they will come' approach of these groups also risks the dreaded 'parachuting in' problem, whereby an outside-the-issue 'player' (the tool developer or non-local NGO) expects already active participants (local activists) to change their existing workflows to use a single platform. By definition, these documentation platforms can only work effectively when *one* is chosen *definitively*; any variance or duplicity of efforts reduces overall impact.

2.3 Targeted Mass Archiving

A targeted mass archive is distinguished from investigative archiving and platform archiving by its approach to ingesting and transforming content. Whereas an investigative archive may archive each of the particular units of user-generated content needed for a particular investigation, and a platform archive solicits user-generated content from a specific and definite user-base, a targeted mass archive will store an indefinite amount of content that falls under a broader topical umbrella.

[14] www.eyewitnessproject.org/.

[15] https://www.aclu.org/issues/criminal-law-reform/reforming-police-practices/aclu-apps-record-police-conduct.

[16] https://www.freepressunlimited.org/en/projects/storymaker-make-your-story-great.

In this approach, all relevant content that *might* advance the archive's intended purposes is ingested as soon as it enters into a collectible domain. This shifts the collection, consolidation and verification efforts from on-the-ground documentation efforts to the archival groups doing the data collection. While the data collectors may have difficulty ascertaining which items hold potential future value, storing and processing at mass scale offers the ability to return to the data set at a later date and comb the set for newly relevant data. Thus, decisions about the relevance of documented content are delayed until *after* archiving, instead of serving to filter what is collected in the first place.

Each large-scale archive can be seen as an archive of a subset of the total stream of digital information that is and has been available. This information is not based on a snapshot of one moment of time, as the targeted mass archive collects data continuously, ultimately providing multiple snapshots at multiple points at multiple times. For example, a YouTube video watched ten times on the original upload date that goes viral three days later will be reflected accordingly in the database.

The goal of targeted mass archiving is to generate a digital collection that is as complete as possible on any given topic. What the end user (audience) sees is not the sum of what has been collected, but what the archival group selects from the ingested content (the complete data population) as the subset most relevant to the issue at hand. There are some YouTube channels, for example, that host valuable videos only a small percentage of the time, while the rest of those channels' content could be disregarded as not fitting the archive's intended purpose. It is important for a targeted mass archive to ingest even the irrelevant content at first, and to filter this data into relevant subsets.

3. Advantages and Disadvantages of the Targeted Mass Archiving Approach

This section briefly discusses how a mass archival approach might prove advantageous for human rights documentation efforts, as well as the disadvantages of the approach.

3.1 Documentation Efforts

Mass archiving offers the benefit of ingesting content sooner and faster than an individual researcher or research team. As explained elsewhere in this book, digital content often disappears from the public-facing internet.[17] The loss of critical content from public platforms is only increasing[18]. Owing to increased pressure from Western governments on glorification of terrorism, human rights videos and photographs are facing increased scrutiny whose often-graphic nature may potentially violate platforms' terms of service and community

[17] A Asher-Schapiro, 'YouTube and Facebook Are Removing Evidence of Atrocities, Jeopardizing Cases against War Criminals' *The Intercept* (2 November 2017) https://theintercept.com/2017/11/02/war-crimes-youtube-facebook-syria-rohingya/.

[18] Although it probably does not disappear from non-public backend storage, which is why YouTube is able to reinstate videos and channels inadvertently flagged for deletion.

guidelines, as well as the introduction of machine-learning algorithms that automatically remove content and sources at a previously impossible speed and scale.[19]

Given these new realities, the collection and ingestion of human rights content has become a race against time. The sheer scale of ingested content can be too difficult to parse through on a short time-scale. A targeted mass archive ensures that relevant information does not become permanently lost before it can be analysed and used.

A benefit of independently operating any archive is the ability to take agency over the longevity, ownership, purpose, and intention of a collection of data. Many platforms (especially social media platforms) offer only particular views of their data to the public. For example, a typical platform user can only search by *some* fields (e.g. place of employment, full name) while restricted from searches of other fields (e.g. past employment, affiliations). When content is stored on a platform, the public permanence of this data is not ensured; rather, permanence is left to the discretion and motivations of the platform operators. Collecting and storing data on an archival group's own server(s) allows the group to investigate, use, and publish data however they want. With a certain amount of technical know-how, custom search entry points can be built to allow for or searches of the data in ways that the original platforms might not easily enable or block altogether.

Assuming that such suitable search entry points have been built, a research or investigative team can find items that they may not have discovered by conducting a search on the open web. In a controlled environment, tools can be tailored to meet specific data needs. It is also possible to conduct analysis on large sets of data—following trends (e.g. use of chemical weapons over time) and providing real-time statistics on, for example, removal rates of content from social media platforms.

Mass archiving also opens up the ability to use machine learning (artificial intelligence) to process the ingested data. While large tech companies like Google and Facebook are already running machine learning algorithms on their own content, they remain opaque about their algorithmic practices and often do not offer taxonomies and classifications that are suited to human rights investigations, if they are offered at all. Additionally, since platforms such as YouTube and Facebook own the infrastructure user-generated content is hosted on, only *they* are able to perform this sort of analysis. Companies do not currently offer this machine intelligence or analysis to human rights groups.

In combination with a mass archive, machine learning has the potential to allow human rights defenders to investigate their own datasets, helping overcome some of the challenges of analysing such huge quantities of material.[20] While still largely untested, machine learning projects promise easier parsing ability and quicker pathways to pertinent content. At the moment, there are few open source software projects available for archival and documentation groups.

One exception is vframe.io, a partner of the Syrian Archive. This software is tailored specifically to the sort of armed conflict seen in Syria. vframe.io,[21] for example, allows Syrian Archive to search the visual content of each video in its dataset (more than 1 million pieces

[19] Kate O'Flaherty, 'YouTube Keeps Deleting Evidence of Syrian Chemical Weapon Attacks' *Wired UK* (26 June 2018) https://www.wired.co.uk/article/chemical-weapons-in-syria-youtube-algorithm-delete-video accessed 11 December 2018.

[20] Kalliatakis G and others, 'Detection of Human Rights Violations in Images: Can Convolutional Neural Networks Help?' [2017] arXiv:1703.04103 [cs] http://arxiv.org/abs/1703.04103 accessed 11 December 2018.

[21] https://vframe.io/.

of content) with textual queries such as 'cluster munition', 'helicopter', or even a vehicle's licence plate number. Researchers can then use these results to construct a shareable list of prioritized videos for use in ongoing investigations. A query such as the following might be constructed: 'Show us screenshots of all relevant videos from YouTube that may contain cluster munitions, with a low view count, and have not been verified yet by our team or a partner's team.'

Human Rights Information and Documentation Systems (HURIDOCS) is another organization that is using machine learning in the form of natural language analysis to analyse large amounts of textual content. Analysing this content helps human rights defenders by automatically tagging and clustering documents based on machine inferred topics (e.g. corruption, hate speech, propaganda) predetermined by a research team.[22] This helps in reducing search costs when working with large amounts of textual data, such as document leaks and dumps.

3.2 Legal Efforts

Archiving and preserving digital materials documenting human rights abuses and war crimes are increasingly being recognized as critical for justice and accountability efforts. Courts and traditional documentation groups have lagged behind in employing the digital tools and methods required to harness this potential. There are, nevertheless, a number of considerations for legal efforts that should be taken into account when automating the archival process. These include issues surrounding transparency, data validation, and questions of applicability.

There is an emerging body of case law in which user-generated content from social media platforms features prominently. The surveillance software company X1 reports there were over 9,500 cases in the United States for 2016 alone in which user-generated content played a prominent role. The group found a more than 50 per cent increase in the use of social media content in US legal contexts between 2015 and 2016 and believes this trend will only increase.[23]

User generated content is also being used in legal contexts outside the United States, even apart from the use in the ICC case against Mahmoud Mustafa Busayf Al-Werfalli reported throughout other chapters in this book.[24] Elsewhere, in 2016 in Sweden a case was concluded against a former Syrian rebel who had previously taken part in the killing of seven captured Syrian soldiers.[25] There, the court relied on Facebook and Twitter posts to identify the time and place where soldiers were captured and establish that only forty-one hours passed between their capture and execution. Facebook was contacted by prosecutors in order to verify the content's metadata.

[22] https://www.huridocs.org/2016/08/applying-machine-learning-to-human-rights-documentation-an-interview-with-natalie/.

[23] https://www.x1.com/products/x1_social_discovery/case_law.html.

[24] *Prosecutor v Mahmoud Mustafa Busayf Al-Werfalli* [2017] International Criminal Court ICC-01/11-01/17.

[25] Christina Anderson, 'Syrian Rebel Gets Life Sentence for Mass Killing Caught on Video' *The New York Times* (22 December 2017) https://www.nytimes.com/2017/02/16/world/europe/syrian-rebel-haisam-omar-sakhanh-sentenced.html accessed 11 December 2018.

Transparency is key to using user-generated content in court. For Syrian Archive, because all stages of its archival work are open source, it is possible to show how the data was discovered, how it was acquired, and the process by which data has been transformed, processed, and analysed.

Third-party data validation is essential to maintain the integrity of the preserved data. For Syrian Archive, this takes the form of hashing and timestamping all content to ensure that the content has not been tampered with after it has been ingested. An independent third party, Enigio,[26] performs this validation process simultaneously. Hashing is a process of computing a unique code for a piece of digital content. The same content will always compute to the same code, but the code cannot be transformed back into the content.

Archiving at mass scale allows for alternative forms of accountability to take form. After the fall of Chile's dictator Augusto Pinochet, for example, investigators collected and sealed the stories of people who had been imprisoned, tortured, killed, or disappeared for political purposes, with the goal of building an evidence base in developing an overall picture of human rights violations committed during the Pinochet years, culminating in the Rettig Report (Report on the Chilean National Commission on Truth and Reconciliation, 2000)[27] and the Valech Report.[28] Although testimony will not be released for fifty years after the commission met, and therefore will not be likely to be used to bring individuals to justice, summary reports have been written and released to the public, and records have been used for reparations purposes. Similarly, in Germany, the Stasi archives have been made available since 1992 for victims to view their own records and, in 2015, the files of those individuals no longer living were made public.

In the case of Syria, large-scale archival preservation allows for the telling of untold stories by amplifying the voices of those on the ground. Not every incident there is reported by journalists (nor can it be), and the challenging conditions of an ongoing conflict have made it especially difficult for the media to collect data and report on their findings. Mass documentation may someday help Syrian citizens in setting up a memorialization process: creating dialogues around issues related to peace and justice, recognizing and substantiating suffering, and providing multiple perspectives on the conflict, helping to prevent revisionist or simplified narratives of the conflict.

3.3 Drawbacks of Mass Archiving

While collecting large quantities of digital data may facilitate analyst sovereignty and allow for new insights into data, it also introduces several challenges to archivists, in particular in terms of scale. To be blunt: running servers and operating a large-scale archive costs a considerable amount of money and effort and requires technical skills to maintain. This is not dissimilar from other sorts of big data projects, however, and touches on many of the same challenges: namely *volume*, *velocity*, and *variety*.[29]

[26] www.enigio.com.

[27] 'Foreword', *Report of the Chilean National Commission on Truth and Reconciliation*, vol I/II (University of Notre Dame Press 1993).

[28] Tom Burgis, 'Chile's Torture Victims to Get Life Pensions' *The Guardian* (30 November 2004) https://www.theguardian.com/world/2004/nov/30/chile accessed 11 December 2018.

[29] Cynthia Harvey, 'Big Data Challenges' *Datamation* (5 June 2017) https://www.datamation.com/big-data/big-data-challenges.html accessed 11 December 2018.

Navigating these shoals with a small human rights team (on a shoestring budget) and in transparent ways is far from easy. In addition, as discussed in the previous section, there is no assurance that user-generated content will find use in courts. This lack of assurance is compounded by the large amount of effort and money it takes to run a large-scale archive. Thus, it can be difficult to know what to prioritize among responsibilities for documentation and ensuring the longevity of the archival content and where to allocate limited resources. As more news sources, human rights groups, and institutions rely on a particular archive, more responsibility and expectation lands on the plate of the archivists. Additionally, there is the risk of an increased interest and scrutiny from governments or institutions that could be considered unsavoury and may not align with the archive's intended use.

It can become difficult to ascertain what use the data will have and which policies need to be developed for data publishing and data sharing. One must consider both the positive and the negative effects the collection might have—possible unintended consequences of releasing public datasets may include doxxing or creating a backlash of disinformation.

4. Considerations for Implementing a Mass Archive

In a mass archive, the amount of ingested content can be overwhelming for a team of researchers to make sense of. To make this easier, it is necessary to establish effective and consistent procedures for how the data is stored and transformed. These transformations, from ingestion to management to publishing, can be called the data pipeline.[30] To establish the process and actions of the pipeline, a data model, operating model, and publishing model must be created. *Data models* concern the structure of individual pieces of archived digital content, the metadata and additional fields about this content, and the technologies and methods that are used for storing it. *Operating models* concern the transformations and processes that ferry information from ingestion to publishing. *Publishing models* concern what is shared from the archive, who it is shared with, and how those entities receive access. Here we focus primarily on data models and the initial stage of the pipeline.

In many discussions, including some in this book, the term *metadata* is used to refer to fields and information added to a unit by a team of researchers.[31] For the purposes of this chapter, however, we refer to this information as 'archival context' or the unit's 'ontology'.[32] Machine created information about files (e.g. duration, file size, device used for capture) will simply be called 'metadata'. Information created by a prior source, before the unit was ingested into the targeted mass archive (e.g. upload date, tags), we refer to as 'original context'.

[30] rDisorder, 'Building a Data Pipeline from Scratch' *rDisorder* (9 August 2016) https://www.rdisorder.eu/2016/08/09/building-a-data-pipeline-from-scratch/ accessed 11 December 2018.

[31] J Riley, *Understanding Metadata: What Is Metadata, and What Is It For? A Primer* (National Information Standards Organization 2017).

[32] N Guarino, D Oberle, and S Staab, 'What Is an Ontology' in Staab S and Studer R (eds), *Handbook on Ontologies* (2nd edn, Springer-Verlag 2009).

4.1 Documentation Tools and Strategies

In the field of human rights reporting there is an abundance of available tools and strategies for documentation produced by a variety of companies, communities, and research institutions. Each of these tools creates a data format and a data pipeline, as well as providing a closed set of workflows. In our view, a technical solution needs to have certain properties. These properties include using open source software—software whose code is transparent, inspectable, and changeable[33] and often free of charge—the freedom of choosing and revising sets of data fields and models, the ability to automate processes within a data pipeline, and the ability to store, manage, and display large amounts of data.

Syrian Archive has chosen to use several open source software tools running on its own infrastructure to address these needs, in lieu of a platform based solution. This has allowed the Syrian Archive to change and iterate on its workflow that was designed in-house, and changes depending on new needs and requirements. Additionally, a variance of tools allows Syrian Archive to host and produce an independent archive, create its own data pipeline, and retain flexibility in its operations.

Furthermore, we would argue that there *can* be no satisfactory one-platform-solution for documentation archives. Human rights use cases—especially (but not exclusively) in the style of targeted mass archival—include a much higher complexity of 'problem' than most commercial tools, interfaces, and platforms are able to solve. Silicon Valley-style approaches to creating platforms often assume a simple problem solved by a technically complex solution (e.g. connecting available drivers and passengers) with the goal of creating user convenience. This convenience drives users to the platforms. For documentation efforts, even correctly identifying the problem(s) or potential users is challenging, causing a tech solution to blossom in complexity.

At the time of writing, there is a shortage of good available tools for research groups to archive on a *large scale*. Although some tools have been created to help meet the needs of open source investigators and journalists, and might include some archiving ability, these tools lack the capacity to automate these processes, store large amounts of data, or otherwise meet the above-mentioned requirements of a targeted mass archive.

Additionally, these tools are rarely open source and thus the data and its metadata are usually stored on technical infrastructure not owned by the research group using the software. This can damage the transparency of the data process, as well as reduce the possibilities in which the data can be accessed and published. Commercial tools, which are often closed source, are often problematic for these reasons.

If using these closed-source tools, it can help to build a business relationship with the relevant company in order to solve some of the above mentioned problems; doing so outsources the automatization, storage, and technical expertise to an external organization in exchange for money. But there is still the consideration of data and documentation existing on technical infrastructure owned by someone else (the business), as well as being locked into a particular platform or workflow. In this model (using closed-source tools), the existence of the archive is directly linked with the business' financial longevity.

While using a range of open source tools and technologies can often solve most of the needs for these use cases, as well as being available free of charge, there is a traded cost

[33] G von Krogh and S Spaeth, 'The Open Source Software Phenomenon: Characteristics That Promote Research' (2007) 16 Journal of Strategic Information Systems 236.

of development and maintenance. Using closed-source commercial products can, therefore, be advantageous for research and documentation groups who have little or no internal technical abilities or whose access to developers or technologists is limited. Ultimately, open source tools often trade the simple, usable user interfaces available in commercial tools for scalability, flexibility, and configuration.[34]

Given these realities, the technical ability of a research team is highly relevant to which tools they should adopt. Team members need to understand a system's daily operation, and be trained into perhaps less than obvious elements of the workflow. Syrian Archive has accomplished this by tightly coupling its technology teams with its research teams. Each research team has a staff technologist to aid in the research process, and each individual member of the research team is trained to use the tech tools. Additionally, toolkits and methods are created, shared publicly, and used to help guide team members.[35]

4.2 Ingesting Content

The first step in designing a model for a mass archive is to identify and create entry points for ingestion of content. This means both identifying the formats *and* the sources that content can be ingested from. This might include, for example, social media platforms (e.g. YouTube), submitted collections (e.g. a UN database or SD card containing images provided by a source), or particular websites (e.g. *The Guardian*). For the purpose of this chapter, these will be called 'mediums'. Additionally, the archivist must define which channels, streams, or sections of these platform sources will be archived. These will be called 'sources'.

4.3 Sources

Syrian Archive has identified more than 3,000 sources by following credible and verified social media accounts and the channels of individual citizen journalists and larger media houses. Many of those sources have content that contains video documentation relevant to the Syrian conflict from as early as 2011 and have published their work on social media channels or through media houses, or in reports.

In an effort to create a comprehensive archive, covering each region in Syria, Syrian Archive identified and collected as many credible open sources as possible. This established a database of trusted sources. Not all of these sources are non-partisan, and thus the information they have provided requires caution and verification after ingestion.

In the case of the Syrian conflict, activists prefer using social media platforms for publishing and publicizing documentation, or at least they use the medium effectively and often.[36]

[34] Timothy B Lee, 'Open User Interfaces Suck' *Bottom-up* (15 November 2010) http://timothyblee.com/2010/11/15/open-user-interfaces-suck/ accessed 11 December 2018.

[35] https://github.com/syrianarchive/toolkit.

[36] Joe Sterling, 'For Syrian Activists, YouTube Is a Sword and Shield' *CNN* (15 March 2012) https://edition.cnn.com/2012/03/14/world/meast/syria-youtube-uprising/index.html accessed 4 June 2018.

As explained in an interview entitled 'Revolutionary Echoes from Syria' (first publication Hourriya),[37] which documents the beginnings of Syria's resistance movements, the respondents state:

> We achieved a point when we realized we should start organizing ourselves, we should start something organized. Because all of the media channels refused to publish this kind of videos, even Al Jazeera, all of the mainstream media actually. There was only one channel called Orient, it belongs to a businessman, who invested his channel in this Syrian revolution for some reason ... There was actually no media coverage, only this one channel and social media, YouTube and Facebook ... Young people cooperated with channels, they made the channels actually, on YouTube ... These were the first local groups based on YouTube. They were organized, they had correspondents everywhere. They collected movies ... the first organized phenomenon in Syria was a media group.[38]

It is important for Syrian Archive (or any large archive ingesting content) to meet the content producers where they are at; utilizing platforms and workflows documentation groups already use and are familiar with. Being as open as possible to as many different formats and deliveries of data is essential when adopting a mass archival strategy to avoid loss of important sources and documentation.

Forming network relationships with some of these sources (e.g. media houses) is important to build trust between an archival group and those documenting on the ground. This ensures a feedback loop between archivist and documenter, demonstrating that uploaded content has been securely preserved and that content has been used for the purposes provided. In this way, social media platforms (e.g. YouTube, Facebook, Twitter) become interfaces for documentation groups to submit content into a larger mass archive, instead of having to interact with the archive directly.

The tendency to use social media platforms is likely to arise because of these tools' ease of use, reliability, shareability, and large existing audiences. They also enable human rights defenders to coordinate with each other (e.g. in authentication, account management), consolidate documentation (e.g. large-scale storage, permission controls, resource management), and publish this information to a wide audience that is already accustomed to using the platform.

4.4 Content Mediums

Social media companies often offer access to content hosted on their platforms through a public application programming interface, otherwise known as an API.[39] APIs offer, amongst other elements, a machine readable and automatizable format of what users upload to the platform, including valuable metadata about each upload. Social media companies

[37] Available to listen to at https://archive.org/details/RevolutionaryEchoesFromSyria.

[38] *Revolutionary Echoes from Syria* (Hourriya 2016).

[39] Jenn Chen, 'What Is an API and Why Does It Matter?' *Sprout Social* (31 January 2018) https://sproutsocial.com/insights/what-is-an-api/ accessed 11 December 2018.

create APIs in the hope that developers will create applications that interact with the social media platform, thereby increasing the value of the data on the platform. For mass archives, this offers the ability to ingest social media content with ease.

Some social media companies do not offer an available API for their platform. In these cases, or when the data provided by their API is unsatisfactory, automated web-scraping technologies can be used. Web scraping is a process in which machine readable data is extracted from the HTML lay-out data of websites delivered to a user's browser and storing that data locally. This process takes data that is meant for display on a user's device and converts it into a format that can be processed. These often require more development time and include less contextual metadata about each unit, but still make efficient ingestion of large quantities of content possible.

Partner documentation groups offer access to their own internal collections; content can also be collected by collaborating, sharing, and ingesting data directly. This type of data usually comes in the form of original image or video files, or spreadsheets. In these cases, direct collaboration is needed to create methods to ingest this information into the mass archive as well.

4.5 Automated Collection

Once mediums and sources have been identified, the mass archive must automate the process of collecting from the sources on a regular basis. Syrian Archive uses an open source software project called SugarCube[40] for many of its entry points. SugarCube enables accessing, transforming, and storing information from many social media platforms, as well as from internet searches, filesystems, and downloads. SugarCube also enables the construction and management of reusable data pipelines, finding relations in the data, and tracking data changes.

For collecting directly from partners and local media groups, Syrian Archive uses a variety of strategies. SyncThing,[41] for example, allows partners and local groups to manage and control their own file system archives, while allowing Syrian Archive access to their collections, preserving them on Syrian Archive infrastructure in the process. Most videos from social media platforms can be downloaded using a popular open source software called YouTube-dl.[42] Despite its name, YouTube-dl also works with Facebook, Twitter, and over 1,000 other websites and platforms. Many commercial preservation tools also use this software in their back end because of its stability, large developer base, and flexibility. As part of its automated process, Syrian Archive also downloads a copy of the relevant media associated with each archived item.

Automating these collection processes is often handled using Cron,[43] a technology that is more than twenty years old and runs on Unix-like systems, such as Linux. Using this software, collection processes can be automated to run on set schedules (e.g. hourly, daily, weekly, or even every full moon on a cloudy night).

[40] https://gitlab.com/sugarcube/.
[41] https://syncthing.net/.
[42] https://rg3.github.io/ YouTube-dl/.
[43] https://en.wikipedia.org/wiki/Cron; https://bscb.cornell.edu/about/resources/linux-cron-and-crontab/.

As data may come from many different sources and in many different formats, it is necessary to model how data will be ingested and stored. Automated processes require standardized transformation practices and clear data models. The following section describes Syrian Archive's data model, which uses a variety of open source tools and strategies to ease the process of storing, accessing, and transforming data into a consumable archive.

5. Designing a Data Model

Although each type of ingested data might take a different format, all must go through archival processes and data pipelines. In the previous chapter, the OAIS system was included as a reference model to create a framework for long-term preservation. From a practical standpoint, this section will describe how data models in the mass archival process have been implemented by Syrian Archive for the ingestion, preservation, and data management processes. The previous chapter also introduces the SPOT (simple property-oriented threat) model for risk assessment. This model's properties (availability, identity, persistence, renderability, understandability, and authenticity) apply to each of the categories in our data model.

Syrian Archive identified four categories of necessary data pertaining to each unit in the archive. Each category utilizes a different structure and achieves a different conceptual purpose. These are: unit, original context, processing, and archival context.

The following unit from Syrian Archive's public database can serve as an example for discussing our data model, which is also available as a permalink.[44]

Figure 8.1

[44] https://syrianarchive.org/en/database?unit=0be73b48.

5.1 Unit

In our data model, the *unit* is the primary piece of information that is stored and referenced. For Syrian Archive, the format of the unit is most often a video or an image file attached to a social media post or submitted directly, though it can also be a text-based social media post.

In our given example, the 'unit' is the downloaded video file. Although the video still exists in a viewable state at the original YouTube link (as of the date of this writing). To give a sense of scale, Syrian Archive ingests roughly 600 new units each day.

In our case, the process of ingesting and storing units on a file system is automated; however, we still needed a strategy for storing and backing up those units. It is important to be able to access each unit easily, as well as to plan for having enough space to store the enormous number of units that may ultimately be ingested.

5.2 Original Context

The *original context* gives information about the environment in which the unit was found and ingested. The original context may not include *the* original file (i.e. from the camera of the documenter or the bytes typed into the computer), but it is important to store the information about the context in which the archivist (or the automated targeted archive process) discovered the unit.

At the point of ingestion, the file has often gone through a data pipeline already (for example, the video file was sent on a USB stick by the original filmer to a media group, converted and uploaded to YouTube, or copied to a hard drive and sent to Syrian Archive as a submission). Our approach attempts to document and store as much information about the unit's origin as possible. Storing data about the original context in which an archivist finds a unit enables a partial reconstruction of this environment in the future. Thus, it is critical to identify what can be stored about the environment, how that storage can be effectuated, and how those processes can be automated.

Fields present in the 'original context' might range from the original URL of the downloaded file or the name of the uploader, all the way to comments on the video, or a screenshot and the source's original HTML code. While the original context might include fields in the (publicly) accessible archival data (such as the source of the data), it also includes data important for potential use in legal proceedings (such as demonstration of origin). Keeping original context information can also aid open source investigations by offering searchable discovery interfaces. Inside of the context of targeted mass archives, it also aids in the parsing and filtering of data.

In our given example, most of the original context is not displayed to the end user. However, (ideally) a screenshot of the YouTube page is generated and stored, the YouTube API response is stored, and source information is correlated to the unit on the back end. All of this information can be made available to the research team or partners to help in creating the public-facing resource.

Each medium offers a plethora of information, though it may vary considerably. YouTube strips uploaded videos of its Exif data, for example, while a similar video from a submission to a different platform might contain all of this important information. Even similar pipelines for similar mediums may include vastly different sets of fields. The data structure of a

Twitter API response and a YouTube API response vary greatly, whereas an anonymously submitted file might have nothing more than the file name. While these fields could theoretically be piped into a standard ontology and the original data structure abandoned, Syrian Archive argues that this initial data structure should be stored in its entirety.

If a unit is reacquired (the same unit is ingested at two points in time), as it can be with automated daily scripts, and the API response or data has changed, both the new response should be stored as well as the old response. For example, the source may have changed the description of a video on YouTube after additional information is known. To further complicate matters, the structure of social media platforms' APIs change over time; the platform might change privacy restrictions or business strategies, or severely restrict access to their API altogether.[45] In this most extreme case, the archiving strategy for a platform source might have to change from API access to web-scraping. Mass archives enacting automated ingestion therefore require continual development and upkeep.

In all of these cases, any technical archival system be able to accommodate easily these and other changes, as well as to accommodate varying data formats. Using an unstructured database approach[46] allows for flexible fields and references, as well as file storage or a mixed strategy to be utilized in storing associated downloads, screenshots, and other extracted files.

Unstructured databases (or relational databases permitting unstructured elements)[47] allow for a disparate and changing array of field sets to be stored without needing to design, alter, or enforce a data schema. This enables, for example, the automated preservation of contextual data. It also ensures the loss of as little data as possible, as the database does not need to be filtered into a standard set of fields. Many available tools marketed to human rights defenders (e.g. Corroborator[48]), as well as larger documentation and archival groups, use relational databases and set schemas as the only datastore, causing important available data to be lost.

This ingested unit and its contextual data generates the collected database. This database serves a different purpose than the public facing resource, which displays the archival context to an archive user. Rather, as an unstructured database of collected content, it serves as a starting point for internal research teams to view, search, and filter for information.

5.3 Processing

The processing phase, as well as the defined methodology of what happens to unit data and original context data must also be seen as part of the archive. The processing phase describes the transformation process of data and fields present in the original unit (original context) to the fields relevant to a user of the archive (archival context).

In the SPOT model described in the previous chapter, this documentation is important in order to ensure authenticity, renderability, and understandability. For a unit's authenticity,

[45] Craig Silverman, 'Journalists Are Criticizing Facebook for Its Data Collection. At the Same Time, They Often Use It to their Advantage' *BuzzFeed News* (11 April 2018) https://www.buzzfeednews.com/article/craigsilverman/facebook-cambridge-analytica-journalism-data-criticism-osint accessed 11 December 2018.

[46] https://ieeexplore.ieee.org/abstract/document/6187357/.

[47] https://www.postgresql.org/docs/current/static/datatype-json.html.

[48] https://equalitie.github.io/open-corroborator/.

it is important to store and be able to show procedural information such as *when* the unit was first discovered and downloaded, *how* it was acquired and *which* software or human methods were used. For the renderability attribute, the documented process of how a unit went from its original environment into the format it is displayed in the consumable archive must also be documented and stored (e.g. file format conversions for viewing a video in a web browser).

Additionally, any processes that used data pipelines to fill in metadata information informing the archival context must also be documented and stored. For example, if time stamps were extracted from an image's Exif data and used to influence a claim on an incident date, the archivist should log the process of extraction. The identifiers of any team members and researchers who made changes to the structure or content of data should also be stored.

Just as it is important to document the process that humans are taking in their investigative models, tools, and methods, it is important to document the process that machines have been set up to take in their data transformation, tools, and methodologies.

Processing information can also include additional steps that were used to ensure authenticity. For example, as previously mentioned, Syrian Archive collaborates with a third party, Enigio, that stores file hashes of each downloaded unit for safe-keeping. This partnership ensures that it can be shown with little doubt that Syrian Archive acquired a file on a particular date, and that the file has remained unchanged since then. The date that this hashing action was taken is stored, as well as the API response from the third party. This allows Syrian Archive to show when and how the action was taken, and which softwares influenced external information about the unit.

Processed data often takes the form of text-based logs, or relations to original files; downloaded copies might also be stored in an unstructured database. It matters little which method of storage is chosen, so long as the process data is always available on future request.

5.4 Archival Context

Finally, the archival information is added to the relevant unit. This information is commonly referred to as 'metadata', but it is actually much closer to a data ontology or annotation schema, as described earlier in this and in other chapters. A data ontology helps frame the purpose of an archive, as well as helps users and intended audiences to find what they need. This ontology might include categories and descriptions not found in the original context or the unit.

Fields in the archival context should be decided early in the archival process, and changed only rarely. For Syrian Archive, fields in this data ontology range from the type of human rights violation observed in content (e.g. violations of children's rights, use of illegal weapons), corroborating data that a research team has discovered and observed in the documentation (e.g. weather conditions, landmarks), to the clustering and relations of each unit to others. This clustering can range from an article or other external resource discussing an alleged incident that a unit pertains to, as well as to the collections for which the unit are a part of (e.g. chemical weapons attacks[49]).

[49] https://syrianarchive.org/en/collections/chemical-weapons.

While the archival context fields will differ from archive to archive, it is important for a documentation group to research similar use cases, or field sets that have been used in the past. In the case of Syrian Archive, this meant discussing field types with various archival institutions and documentation groups, including the NIOD Institute for War, Holocaust, and Genocide Studies.[50]

Internal standardization of fields will aid in data sharing and data consolidation, and will give a common frame of understanding to visitors of the archive. Imagine a library without a classification system—it would just be a pile of books. In a user-generated documentation situation, without a consistent latitude and longitude, a system would not be able to map a collection of units digitally, which can aid researchers in identifying location trends. External standardization would be ideal. But we acknowledge this has political consequences and also brings its own set of challenges. The international standard book number (ISBN) classification works in the case of books, but developing a standardized universal list and definitions of disabilities is not an easy task.[51]

Whatever the chosen ontology, or standardized field set, from a technology perspective, a structured data storage solution should be chosen. Structure data is easy to index, search, and build methods of replicable display. Many efficient, mature, free, and open source solutions exist for structured databases (e.g. Postgresql,[52] Mysql,[53] and sqlite[54]).

For smaller documentation efforts using relatively low-tech approaches, a spreadsheet in CSV format, or a free, cloud-based solution such as Google Sheets can suffice as long as the data is clean, machine readable, and fields are pre-established and validated. This will aid in filtering and searching data.

Maintaining the archival context requires the largest amount of human labour in an archive. Standardized methods for annotation should be developed to aid researchers in this process. Both old and new technologies covered earlier in this chapter can assist researchers in discovering new content in own their archives, in collaborating with others, and in effectively publishing information in line with an archive's intended purpose.

6. Conclusion

In this chapter, we covered considerations, strategies, benefits, and disadvantages of targeted mass archival strategies used by human rights documentation groups, particularly Syrian Archive, and how this compares to manual, investigative, or platform archival practices used by a large part of the human rights sector.

User-generated content is at this point an important part of the memory of those affected by conflicts. It is hoped this will also become an important part of accountability processes in the near future. While most users of an archive will only ever see the unit and the archival context data, it is important that documentation groups also archive the additional data types: the process and the original context.

50 https://www.niod.nl/en.
51 Disability is environmental; a disability in one location might not be so in another.
52 https://www.postgresql.org/.
53 https://www.mysql.com/.
54 https://www.sqlite.org/index.html.

As the amount of discoverable documentation continues to increase, it is important for the human rights sector to utilize emerging technologies effectively in the same way that governments and private institutions are using these technologies for surveillance and exploitation.

The worlds of investigations, research, documentation, and technology are coming ever closer together, and a meaningful effort in any one of these is likely to contribute to all other related disciplines. In the near future, documentation efforts in the realm of open source investigations must take these changes into consideration, form interdisciplinary and collaborative teams, and work with each other in partnerships to delegate work to the most appropriate group.

9
How to Verify and Authenticate User-generated Content

Aric Toler

After discovering instances of suspected human rights abuses, the next step in verification is affirming the veracity of user-generated content, namely the content, place, time, and originality of a photograph or video. The process of verification allows researchers to use discovered materials with confidence for either human rights advocacy or as evidence in attempts to bring perpetrators to account. The challenges of verifying a piece of user-generated content can differ in each case, with no single 'silver bullet' to solve every problem. Because of this, patience and creativity are just as important as the digital toolset in conducting verification. The process of verification can be made easier with the help of algorithms and proven methods, but a researcher must be able to improvise, as there are clear limitations with existing tools and methods.

This chapter takes us through a systematic consideration of verification, covering why verification is an essential step in human rights investigations, how to determine the original source of a material, and methods that can be used to ascertain that a photograph or video was captured at the same time and place of the incident under question.

1. Why Verify?

For human rights researchers, the answer to the question of 'why verify?' is simple—to assess user-generated content documenting possible human rights abuses and even, potentially, use that content as evidence in courts of law. Any user-generated content introduced in an investigation alleging human rights abuse must be trustworthy, not only for the integrity of the investigation itself, but also for the risk false information poses to one's credibility and reputation in the field. Using a staged photograph or video can damage the reputation of a human rights researcher or institution not only in present and future investigations; it can also cause previous, unrelated findings to come into question. Verifying content can often seem more of a hassle than an essential step to research, as a photograph or video appears to be self-evident in its originality. Regardless, especially in a legal context, every piece of evidence must be verified for both the integrity of the investigation at hand and of previous work. And appearances are occasionally deceiving.

User-generated content is more often than not correctly labelled and not intentionally misleading. For example, a photograph on Instagram will have a correct geotag, streaming video on Facebook Live will be in the location given by the Live Map, or the time and/or place in the description of a YouTube video will correspond with the content. However, verifying all user-generated content is necessary for journalism and human rights research, both for correctly reporting information and to halt the unintentional spread of mislabelled or fabricated materials—misinformation—and the intentional spread of these materials—disinformation.

2. Misinformation v Disinformation

The Council of Europe's 2017 report on 'information disorder' details the differences between these two concepts, defining disinformation as material that is 'false and deliberately created to harm' a range of targets, and misinformation as 'false, but not created with the intent of causing harm'.[1]

The methods and techniques employed in verifying user-generated content are often the same when dealing with misinformation and disinformation, but there can be some key differences. For example, the approach in determining the provenance of a photograph or video can differ depending on the intent of those sharing it.

Misinformation and disinformation thrive during events with a significant public appetite for any new information, such as conflicts and breaking news events. For an example of by-the-book misinformation, while Hurricane Irma was beating down on Florida, United States, in September 2017, the White House Director of Social Media Dan Scavino tweeted out a video from his government account (@Scavino45) that he claimed was from Miami International Airport, showing severe flooding.

If the White House official had attempted to verify this video, he would have seen that it was actually filmed in Mexico City[2] several weeks prior to Hurricane Irma's descent on Miami. Scavino later reported that he had been unaware of the real location of the video, as he received it 'from [the] public',[3] which would make this a case of misinformation, rather than disinformation.

The average social network user may be guilty of spreading misinformation, but these shares are usually honest mistakes rather than purposeful attempts to muddy the information space. A far smaller online population, whom we can call 'bad actors' in the digital information space, is committed to spreading misinformation's more insidious cousin, disinformation—intentional false information, including purposefully mislabelled, incorrectly contextualized, and even fabricated photographs and videos.

The origin of specific pieces of disinformation can be traced to malicious actors in the information space ranging from a prankster re-uploading an old video that could pass for a more recent event, to state-sponsored campaigns to create and disseminate incorrect or fabricated information. In cases of armed conflicts, disinformation thrives when being spread by ideologically motivated actors and networks. Similarly, when

[1] Claire Wardle and Hossein Derakhshan, 'Information Disorder: Toward an Interdisciplinary Framework for Research and Policy Making' Council of Europe Report DGI (2017) 9, 20 https://rm.coe.int/information-disorder-report-november-2017/1680764666 accessed 30 December 2018.

[2] David Mack, 'Trump's Social Media Director Is Sharing Fake News about Irma with President' *Buzzfeed* (12 September 2017) https://www.buzzfeed.com/davidmack/scavino-irma-tweet?bftw&utm_term=.lem6VqlEjv#.bfe42EQXG5 accessed 30 December 2018.

[3] https://twitter.com/Scavino45/status/906979635858210817 accessed 30 December 2018.

Figure 9.1

genuine digital evidence of human rights violations is introduced, a strict regime of verification must be applied to protect the investigation from harsh scrutiny from politically motivated individuals, networks, and even governments seeking out a weak link in a chain of evidence.

The war in eastern Ukraine, which erupted following the 2014 ousting of ex-president Viktor Yanukovych and Russia's annexation of Crimea, is the first European war fought in the ubiquitous presence of the internet, including citizens and combatants armed with smartphones. Because of this, human rights abuses from the war are often recorded and put online on both Western social media platforms, such as YouTube and Facebook, and ones with mostly Russian-speaking user bases, such as Vkontakte and Odnoklassniki. However, not all materials showing alleged human rights abuses are as straightforward as they may at first seem. A particularly strange case of disinformation is a June 2014 video with Igor Bezler, a commander in the self-proclaimed Donetsk People's Republic (DNR) in eastern Ukraine. In the video, Bezler appears to order the execution of two Ukrainian hostages in order to pressure Ukrainian authorities to exchange their hostages for other men that Bezler is holding. The taking and extra-judicial killing of these hostages would be a clear violation of international humanitarian law.[4]

[4] https://www.youtube.com/watch?time_continue=101&v=OUWtEyfhu98&has_verified=1 accessed 30 December 2018.

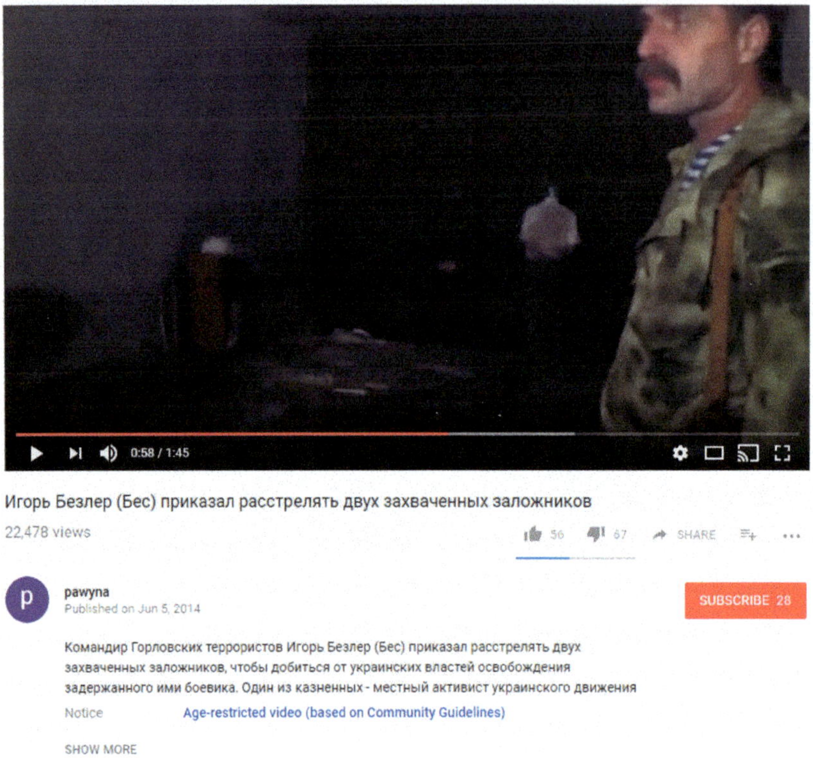

Figure 9.2

After Bezler gives the command to execute two of the hostages, shots are heard and two men fall down, apparently dead. The video, though widely shared in both Russian and Ukrainian media, is staged and does not actually show the execution of hostages—there is no blood, and the 'executed' hostages fall in a way that is not congruous with the direction of the fire, as has been shown by StopFake, a Ukrainian fact-checking organization based out of the Kyiv-Mohyla School of Journalism.[5] After the 'execution' video was published, Ukrainian journalists spoke with one of the men who was 'killed' by Bezler, who confessed that the video was a stunt.

When it comes to rudimentary recycling of videos, there are relatively straightforward methods to determine the provenance of the materials. In contrast, in the case of organized disinformation campaigns, journalists and researchers may have to spend almost as much time debunking the fake as the creators took in making it in the first place. As will be seen later in this chapter, there is no indisputable solution to debunk every online hoax, but the toolbox of methods and the lessons learned from analysing disinformation campaigns so far can inform future verification efforts.

[5] 'Execution of Hostages by Colonel of the Russian Main Intelligence Directorate Proved to de staged' *StopFake.Org* (11 June 2014) https://www.stopfake.org/en/execution-of-hostages-by-colonel-of-the-russian-main-intelligence-directorate-proved-to-de-staged/ accessed 30 December 2018.

3. Verification Technique: Determining Provenance

The simplest method of verifying user-generated content is simply to 'reverse search' the material in order to determine its provenance. This technique can be done with various reverse image search engines, including Google, Yandex, and TinEye, that allow you to upload a photograph into a search engine that uses an algorithm to find similar photographs, thus allowing you to find previously uploaded copies of the same image.

While many of the techniques described in this chapter do not rely on online tools, reverse searching multimedia is heavily reliant on the proficiency of websites such as Google Image Search and TinEye, along with other services that are being developed and improved. The algorithms used by these sites are constantly being tweaked, with both improvements and deficiencies for verification; therefore, one should use the reverse search engines of Google, Bing, Yandex, and TinEye in tandem for the best results.

When using the Chrome web browser, reverse image searching is a two-step process: right click an image and select 'Search Google for image'. In the case illustrated here, a suspiciously professional-looking photograph is being displayed by a Twitter user, raising the question of whether the profile picture is really of the person described.

Figure 9.3

Certainly, reverse image search results show that the person portrayed in the photograph, purportedly 'Zach Wellz', is actually a professional model, making it unlikely that the Twitter user is using his or her actual photograph.

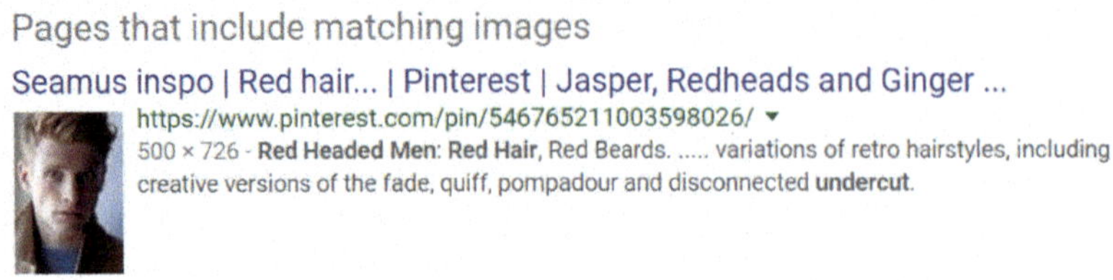

Figure 9.4

<Caption>One of the results from a reverse Google Images search, showing that this Twitter profile picture was taken of a professional model.</Caption>

A manual upload of a photograph can also be conducted from the Google Images page (images.google.com), rather than the two-click method within Chrome.

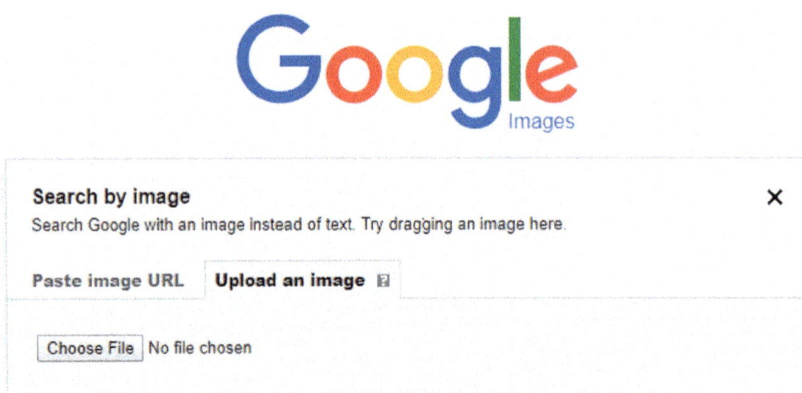

Figure 9.5

Alternative reverse image search sites include TinEye (tineye.com), Yandex (yandex.com/images), and Bing (bing.com/images). When analysing user-generated photographs, all of these sites should be used as a first step of verification to ensure the originality of the image.

Conducting a reverse search on videos in the same way we do with images is currently not possible with any functional and cheap tools, but it is possible to find alternative solutions by running a reverse image search for a video's thumbnails, rather than the video itself.

The InVid tool,[6] developed in 2016 after a grant from the European Union's Horizon 2020 programme, provides a browser plug-in that can assist a researcher in user-generated content verification. After installing the plug-in or using the InVid application,[7] the user

[6] InVID http://www.invid-project.eu/ accessed 30 December 2018.

[7] InVid, 'InVID Verification Application' http://www.invid-project.eu/invid-verification-application/ accessed 30 December 2018.

can view the detailed metadata for a video and see a number of thumbnails that can be reverse searched. Below, the metadata for a video that claims to show a number of executed solders in Syria is visible, including the exact upload time. While Amnesty International's YouTube DataViewer only provides reverse search links for Google Images, InVid also provides search options for Yandex, TinEye, and Twitter.

Video:

Video title	قتلى عصابات الطاغية في السرية الرابعة التابعة للواء 61
Video description	لواء تبارك الرحمن بالاشتراك مع لواء السبطين و تجمع ألوية أحفاد الرسول بعد تحرير العديد من الس رايا التابعة للواء 61 في محافظة القنيطرة و إكمالاً لأعمالهم العسكرية يزفون إليكم نبأ تحرير السرية الرابعة المعروفة بسرية خلدون و السيطرة عليها بالكامل

Video view count	3141
Like count	19
Dislike count	2
Duration	00:59
Licensed content	false
Description mentioned locations	
Recording location description	
Upload time	2013-11-11, 19:27:42 (UTC) Convert to local time

Channel:

Channel description	
Channel created time	2013-09-07, 00:08:07 (UTC)
Channel view count	128078
Channel page	https://www.youtube.com/channel/UCHjbV_Lq3fBS9fkQ58CI1QQ
Channel location	Not available

Comments:

Video comment count	3
Number verification comments	0

Figure 9.6 Information provided by InVid for videos uploaded to YouTube.

3.1 Interpreting Video Upload Time

The exact time given that a video was uploaded can be deceptive, as various platforms may render the upload date of user-generated content based on the local time of the user or server. In the case of YouTube, video upload dates will be in line with that of YouTube's servers in California. Because of this confusion, services like InVid are important in obtaining an exact capture time—not just the date—of a video upload.

Russian Foreign Minister Sergey Lavrov, for example, fell victim to this practice of YouTube when he claimed that videos uploaded to the platform on 21 August 2013 showing a Sarin attack in a Syrian village were not to be trusted because of the upload time: 'There is information that videos were posted on the internet hours before the purported attack, and other reasons to doubt the rebel narrative.'[8] However, this conclusion was false—some videos could show their upload date as the previous day, 20 August 2013, owing to the fact that YouTube's servers were in California in Pacific Daylight Time (GMT-7), ten hours behind Syria's time zone (GMT+3).[9] The Sarin attacks of 21 August took place in the early morning (2:30 am–5 am[10]) Syrian time, meaning that initial reports and videos describing the incident would have been published when it was still 20 August for YouTube's servers. To the average user unfamiliar with YouTube's upload date practices, it would be confusing to see videos showing an incident from 21 August 2013 be uploaded on 20 August 2013, giving rise to both misinformation—purely mistaken users questioning the upload times—and disinformation—users, networks, and governments taking advantage of this time zone differences to deceive others.

Instagram, Facebook, and Twitter will show the local time of the user for the upload date. On Facebook, hold your mouse over the text showing the approximate time of upload to see an exact date and time, adjusted to the local time zone of the user.

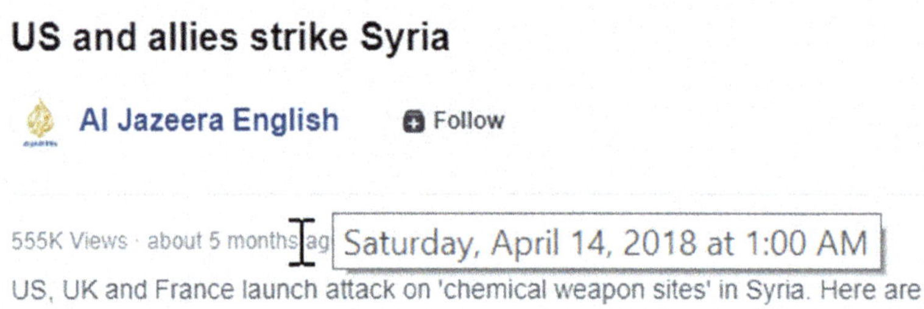

Figure 9.7 The exact upload time of a Facebook video, made visible by holding your mouse of the upload date.

On Twitter, the exact time and date are noted, the same as occurs on a normal tweet, again adjusted to the user's local time zone.

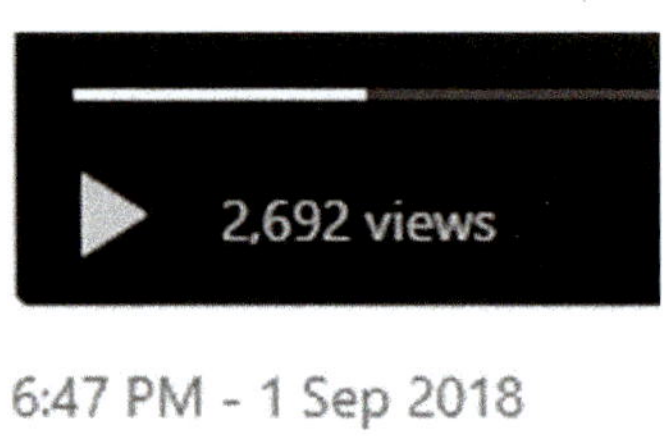

Figure 9.8 The exact upload time of a video in a tweet, visible within the Twitter user interface.

[8] 'Hysteria around Chemical Attack Suits Those Who Want Military Intervention in Syria: Lavrov' *RT* (26 August 2013) https://www.rt.com/news/lavrov-syria-press-conference-003/ accessed 30 December 2018.

[9] Robert Mackey, 'Confused by How YouTube Assigns Dates, Russians Cite False Claim on Syria Videos' *The New York Times* (23 August 2013) https://thelede.blogs.nytimes.com/2013/08/23/confused-by-how-youtube-assigns-dates-russians-cite-false-claim-on-syria-videos/?mtrref=www.google.com&gwh=841330C228D5E2F34AD25A3C72F5AF24&gwt=pay accessed 30 December 2018.

[10] Bridget Kendall, 'Syria "Chemical Attack": Distressing Footage under Analysis' *BBC News* (23 August 2013) http://www.bbc.co.uk/news/world-middle-east-23806491 accessed 30 December 2018.

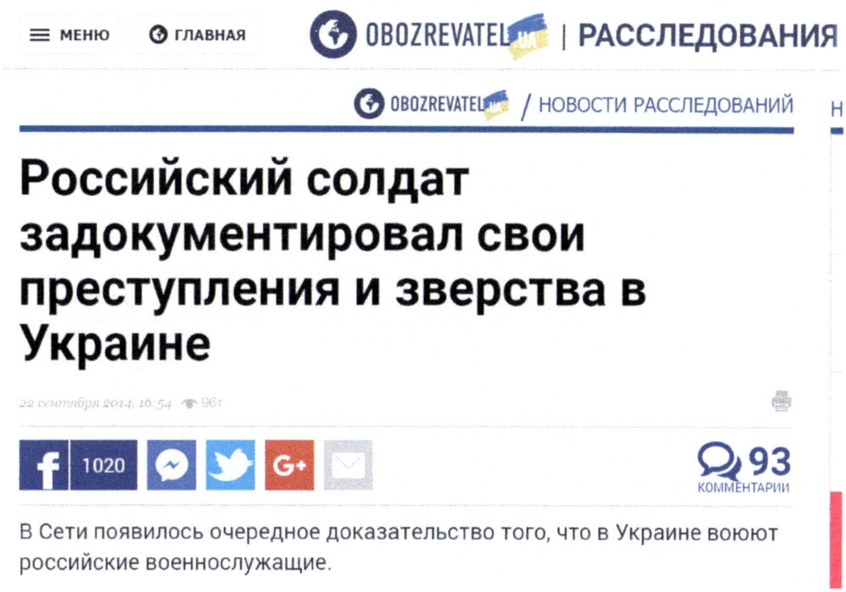

Figure 9.9

3.2 Image Manipulation

Simple reverse image search is not always completely effective, however, as some clever fakers have figured out ways to bypass algorithms and make their uploads seem genuine. Malaysian Airlines Flight 17 (MH17) was downed on 17 July 2014 over eastern Ukraine, killing all 298 passengers and crew members. Two months later, on 20 September 2014, a profile for a 'Russian soldier' on Vkontakte, a Russian social network modelled after Facebook, shared a number of photographs, along with a confession of launching the missile that downed the passenger plane. One photograph, showing a Russian missile system, had a geotag for the Ukrainian city of Donetsk. If an active Russian serviceman was present in Donetsk with this missile system, it would seriously implicate the Russian Ministry of Defence. A number of Ukrainian news sites saw this photograph, and others, and published stories detailing how a Russian soldier revealed his involvement in the war in eastern Ukraine. For example, the popular Ukrainian news site *Obozrevatel* received nearly 100,000 views when detailing this soldier's social network profile, which included the missile launcher photograph.[11]

[11] https://www.obozrevatel.com/crime/20897-rossijskij-soldat-zadokumentiroval-svoi-prestupleniya-i-zverstva-v-ukraine.htm accessed 30 December 2018.

Figure 9.10

When this photograph was taken, a reverse image search on Google would not bring up any results, leading to the possible conclusion that this user-generated content was original, and thus real. However, a close look at the licence plate of the missile launcher reveals a trick that the faker used: mirroring.

Figure 9.11

The licence plate should read '2053 EP', but the image has been mirrored, or flipped 180 degrees horizontally, preventing the reverse image search algorithms from locating the original source of the photograph. If the image is flipped back to its original position, a number of results showing the real photograph appear in Google reverse image searches, including one in a video showcasing Russian-made military equipment.[12]

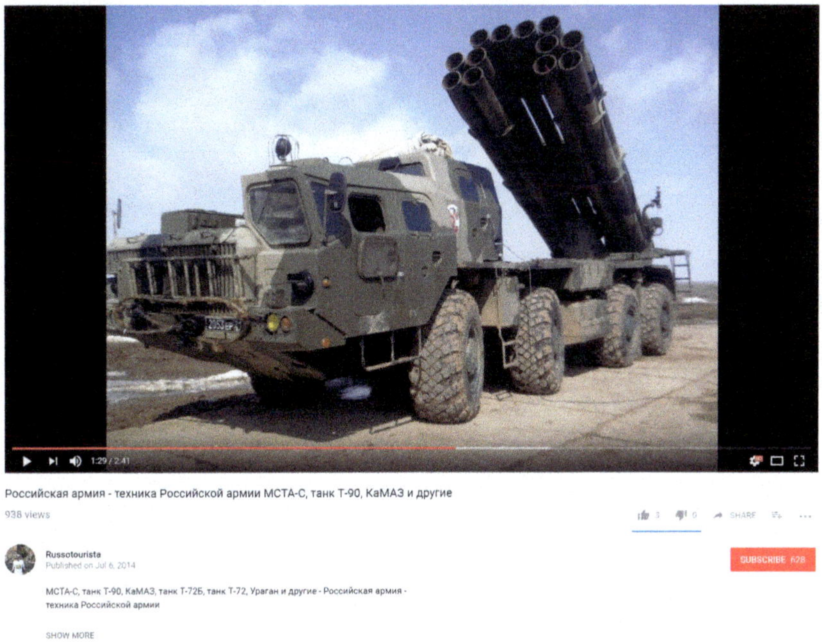

Figure 9.12

While the free tools that find the original source of photographs are useful, in this case, the verifier needs an extra dose of creativity, along with an attentive eye, not to be fooled by a doctored image.

4. Recycled Content

In the immediate aftermath of major incidents gaining swift international attention, such as a suspected terrorist attack or a plane crash, a number of old videos are typically shared online under the guise of showing first pictures of the breaking news event. For example, images that were actually from a 2011 explosion in Moscow's Domodedovo Airport and a 2011 explosion in a Minsk metro station were 'recycled' in 2016 after an explosion in the Malbeek metro station in Brussels. This fooled the global news channel CNN into broadcasting the Moscow and Minsk footage as being from Brussels.[13]

[12] https://www.youtube.com/watch?v=OCHTJig2Pjk accessed 30 December 2018.
[13] https://twitter.com/DavidClinchNews/status/712263834006896643 accessed 30 December 2018.

Figure 9.13

An extreme example of video recycling can be seen in the case of a 2009 video filmed in Utah of a group of people playing with Airsoft guns—mostly harmless replica weapons that can look and sound like actual guns.

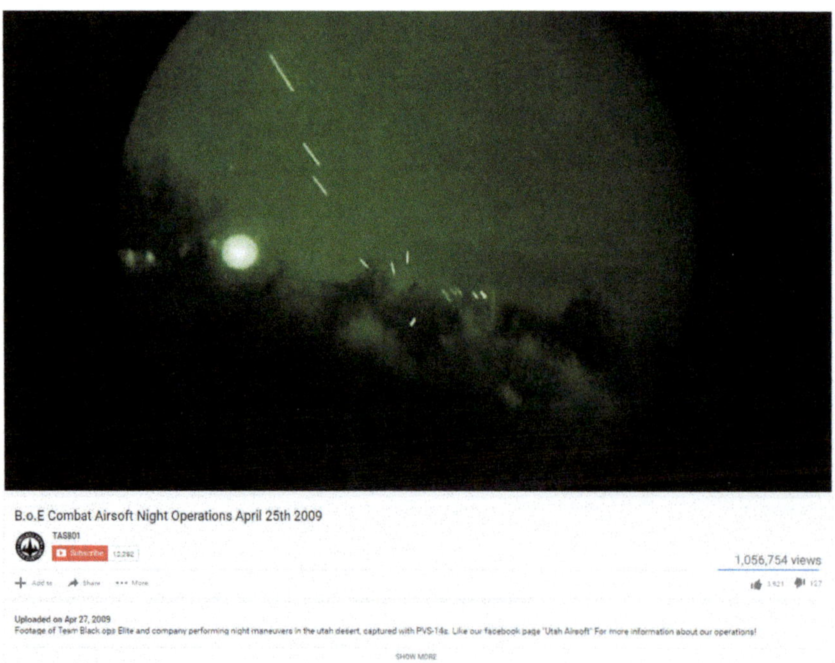

Figure 9.14

The original video was filmed with night vision and was eight minutes long, with English-speaking voices throughout the clip. The clip showing a group of people playing a game with replica weapons, however, has been repurposed and used in dozens of videos to fool others into believing it depicts actual conflict.

When conducting reverse image search on screenshots from the video, researchers have discovered that abbreviated versions of this video, often with the English voices cut out, have appeared on YouTube and other video hosting sites. Locations where this video was purportedly 'filmed' include Iraq, Syria, and Ukraine.

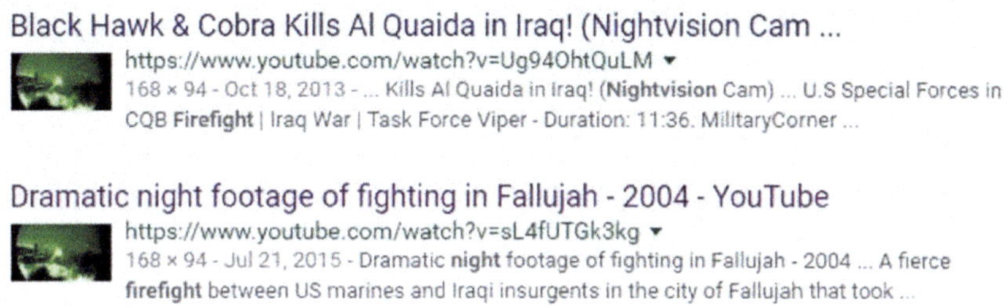
Black Hawk & Cobra Kills Al Quaida in Iraq! (Nightvision Cam ...
https://www.youtube.com/watch?v=Ug94OhtQuLM ▾
168 × 94 - Oct 18, 2013 - ... Kills Al Quaida in Iraq! (**Nightvision** Cam) ... U.S Special Forces in CQB **Firefight** | Iraq War | Task Force Viper - Duration: 11:36. MilitaryCorner ...

Dramatic night footage of fighting in Fallujah - 2004 - YouTube
https://www.youtube.com/watch?v=sL4fUTGk3kg ▾
168 × 94 - Jul 21, 2015 - Dramatic **night** footage of fighting in Fallujah - 2004 ... A fierce **firefight** between US marines and Iraqi insurgents in the city of Fallujah that took ...

Figure 9.15

War in Ukriane: Firefight in Shyrokyne - YouTube
https://www.youtube.com/watch?v=zCLR2EE7h9s ▾
168 × 94 - May 1, 2015 - **Fire fight** on front lines in Shyrokyne near Mariupol east Ukraine. Fight between DNR/Russia vs Azov Regiment. Filmed by Noah Brooks.

Figure 9.16

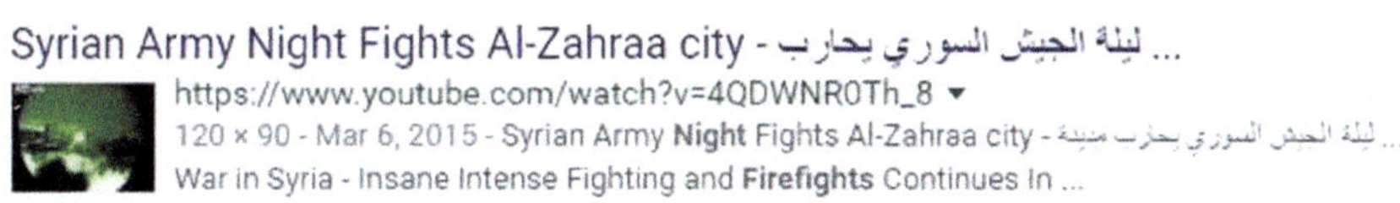
Syrian Army Night Fights Al-Zahraa city - ليلة الجيش السوري يحارب ...
https://www.youtube.com/watch?v=4QDWNR0Th_8 ▾
120 × 90 - Mar 6, 2015 - Syrian Army **Night** Fights Al-Zahraa city - ليلة الجيش السوري يحارب مدينة ...
War in Syria - Insane Intense Fighting and **Firefights** Continues In ...

Figure 9.17

There are also versions of this video clip online so heavily modified that it prevented verifiers from easily determining the original source. In one example, a Ukrainian television channel found a heavily edited version of the 2009 AirSoft game that was attributed to a December 2016 battle in Ukraine.

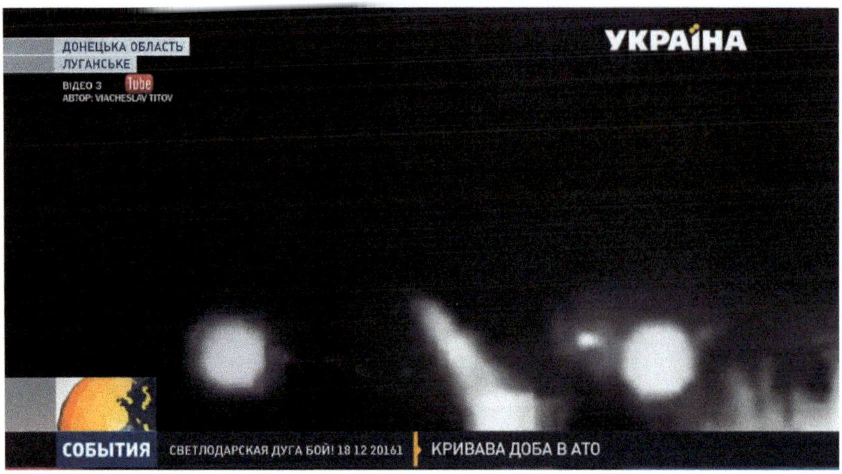

Figure 9.18

The AirSoft video has been significantly modified before it appeared on Ukrainian television: the green-hued night vision of the original video is now black and white and the video is zoomed-in dramatically, leaving only a low-resolution series of tracers and, apparently, explosions visible. Even so, the video was still believable enough in its recycled form to be aired on a major Ukrainian television channel. This practice is common everywhere now, with videos being recycled across events around the world, and it is one of the most important issues that open source human rights investigators need to be aware of.

5. Verification Technique: Geolocation

Perhaps the single most powerful verification method is geolocation—the determination of the exact location where a photograph or video was recorded. For most user-generated content that is recycled—such as an old video of an explosion at an airport, repurposed for a breaking news event—carrying out geolocation analysis on the material will provide a definitive debunking. For materials that are likely to be genuine, such as a credible witness video of a recent event, geolocation is also the quickest way to establish a higher degree of confidence that the piece of user-generated content is from the place and time claimed.

The fundamental process of geolocation is simple: cross-reference geographic details found in a piece of user-generated content with reference materials, such as satellite imagery, street-level photographs, or other visual materials that are confirmed to be from a particular location. When geolocating a video that was allegedly taken in London or another large urban area, the process of geolocation is usually simple, owing to the seemingly endless amount of potential reference materials available. These reference materials can include historical imagery from Google Street View, high-resolution overhead imagery from satellites and drones, and thousands of geotagged photographs on Instagram and other social platforms.

5.1 Reference Materials: Street-level Imagery

One of the most useful tools in quickly verifying photographs is a street-level imagery service such as Google Street View. The other two largest services that provide street-level imagery are Bing Streetside and Yandex Panorama. Bing Streetside (https://www.bing.com/maps) has extensive coverage in the United States and some urban areas in western Europe, while Yandex Panorama (https://maps.yandex.com) has extensive coverage in Russia and other former Soviet states and in some areas of Turkey, such as Istanbul and Ankara.

Often with user-generated content recorded in towns, there will be details that can be easily traced, such as shop fronts, recognizable structures, or street signs. Even if you are not familiar with the language in the photograph, search algorithms on Bing, Yandex, and Google are usually clever enough to bring you a useful result.

An example is a photograph below showing a building with the words 'RESTAURACE U DVOU KOCEK'.

Figure 9.19

Even if you did not know that this is the Czech language, you can easily search this phrase to find the location of the photograph. Searching on Google Maps gives us two results—one restaurant in Prague, and the other in Tabor—both in the Czech Republic (Czechia).

Figure 9.20

After bringing up the available Google Street View imagery, we can easily cross-reference the photograph with the same restaurant in central Prague, with matching storefronts. If we were to look closer, we could match plenty of other details.

Figure 9.21 Composite showing an original photograph (top) and the same scene in Google Street View (bottom), matching up the common details.

This example can be solved with a very simple geolocation analysis owing to the clearly visible geographic details and the availability of street-level imagery taken just a few metres away from the source material. However, sometimes using street-level imagery is just part of a larger, more difficult verification process.

In October 2017, the international criminal investigation into the downing of Malaysian Airlines Flight 17 (MH17), which, as mentioned earlier, crashed in eastern Ukraine in 2014, published a photograph of the weapon used to down the passenger plane. There were a number of previous photographs and videos recorded of this missile launcher taken on the day of the tragedy; however, this photograph, which was sent to the investigation by a witness in eastern Ukraine, had never been seen by the public before. The investigation asked anyone who had additional information about the photograph, including its exact location, to contact them. Verifying the location of this photograph is much more difficult than a restaurant in central Prague, but some of the basic methodology is the same.

Information about photograph BUK-Telar

Recently the JIT has received a new photograph of a BUK-TELAR. This picture was probably taken on July 17, 2014 in the town of Makeevka, Ukraine. The JIT presumes that the picture contains the BUK-TELAR which is responsible for downing flight MH17.

The JIT requests anyone who has any kind of information about the picture, the vehicles on it and the location where the picture was taken to contact the JIT. We will handle your information with ultimate care. JIT investigators are available to help you in several languages including Russian and Ukrainian.

Figure 9.22 Photograph shared by the Dutch-led criminal investigation into the downing of MH17. The investigation asked the public for help in determining the exact location where the image was captured.

Determining the potential location of this photograph required close analysis, which was carried out with online crowd-sourcing after the MH17 investigation's request was publicized. A keen eye on this photograph will reveal more than is initially visible: for example, all three vehicles in the photograph seem to be in different lanes, all facing the same direction—probably indicating that they are on a one-way street with at least three lanes. The MH17 disaster took place late in the afternoon, long after the missile launcher would have been unloaded from the red trailer that is visible in this photograph, meaning that this snapshot was probably taken in the morning. With the sun shining from the left of the image, this indicates that the vehicles are facing west. Furthermore, the background suggests there is a small park or perhaps a tree-lined area of green space in between the road on which the vehicles can be seen and a corresponding one-way street in an eastward direction, not in view.

Figure 9.23

There are not many three-lane one-way streets with green space in between them in the cities where this missile launcher was spotted on the day of the MH17 downing. Just by surveying satellite imagery of this area, there is only one city—Donetsk, the largest in the region—that has more than one street that would resemble the one seen in the published photograph.

By going onto Google Street View and Yandex Panorama, we can 'drive' up and down the multi-lane, one-way streets in Donetsk, hoping to find a match to the area in this photograph. If we do this for long enough, we eventually find a road that seems like a match: Prospect Ilicha, in central Donetsk. Much like the Google Street View interface, you can 'drive' up and down the street on Yandex's street view function using your keyboard or clicking onto the screen. However, the number of snapshots published by Yandex on each street is smaller than that of Google.

To find the street-level imagery on Yandex, select 'Panoramas' in the upper-right part of the user interface, which will then highlight streets in blue for available imagery.

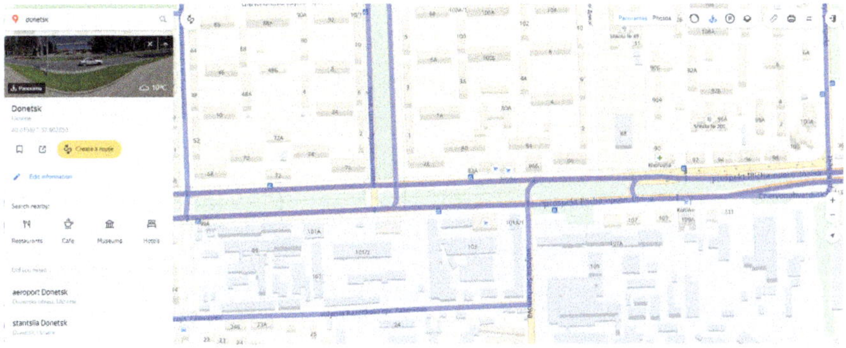

Figure 9.24

Once on the westward (northern) lane, the general lay-out matches that of the photograph published by the MH17 investigators: multi-lane one-way road headed west, and trees and green space in the median.

Figure 9.25

A close analysis of the photograph will reveal what appears to be a metal fence along the road just barely visible in between the trailer hauling the missile launcher and the ground. In the street-level imagery, a fence is also visible in roughly the same area, though it is difficult to ascertain the exact design on the gate to compare it with the Yandex Panorama image.

Figure 9.26 Magnification of the metal fence visible between the road and the bottom of the trailer.

After this resemblance of the general area was determined via street-level imagery, locals in Donetsk surveyed the area along this street, eventually finding the exact spot, as revealed by a decorative rock in the bottom-right part of the photograph.

Figure 9.27

Thus, the photograph was verified as genuine, as the timing, location, and contextual information for this photograph matched the known route of the missile launcher on the day of the MH17 tragedy.

The street-level imagery services of Google and Yandex may not always be the sole solution to verifying images, but are often the quickest way—with visible, relatively unique details such as shop fronts and street signs—or they at least provide valuable supplemental information, such as determining potential locations for a photograph or video, even if the exact details are not all visible.

5.2 Reference Materials: Satellite Imagery

While street-level imagery can provide a similar perspective to that of the user-generated content to be verified, using such reference materials is dependent on the presence of coverage from Google, Yandex, and Bing. If the user-generated content to be verified shows an outdoor scene, then satellite imagery can and should also be used in the verification process.

The most useful tool in conducting verification with satellite imagery is Google Earth, which is free to download on Windows, Mac, and other platforms.[14] Satellite imagery on Google Earth is not from any satellite operated by Google itself, but instead from a variety of organizations that provide satellite imagery either as a public service or for profit.

[14] 'Google Earth Pro' https://www.google.com/earth/download/gep/agree.html accessed 30 December 2018.

Figure 9.28

The 'Historical Imagery' option of Google Earth is vital to conducting verification, as it allows comparison of multiple satellite images in the same location.

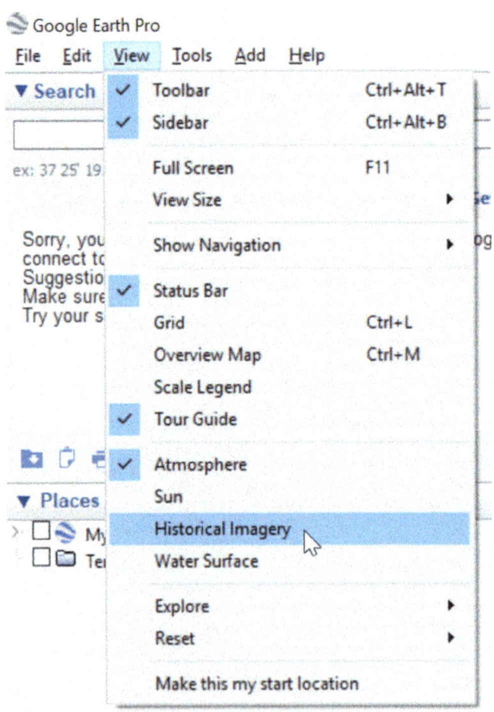

Figure 9.29

By changing the date of the satellite image in the top-left of the user interface, Google Earth will display all available satellite imagery in its database for the location. For example, the Barra Olympic Park in Rio de Janeiro, which was built for the 2016 Summer Olympics, can be viewed during its early construction through to its completion.

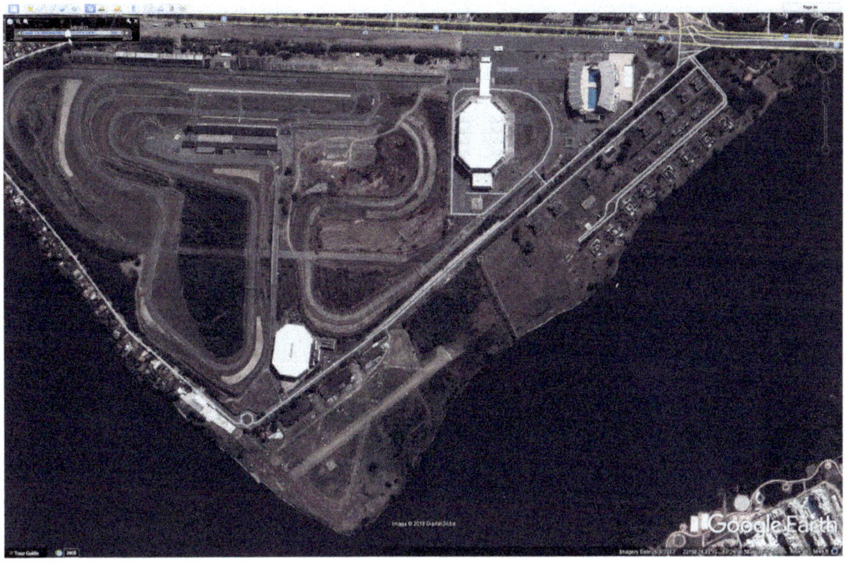

Figure 9.30 *Barra Olympic Park in 2012, on Google Earth*

Figure 9.31 *Barra Olympic Park in 2016, on Google Earth*

There are a multitude of services that provide free satellite mapping, including Google Maps, Google Earth, Bing Maps, Yandex Maps, USGS Earth Explorer, the European Space Agency's

Sentinel Mission, Here Maps, and Apple Maps. Google Earth is the most commonly used satellite service in verification because of its powerful historical imagery and user interface.

Wikimapia, hosted at wikimapia.org, is another valuable resource. It does not have satellite imagery of its own, but it consolidates multiple services, including Yandex Maps and Bing Maps, onto one website, along with user-submitted metadata for locations that can be seen by anyone accessing the site. This service allows a user to view multiple satellite imagery sources on overlaid onto one map, instead of juggling multiple websites simultaneously.

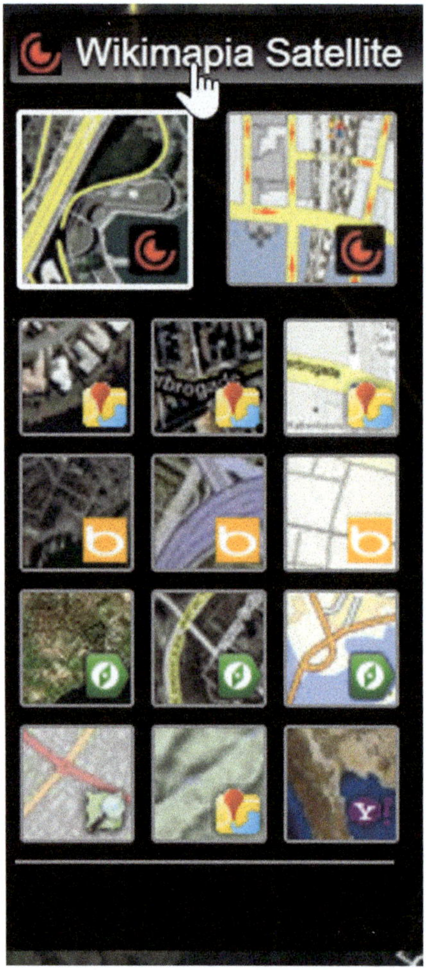

Figure 9.32 *Available layers of satellite imagery on Wikimapia, which includes Bing Maps and Yandex Maps.*

The user-submitted classification of locations also allows verification based on small amounts of information. For example, if a user-generated photograph or video claimed to be in or near a hospital in Berlin, Wikimapia is able to highlight all of the locations tagged as 'Hospital' on its map, allowing a verifier to analyse potential locations for a match quickly.

To do this, the user must select the 'Categories' option in the top-left of the Wikimapia user interface, and then either select the relevant category from the list, or search for it.

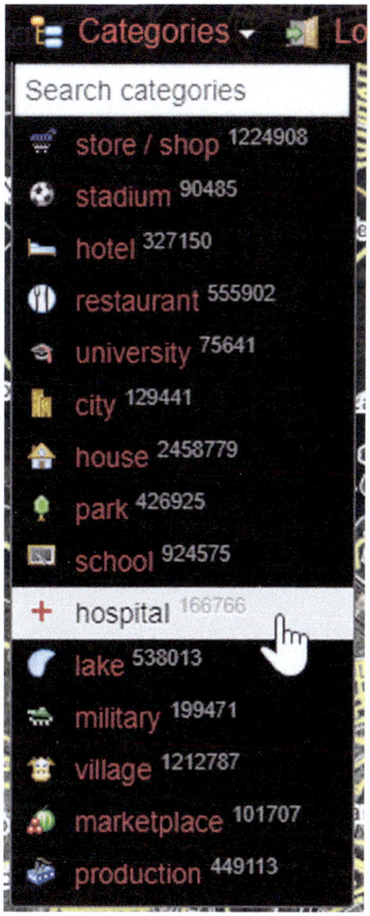

Figure 9.33

Each location tagged in the selected category—in this case, 'hospital'—is marked by a small red box on the map.

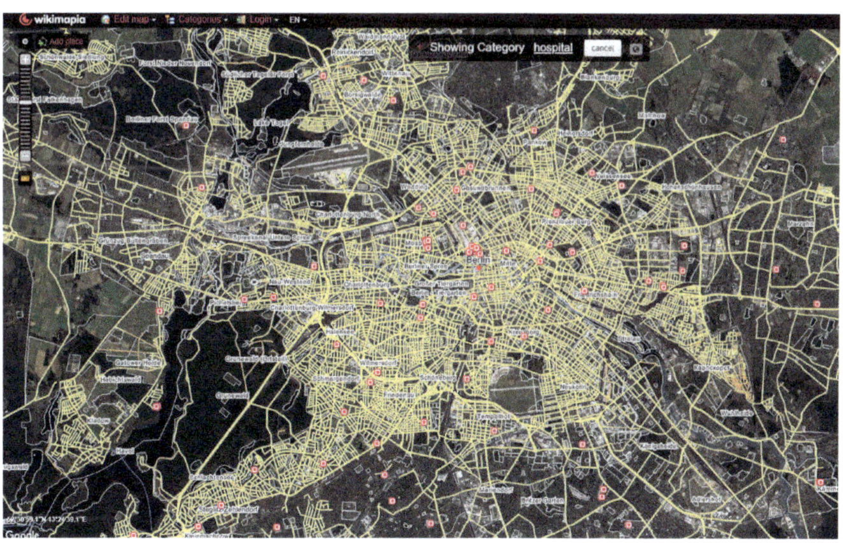

Figure 9.34

While Wikimapia has an enormous amount of information about millions of locations, according to its database, not all of the information should be trusted completely—Wikimapia works in a similar way to Wikipedia in how it relies on users to submit, edit, and curate large amounts of information on its platform.

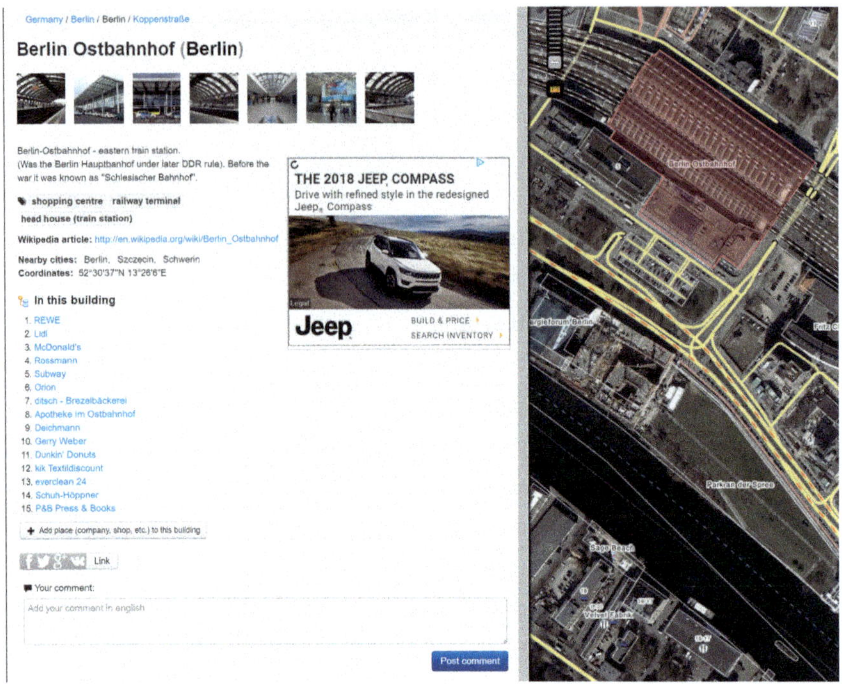

Figure 9.35 *User-submitted metadata for the Ostbahnhof station in Berlin, which includes category tags, geographic coordinates, descriptive information about the location, and user-submitted photographs.*

An example of how satellite imagery can be used to verify materials can be seen in geolocating footage released of the air campaigns being waged in Syria by the America-led Coalition and the Russian Air Force. Both of these countries publish videos of air strikes against targets in Syria, but often the locations or targets are incorrectly described by the parties carrying out the attack.

A January 2016 air strike from the US-led Coalition was reportedly north of the town of Abu Kamal in Syria.

A number of researchers found[15] this location on satellite imagery, confirming the location the US-led Coalition had indicated. By searching along the Euphrates River north of Abu Kamal, a landscape similar to the one in the air strike photograph becomes visible, with a number of matching features.

[15] https://twitter.com/obretix/status/685175492320882688 accessed 30 December 2018.

Figure 9.36 Comparison of the video shared by U.S.-led Coalition (top) with the same location visible on satellite imagery, via Google Earth (bottom).

This match shows us that the location described by the US-led Coalition is correct, and it enables journalists and researchers to follow up with additional research to verify the Coalition's claims that the so-called Islamic State was operating in this area.

Verifying images from the ground is more difficult than from aerial shots such as in the air strike footage. In the photograph below, from a 2016 papal visit in Tbilisi, Georgia, there is no available street-level imagery from Yandex or Google, making satellite imagery vital in determining the location of the photograph.

Figure 9.37

With only a few Catholic churches present in Tbilisi, we can compare the street lay-out and large buildings visible in this image with satellite imagery to determine the likely location. When attempting to verify especially difficult content, it can be useful to sketch a general lay-out of the area, as you would expect to see it in satellite imagery. In the photograph above, we can make a rough sketch of the area based on the visible buildings (especially their roof shapes), street lay-out, and presence of vegetation, as shown below. A photograph like this by itself may not tell us which direction is north, though we might be able to ascertain this based on the direction of the sun's light if we were aware of the time of day the photograph was taken.

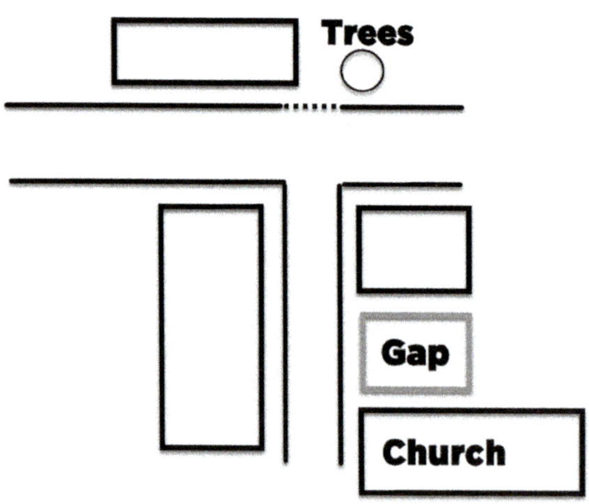

Figure 9.38

The next step is to compare this general outline and the actual photograph with various Catholic churches throughout Tbilisi. One of the largest Catholic churches in Tbilisi, the Saints Peter and Paul Church, is not a match to this outline: there is a heavy presence of trees near the Saints Peter and Paul Church and the general street lay-out does not match that seen in the photograph.

Another Tbilisi Catholic Church, the Cathedral of the Assumption of the Virgin, makes a more compelling match to the street lay-out sketch. The schematic of the area drawn from the photograph is not an exact match with the satellite image, but the general features are present: the gap between the church and the neighbouring building, a lack of trees in the immediate sight-line of the camera, and the 'T-shaped' street lay-out in front of the photographer.

Figure 9.39

There are a few major issues when working with satellite imagery in video and image verification: availability of relevant images at a sufficient resolution, the price of acquiring the correct satellite images, and interpreting satellite imagery that may be ambiguous or difficult or decipher.

In many locations, free historical satellite imagery is plentiful. With more satellite images, the problem of ambiguous imagery may be solved by viewing the same scene from multiple angles. An example of how multiple satellite images taken in the same year can show much different perspectives can be seen below, with the Eiffel Tower in 2014 on Google Earth, taken from different angles:

Figure 9.40

Figure 9.41

In downtown Manhattan, to take another example, Google Earth provides six satellite images taken in 2017 alone, many of which are in an extremely high resolution. However, in Erbil, Iraq, there is only *one* image—taken on 8 June 2004. When conducting verification for user-generated content in Erbil, the only available satellite image on Google Earth being well over a decade old presents significant challenges. Fewer satellite images result in a larger margin of error for a verifier, and a much more difficult challenge for geolocation.

In some rare cases, satellite imagery can provide unexpected information to an investigation to uncover human rights abuses, once user-generated content depicting the abuse is geolocated. In August 2017, the International Criminal Court (ICC) issued a warrant for a commander of the Libyan National Army, Mahmoud Mustafa Busayf Al-Werfalli, as described in Chapter 1

One of the ways this user-generated content can be verified, after being geolocated,[16] is by finding the exact locations of the executions near Benghazi through details in historical satellite imagery. As detailed[17] in 2017, the execution site was geolocated near to the Benghazi Airport after a lengthy crowd-sourcing campaign.[18] Below, many of the geographic details seen in the video cited by the ICC as evidence of extrajudicial executions are visible in satellite imagery.

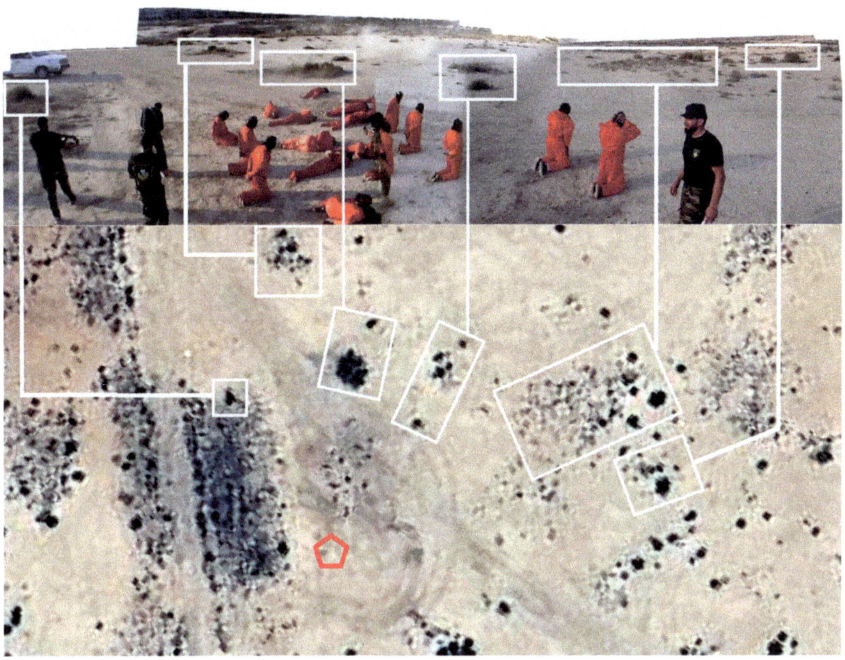

Figure 9.42

In a coincidence that rarely occurs during human rights abuse investigations, a satellite image was taken just hours after this incident, revealing additional evidence. Below, the image on the left shows the site on 11 July 2017, while the one on the right shows the same location on 17 July 2017. Extrajudicial executions took place at this location early in the morning on 17 July 2017, hours before the second satellite image was taken.

[16] 'How a Werfalli Execution Site Was Geolocated' *Bellingcat* (3 October 2017) https://www.bellingcat.com/news/mena/2017/10/03/how-an-execution-site-was-geolocated/ accessed 30 December 2018.

[17] ibid.

[18] Christiaan Tribert, 'Geolocating Libya's Social Media Executioner' *Bellingcat* (4 September 2017) https://www.bellingcat.com/news/mena/2017/09/04/geolocating-libyas-social-media-executioner/ accessed 30 December 2018.

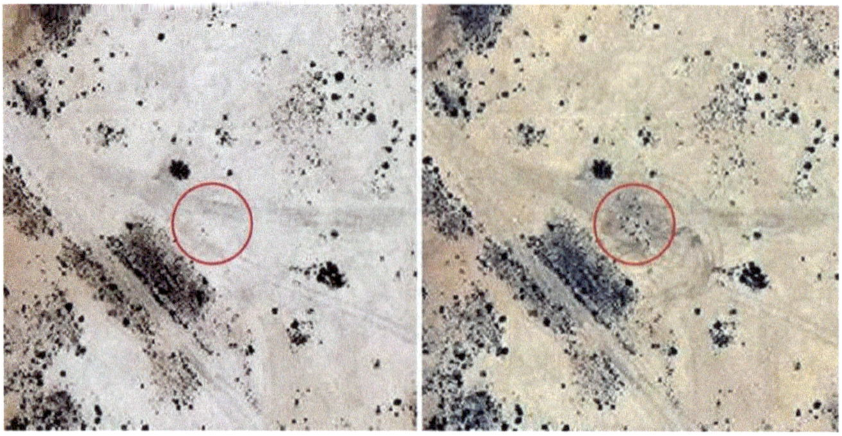

Figure 9.43

After meticulously aligning the perspective of the camera showing the executions, along with the same approximate perspective overlooking the 17 July 2017 satellite image, the dark spots reveal themselves as blood—the bodies of the executed prisoners, as seen in the user-generated content cited by the ICC as evidence, aligns almost exactly with the dark spots on the satellite image.

Figure 9.44

If a verifier has sufficient resources, satellite imagery for purchase may be available for a particularly difficult geolocation challenge when free satellite imagery does not pose a solution. The following sites are some of the most useful for verification but require either a subscription or one-time payment for a satellite image with varying availability and resolution: DigitalGlobe (digitalglobe.com); Planet, which offers a very high number of satellite images, but at a low resolution (planet.com); and TerraServer, with higher resolution imagery than Planet, but with fewer satellite images available (terraserver.com).

6. Verification Technique: Determining Time

Geolocation, the determination of the location of a photograph or video, is often only part of the verification equation. Verifying user-generated content often requires the determination of time as well as place, though this process is often much less precise. In the case of human rights investigations, often multiple incidents occur in the same location—for example, on the front-line of conflicts, meaning that the time of user-generated content showing an event can be more important than the location. Outside of a visible clock in the background, there are few infallible methods to determine the time of an uploaded (non-live streamed) photograph or video precisely, but there are a handful of methods that allow an approximation to assist in verification.

6.1 Time Determination: Weather

One of the most important temporary indicators in user-generated content is weather. When verifying user-generated content, knowing the supposed date and general location is enough to cross-reference the weather information. Wolfram Alpha, accessed at wolframalmpha.com, provides historical weather information going back decades, with a wealth of accessible data.

Not only can Wolfram Alpha provide information about the general conditions on a day, but also an hour-by-hour account of the cloud cover, precipitation rate, wind speed, and temperature. For most verification cases, the presence of rain and cloud cover are the most important details to reference, but circumstantial evidence can be gleaned from other details, such as clothing worn by people visible in user-generated content that is incongruous with the temperature recorded on the reported day of the photograph or video.

For example, this photograph in Prague was uploaded on 5 May 2018.

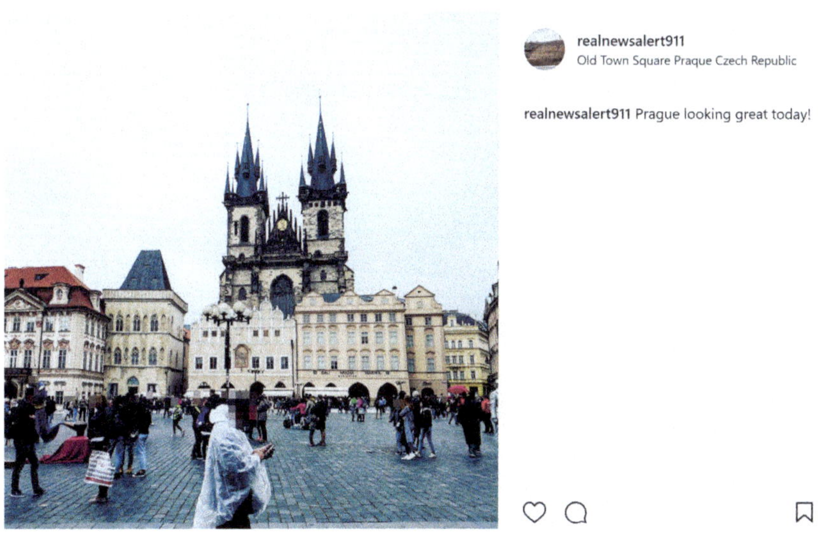

Figure 9.45

It takes just one minute to load up Google Street View to geolocate the photograph and verify the location as Old Town Square in central Prague, matching the geotag accompanying the Instagram post.

Figure 9.46

But verifying the location is only half of the problem. The scene in the Instagram photograph is an overcast day with one person wearing a poncho and others wearing jackets and holding umbrellas.

Checking the Wolfram Alpha database for historical data on the weather in Prague allows additional verification possibilities for this photograph. By searching the phrase 'Weather in Prague on May 5, 2018' on the site, the historical data will appear, including the relevant precipitation and cloud cover information for this day.

Figure 9.47

The results show that there was minimal cloud cover throughout the day, and no recorded precipitation.

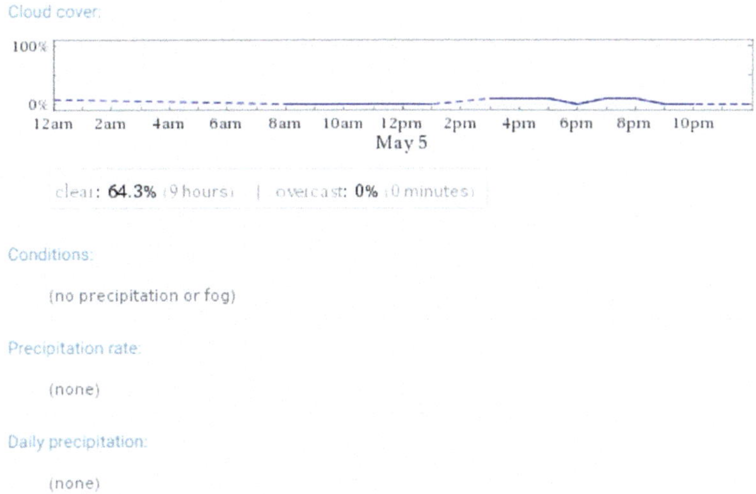

Figure 9.48

While the photograph was indeed taken in the geotagged location of Old Town Square in Prague, it was not taken on 5 May 2018, when it was uploaded.

6.2 Time Determination: Temporary Details

Temporary details, such as advertisements and construction, can provide vital clues about when user-generated content was captured. Many of these details can be seen on Google Street View, which includes a valuable chronological feature that allows the user to view how an area changes over time if multiple snapshots have been taken. This feature was used in October 2017 to analyse a photograph shared by a former adviser to US President Trump, George Papadopoulos, who, just a week earlier, was revealed to be cooperating with the FBI regarding meetings connected to Russia and the Trump campaign.[19]

[19] https://twitter.com/GeorgePapa19/status/923078894634270720 accessed 30 December 2018.

Figure 9.49

This photograph was notable because it was sent out while Papadopoulos was still cooperating with the FBI and did not have access to his passport, keeping him in the United States. Most people would recognize this scene as the United Kingdom, owing to the iconic double-decker red bus popular in London and the fact that the vehicles are driving on the left side of the street. So, how could Papadopoulos be in London in October 2017 when he had surrendered his passport to the FBI months prior?

Google Street View's chronological feature allows us to determine when this photograph was taken—more than three years before it was tweeted out. Many who have visited London will recognize the location of the photograph as Harrods, a popular department store in the city centre. While many of the details around Papadopoulos do not change with time, there is something that does—the stickers on a pole directly behind him, which are cleaned off occasionally by city workers. In particular, there is one large sticker with what appears to be the wings of a bird, and two stickers (and the remnants of a third) below it.

Figure 9.50

By selecting the timeline feature of Google Street View in the top-left of the user interface, we can scroll through captures of the area from 2008 (left-most option) and 2016 (right-most option).

Figure 9.51

In May 2016, the stickers from the Papadopoulos tweet have been scraped off, with only remnants of the stickers' adhesive remaining.

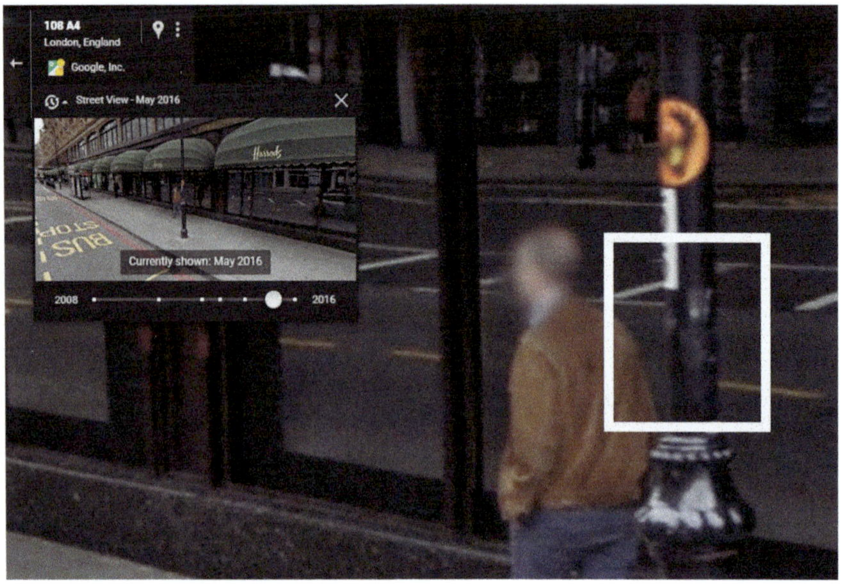

Figure 9.52

However, in August 2014, the stickers are still present.

Figure 9.53

Figure 9.54

In May 2015, the stickers are gone, just as they were in the most recent (2016) snapshot of the pole outside the London department store.

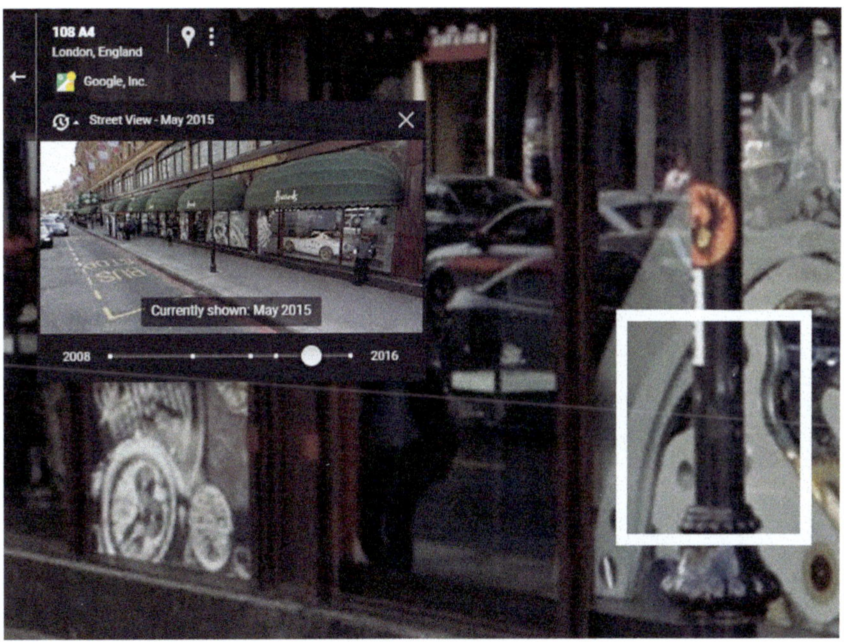

Figure 9.55

What does all of this mean? In short: Papadopoulos purposefully selected a photograph of himself abroad as if he were there at the time, even though the photograph was taken some time before May 2015, when we can no longer observe the sticker from his photograph on the pole.

6.3 Time Determination: Shadows

Observable shadows allow a more exact determination of time than details such as weather and temporary features. In order to determine the approximate time of user-generated content from the observable shadows, the exact location and approximate date are necessary. There are a handful of online tools to assist the verifier in the process, but the naked eye can make a broad judgment if the user-generated content has been geolocated. For example, as anyone knows, a long shadow facing to the east means that the sun is low in the western sky, meaning that the material was taken in the late afternoon. Determining the time of a photograph or video using shadows is greatly assisted by a versatile digital toolset, but it is not required to make general assumptions if a clearly cast shadow is visible and the cardinal directions have been determined.

An example of using shadows to verify user-generated content can be seen in a video uploaded by the Indian news agency *ThePrint*, presumably received from a soldier or officer in the area, showing a brawl between Indian and Chinese soldiers. The video was reportedly filmed in the morning of 15 August 2017 as detailed in further reporting from *ThePrint*.[20]

Figure 9.56

[20] https://twitter.com/ThePrintIndia/status/898871876813967361 accessed 30 December 2018.

The time of the video can be verified by the long shadows visible throughout the video. First, geolocation of the video is necessary to confirm the location and, if the location is correct, we can measure the angle of the shadows to help estimate the time of day.

Satellite imagery on Google Earth from 14 July 2017 shows the same location in the video on Pangong Lake, as described in the original tweet. Below, an arrow indicates the same direction, with the camera on an elevated location near the shore on the right-hand part of the satellite image.

Figure 9.57

The website SunCalc (suncalc.org) allows the virtual casting of shadows onto a satellite image, with the cast shadow allowing for the astronomical data of any day. By selecting the correct day, the correct data for the sun on that day—down to the exact second of sunrise, sunset, and the solar azimuth—is included in calculations. If we select the correct location (Lake Pangong) and date (15 August 2017), SunCalc can replicate how the shadows in the video appeared, providing an approximate time in which the shadows would have appeared in a similar location.

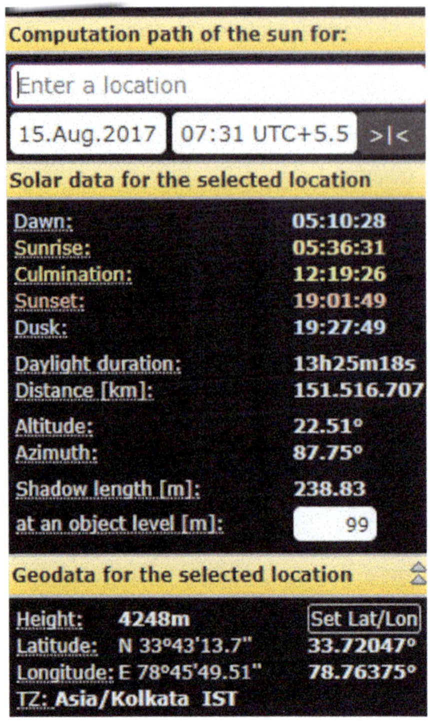

Figure 9.58

The shadow for approximately 7.30 am local time would have appeared as such, with the shadow cast towards the right-hand shore in the satellite image. (We have rotated the satellite image 180 degrees to match the perspective of the video, and thus the white arrow is facing south, not north.)

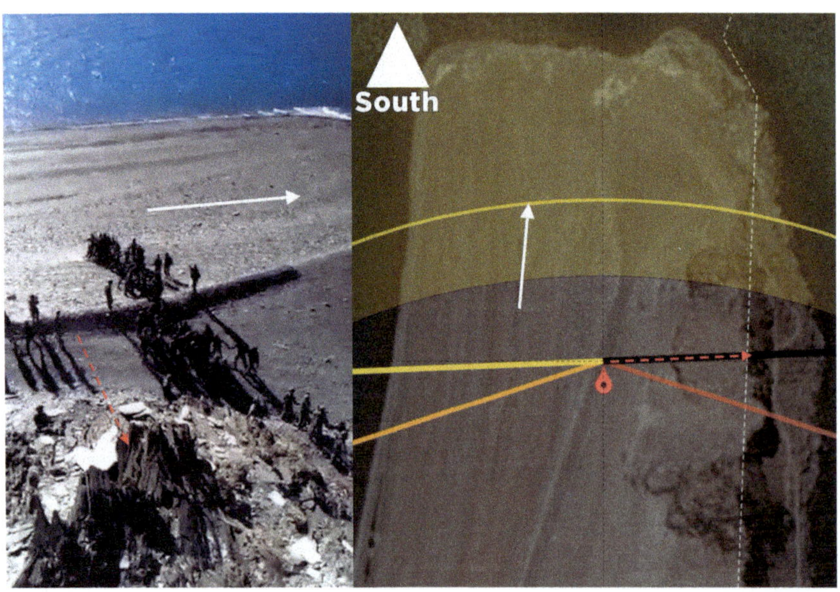

Figure 9.59

While determining the exact minute that the video was taken is difficult by only analysing the visible shadows; however, it is possible to determine conclusively that the video was shot early in the morning owing to the fact that the long shadows are cast westward (towards the camera).

7. Holistic Verification Regime

While a number of verification methods and tools can be the first and last step to verifying some user-generated content, a verifier should not rely on a small selection of online tools and methods alone. Even the most proficient users of digital tools and purveyors of satellite imagery will be a step behind those with strong regional familiarity for the area that the user-generated content was taken. For example, in verifying a photograph in the war zone of eastern Ukraine, large slag heaps from coal mines, which are frequently seen in this area of eastern Europe, are often the best guidelines for geolocation, while one should look for the minarets of mosques to pinpoint the location of materials from Syria.

The most effective verification regime combines regional expertise, an analytical eye, proficiency in digital tools, and proven verification methods. Digital tools will come and go, but there is no expiration date on the necessity of understanding how to approach each methodological step of verification, such as determining provenance, time, and location of user-generated content.

8. Index of Tools

Not all of these tools may be online indefinitely. For an up-to-date, curated listed of tools that are online, refer to the Bellingcat Digital Toolkit on Google Docs, found at bit.ly/bcat-tools.

Mapping Services

Wikimapia: wikimapia.org
Google Maps: maps.google.com
Yandex Maps: maps.yandex.com
Bing Maps: maps.bing.com
Google Earth: google.com/earth

Reverse Search and Image Verification

Reverse Google Image Search: images.google.com
Reverse Yandex Image Search: Yandex.com/images
Tineye: tineye.com
Invid: invid-project.eu
Jeffrey's Image Metadata Viewer: exif.regex.info/exif.cgi
SunCalc: suncalc.org

10

The Role and Use of Satellite Imagery for Human Rights Investigations

Micah Farfour

Remote sensing is the measurement of an object from a distance. While there are many kinds of measurement that could fall under that broad definition, the main interest for human rights research is the measurement of the earth's surface using optical sensors producing a two-dimensional spatial grid referred to as satellite imagery. The sensors detect radiation reflected from the earth at different wavelengths to form an image that can be interpreted by machines or human analysts. In the past, the military was the predominant consumer of high-resolution satellite imagery, but as more commercial imagery becomes available, prices have become more competitive and, in some cases, free, allowing other interested parties, such as human rights researchers, to explore potential applications.

There are three main categories to consider when working with satellite imagery: spatial resolution, spectral resolution, and temporal resolution. Spatial resolution is the size of the smallest feature that can be detected. Spectral resolution is defined by the sensors' ability to measure different wavelengths in the electromagnetic spectrum. Temporal resolution, or revisit rate, is the time that elapses between different images in the same geographic location. All these factors contribute to the potential for clear and accurate documentation of human rights abuses. Higher spatial resolutions allow more accuracy in visually confirming events while faster revisit rates allow the timeframe of activities to be narrowed, possibly aligning with the reported presence of specific actors. Higher spectral resolution is less often needed, though bands outside of the visible wavelengths are often utilized to detect such things as recently burned areas or changes in crop health. While each category has benefits, imagery most often used in the documentation of human rights abuse must be of high resolution and quality to be an acceptable form of evidence in a court of law.[1]

Over the years, spatial, spectral, and temporal resolutions have advanced dramatically from the first Landsat Multispectral Scanner System (MSS) launched in 1972 with 80m spatial resolution, four spectral bands, and a revisit rate of eighteen days to today's commercially available satellite imagery with spatial resolution of up to 31 cm, spectral resolutions with hundreds of bands and daily revisit rates. In the last decade, more and more commercial earth observing satellites have been launched and the price for imagery has

[1] *Prosecutor v Ahmad Al-Faqi Al-Mahdi* (Judgment and Sentence) ICC-01/12-01/15-171 (27 September 2016).

decreased. This has allowed the science community to explore other applications ranging from analysis of global deforestation and monitoring the aftermath of a disaster to mapping forced human migrations and the razing of villages. The American Association for the Advancement of Science (AAAS) has been at the forefront in using satellite imagery for human rights investigations.[2]

Since the first commercially available satellite imagery became available, not only have the spatial, spectral, and temporal resolutions advanced significantly, but the number of commercial satellites in space has also increased dramatically. In the past five years, many new companies and countries have joined the rush for space. These new companies are challenging the remote sensing industry, forcing innovation and changing the face of satellite imagery in the United States and across the world. Countries formerly under strict government control—such as China, Brazil, and India—are launching their own commercial satellites and increasing the use of imagery across the globe. With all these new companies, not only is the cost of imagery dropping, but the extraordinary amount of data being collected has led to a new problem: too much data for the capacity available to make sense of all of it. A variety of new research and companies have been formed specifically to handle this influx of data.

In this chapter, we will look more closely at the history of satellite imagery, some of the various applications, and their importance in human rights investigations. Five case studies will be presented. There will also be a quick look at new things in the industry and where to access remote sensing data.

1. History of Satellites

Earth-monitoring satellites—colloquially referred to as spy satellites—were first developed for military purposes to monitor perceived enemies in the 1960s. The first earth-observing non-military satellite was launched in 1972 by the United States Geological Survey (USGS)[3] to monitor the earth's terrain at 80m spatial resolution, marking the start of the Landsat programme. Since that time, seven more Landsat satellites have been launched with the latest, Landsat 8, launched in 2013. Landsat 8 sensors can measure eleven spectral bands with spatial resolution of 30m. Landsat 9 was previously planned to be launched in 2020 but current government funding has not made its construction a priority.

While Landsat provides the most historically comprehensive dataset of earth monitoring measurements, other satellites have also been launched since 1972. In 1986, for example, the French launched their first earth observing satellite, Satellite pour l'Observation de la Terre (SPOT) with 10m resolution. At the time, it had the highest resolution commercially available. Since the first SPOT satellite, six more have been launched with the latest resolution up to 1.5m.

These developments, along with a few changes in law to stimulate the US commercial market,[4] led to the launch, in 1999, of the first high-resolution satellite, Ikonos,

[2] 'SRHRL Past Projects: Geotech & Human Rights: Case Studies' (*American Association for the Advancement of Science*) https://www.aaas.org/programs/scientific-responsibility-human-rights-law/geotech-human-rights accessed 10 September 2018.

[3] 'History' (*NASA Landsat Program*) https://landsat.gsfc.nasa.gov/about/history/ accessed 20 September 2018.

[4] 'Presidential Decision Directive/NSC-23' https://fas.org/irp/offdocs/pdd/pdd-23.pdf accessed 10 September 2018.

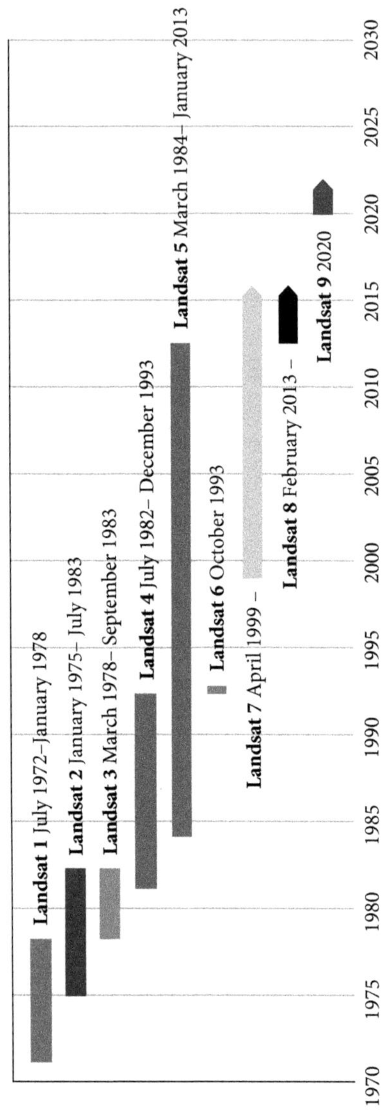

Landsat 1 July 1972–January 1978
Landsat 2 January 1975– July 1983
Landsat 3 March 1978– September 1983
Landsat 4 July 1982– December 1993
Landsat 5 March 1984– January 2013
Landsat 6 October 1993
Landsat 7 April 1999 –
Landsat 8 February 2013 –
Landsat 9 2020
1970
1975
1980
1985
1990
1995
2000
2005
2010
2015
2020
2025
2030

Figure 10.1

by GeoEye. At a maximum of 1m resolution, Ikonos provided the first commercially available high-resolution satellite imagery and was the catalyst for what became a wave of innovation in satellite imagery. Soon after the launch of Ikonos, the company DigitalGlobe successfully launched Quickbird 2 with a spatial resolution of just 60cm.

From 1999 to 2012, GeoEye and DigitalGlobe dominated the market for high-resolution imagery with the launch of three more satellites, each with 50cm spatial resolution. In 2012, DigitalGlobe acquired GeoEye and in 2014, DigitalGlobe pushed the bar even further by gaining a licence from the US government to sell 31cm imagery.

With DigitalGlobe leading the market on the highest resolution of commercially available satellite imagery, new companies have joined the race to fill in where there might be gaps. Planet, for example, developed a group of smaller, less expensive satellites, referred to as micro-satellites,[5] which can be launched into space in large numbers. At the time of writing, Planet has over 175 micro-satellites in orbit, making it the largest constellation. The micro-satellites capture 3m spatial resolution imagery with four spectral bands. The company's goal is to push temporal resolution and document all of earth's land surface daily.

In recent years, many more countries have begun building their own satellites, trying to find a niche in a burgeoning market. There are currently at least twenty-three commercial satellites capturing imagery under 1m resolution. All of these new satellites have led to a new wave in human rights research. Today, when an event happens, there is likely to be an image of the location, albeit of varying resolution, that will be taken within a week.

2. Satellite Imagery Applications

The uses for satellite imagery have expanded greatly since the first Landsat was launched to monitor large changes on the earth. With the vast library of historical imagery dating back to 1972, global change detection and monitoring have detailed over four decades of changes on the planet including global warming, deforestation, and ozone depletion.[6] Companies such as Google have developed simple tools, such as Timelapse, to look quickly at some of these large changes over time.

Specific areas of the environment can also be monitored to look at urban growth or assess hazardous waste. AAAS, for example, conducted an analysis of oil spills in the Niger Delta, near Bodo, Nigeria and found thousands of acres of landscape contaminated.[7]

[5] 'Goldilocks Deep Dive Micro-satellite Data: Measuring Impact from Space' (February 2016) https://www.poverty-action.org/sites/default/files/publications/Goldilocks-Deep-Dive-Micro-satellite-Data-Measuring-Impact-from-Space_5.pdf accessed 10 September 2018.

[6] LuAnn Dahlman, 'Climate Change: Spring Snow Cover' *Climate.gov* (22 August 2018) https://www.climate.gov/news-features/understanding-climate/climate-change-spring-snow-cover accessed 10 September 2018.

[7] 'AAAS Analysis of Satellite Images Confirms Devastating Oil Spills around Nigerian Town' *American Association for the Advancement of Science* (10 November 2011) https://www.aaas.org/news/aaas-analysis-satellite-images-confirms-devastating-oil-spills-around-nigerian-town accessed 10 September 2018.

Such satellite imagery assessments can provide scientists or those conducting remediation, important information on how far the waste may have spread and those areas most affected.

The agriculture industry is also one that can benefit from the use of satellite imagery to monitor soil quality, crop health, and to forecast crop yields. In areas of the world where small-scale agriculturalists are dependent on crops for their livelihoods, satellite imagery provides information on crop health to determine potential decreases in food security.[8]

The many spectral bands available in satellite imagery allow industries to conduct exploration remotely to detect specific minerals, commonly found in areas with other non-renewable resources. Similarly, renewable natural resources such as forests and wetlands can be assessed and monitored using satellite imagery to determine viability and health.[9]

Satellite imagery of course is also used for mapping. Groups such as OpenStreetMaps have been bringing together volunteers and using satellite imagery to fill in areas of the world that had remained unmapped and document changes in the environment after disasters. Many people can benefit from these maps, especially in situations of crisis where roads may be impassable, and people have been stranded, such as during the aftermath of the April 2015 earthquake in Nepal.[10]

News and other media use satellite imagery to demonstrate analysis and provide visuals to tell the story. While words can be engaging, satellite imagery can help to explain the story, allowing to visualize and potentially relate better to the story. There is also possible information within the data from a satellite image that can explain the situation better than any words.[11]

Finally, satellite imagery is often used for other aspects of safety and security than disaster recovery. This often entailed military applications, but others, including human rights organizations, began to take on projects such as mining natural resources in conflict zones, protection of at-risk populations from further violence, monitoring detention facilities for changes in population, and many other situations.

All of these specific applications can be used in investigating human rights abuses. Looking at global change over time could indicate water resources are being directed to specific groups of people at the expense of others. Documentation of hazardous waste could

[8] Hafizur Rahman, 'Satellite Based Crop Monitoring and Estimation System for Food Security Application in Bangladesh' (Food and Agriculture Organization of the United Nations 2014) http://www.fao.org/fileadmin/templates/rap/files/Project/Expert_Meeting__17Feb2014_/P2-5_BANGLADESH_PAPER_BY_HAFIZUR_RAHMAN.pdf accessed 10 September 2018.

[9] Brian David Woodward, Paul Harrison Evangelista, and Anthony Grant Vorster, 'Mapping Progression and Severity of a Southern Colorado Spruce Beetle Outbreak Using Calibrated Image Composites' (2018) 9 Forests 336.

[10] Annie Sneed, 'The Open Source Maps that Make Rescues in Nepal Possible' *Wired* (8 May 2015) https://www.wired.com/2015/05/the-open-source-maps-that-made-rescues-in-nepal-possible/ accessed 30 December 2018.

[11] Ethan Siegel, 'NASA Images Show a Record Recovery from History's Worst National Park Wildfire' *Forbes* (3 September 2018) https://www.forbes.com/sites/startswithabang/2018/09/03/nasa-monitors-record-recovery-from-worst-national-park-wildfire-in-history/ accessed 10 September 2018.

help provide evidence for accountability in oil spills,[12] while changes in agricultural activities and health of crops could indicate the starvation of a population.[13]

3. Importance in Human Rights Research

Satellite imagery can provide an unbiased, scientific analysis of an area on the planet. And the methodology used to analyse the imagery can also be replicated to verify analytical findings. The actual interpretation of satellite imagery can lead to certain biases, but in the case of human rights research, many other datasets are typically incorporated to triangulate a responsible understanding of the situation.

A satellite is also able to access visually areas of the globe that are often inaccessible to human rights abuse investigators, such as North Korea, Rakhine State, Myanmar, and Jebel Marra, Sudan. In other instances, satellite imagery can provide a very prompt look into a remote region after, for example, a massacre, before a researcher is able to visit the area.

The ability to look back in time, pinpoint activities geospatially, detect changes unobservable by the human eye, and use high-resolution imagery to see specific items provides an incredible advantage to information collected in human rights investigations. When compared with traditional styles of evidence gathering, which relied heavily on witness testimony, satellite imagery offers a check of visual evidence over time that may run counter to the effects of trauma on a person's memory of events or the ulterior motives of a perpetrator to insist upon a different sequence of events on the ground. Satellite imagery, in most situations, cannot independently prove an abuse has been committed, but it can add—sometimes essential—information to what may have transpired. Advancements in spatial, spectral, and temporal resolutions, as mentioned earlier, have led to increased and more accurate documentation of situations involving environmental rights, indiscriminate violence, forced relocation, and violence visited upon civilians, along with other human rights abuses.

3.1 Spatial Resolution

The highest spatial resolution of satellite imagery allowed commercially in the United States is 31cm. Before 2014, laws only allowed the public to view imagery at 50cm resolution. Though the technology is available to capture higher resolutions of satellite imagery, the government restricts the satellite imaging companies.

However, the leap from 50 to 31cm resolution is making satellite imagery into a more robust piece of information difficult to deny. In an increasing number of situations, the higher resolution imagery is making its way into court cases as evidence, such as in the *Al-Mahdi* case at the International Criminal Court (ICC) (see Chapter 1).

[12] '(S)Hell in the Niger Delta: Satellite Images Document Oil Spills' Amnesty International (2011) https://www.amnestyusa.org/shell-in-the-niger-delta-satellite-images-document-oil-spills/ accessed 10 September 2018.

[13] '"We Leave or We Die": Forced Displacement under Syria's "Reconciliation" Agreements' Amnesty International (2017) https://www.amnesty.org/en/documents/document/?indexNumber=mde24%2f7309%2f2017&language=en accessed 10 September 2018.

Figure 10.2 Examples of 50 centimeter (left) and 30 centimeter (right) over the same location in Raqqa, Syria. Imagery: © DigitalGlobe, 25 August 2017, 35.9421°, 39.9908°

3.2 Spectral Resolution

Satellites are measuring the reflectance of light off the surface of the earth in many different wavelengths apart from the visible, red, green, and blue bands. This allows analysts the ability to detect reflectance in other wavelengths invisible to the human eye. Though there are satellite sensors with the ability to measures hundreds of bands, only a few are used regularly in documenting human rights abuses.

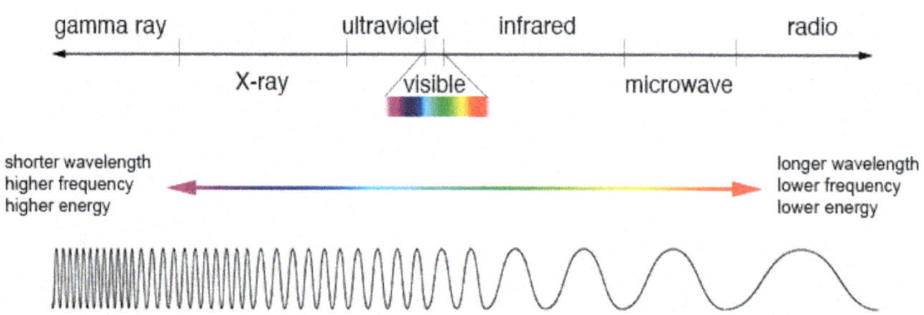

Figure 10.3 Source: Comparison of wavelength, frequency and energy for the electromagnetic spectrum." Digital image. The Electromagnetic Spectrum. March 2013. Accessed June 2017. https://imagine.gsfc.nasa.gov/science/toolbox/emspectrum1.

The main band, not in the visible range, utilized is the near infrared (NIR) band. The NIR band is helpful when looking at vegetation since plants reflect this wavelength through the water in their leaves. Healthy plants will appear brighter than unhealthy plants.[14]

Places such as the Niger Delta have been horribly polluted by oil spills, which has had a grave impact on the local communities reliant on the land and water. In many spill areas,

[14] Mausi Segun, 'Dispatches: What Really Happened in Baga, Nigeria?' *Human Rights Watch* (14 January 2015) https://www.hrw.org/news/2015/01/14/dispatches-what-really-happened-baga-nigeria accessed 10 September 2018.

vegetation has completely died out, and the impact is readily visible in satellite imagery highlighting the NIR band. Information like this is helpful in building cases against the oil companies in the region that allowed oil spills to occur and did not provide sufficient clean-up and the remediation needed to preserve the ecology of the region.

The NIR band is not only helpful in seeing vegetation health, but also highlights areas that have been burned. The band can be used to increase visibility through certain types and thicknesses of smoke, possibly allowing a better view of the ground. In some cases, active fires are also visible that would not be apparent in natural colour imagery.[15]

Since the NIR detects in the spectrum reflected by plants, manmade objects often appear differently than in natural colour images. Manmade materials in vegetated areas tend to pop out of the area making them easier to detect. Vehicles under trees can become more apparent, and detectable materials of a structure's roof could distinguish it from other common roofs in the area. Tarpaulins used by internally displaced people can easily be seen by looking at the NIR band.

Another useful combination of spectral bands is developed from a combination of the NIR and Red band, where the normalized difference vegetation index (NDVI) can be determined with the formula NDVI = (NIR - Red)/(NIR + Red). This index indicates changes in vegetation in considerable detail. Amnesty International and Forensic Architecture have used this index, for example, in determining the path Israeli tanks took in the 2014 conflict in Gaza.[16]

Research has also been conducted to determine areas of potential mass graves using satellite imagery and other remotely sensed data.[17] At this time, this research has not become common in the documentation of human rights abuses, but it may in the future.

3.3 Temporal Resolution

In many cases of human rights abuse, there is a delay between when the event occurred and when it comes to light. In some instances, the abuses occurred many years earlier and the people affected may not have been aware of their rights or that information was available to protect their rights in retrospect. In other instances, the abuses might span a long time period where looking at a range of historical data is needed to understand events happening now, including the long-term effects of mining on a village.[18]

Today, with so many commercial satellites covering the globe, capturing a weekly image of a location on the planet is feasible. Compared with the original revisit rate of eighteen days, the better temporal resolutions are leading to more accurate documentation of when events happen, potentially aligning with certain actors being present in an area.[19]

[15] 'Nigeria: Satellite Images Show Horrific Scale of Boko Haram Attack on Baga' Amnesty International (2015) https://www.amnesty.org/en/latest/news/2015/01/nigeria-satellite-images-show-horrific-scale-boko-haram-attack-baga/ accessed 10 September 2018.

[16] '"Black Friday": Carnage in Rafah during 2014 Israel/Gaza Conflict' Amnesty International (2014) https://blackfriday.amnesty.org/report.php accessed 10 September 2018.

[17] Hannah Hoag, 'Using Technology to Find Hidden Graves' *Discover* (8 September 2015) http://discovermagazine.com/2015/oct/14-body-of-evidence accessed 10 September 2018.

[18] '"Our Lives Mean Nothing": The Human Cost of Chinese Mining in Nagohna, Mozambique' Amnesty International (2018) https://www.amnesty.org/en/documents/document/?indexNumber=afr41%2f7851%2f2018&language=en accessed 10 September 2018.

[19] 'Architects of Atrocity: The Sudanese Government's War Crimes, Crimes against Humanity, and Torture in South Kordofan and Blue Nile States' The Enough Project and the Satellite Sentinel Project Teams (2013) http://www.satsentinel.org/sites/default/files/Architects_of_Atrocity.pdf accessed 10 September 2018.

With such a growing library of imagery, events and changes detected can be mapped at a larger scale with more frequency. Geospatial patterns over space and time can be used to better understand the situation and the factors that might be involved. If a group has been committing human rights abuses for some time, it is possible to understand the specific types of people that are at risk and predict sensitive areas for future monitoring. For example, the people in Jebel Marra have been subjected to military operations against them year after year. This knowledge, along with frequent revisit rates of satellites, allows researchers to monitor the areas for potential increases in troops and the potential for further human rights abuses to be committed. This documentation could also be used to show the scale of a problem and to create pressure to protect the population against future attacks.

4. Case Studies

To explain the use of satellite imagery better in recent human rights abuse events, five case studies are discussed here briefly. They span a range from environmental rights, indiscriminate violence, forced relocation, violence against civilians, and crimes against humanity.

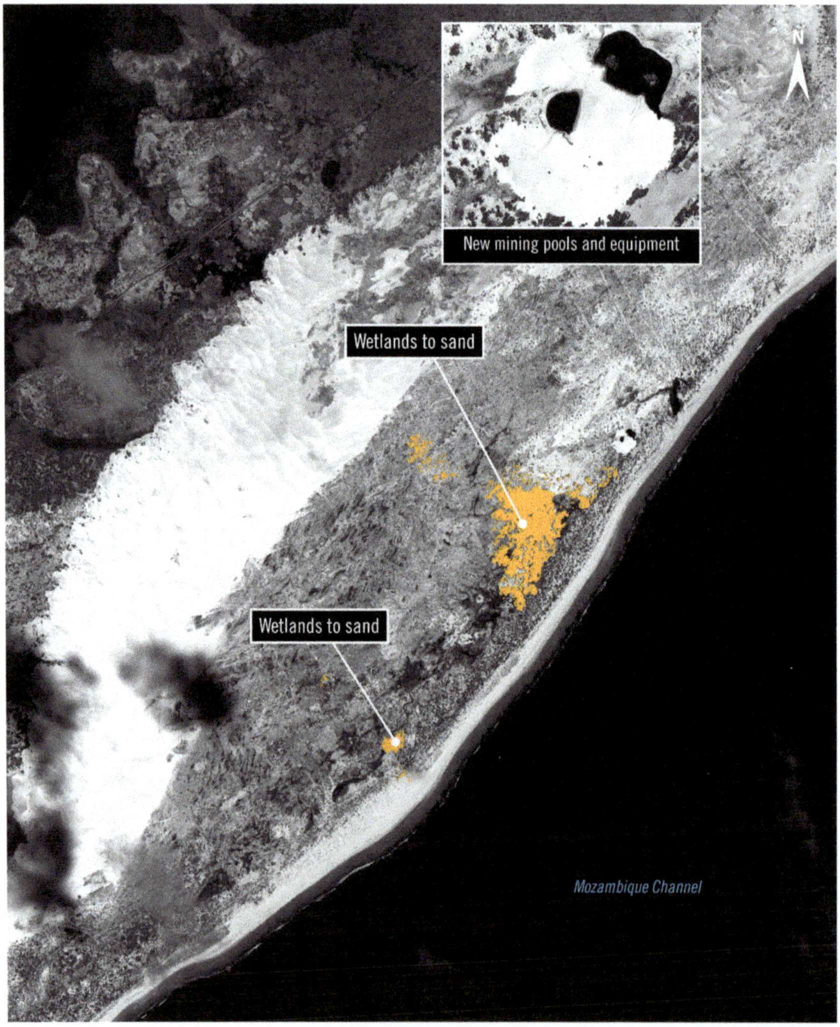

Figure 10.4 Imagery: © DigitalGlobe, 6 April 2015, -16.1139°, 40.0699°

Environmental Rights

Mozambique: 'Our Lives Mean Nothing': The Human Cost of Chinese Mining in Nagonha, Mozambique*

Publication Date: 27 March 2018

A Chinese mineral mining operation located in a remote area of Mozambique began operation in 2010. In 2015, a flash flood moved through the village south of the operations, Nagonha, and led to the destruction of forty-eight homes, leaving 290 people homeless. Amnesty International analysed imagery from 28 February 2010 to 6 April 2015 to determine if the mining activities contributed to the flash flood forming a new path and destroying the homes.

Satellite imagery was able to confirm increased deposits of sand from mining related activities that appeared to block natural stream flow north of the village. Without the natural path present, it is likely the water created a new path through the village where the sand deposits were not present.

* '"Our Lives Mean Nothing": The Human Cost of Chinese Mining in Nagohna, Mozambique' (n 18) .

Indiscriminate Violence

Syria: Un Must Act to End Onslaught Aimed at Purging Civilians from Eastern Aleppo

Publication date: 20 October 2016

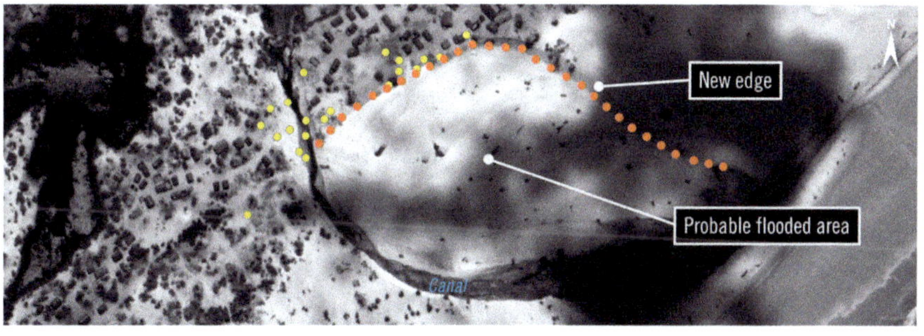

Figure 10.5 Image: © 2018 DigitalGlobe, 4 August 2016, 41.8326°, 129.7294°

Attacks in Aleppo, Syria continue to target the civilian communities. Before a UN General Assembly (UNGA) in 2016, Amnesty International issued a statement requesting action to end the indiscriminate violence impacting the civilians in eastern Aleppo.

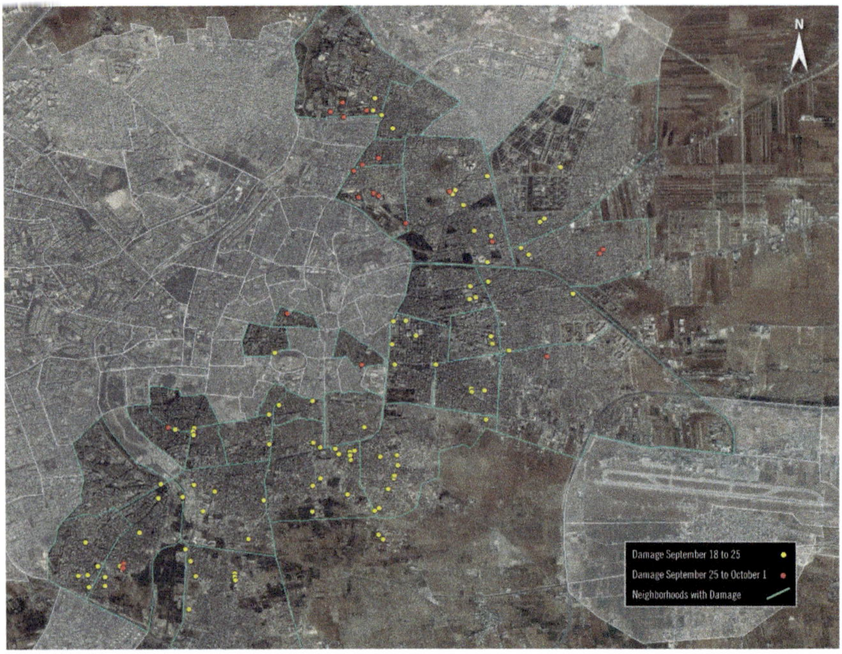

Figure 10.6 Image: © 2018 DigitalGlobe 21 January 2018, 4.5832°, 9.3012°

Satellite imagery was used to demonstrate the continued destruction throughout eastern Aleppo from 18 September 2016 to 1 October 2016. During that time, over 110 locations appeared damaged.

Figure 10.7 Image: © 2018 DigitalGlobe, 25 September 2016, 41.8326°, 129.7294°

Forced Relocation

Swaziland: 'They don't see us as People'. Security of Tenure and Forced Evictions in Eswatini*
Publication date: 30 August 2018

Figure 10.8

Amnesty International travelled to Swaziland to document forced evictions in the country. While investigating, it was able to uncover the lack of land tenure rights in the country since most of the land is held in trust by the king. Though access to the people and locations were feasible in most cases, for the Nokwane community, outside of Manzini, historical imagery needed to be analysed to corroborate testimony of homes being in the area.

Figure 10.9 Imagery: © DigitalGlobe, 25 September 2016, 36.1913°, 37.1792°

Satellite imagery analysed between 2002 and 2017 shows over 200 structures are missing, while a new biotechnology park is constructed.

* 'Swaziland: "They Don't See Us as People": Security of Tenure and Forced Evictions in Eswatini' Amnesty International (2018) https://www.amnesty.org/en/documents/document/?indexNumber=afr55%2f8785%2f2018&language=en accessed 12 September 2018.

Violence on Civilians

Cameroon: 'A turn for the worse: Violence and human rights violations in Anglophone Cameroon'*
Publication date: 11 June 2018

Figure 10.10 Images: © 2018 DigitalGlobe, Source: Google Earth, 20 October 2002 & 12 October 2017, -26.5295°, 31.2709°

The Anglophone region in Cameroon has seen a surge in violence, with armed separatists attacking security forces and civilians not joining the strikes and protests. The military has reacted by designing operations leading to arrests, torture, unlawful killings and destruction of property.

The Anglophone region of Cameroon is remote and often cloudy. High-resolution imagery, when captured over the area is often riddled with clouds, which is one of the few limiting factors for satellite imagery, though radar imagery is challenging that. In the case of the locations of reported abuses, cloud-free imagery was limited so lower resolution imagery was often used where possible. With 3m resolution imagery from Planet, active fires were visible using the NIR band on 18 January 2018 over Kwakwa. Another satellite sensor detected hotspots in the area on the same day. With this information, we were able to corroborate testimony of when the village was burned.

*'A Turn for the Worse: Violence and Human Rights Violations in Anglophone Cameroon' Amnesty International (2018) https://www.amnesty.org/en/documents/document/?indexNumber=afr17%2f8481%2f2018&language=en accessed 10 September 2018.

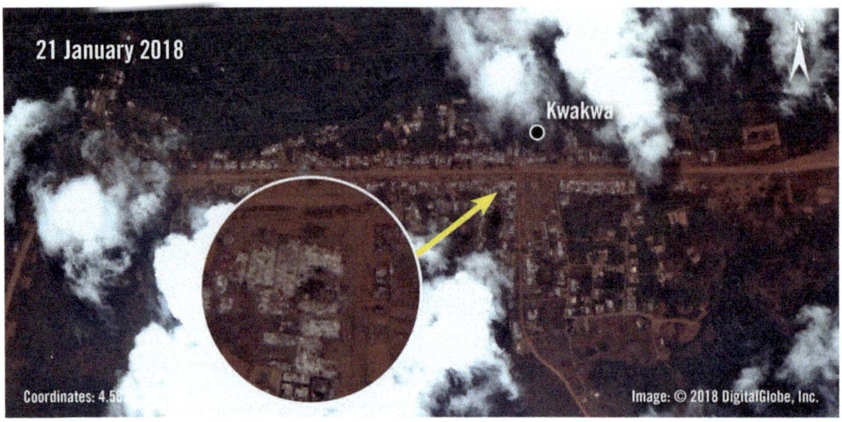

Figure 10.11 Image: © 2018 DigitalGlobe 21 January 2018, 4.5832°, 9.3012° 4.5832°, 9.3012

Crimes against Humanity

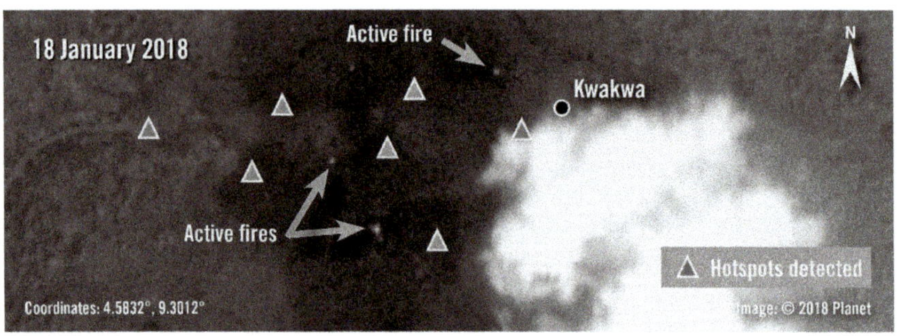

Figure 10.12 Image: © 2018 DigitalGlobe 21 January 2018, 4.5832°, 9.3012°

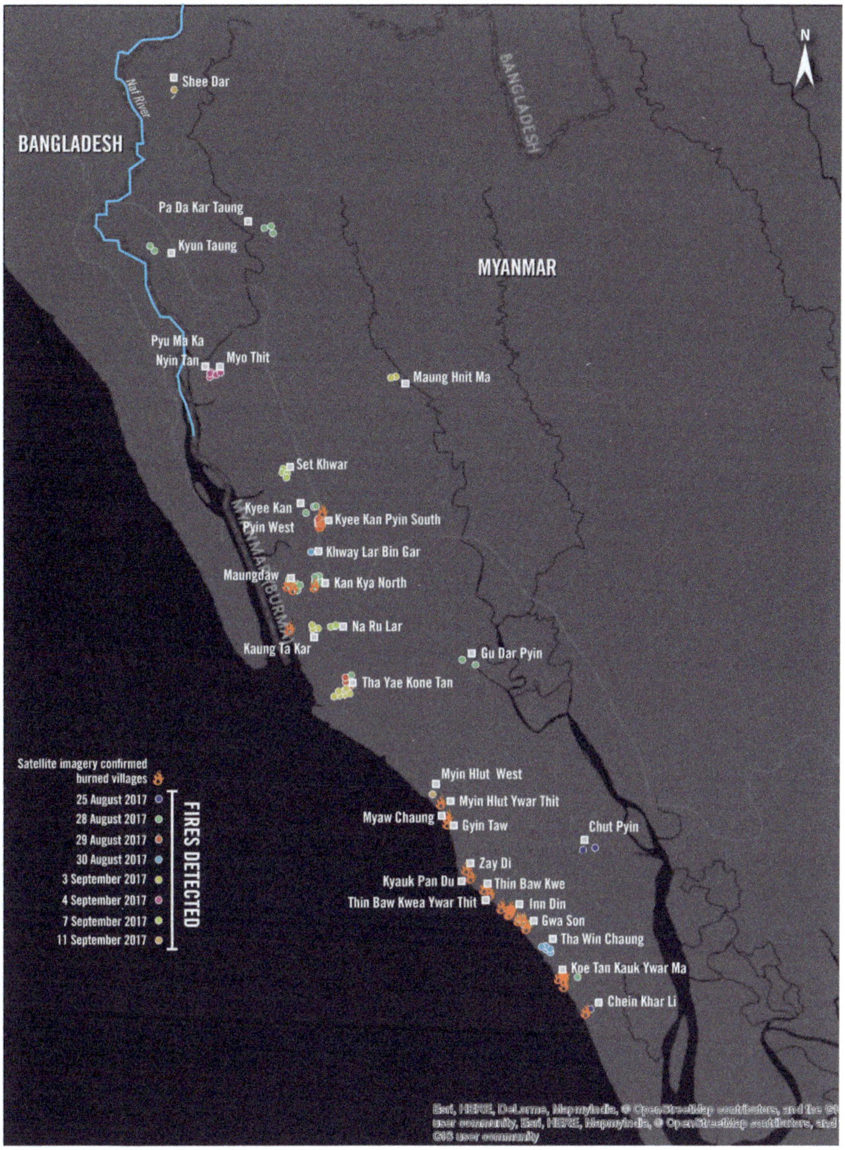

Figure 10.13

Myanmar:* 'My World is Finished'. Rohingya Targeted in Crimes Against Humanity in Myanmar
'We will Destroy Everything'
Military Responsibility for Crimes Against Humanity
In Rakhine State, Myanmar
Remaking Rakhine State

In August 2017, a large-scale military operation swept through Rakhine State in north-western Myanmar. The government of Myanmar does not allow access to Rakhine State by any foreigners or tourists without a permit. Foreign aid agencies do not operate in the region and access is extremely restricted. With numerous reports of entire villages being burned and Rohingya people fleeing, the quickest way to understand what was happening on the ground was to use remote sensing technologies.

In August, Rakhine State is typically saturated with clouds. High-resolution satellite imagery was limited and, when images were taken, clouds covered the region. Environmental satellite sensors used to detect hotspots were the first clues that testimonies and reports could be true. As Planet continued to capture imagery over the area, despite the clouds, gaps in the clouds slowly began to appear day by day and eventually the stark reality of the situation began to be confirmed village by village.

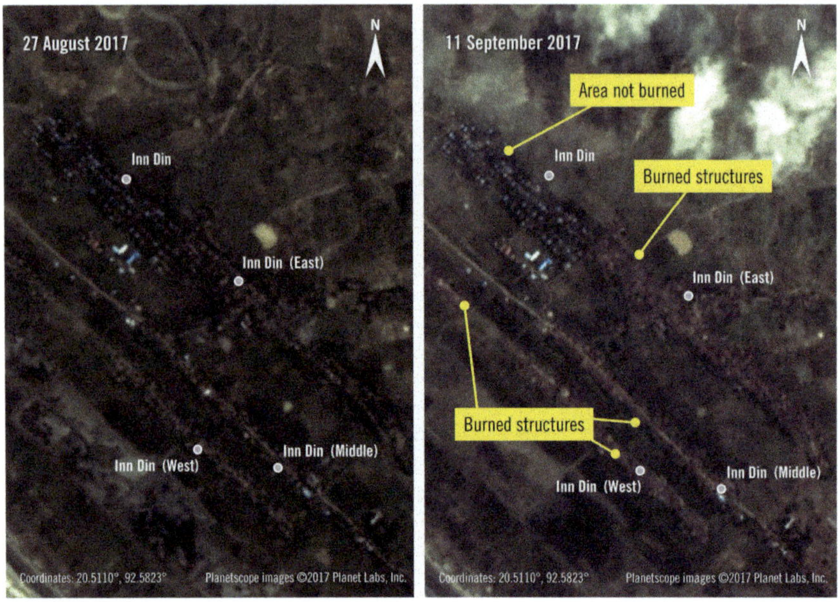

Figure 10.14 Images: ©2018 Planet, 27 August 2017 and 11 September 2017, 20.5126°, 92.5826°

Satellite imagery was used to document the sheer scale of the villages burned and confirm allegations that the Rohingya villages were targeted. As the situation began to unfold over the following months, villages were shown being razed and, in some areas, new construction showed security force bases, repatriation camps, and other unconfirmed structures.

Figure 10.15 Image: © 2018 DigitalGlobe, Source: Google Earth, 25 April 2018, 20.8268°, 92.3916

Since these events began in August 2017, no Amnesty International researcher has been able to access the Rakhine State area. Through interviews, photos, videos, and remote sensing, multiple reports document the various crimes against humanity directly committed by specific members of the Myanmar military. The events have been deemed a genocide by a recent United Nations report.**

*'*Myanmar* 2017/2018' Amnesty International (2018) https://www.amnesty.org/en/countries/asia-and-the-pacific/myanmar/report-myanmar/ accessed 10 September 2018.

** 'Report of Independent International Fact-Finding Mission on Myanmar' Independent International Fact-Finding Mission on Myanmar (2018) A/HRC/39/64 https://www.ohchr.org/Documents/HRBodies/HRCouncil/FFM-Myanmar/A_HRC_39_CRP.2.pdf accessed 12 September 2018.

5. New Advances in Remote Sensing

The commercial remote sensing and especially satellite imagery industry has grown significantly in the last five years. Open source tools such as Google Earth and Open Street Maps now enable any interested party to use and understand satellite imagery on a basic scale. As noted above, companies such as Planet have changed the idea of satellite imagery only coming from US$600 million, highly sophisticated satellites launched into space every five years to multiple small satellites being sent up at one time for only US$25,000 each. Planet was not trying to win the game in spatial resolution but instead wanted to win on temporal coverage.

Another company, ICEYE, is building the first constellation of eighteen radar cubesats to be launched in 2020. These small satellites could open another arena where the spectral bands are able to see through most clouds, allowing the ability to see the ground in very cloudy areas of the world like Colombia. Meanwhile, countries previously uninterested in the race for space like Australia have even joined in, establishing their first space agency in 2018.[20]

An entire industry has now formed to work out ways to analyse satellite imagery quickly using crowd sourcing, machine learning algorithms, and neural networks. Companies such as Orbital Insights and Descartes Labs have formed to assist in making sense of the overwhelming satellite imagery data deluge. In the typical fashion of the GIS industry, groups have also created open source machine-learning platforms like Skynet from DevelopmentSeed.[21]

These new developments have the capacity to allow a single analyst to document possible human rights abuses over a much larger area at a faster rate. Other forms of data, beyond satellite imagery, could also be incorporated into the algorithms to develop a more comprehensive view of the situation. These new advances could also help predict future outbreaks of abuses, possibly preventing them before they happen.

[20] Innovation and Science Department of Industry, 'Australian Space Agency' Department of Industry, Innovation and Science (18 June 2018) https://www.industry.gov.au/strategies-for-the-future/australian-space-agency accessed 10 September 2018.

[21] 'Skynet: Machine Learning for Satellite Imagery' (*Development Seed*) https://developmentseed.org/projects/skynet/ accessed 30 December 2018.

6. How to Access Satellite Imagery and Remote Sensing Tools

There are many sources for free, relatively low-resolution imagery. Sentinel 2A has the best spatial resolution of any freely available imagery, but Landsat tracks events happening over a relatively long period of time.

For high-resolution imagery, Google Earth Pro Desktop is the best source available. The Historical Imagery tool allows one to look back in time through all of the imagery available on Google's platform.

Below in table 10.1 is a select list of the variety of tools open source satellite imagery analysts use to find and pinpoint areas of interest.

Table 10.1

Remote Sensing Tool/ Website	Cost	Notes
Google Earth Pro	free	Look at the 'historical imagery' tool
Bird.i	free trial	New, coverage is limited
Terraserver	US$299/year	Free to view with subscription, pay to download
Sentinel Hub Playground	free	10m resolution
Planet	Varies	
Imagehunter	free	Tool to see coverage of satellite imagery. Must purchase imagery.
Fire Data	free	Detects large fires
DigitalGlobe	Free overviews	Tool to order imagery from DigitalGlobe. Images are approximately US$400 per 25 km^2
Airbus	free	Tool to order Airbus imagery. Images are approximately US$350 per km^2.
QGIS	free	Open source Geographic Information System used to view satellite imagery

There are many resources available to explain how to use satellite imagery, for example:

- Satellite Imagery Interpretation Guide: Intentional Burning of Tukuls https://hhi.harvard.edu/publications/satellite-imagery-interpretation-guide-intentional-burning-tukuls
- Satellite Imagery Interpretation Guide: Displaced Population Camps https://hhi.harvard.edu/publications/satellite-imagery-interpretation-guide-displaced-population-camps
- How to Interpret a Satellite Image: Five Tips and Strategies https://earthobservatory.nasa.gov/Features/ColorImage

PART III

11
Ethics in Open Source Investigations

Zara Rahman and Gabriela Ivens

Open source investigation is a powerful source for uncovering human rights violations. However, the techniques that are used, the data that are gathered, processed, verified, and published, and the actions of the people who play various roles within these investigations all pose potential ethical challenges.

There are deep power disparities between the various actors engaged in open source investigations, from the investigators themselves to the people represented in the information gathered and those responsible for the data being uploaded to the internet. These disparities combined with the responsibility that human rights practitioners have towards the people they work with—and for—sometimes result in serious ethical challenges. These challenges are made more difficult by the fact that many of the non-state actors engaging in open source investigation are not subject to institutional guidelines, and face little or no formal accountability for their actions.

In this chapter, we take a rights-based approach to ethics, considering how people's rights are affected by both the process and the end result of open source investigations. Underlying our discussion are two underlying principles:

(1) Just because you can does not mean you should.
(2) The ends do not necessarily justify the means.

We argue against a utilitarian approach[1] which would maintain that it is the consequences and effects of the actions and methods employed that determine whether they are morally right or wrong. Instead, we believe that, regardless of the end goal, human rights should be respected and protected throughout the collection, verification, and presentation stages of an investigation.

Further, we believe that the foundation of an ethical approach lies in understanding the context of a situation, how information was obtained, and the uses to which its publication might be put. We suggest that context is so crucial that no 'cookie-cutter' approach to ethical judgment is possible, leaving the investigators themselves often in the best position to decide the best course of action in the face of ethical dilemmas. For this reason, our approach focuses on supporting individual investigators and organizations to make the best possible judgments in their particular context, rather than recommending generalized guidance.

[1] First introduced by Jeremy Bentham in 'An Introduction to the Principles of Morals and Legislation', first published in 1789, available at http://www.koeblergerhard.de/Fontes/BenthamJeremyMoralsandLegislation1789.pdf.

We drew inspiration from scenarios such as the following:

- Carrying out an investigation might involve looking into all sorts of data, particularly social media data, in order to verify that a person of interest was at a place at a particular time. Profiles that might be of interest in an investigation are not just those of the targets themselves, but also people within their close network—such as their children.[2] In some cases, minors could unknowingly be posting incriminating images—for example, a photo with two people which shows they have an existing relationship. What are the limitations (if any) of using social media profiles of minors as part of an investigation?
- When the data have been put online without the visible knowledge of the people whose data it is, for example via a data breach—is that information still considered 'fair game' for the purposes of an open source investigation? Is there a 'duty of care' to notify the responsible parties of the data breach, if it is reasonable to expect they do not already know?
- Many, if not all, of the websites through which mass amounts of data are gathered are not designed for the purpose of open source investigation. They might have access or use restrictions on their platforms or make it explicitly difficult for people to gather data that have been online for longer than a certain amount of time. Breaching a website or a company's 'Terms of Service' is often considered necessary in carrying out an investigation. Does breaching what is effectively a contract between company and user in this context undermine the mission of the investigation?

We begin in this chapter by interrogating the purpose of investigations, noting that the methods for open source investigations in pursuit of human rights are, for all intents and purposes, the same methods that can be used by malicious actors in pursuit of the exact opposite—of surveillance, invading privacy, and tracking people without their knowledge. With this in mind, we consider with whom the responsibility lies in the case of unintended negative consequences. We then consider the ethics of how these distinct actors are treated, the power they hold, and the risks they face. We use the term 'human infrastructures'[3] to describe the human labour that creates this environment. We follow this with a section on the built infrastructures of an investigation,s including ethical implications of the physical and digital infrastructures used in investigations, such as areas with particular inequalities like user consent, access to data, and changing visibility of content.

A discussion of the ethical considerations of data processes follows, from the creation and collection of data itself, through to verification, preservation, and publication. Finally, we conclude with a short discussion of what ethical challenges might arise in the future, considering that the amount of data available about almost every single one of us is vastly increasing.

[2] For more on this see the discussion by Paul Myers in ch 6.

[3] We adapt this term from a paper by MC Elish, '(Dis)Placed Workers: A Study in the Disruptive Potential of Robotics and AI' *WeRobot* (2018).

1. The Purpose of an Investigation

Diverse actors are involved in open source investigations, and their motivation for participating varies widely. These motivations can include, for example: working on an investigation as an organizational priority, as a personal priority, or as a technological challenge.

Despite this diversity in purpose, the methods used by different actors are very similar. A how-to guide for finding the location of a person using only their social media data could be a vitally important piece of advice for someone working on a human rights investigation. But that same how-to guide could be invaluable to someone engaged in domestic abuse trying to locate a former partner who is hiding from them.

To what extent, then, does the mission of revealing human rights violations via open source investigations justify the means and methods of carrying out the investigation?

1.1 The Mission and the Methods

In an investigation, there is an individual, group of individuals or entity being investigated. Usually somewhere among these actors, there is someone or multiple people trying to hide that information from being revealed, for varying reasons. In essence, one person's open source investigation could be another person's 'doxxing'—a term used to describe publicly identifying or publishing private information about another person, usually done in a malicious way as a form of punishment or revenge.

The once-public Tumblr site 'Racists Getting Fired' worked under the idea of 'doxxing for good', that is, sharing the personal information of someone who has displayed racist behaviour with the intention of pursuing social justice and, ultimately, retribution for the culprit. The contributors of the blog located individuals in the United States who posted racist comments online, found out as much information as possible about them from online sources, and then passed on these comments to their workplaces, along with a suggestion they be fired. Reportedly, the site became hard to manage, with trolling groups such as 4Chan becoming involved, along with the wrongful inclusion of someone whose public profile and racist comments were fabricated by her ex-boyfriend.[4] By the time a retraction was posted, she was facing multiple investigations by her employer and university.

This case provides us with an example of how open source investigation techniques can be weaponized or inadvertently cause harm to people if ethical impacts are not carefully considered. This kind of action can violate the human rights of an individual or a group, and ultimately can have a chilling effect[5] on their freedom of expression. Journalist Ijeoma Oluo, writing about the 'ethics of doxxing',[6] notes 'what separates us from what we say we stand for and what we actually stand for are our actions.'

[4] S McDonald, '"Racists Getting Fired" Exposes Weaknesses of Internet Vigilantism, No Matter How Well-Intentioned' *Washington Post* (2 December 2014) https://www.washingtonpost.com/news/morning-mix/wp/2014/12/02/racists-getting-fired-exposes-weaknesses-of-internet-vigilantism-no-matter-how-well-intentioned/ accessed 9 May 2018.

[5] J Townend, 'Freedom of Expression and the Chilling Effect' in H Tumber and S Waisbord (eds), *The Routledge Companion to Media and Human Rights* (Routledge 2017).

[6] I Oluo, 'Taking Down Bigots with their Own Weapons Is Sweet, Satisfying—and Very, Very Wrong' *Medium* (6 April 2015) https://medium.com/matter/actually-it-s-about-ethics-in-doxxing-1651b3deac77 accessed 9 May 2018.

In the context of open source investigation for human rights research, those ethical boundaries blur. How do human rights principles translate into carrying out online investigations? And to what extent does the mission of revealing human rights violations justify the means?

For human rights practitioners, the pursuit of truth may well be thought of as more important than, for example, violating an 'adhesion contract', a contract, such as terms of service of one's use of digital platforms. Adhesion contracts are usually drafted by one party who holds considerably greater bargaining power over the other contracting party. Owing to this power disparity, the weaker party 'adheres' to the contract without the opportunity to negotiate or change the terms of the contract or its provisions. For example, in order for human rights practitioners automatically to gather information from Facebook, they are often violating these contracts of adhesion that they 'signed' by clicking 'I agree' when registering onto the platform.

Some could say that violating Facebook's Terms of Service is justified if it means gaining access to a potentially vital piece of information. The investigator might, for example, create a Facebook profile under a pseudonym in order to gain access to closed groups. Such a move might seem particularly tempting when that privacy violation is likely to remain secret, without the company itself, or any individuals involved, ever needing to know. But even if this remains a secret, with no (visible) negative consequences, does the end justify the means? We suggest that in taking an ethical approach to open source investigation, particularly in the human rights sphere, the answer is no.

Legal consequences of these violations are relatively unknown thus far; for example, how enforceable these adhesion contracts are and in what situations, and whether violating such contracts is a question of civil versus criminal liability.

Ethical principles, however, should not be conflated with legal principles, although the legal aspects of open source investigations should be considered along with ethical concerns when assessing risks to those conducting an investigation. As the primary authors of Brown University's 'A Framework for Making Ethical Decisions', Sheila Bonde and Paul Firenze, put it: '[b]oth law and ethics deal with questions of how we should live together with others, but ethics is sometimes also thought to apply to how individuals act even when others are not involved.'[7]

An underlying assumption of this chapter is that investigators would, in the spirit of acting ethically, actively choose not to carry out certain activities even if these activities were within reach. This is a big assumption to make, and one that some investigators might challenge, particularly in cases where the actual steps an investigator takes are not likely to come under scrutiny.

A common argument against the approach we recommend is that in a situation where human rights could apparently be advanced, 'not acting is unethical'. Suppose, for example that accessing the social media account of a politically exposed persons young child could provide crucial evidence; or that a certain person's image could be a valuable piece of the puzzle, regardless of whether their consent is obtained or not. In these cases, a utilitarian approach would allow an investigator to focus on the greater good—in this case, completing

[7] Brown University, 'Making Choices: A Framework for Making Ethical Decisions' Brown.Edu (2013) 1 https://www.brown.edu/academics/science-and-technology-studies/framework-making-ethical-decision accessed 11 May 2018.

the investigation, or gathering as much evidence as possible—above considering the ramifications of the steps taken.

To take another example, if an investigator were to receive an unverified dataset from an anonymous source which, if accurate, contained a seemingly valuable piece of evidence for an investigation. If verifying that dataset is not possible, we would suggest not using anything from it in the investigation—that is, not acting, rather than focusing on the end goal—because it could risk undermining the whole investigation if that one piece of evidence were proved to be false.

Focusing on the 'greater good' is, in some ways, a false flag.[8] It is perfectly possible to carry out an investigation with a clear mission, while also respecting the rights of those affected by that investigation. We suggest that arguments that lean on the consequences of 'not acting' are, intentionally or not, seeking to provide an excuse for not respecting fundamental human rights.

We can draw parallels here with what is known as 'white-hat' and 'black-hat' hacking in the field of cybersecurity. White-hat hackers are typically hired by a company to test the security of a system, within specified boundaries. They notify the company of vulnerabilities they find, for example, so that the company can strengthen their systems in response. Conversely, black-hat hackers are people whose work is unauthorized by the company in question, who test the security of systems for personal gain, malicious motives, or curiosity.

As writer Aidan Knowles explains on IBM's Security Intelligence blog, attention to guidelines plays a crucial role in distinguishing between the two groups: '[w]ithout clear ethical standards and rules, cybersecurity professionals are almost indistinguishable from the black-hat criminals against whom they seek to protect systems and data.'[9]

Some associations that work with white-hat hackers, such as the Information Systems Security Association, a non-profit international organization of information-security professionals and practitioners have developed codes of ethics in response to this situation. Their brief code of ethics,[10] which all members have to agree to, includes a promise to 'perform all professional activities and duties in accordance with all applicable laws and the highest ethical principles'. Such a vow of course may be interpreted in vastly different ways by different individuals, based on their own moral beliefs, education, and personal situation. Similarly, (ISC)^2, an international, non-profit membership association for information security leaders, asks members to adhere to 'the highest ethical standards of behavior',[11] though they provide a little more guidance as to what that might mean, including:

- to protect society, the common good, necessary public trust and confidence, and the infrastructure
- to act honourably, honestly, justly, responsibly, and legally.

[8] B Williams, 'A Critique of Utilitarianism', in J.JC Smart and B Williams, *Utilitarianism: For and Against* (Cambridge University Press, 1973).

[9] A Knowles, 'Tough Challenges in Cybersecurity Ethics' *Security Intelligence* (12 October 2016) https://securityintelligence.com/tough-challenges-cybersecurity-ethics/ accessed 9 May 2018.

[10] Information Systems Security Association, *Issa.Org* http://www.issa.org/?page=CodeofEthics accessed 9 May 2018.

[11] Isc2, 'Code of Ethics | Complaint Procedures | Committee Members' *Isc2.Org* https://www.isc2.org/Ethics# accessed 9 May 2018.

In the case of open source investigation for human rights research, there is a clear need to abide by ethical boundaries, regardless of whether or not those choices will be open to scrutiny. This is for two reasons in particular: first, that there is always the risk that a perceived 'small' violation—for example, of the privacy even of a suspected abuser—might have unintended consequences down the line if, for instance, the information gained was later used in a legal claim and the chain of custody had to be demonstrated in a court of law.

The second reason, as we indicated above, is that actions in pursuit of defending human rights need to be in support of human rights throughout the process in order to maintain legitimacy and credibility of the human rights endeavour. This approach, however, relies upon a solid and clear understanding and agreement of what 'human rights' actually are, as well as alignment of an individual's working conception of rights with it. In the Racists Getting Fired example above, the creators of the blog could argue that they were working towards furthering human rights and justice. What form 'justice' takes, however, can look very different—mediated by a criminal court, for example, compared with taking the law and licence into one's own hands and opting for 'vigilante' justice.

1.2 Investigation and Responsibility

The purpose of an investigation is further complicated when institutional guidelines or a framework to rely upon is lacking. Hamilton Bean, a professor in the fields of organizational discourse and security, describes the role organizations should play in these situations: '[w]hile individual open source analysts must be 'sensitive' and 'careful' about collecting information about U.S. Persons, it is ultimately the organization's legal and ethical responsibility to ensure compliance with institutional standards.'[12]

Given the ad hoc nature of many investigations and absence of such organizational responsibility for many of those involved, however, the question becomes: in the case of (negative) unintended consequences as a result of open source intelligence investigations, with whom does responsibility lie?

We suggest it lies with the investigators themselves, who must consider the implications (unintended or not) of their efforts within the context in which they are working. In open source investigations particularly, which are already pushing boundaries of conventional practice compared to more established methods of human rights research, credibility matters. Depending on the intended end use of the investigation (or the pieces of information within it), breaking Terms of Services or carrying out illegal activities might even invalidate the information gathered, thus putting the whole investigation at risk. Taking an ethical approach in these circumstances means that investigators should make a concerted effort to actively understand the risks involved for themselves, and for those they are working with and on behalf of.

[12] H Bean, 'Is Open Source Intelligence an Ethical Issue?' in Susan Maret (ed), *Government Secrecy (Research in Social Problems and Public Policy, Volume 19)*1 (Emerald Group Publishing Limited 2011) 394.

2. The Human Infrastructure of an Investigation

An investigation is made up of many different people, who receive differing amounts of attention and wield differing amounts of power. Anthropologist M.C. Elish uses the term 'human infrastructure' to refer to the human labour that goes into creating machine-led systems.[13] Here, we adapt this term to refer to the frequently overlooked human labour that goes into creating the overall environment in which open source investigation can take place. In this section, we explore the human labour and the ties between individuals that make an investigation possible. We suggest that the current tendency to glorify the work of investigators is a misdirection of attention, undervaluing the less visible work of others who work on open source investigations. This hidden labour is what makes open source investigations possible, and where more of the front-line risks lie.

2.1 The Hidden Labour of Investigations

Any open source investigation is made up of data, and these data are the result of labour by people who create, upload, appear in, find, tag, translate, and curate. Often, these roles are far less visible than that of the investigator or investigation group, the people who are typically tasked with piecing these fragments together. It is the names of the investigator (or the investigation groups) who appear on the public-facing report, or who are quoted in the media, not the people who appear in or who uploaded the data being used. This focus of attention ignores that the fragments would not exist were it not for this hidden human infrastructure behind the scenes of an investigation, creating and preparing that data in a way that makes it legible to the investigator/s.

The most visible actors within the world of open source investigation are the investigators. The investigators will be likely to get the credit for an investigation, have better access to job opportunities as a result of their labour, and are typically better prepared to receive compensation for their work, for example by being part of a formal institution that is organized to receive philanthropic grant funding.

As academics Catherine D'Ignazio and Lauren F. Klein write with regard to feminist practices for data visualization, '[m]aking labor visible also has implications for fair attribution and credit for the resulting artifact, especially in light of the fact that women and other underrepresented groups have been notoriously excluded from sharing in credit for scientific work."[14] We can commonly observe high-profile investigators receiving accolades for their valuable investigative work, while the people who made that work possible remain unacknowledged, perhaps even unaware that the video or image that they recorded was even used.

[13] Elish (n 3)I8.

[14] C D'Ignazio and LF Klein, 'Feminist Data Visualization' *VIS4DH: 2016 Workshop on Visualization for the Digital Humanities* (2016) 3.

2.2 If Everyone Can Contribute, Why Aren't They?

One refrain often heard within open source communities and peer-production communities, is that 'anyone can contribute'. As we see from peer-production spaces such as Wikipedia, however, 'open for everybody' to participate often has a significant skew towards certain demographics.[15]

As Astra Taylor writes in her book, *The People's Platform*, '[m]otivation and resources, time and power—these are assets that are not evenly distributed, even if the Internet has removed many of the old barriers to entry. They are inequalities that we must take into account when we talk about the network's "level playing field"'.[16] It is these inequalities that are often forgotten in the claims of how internet access and the spread of digital technologies have 'democratized' involvement in activities like open source investigations.

In 2017, for example, open source code platform GitHub carried out a survey[17] of 5,500 randomly sampled GitHub contributors and 500 people from communities who work on other platforms. Of these respondents: 95 per cent of respondents were men; women were more likely than men to encounter language or content that made them feel unwelcome; and 50 per cent of people had witnessed a negative interaction with another user.

Of course, the investigator space is quite different than GitHub in a number of respects. The biggest difference between the two communities is that open source investigation has a significantly lower barrier to entry than contributing code to an open source project. The fact that investigations can be carried out entirely individually, without having to share or show methodology to others, also provides more space and time for people learning open source intelligence techniques to experiment with their own approaches privately. As explored in a workshop on information collection and legal accountability held at the Rockefeller Foundation Bellagio Center in Italy in 2017, this may change with the issuance of the Protocol on Open Source Investigations, which calls for methodological transparency and peer review.[18]

Even though there is no representative sample for open source investigations similar to that for GitHub, we suggest there are nevertheless some similarities between the two spaces.

Similar to open source coding, there are a number of privileges required in order to contribute—as Taylor describes above. A number of additional factors may be mentioned, for example having in-person connections to people, or attending in-person trainings, conferences or events. This naturally disadvantages people who are outside of more prominent (and typically Western) cities.

In both communities: certain roles are more valued than others (in open source coding, the coders, and in open source investigation, the investigators); it has a similar ethos in that, in principle, anybody is able to contribute (but actual participation is dependent on a variety of existing privileges and factors); the majority of documentation on the topic is in English;[19] and a tendency towards trolling or harassment as a result of contributions.

[15] See the Wikipedia Human Gender Indicators (WHGI project) for a weekly data update of the gender gap in Wikipedia contributors http://whgi.wmflabs.org accessed 22 August 2018 for one such example of this.

[16] A Taylor, *The People's Platform: Taking Back Power and Culture in the Digital Age* (Picador 2014) 220

[17] GitHub, Open Source Survey (2017) http://opensourcesurvey.org/2017/ accessed 9 May 2018, https://securityintelligence.com/tough-challenges-cybersecurity-ethics/ accessed 9 May 2018.

[18] Human Rights Center School of Law University of California, Berkeley (2017) https://www.law.berkeley.edu/wp-content/uploads/2018/02/Bellagio_report_2018_9.pdf accessed 20 August 2018.

[19] For example, to date there is no tutorial on how to conduct open source investigations in Arabic.

Tactics used by 'trolls' seeking to attack investigators include creating fake accounts to impersonate a person's avatar, as happened to Bellingcat's Aric Toler throughout the course of 2017.[20] At the time of writing in 2018, there are at least twelve accounts with his name, copied bio, and avatar photo.

In an interview in 2017, Bellingcat founder Eliot Higgins described the organization's interaction with trolls in this way: 'We've had the Russian Minister of Defense attack our work, we've had the Russian Foreign Ministry attack our work, and we had the hackers from the Podesta emails and DNC leaks target us for hacking.'[21] Higgins himself took the attacks as a kind of compliment to the effectiveness of his work: '[t]he reaction from Russia and trolls was one of the most rewarding things.'[22] Instead of being put off by this kind of attack, investigators are forced to reckon with these risks, and, presumably, accustom themselves to them.

Higgins' reaction is unlikely to be shared by people already subject to harassment and trolling attacks simply for being of a certain identity and active online. Women, people of colour, and members of marginalized communities already face far more abuse and hate speech on social media platforms and forums such as Reddit than other demographics.[23] Researchers Alice Marwick and Robyn Caplan write, '[h]arassment is often used to police women's online behavior, and may have a chilling effect on women's participation in the public sphere both off and online.'[24] Seeing the consequences for more well-known investigators, however, could result in those thinking about learning requisite skills being discouraged before they even begin. Owing to a lack of research and evidence in this area, however, this is currently only a hypothesis.

2.3 Risk and Safety

The roles that combine the highest risk and the least agency are those at the very beginning of the chain: the witness, the person recording the event, and the one uploading the data (roles that are sometimes, but not always, performed by the same person). In Syria for example, people have been killed, displaced, tortured, and imprisoned for recording footage or publicizing events where human rights have been violated. Thus, in some cases, the individuals involved may hope their names are never disclosed.

This leads to some concerns around the ethics of representation. Who is in a position to make the decision regarding how a video is shared, used, and who else gets to see it? This decision is rarely made by the person who is in the video, nor the person who captured the image or made the video itself. Nevertheless, it is the person represented, or the person

[20] J Cox, 'Dodgy "Hackers" Target Bellingcat Investigators Who Call BS on Moscow' *The Daily Beast* (17 November 2017) https://www.thedailybeast.com/polish-hackers-target-investigators-who-call-bs-on-moscow accessed 9 May 2018.

[21] K Johnson, 'Why Bellingcat Wants to Teach Normal People to Be Investigative Journalists' *Throughcracks.Com* (31 March 2017) http://throughcracks.com/why-bellingcat-wants-to-teach-normal-people-to-be-investigative-journalists/ accessed 9 May 2018.

[22] ibid.

[23] M Duggan, 'Online Harassment 2017' Pew Research Center: Internet, Science & Tech (11 July 2017) http://www.pewinternet.org/2017/07/11/online-harassment-2017/ accessed 11 May 2018.

[24] AE Marwick and R Caplan, 'Drinking Male Tears: Language, the Manosphere, and Networked Harassment' *Feminist Media Studies* (26 March 2018) 1.

carrying out the on-ground work, whose potential safety is affected, in many cases without their awareness or ability to consent.

As a video or investigation is made public, the threat model[25] of investigators also changes. The key difference in this case is that the investigators have the agency to be able to make a change, to remove their name from the final published product, or to take other precautions if necessary, whereas others at different points of that chain are typically not asked for, nor have any option to remove, their consent.

In cases where contacting those represented in the data might be possible—for instance to seek clarification, check sources, or ask for consent—new risks arise. These risks could potentially affect those asking for the information, those receiving the request and others involved in the investigation. Here, an investigator will have to decide how forthcoming to be when contacting sources; how open to be about details concerning the investigation, and how most safely to contact them, to name just a few considerations.

This brings up ethical dilemmas, particularly for investigators who simply cannot know whether or not the risks faced by the people represented in the digital and photographic information have changed, and who logistically would struggle to request informed consent from those appearing in the imagery.

However, as conflicts progress, the risks a person faces can dramatically change, especially in conflict zones or unstable political situations. Issues of appropriate representation of those at risk become ever more important in these conditions of deep power asymmetry and exclusion, where some are in the position of making decisions on behalf of others (or themselves), in spite of not being able to truly understand what the consequences of those decisions might be. In almost every human rights case, an inherent part of an investigation means that an investigator has chosen to work on or represent a human rights case, often without the knowledge or consent of those who were directly involved, who might have far less agency than the investigator themselves.

The networked nature of open source investigations allows people who sit far away from the site of conflict to become involved. This means that in the most extreme of cases, serious risks or danger can arise from their open source investigation even if they do not leave the assumed safety of their own home. If the research is revealed, the investigators could become the target of others' investigations, and, as Bellingcat investigations in particular have shown, risk having their own personal information revealed online. When malicious actors come to use open source investigation against others, it seems fairly obvious that the ethical concerns and considerations that we elaborate upon here are of little consequence to them.

2.4 Gamification of Investigations

As discussed in previous sections, among the variety of different actors who are becoming involved in open source investigations are interested members of the public willing either to volunteer skills or unskilled time as part of micro-tasking or crowd-sourcing campaigns. These campaigns often target an undefined, large group of people in an open call[26] for

[25] Electronic Frontier Foundation, 'Threat Model' https://ssd.eff.org/en/glossary/threat-model accessed 24 August 2018.

[26] J Howe, 'The Rise of Crowdsourcing'6 *Wired* (2006) www.wired.com/wired/archive/14.06/crowds.html accessed 20 July 2018.

volunteers and range from asking them to identify objects in satellite imagery, to categorizing leaked documents.

For human rights practitioners and organizations using such campaigns, one option sometimes considered is to introduce gamification techniques as a low-cost method to attract, motivate, and engage people to join the campaign. 'Gamification' is the use of gameplay mechanisms in non-gaming contexts to encourage desired behaviours.[27] In this context, gamification might include features like awarding 'top tagger' statuses, leaderboards to show progress against other people, progress bars, or other ways of showing competition against others.

Reasoning behind using these methods is varied, from encouraging greater engagement from non-experts, to introducing incentives in an attempt to make what could otherwise be repetitive labour more interesting. However, the gamification aspect of crowd-solving compounds two existing challenges within open source investigative practices.

First, the perceived higher number of men taking part in open source investigation practices.[28] A study conducted in 2006 revealed that female respondents were less attracted to competitive elements in video games than male respondents.[29] Though this study was not conducted with gamification of open source investigations in mind, it suggests a bias towards male respondents being more attracted to gamification aspects of investigations and thus have an unintended side-effect of increasing male participation.

Secondly, many investigators are already somewhat removed from the human rights issues they are researching. Gamification techniques rely upon extrinsic motivators,[30] such as the consequences of the activity, rather than intrinsic motivation—the activity itself.[31] Studies have shown that intrinsic motivation is more effective than extrinsic motivation; and, in some cases, that a focus on extrinsic motivators has led to decreased motivation in the long run.[32] After all, where extrinsic motivators are used to increase participation in open source investigations, the focus is on prestige, rewards, or points—a far cry from the grave human rights issues that are at the heart of this work.

Despite the lack of research currently available on how gamification affects participants' perceptions of the issues, we suggest that caution should be taken when using gamification as a technique to help ensure that its use does not trivialize the violations of human rights that are being researched or the work of those who may have undergone huge risks to produce the content being used.

27 K Werbach and D Hunter, *For the Win*, (Wharton Digital Press 2012).

28 R Stamboliyska, 'Women in OSINT: Diversifying the Field, Part 1'5 *Bellingcat* (8 December 2015) https://www.bellingcat.com/resources/articles/2015/12/08/women-in-osint-diversifying-the-field/ accessed 18 August 2018

29 T Hartmann and C Klimmt, 'Gender and Computer Games: Exploring Females' Dislikes' (2006) 11(4) Journal of Computer-Mediated Communication1p 910.

30 H Zheng, D Li, and W Hou, 'Task Design, Motivation, and Participation in Crowdsourcing Contests' (2001) 15(4) International Journal of Electronic Commerce5. 57.

31 M Gagne and E.L Deci, 'Self-determination Theory and Work Motivation' (2005) 26(4) Journal of Organizational Behavior6. 331.

32 MD Hanus and J Fox, 'Assessing the Effects of Gamification In The Classroom: A Longitudinal Study on Intrinsic Motivation, Social Comparison, Satisfaction, Effort, and Academic Performance' (2015) 80 Computers & Education. 152.

3. The Built Infrastructure of an Investigation

The human infrastructures of investigations discussed above are facilitated, supported, and affected by physical and digital infrastructures—what we refer to as the 'built' infrastructures of investigations. There is relatively little technical infrastructure built specifically for open source investigators; rather, human rights researchers must generally rely on infrastructures built by large tech companies or technologists with other purposes in mind. While open source investigators can choose from a variety of data collection and analytical tools and online platforms, in reality, they have very little control over this environment.

This section covers ethical concerns with the use, development, and spread of physical and digital infrastructures used in investigations, from the historical roots of information asymmetry in different regions of the world to the influence of corporations who control much of the digital infrastructure used in investigations.

3.1 Information Asymmetry

Certain areas of the world are home to stronger and more comprehensive internet and data infrastructures than others. This asymmetry in infrastructure reflects itself in two key ways: first, in that people living in well-served areas of the world have better access to the internet in order to carry out investigations; and second, that certain areas of the world have more data available online about them and their surroundings.

In the case of crowd-sourced data, such as flight and marine tracking datasets, there are entire areas of the world with very low levels of coverage due to low participation levels by people in those areas, for whatever reason—from lack of knowledge of the platform or lack of availability in other languages beyond English, to lack of access to digital infrastructure required to contribute.[33] Similarly, some governments have considerably more datasets online in machine-readable formats in ways that can support investigations than do others.[34] In some cases, communities do not want data about their lives and livelihoods online for others to browse outside of their direct control, such as indigenous communities for whom data sovereignty is considered a fundamental right.[35]

As a consequence of such information asymmetry, investigations are easier to carry out on certain areas of the world than others. Here, we often see colonial divisions replicated—with rich, former colonial powers in possession of strong internet coverage and wider availability of data, relative to the poorer, formerly colonized nations.

One could compare the way in which data infrastructures and digital technologies designed largely in Western nations have been 'forced upon' formerly colonized nations, with the critique and movement Third World Approaches to International Law (TWAIL).

[33] For example, flight and marine tracking websites often only have receivers in built-up and populated areas, leaving other areas with little or zero coverage.

[34] See the following tracking portal that tracks the state of open government data—Open Knowledge, 'Global Open Data Index' *Open Knowledge Foundation* https://index.okfn.org/place/ accessed 11 May 2018.

[35] S.C Rainie, D Rodriguez-Lonebear, and A Martinez, 'Policy Brief: Data Governance for Native Nation Rebuilding' (2017)n Native Nations Institute http://usindigenousdata.arizona.edu/sites/usindigenousdata/files/spotlight/files/policy_brief_data_governance_for_native_nation_rebuilding_version_2.pdf accessed 29 August 2018.

A movement dating back to 1955,[36] TWAIL argues that international law created during the colonial era was forced upon Third World countries, 'legitimising, reproducing and sustaining the plunder and subordination of the Third World by the West'[37] and is therefore illegitimate. Their critique focuses on the challenges that arise after colonialism ended, and they identify international legal studies and praxis as a particular place where these challenges arise.

Digital space is another site in which similar dichotomies are being furthered, such as the labour of content moderation for Western users of social media being outsourced to countries like the Philippines and Bangladesh, where such labour is far cheaper and easier to exploit;[38] the structure of governance bodies of the internet itself, such as the Internet Governance Forum; and the questions surrounding who profits from different domain names.[39] These inequalities create the environment in which open source investigations are taking place.

3.2 Tools for Investigations

Investigators end up using many tools that are not designed for them, which naturally limits their usefulness. Tools, platforms, training material, and relevant documentation are often available only in English. For some, using an anonymity-enhancing tool such as Tor[40] would in fact endanger them, as it would alert authorities to the fact that they may be trying to evade detection. It is worth remembering here, as ever, that security measures should be decided upon in response to the potential attacks or risks faced by an individual.

Some tools are managed not by commercial entities, but by open source communities, often not supported by either viable commercial models or institutional support.[41] Non-commercial tools come with their own set of challenges, though as we discuss below, many tools create precarity within investigator workflows. A key difference between open source and proprietary tools, however, is that open source tools can be picked up and continued regardless of a certain company or individual's association with it; whereas proprietary tools, where the code is not available publicly, are no longer usable if the main actor behind it suspends work on the tool, or shuts it down completely.

One concrete example of the power that companies hold over investigators, and the quality of an investigation itself, can be seen if we consider application programming interfaces (APIs), which are a crucial entry points for researchers, and usually the only way to gain access to data on closed platforms. In 2018, following the Cambridge Analytica scandal,[42] Facebook considerably restricted access to their API. Leading internet researchers have

[36] M Mutua and A Anghie, 'What Is TWAIL?' Proceedings of the Annual Meeting (2000) 94 American Society of International Law40 31.

[37] ibid.

[38] *The Cleaners* (dir Hans Block and Moritz Riesewieck, Gebrueder Beetz Filmproduktion 2018).

[39] J Bridle, Citizen Ex [Website] (2016) http://citizen-ex.com/stories/io accessed 3 September 2018.

[40] See Tor Project https://www.torproject.org/.

[41] N Eghbal, 'Roads and Bridges: The Unseen Labor behind Our Digital Infrastructure' (2016) 2–5 https://www.fordfoundation.org/media/2976/roads-and-bridges-the-unseen-labor-behind-our-digital-infrastructure.pdf accessed 10 May 2018.

[42] C Cadwalladr and E Graham-Harrison, 'Revealed: 50 million Facebook Profiles Harvested for Cambridge Analytica in Major Data Breach' *The Guardian* (17 March 2008) https://www.theguardian.com/news/2018/mar/17/cambridge-analytica-facebook-influence-us-election accessed 29 August 2018.

suggested that other platform providers are likely to follow suit.[43] Already, differences in Twitter's API access in comparison to Facebook's mean that considerably more research has been done on Twitter than on Facebook. This suggests that more evidence may have been drawn from one platform than the other, which again brings up issues of information asymmetry, as Facebook is the most used social media platform in many areas of the world.

3.3 (In)visible Social Media Data

Scholar Zeynep Tufecki writes on how the 'social commons' of the 21st century—that is, social media platforms—are now owned by corporations, rather than being the public spaces that they are typically perceived to be.[44] Many users do not realize that social media companies typically have access to all of the content they produce on the site, and that these companies will use this content for their own ends. Investigators must be conscious of this common lack of literacy, and factor that into decisions about use of social media posts.

There is usually a difference in using social media data for the discovery and collection phase of an investigation and using that data in the publication phase. This difference is lessened considerably if the investigation goes to court, where all associated information found and used in earlier phases will have to be released to the court. But in cases where the investigation is part of an advocacy campaign, for example, it is rare that the data used in discovery and collection would have to be published explicitly.

As with most of the ethical situations described in this chapter, however, consideration of the context is essential, and for this reason, we do not suggest strict rules that should be applied in all situations. If, for example, the social media user in question is a potential perpetrator of a human rights violation, guidelines on consent must be adapted accordingly: asking their consent would alert suspected perpetrators that an investigation is underway, and not capturing the full text of their social media entry would allow them to delete their post, thus destroying the evidence.

We can look towards larger human rights organizations for guidance on some of these issues. For Amnesty International, for instance, its guidelines include never to use subterfuge, or digital trespassing, when it comes to a victim or potential victim.

4. Data Processes

There are always limits to what data can tell us. Quantitative data are the result of a series of human decisions—what to collect, what not to collect, how to categorize, sort, or analyse. In the case of open source investigations, these pieces of data are put together to reveal a particular conclusion. However, this conclusion may also be a result of not having access to all relevant pieces of information, and so the conclusion may be provisional. In this section, we focus on the ethical dilemmas that arise during an open source investigator's

[43] A Bruns, 'Facebook Shuts the Gate after the Horse Has Bolted, and Hurts Real Research in the Process' *Internet Policy Review* (2018) https://policyreview.info/articles/news/facebook-shuts-gate-after-horse-has-bolted-and-hurts-real-research-process/786 accessed 9 May 2018.

[44] Z Tufekci, 'Google Buzz: The Corporatization of Social Commons' *Technosociology* (2010) http://technosociology.org/?p=102 accessed 11 May 2018.

work from discovery of data, to verification, preservation, and publication. To highlight the range of processes at play, consider the different types of labour and the various data processes that typically take place from an event happening, to, for example, a video appearing in an investigation:

- Event happens.
- Someone—perhaps the witness, perhaps someone alerted by the witness—records the video or creates the content.
- Someone uploads the video to the internet, ideally tagging it with relevant metadata to facilitate someone else finding it.
- Once the video is online—presumably through YouTube—it has to be found by the investigator. This discovery step is often facilitated by someone sharing the video via social media (perhaps someone whose online/offline networks are already known to the investigator, or someone who curates playlists around certain themes).
- Verification: once the video is found, someone (or multiple people) needs to verify it, perhaps checking with other videos taken at similar times, or with other digital data to corroborate the details found in the video.
- The video itself forms just a piece of the overall investigation—usually made up of different types of digital content. Someone (perhaps the author of the investigation, or the lead investigator) needs to draw all of these pieces together in order for the single video to reach its full potential in establishing the underlying facts of the original event.

4.1 Discovery

There are an ever-growing number of data sources that could be used for open source investigations. Here, we focus on two main categories that often bring with them ethical dilemmas: social media data and data from leaks, breaches, or hacks. We also consider what other issues arise when discovery takes place in real-time.

A major source of current concern when it comes to consent and using other people's data in an ethical way lies within platform infrastructure. Aside from individual sharing preferences that define visibility of a post, there is no way for people who are on social media platforms to indicate preferences as to how they would like others to be able to use or not use their data. This lack of mechanism to actively contribute to investigations means that this consent is currently taken for granted. As a result, credit to the people who created the data are not, and in many cases, cannot, be easily given.[45]

Because of this, the default is that if data are contributed online through social media platforms (e.g. photos uploaded; event updates tweeted) they are generally considered to be 'fair game' by investigators, and explicit consent for this purpose is usually not gathered.

[45] Currently, the only way to do this would be individually and manually to request the permission of everyone whose social media data are used—noting that many will not know of the existence of open source investigations, let alone have an understanding of what the consequences of giving consent might be. Getting permission or consent would be a long process indeed in most cases.

Similarly, people have little or no control over the dissemination of their personal information accessed through leaks, breaches, or hacks, which can be made public without warning, context, or moderation. This often happens in the form of document dumps, email breaches, or making documents available to selected outlets.[46]

In most cases, but not all, data released through leaks, breaches, or hacks, were never designed to be open to the public and shared publicly without the consent of the data's creators or owners. In considering whether or not to make use of information gained by a leak, we encourage interrogating the intent of those who made the data public, as well as the means they used. Using this data in an ethical way means considering the duty of care to not cause further harm with this data, for example by following these steps:

- verifying the data prior to publication or use, making that process of verification available in a transparent way
- redacting versions of the dataset before publishing it publicly
- assigning a trusted institution as the 'gatekeeper' of a particular dataset, which ensures that others wanting access have to go through an institution that has the capacity and knowledge to prevent access to any data that might cause harm to the people involved
- putting extra effort into explaining where the data comes from for viewers of the data, ensuring that viewers understand the limitations and provenance of the data.

Real-time investigations bring their own set of ethical challenges. There have been various online investigations that have taken a real-time approach to discovery, via platforms such as Twitter, Medium, and Reddit, which make possible 'live' sharing of information that can be taken and built on by other online investigators.

An example of this is the Ghost Boat, an open investigation into the disappearance of 243 women, children, and men who were on a boat in the Mediterranean Sea in 2014. The investigation was hosted on Medium, an open publishing platform, and included a number of authors and investigators. Information was put online, and readers were encouraged to dig in to see if they could find anything else; in some cases, they were assigned small tasks such as collating a machine-readable database of refugee arrivals from a series of other databases.[47]

This type of crowd-solving, as many of the web-sleuthing communities refer to it, has few checks and barriers with respect to the ethical consequences in place. There are a number of trade-offs with this kind of 'radical presentation' that are echoed in the radical transparency field.[48] Radical discovery enables real-time collaboration, facilitates somewhat live reporting, and offers the investigation to the commons for involvement by anyone who was following the investigation. Individuals visibly credit the work they are building on and they get credited in return when the next web-sleuth cites their work.

But the subsequent lack of curation or moderation results in many cases of invasion of privacy of sources. In effect, the focus of these investigations is on speed and reaching the

[46] A Dunn and R Miller, 'Responsible Data Leaks and Whistleblowing' *The Engine Room* (26 October 2016) https://www.theengineroom.org/responsible-data-leaks-and-whistleblowing/ accessed 12 May 2018.

[47] Ghost Boat, 'How 30 Seconds of Your Time Could Help Find the Ghost Boat' *Medium* (2015) https://medium.com/ghostboat/how-30-seconds-of-your-time-could-help-find-the-ghost-boat-33bcbd7a0219 accessed 14 May 2018.

[48] M.L Sifry, 'In the Age of Wikileaks, the End of Secrecy?' *The Nation* (3 March 2011) https://www.thenation.com/article/age-wikileaks-end-secrecy/ accessed 9 August 2018.

goal; not on ensuring an ethical process, which takes time and intentional care. Crowd-solving projects also often have a heavy gamification and competitive aspect to them, for example having visible reward systems such as 'likes', 'mentions', and competitions to find the next key detail.

4.2 Verification

Perhaps the crux of open source investigations lies in verification. There is a duty of care to verify information that has been discovered and collected as accurately as possible, at risk of damaging the credibility of the entire investigation, not to mention the people involved. The verification process also offers an opportunity to ensure that unnecessary personal identifying and sensitive data are not incidentally being included within sets of data being published.

Verification and corroboration of videos is a huge task requiring many hours of human labour, which time-strapped researchers often struggle with. In response to this need, Amnesty International set up the Digital Verification Corps (DVC)[49] to train and enlist students in undertaking and supporting verification work, as discussed in Chapter 10. Much of the content being verified can feature graphic images or descriptions of graphic content which, when studied over a period of time, can lead to vicarious trauma.[50] The DVC, in its structure, governance and priorities, has built in concerns for vicarious trauma students may suffer, providing training on how best to 'disconnect' from the content itself, providing access to professional support, and encouraging a culture where students can talk about the mental health concerns they might be having.

Though the culture of human rights organizations is slowly shifting, building in explicit support for the well-being of investigators is still not the norm however. This means that people may be tasked with verification or viewing video, with little or no support available. This distribution of labour can be described as outsourcing trauma. We suggest that this is another tangible consequence of the distributed labour of open source investigations, in which trauma and risk are distributed throughout the chain. If anything, Amnesty's DVC is the exception, rather than the rule when it comes to paying attention to the psycho-social aspects of the investigatory process and considering what ethical verification processes look like.

4.3 Preservation

Sherri Berger writes in 'The Evolving Ethics of Preservation' that the library community is far from being in agreement as to what 'should be saved, how it should be done, and who is responsible'.[51] The same might be said of the open source intelligence community.

[49] S Dubberley and M Grant, 'In the Firing Line: How Amnesty's Digital Verification Corps Changed Official Narratives through Open Source Investigation' (18 May 2017)t https://citizenevidence.org/category/verification-corps/ accessed 16 August 2018

[50] S Dubberley and M Grant, 'Journalism and Vicarious Trauma'7 *First Draft News* (2017)t https://firstdraftnews.org/wp-content/uploads/2017/04/vicarioustrauma.pdf accessed 10 August 2018.

[51] S Berger, 'The Evolving Ethics of Preservation: Redefining Practices and Responsibilities in the 21st Century' in RJ Black (ed), *The Voices of the Future* .k(Routledge 2009) 67.

There is little funding and few agreements regarding what data should be preserved and archived, or how. One of few archiving tools available is the Internet Archive, a non-profit digital library,[52] though their goal is much broader than just archiving digital human rights information.

At a time of rapidly shifting digital landscapes, the preservation and safeguarding of public information online is crucial to investigations—for the sake of our collective memory and to strengthen investigations in the future.[53] It is essential to safeguard relevant public information so it can be used in other contexts and, where appropriate, one day be used in bringing perpetrators to account. Individuals may have risked their personal safety to highlight particular human rights violations; memorializing and safely preserving their contributions is an ethical imperative.

YouTube, for example, hosts approximately 4 million videos related to Syria that have been uploaded since 2011. In 2017, YouTube introduced a machine-learning algorithm designed to flag propaganda videos posted by extremist groups such as the Islamic State in Iraq and al-Sham.[54] Within a few days of the algorithm being introduced, 400,000 videos were taken down, many of which were videos documenting human rights violations. After a large outcry, YouTube reinstated nearly half of those videos by the time of this writing. This is one of the reasons that the Syrian Archive,[55] a small group of activists, has been working since 2014 to collect visual documentation of the Syrian conflict and store it in a safe and publicly accessible database. To date, they have securely archived and preserved 1.4 million videos.

As the availability of date and online tools change, investigation groups or individuals might find themselves in the unintended role of being the gatekeepers for important and sensitive datasets, and thus responsible for the preservation, at least temporarily, of unique archives. Evan Hill described this phenomenon for *BuzzFeed*: 'Smartphones and social media have created an archive of publicly available information unlike any in human history—an ocean of eyewitness testimony. But while we create almost everything on the internet, we control almost none of it.'[56] This mismatch between creation, control, and preservation responsibility is difficult to manage, and without a concerted adjustment in how YouTube interprets its responsibility, will undoubtedly lead to more mistaken deletions in the future. Paradoxically, platforms such as YouTube who individuals trust with their videos are the ones who delete the content in an irresponsible way—but the people who create the content do not see any other viable alternative but to use those platforms, despite their shortcomings.

[52] Internet Archive is a non-profit digital library of internet sites and other cultural artifacts in digital form https://archive.org/about/.

[53] See the above-mentioned Protocol on Open Source Investigations and also 7Ch 7 in this book by Yvonne Ng.

[54] A Rosen, 'Erasing History: YouTube's Deletion of Syria War Videos Concerns Human Rights Groups' *Fast Company* (2018) https://www.fastcompany.com/40540411/erasing-history-youtubes-deletion-of-syria-war-videos-concerns-human-rights-groups accessed 12 May 2018.

[55] See the Syrian Archive project here https://syrianarchive.org/en.

[56] E Hill, 'Opinion: Silicon Valley Can't Be Trusted with Our History' *Buzzfeed* (2018) https://www.buzzfeed.com/evanhill/silicon-valley-cant-be-trusted-with-our-history?utm_term=.sxJ9wjkwz#.iv1PzEez3 accessed 12 May 2018.

4.4 Publication

Publication, or presentation of data, is the last step in an investigation. At this stage, investigators review the data collected and assess what is essential to make public, versus what information is purely useful for the discovery phase of an investigation. A key part of this assessment should be consideration of what data might cause harm to those included or represented if published. This includes not only those directly affected by the issue being investigated but also those being implicated within the investigation itself.

Many human rights organizations work with degrees of certainty for publication, knowing that they may never be 100 per cent accurate but are confident publishing within, for example, an 80 per cent degree of certainty. Key processes here include establishing standards and a review and vetting process and asking how investigators reached their conclusions.

There are many different ways of presenting investigations, ranging from written documents such as reports, articles, and legal briefs to visual content such as videos, data visualizations, and images. Each presentation style necessitates decisions about how the data are represented, how the labour behind the investigation is presented, and what should be left out.

In the case of investigations, visual presentation can sometimes provide a more powerful demonstration of human rights violation than simply stating it in words. In some cases, the presentation method can also be part of the analysis itself. For example, SITU Research used an archive of eye-witness videos to reconstruct three protester deaths at the Euromaidan protests in Ukraine.[57] Their tool for the presentation of evidence in court has also been used in mainstream media reporting,[58] and is a powerful example of how digital data can be employed to tell a story and reveal truths.

But an approach of presenting information as having one objective and universal truth can hide a more complex, multi-perspective, murky and emotional reality. In some cases, presenting just one truth is a key part of the investigation—for example, demonstrating who is responsible for the deaths of protestors. But in others, representing that blurry and emotional reality can be just as valuable. An illustration of this can be seen through Periscopic's emotion-based[59] visualization focused on the number of gun deaths in the United States.[60] Rather than providing an overview of gun violence or of active shooters, they plotted out the years lost, or stolen as they refer to it, from people due to gun violence. After a few minutes, the moving visualization comes to an end and the final figures for 2013 show 11,419 people who had died, the age in which they had died, and a predicted age that they might have lived to. A total of 502,025 stolen years were plotted out.

Data is not a truth so much as it is a rhetoric, gathered with inherent biases built in.[61] As D'Ignazio and Klein write, a central premise of feminist theory is that all knowledge is situated where 'situated refers to the particular social, cultural and material context in

[57] See https://situ.nyc/research/projects/euromaidan-event-reconstruction.

[58] M Schwartz, 'Who Killed the Kiev Protesters? A 3-D Model Holds the Clues' *The New York Times* (30 May 2018) https://www.nytimes.com/2018/05/30/magazine/ukraine-protest-video.html accessed on 14 August 2018.

[59] A Cairo, 'Emotional Data Visualization: Periscopic's "U.S. Gun Deaths" and the Challenge of Uncertainty' *Peachpit* (3 April 2013) http://www.peachpit.com/articles/article.aspx?p=2036558 accessed 16 December 2018.

[60] Periscopic, 'U.S. Gun Deaths' (2013) https://guns.periscopic.com/ accessed 15 December 2018.

[61] D'Ignazio and Klein (n 14)n. 1.

which that knowledge is produced'.[62] Distributing power throughout the design process and including more voices and alternative perspectives in the design project will also facilitate pathways to multiple truths.

5. Future Challenges

With the development of new technologies, the retiring or archiving of older ones, and ever-increasing amounts of personal data appearing online, internet researchers and investigators face rapidly changing challenges.

Alongside these emerging challenges new ethical dilemmas may emerge. Methods of data collection, anonymization, and publication that might be sensitively and thoughtfully undertaken today, might, in the future, put people at risk. Technology now used to blur faces within video footage may, for example, be able to be 'de-blurred' in the future.[63] Individual pieces of anonymized, or de-personalized, data may be pieced together to produce a comprehensive picture of someone, which is known as the mosaic effect.[64]

Particular ethical worries are likely to arise with developments in digital imagery. New digital camera technology will be likely to have facial recognition built into it and/or produce images of such high quality that people in the background of photos could be subject to facial recognition. Synthetic imagery, particularly 'deep fakes' (a combination of 'deep learning' and 'fake videos') are becoming ever-easier to produce, and it is as-yet unknown if, or how, humans will be able to separate these artificially generated videos from authentic ones.[65] As campaigns of misinformation and threats of synthetic imagery continue to spread—images, video, and audio will become easier to discount. Marginal voices will likely be impacted as those in power will be able to better deny the plausibility of incriminating media and access to more advanced methods of verification and tools for assessing authenticity could become out of reach.

While privacy-invasive technology will undoubtedly continue to be developed in the future, data protection and platform regulation—however welcome in some respects—may well reduce the amount of data or personal information that investigators can use.[66] Already, as the European General Data Protection Regulation (GDPR) comes into force, investigative journalists are worried that the regulation will be used to force media outlets to disclose crucial investigations research that they hold, or that malicious actors may use the

[62] ibid.o.n"s6.

[63] R McPherson, R Shokri, and V Shmatikov, 'Defeating Image Obfuscation with Deep Learning'6 ArXiv (2016) https://arxiv.org/pdf/1609.00408v2.pdf accessed 20 August 2018.

[64] A Howard, 'Open Government Experts Raise Concerns about "Mosaic Effect" in Open Data Policy' *E Pluribus Unum* (20 May 2013) http://epluribusunum.org/2013/05/20/open-data-mosaic-effect/ accessed 23 May 2018.

[65] R Chesney and D Citron, Deep Fakes: A Looming Challenge for Privacy, Democracy, and National Security (July 14, 2018). 107 California Law Review (2019, Forthcoming); U of Texas Law, Public Law Research Paper No. 692; U of Maryland Legal Studies Research Paper No. 2018-21. Available at SSRN: https://ssrn.com/abstract=3213954 or http://dx.doi.org/10.2139/ssrn.3213954

[66] C Silverman, 'Journalists Are Criticizing Facebook for Its Data Collection. At the Same Time, They Often Use It to their Advantage', *Buzzfeed* (11 April 2018) https://www.buzzfeednews.com/article/craigsilverman/facebook-cambridge-analytica-journalism-data-criticism-osint accessed 17 August 2018.

GDPR to force platforms or outlets to delete material that might otherwise form valuable pieces of evidence in future investigations.[67]

In the absence of viable alternatives, the practice of investigators using and effectively co-opting tools from large companies will be like likely to continue. Whether or not such companies are receptive to the needs of efforts on behalf of human rights—for example, whether YouTube reinstates the deleted videos from Syria, or whether it makes the case that being a digital archive of human rights information is not, and has never been, its main use case—remains to be seen. Major social media platforms are battling with their responsibilities on many fronts, be it involvement or complicity in duplicitous election practices, or, as in this instance, accepting that their use cases have expanded significantly from their beginnings, and taking responsibility for those new cases.

As open source intelligence techniques become more widely known and understood, there will also be future challenges in providing clear frameworks for ethical practices in these investigations. Taking the time to consider the potential unintended consequences of an investigation, to obtain consent where necessary, and to respect the rights of those involved in an investigation, takes time and money. Beyond acknowledging that ethical approaches need to be part of a human-rights focused investigation, a key future challenge will be providing the resources necessary to build in those ethical approaches in a meaningful and ongoing way.

6. Conclusion

We have argued in this chapter for a rights-based approach to conducting open source investigations. Two core principles are woven through the chapter—first, just because you can, does not mean you should; and, secondly, the ends do not necessarily justify the means.

In writing about the use of big data by academic researchers, researchers danah boyd and Kate Crawford argue that 'it is unethical for researchers to justify their actions as ethical simply because the data are accessible. Just because content is publicly accessible doesn't mean that it was meant to be consumed by just anyone.'[68] The end mission of defending human rights and revealing rights violations means that investigators should be particularly cautious about their actions and understand the responsibility they carry. In essence: human rights should not be violated during the process of a human rights investigation.

Support is needed for the less visible parts of open source investigations—notably, the less visible roles in the human infrastructure, and the parts of the built infrastructure that are overlooked, such as the development of sustainable tools and the preservation of critical material. As open source investigation techniques become more widespread and normalized within human rights research, it is important that we take an approach that understands and values what makes them possible and appreciate all of those parts.

Ethical considerations are an essential aspect in both planning and conducting open source investigations. As with many ethical areas, there are few concrete rules, but rather

[67] P Chadwick, 'Don't Let Data Protection Undermine Journalism' *The Guardian* (10 June 2018) https://www.theguardian.com/commentisfree/2018/jun/10/data-protection-press-freedom accessed 10 August 2018.

[68] d boyd and A Marwick, 'Social Privacy in Networked Publics: Teens' Attitudes, Practices, and Strategies,' paper given at Oxford Internet Institute 'Decade in Time' Conferenced (2011).

questions to be considered and addressed on a contextual basis. Throughout each stage of an investigation, human rights researchers and investigators must keep asking themselves and those around them about the potential consequences of their collection, verification, analysis, preservation, and publication processes, with their particular contexts in mind.

Those involved in investigations and research using open source material have an ethical responsibility not just as part of the end result, but with regard to the methods, techniques, and data being employed, from beginning to end.

12

Digital Human Rights Investigations

Vicarious Trauma, PTSD, and Tactics for Resilience

Sam Dubberley, Margaret Satterthwaite, Sarah Knuckey, and Adam Brown

1. Introduction

Human rights investigations have often relied heavily on interviewing witnesses and survivors, visiting the sites of abuse, and analysing physical evidence.[1] Now, new technologies, such as the increased availability of cheap mobile phones with cameras and improved network connections, mean that some elements of a human rights investigation—whether about the conflict in Syria,[2] extra-judicial killings in Nigeria,[3] or the conditions in which refugees are forced to live in Australia's unlawful offshore detention centres in Papua New Guinea[4]—can be carried out by researchers located anywhere in the world, including those far away from the site of abuse.

When human rights investigators are removed from zones of violence or conflict, they are generally not targets of physical attack themselves.[5] Yet their work is not risk-free. Investigators may be subjected to digital attacks such as threats, harassment, trolling, phishing, or the intrusion of spyware. And, in the course of their digital fact-finding, investigators can be exposed to significant amounts of distressing and traumatic photographs, video, or other materials, creating a risk that they will experience high levels of stress, compassion fatigue, burn-out, depression, substance abuse disorders, and post-traumatic stress disorder (PTSD).

The work of the digital and open source investigator may include, for example, sifting through a database of hundreds of videos of airstrikes, searching in real time on Twitter for photos showing police beatings during a protest, or closely and repeatedly examining

[1] Margaret L Satterthwaite and Justin Simeone, 'A Conceptual Roadmap for Social Science Methods in Human Rights Fact-Finding' in Philip Alston and Sarah Knuckey (eds), *The Transformation of Human Rights Fact-Finding* (Oxford University Press 2016).

[2] Dima Saber and Paul Long, '"I Will Not Leave, My Freedom Is More Precious than My Blood": From Affect to Precarity: Crowd-Sourced Citizen Archives as Memories of the Syrian War' (2017) 38 Archives and Records 80.

[3] C Koettl, 'Sensors Everywhere: Using Satellites and Mobile Phones to Reduce Information Uncertainty in Human Rights Crisis Research' (2017) 11 Genocide Studies and Prevention: An International Journal 36.

[4] Sam Dubberley, 'In the Firing Line: How Amnesty's Digital Verification Corps Changed Official Narratives through Open Source Investigation' *Lemming Cliff* (18 May 2017) https://medium.com/lemming-cliff/in-the-firing-line-how-amnestys-digital-verification-corps-changed-official-narratives-through-23aee8bf415d accessed 18 June 2018.

[5] Agnieszka Bieńczyk-Missala and Patrycja Grzebyk, 'Safety and Protection of Humanitarian Workers' in Pat Gibbons and Hans-Joachim Heintze (eds), *The Humanitarian Challenge: 20 Years European Network on Humanitarian Action (NOHA)* (Springer 2015).

one video of a massacre. Investigators may view large quantities of raw, often bloody and graphic, content in their quest to assess if such content can be turned into evidence for reporting, advocacy,[6] or legal action.[7] Their workdays may include extensive and repeated exposure to 'intense visual material', and they may view scores of incidents of abuse each day.[8] Investigators may be exposed largely to traumatic material via digital sources, or such exposure may occur alongside exposure through interviewing, site visits, or personally experiencing insecurity.

The considerable risk of psychological distress through secondary experiences of potentially traumatic events has been under-addressed in the human rights field for various reasons. These include the relative recency in which viewing traumatic photos and video has been incorporated in the definition of PTSD; the generally poor response of the human rights field to the mental health risks of advocacy; and the far more rapid growth of fact-finding with online and digital content compared to the strategies designed to counter its ill-effects.

In bringing insights from psychology together with experience of the challenges which human rights researchers face in researching with new technologies, the aim of this chapter is twofold: to show that secondary trauma is a real risk for human rights researchers in the digital age; and to introduce human rights researchers and organizations to techniques and methods for mitigating harm and building resilience.

In section 1 of this chapter we outline the general criteria, symptoms, and risk factors for PTSD, and discuss the potential link between viewing photos or video of abuse and PTSD. We focus on PTSD because it is one of the most common types of adverse outcomes which can follow exposure to potentially traumatic events. Other mental health issues can arise in the course of human rights work—such as burn-out and depression—and while we discuss techniques aimed at preventing PTSD, the practices outlined may help some people to mitigate the broad range of negative psychological outcomes. In section 2, we discuss why digital and open source investigations pose a unique challenge to the mental health of human rights researchers. In section 3, we share various tactics which investigators can adopt to help prevent, mitigate, and respond to stress related to exposure to traumatic material. Section 4 turns to organizational strategies for working with potentially traumatic material, and section 5 addresses the impact of technological choices on exposure to distressing material, suggesting that developers need to confront and design with the risk of PTSD and other adverse effects in mind.

[6] Jay Aronson, 'Preserving Human Rights Media for Justice, Accountability, and Historical Clarification' (2017) 11 Genocide Studies and Prevention: An International Journal 82.

[7] Alexa Koenig and others, 'Open Source Fact-Finding in Preliminary Examinations' in Morten Bergsmo and Carsten Stahn (eds), *Quality Control in Preliminary Examination: Volume 2* (Torkel Opsahl Academic EPublisher 2018).

[8] Sam Dubberley, Elizabeth Griffin, and Haluk Mert Bal, 'Making Secondary Trauma a Primary Issue: A Study of Eyewitness Media and Vicarious Trauma on the Digital Frontline' *Eyewitness Media Hub* (2015) http://eyewitnessmediahub.com/research/vicarious-trauma accessed 28 November 2018.

2. PTSD: Criteria, Symptoms, and Risk Factors

2.1 PTSD Criteria and Symptoms

Enduring negative psychological consequences of war, sexual violence, environmental disasters, and loss of loved ones have long been documented and depicted.[9] For some individuals, exposure to traumatic events or material may contribute to the onset of mental health problems such as anxiety, depression, substance abuse, burn-out,[10] and PTSD. Alongside such experiences of psychological distress, individuals may experience impairments in occupational and interpersonal functioning.

PTSD was first formally recognized by the American Psychiatric Association in 1980, when the term was added to the third edition of the Association's Diagnostic and Statistical Manual of Mental Disorders (DSM).[11] The DSM provides standard and common terminologies for mental health disorders. While the specific criteria used to classify PTSD evolves with each iteration of the DSM, the consensus is that a diagnosis of PTSD represents the presence of a constellation of symptoms that can emerge following an individual's exposure to one or more potentially traumatic event(s). For a diagnosis of PTSD, the exposure must be followed by significant impairment in social and occupational functioning and be present at least thirty days after trauma exposure. In the fifth and current edition of the DSM,[12] a diagnosis of PTSD requires individuals to report symptoms in four categories: re-experiencing (e.g. nightmares or flashbacks related to the original trauma), avoidance (e.g. of people or places that remind the individual of the traumatic event), alterations in cognition and mood (e.g. persistent negative beliefs about oneself or the world), and hyper-arousal (e.g. exaggerated startle reflex). Additionally, individuals diagnosed with PTSD frequently report feelings of depressed mood, anger, guilt, shame, and alienation. After exposure to a traumatic event or material, many people may temporarily experience some symptoms associated with PTSD. However, for a diagnosis of PTSD, these symptoms must be present thirty days following trauma exposure and must be severe and persistent enough to have a significant impact on the person's day-to-day life. In addition, unlike other mental health issues such as depression, general anxiety, and obsessive-compulsive disorder (OCD) that do not require a known etiology for a diagnosis, a diagnosis of PTSD is made when symptoms are believed to have emerged in response to an event or series of events.

[9] Marc-Antoine Crocq and Louis Crocq, 'From Shell Shock and War Neurosis to Posttraumatic Stress Disorder: A History of Psychotraumatology' (2000) 2 Dialogues in Clinical Neuroscience 47; Judith Lewis Herman, *Trauma and Recovery: The Aftermath of Violence—From Domestic Abuse to Political Terror* (Basic Books 1992); Derek Summerfield, 'Addressing Human Response to War and Atrocity' in Rolf J Kleber, Charles R Figley, and Berthold PR Gersons (eds), *Beyond Trauma: Cultural and Societal Dynamics* (Springer US 1995).

[10] Burn-out is described as a set of negative behavioural, emotional, and cognitive changes in response to occupational stress, characterized by emotional exhaustion and depersonalization, as well as a reduction in perceived levels of personal accomplishment. Burn-out is also associated with feelings of cynicism, detachment, and a lack of agency. See: Christina Maslach, Wilmar B Schaufeli, and Michael P Leiter, 'Job Burnout' (2001) 52 Annual Review of Psychology 397.

[11] American Psychiatric Association, *Diagnostic and Statistical Manual of Mental Health Disorders* (3rd edn, American Psychiatric Association 1980).

[12] American Psychiatric Association, *Diagnostic and Statistical Manual of Mental Health Disorders* (5th edn, American Psychiatric Association 2013).

2.2 PTSD Research on Human Rights Advocates

The inclusion of PTSD in the DSM resulted from the efforts of both feminist groups and US military veteran groups following the Vietnam War to document and raise awareness about the negative psychological impact of domestic violence and war.[13] Since then, PTSD research has expanded to include the impacts of experiencing traumatic events in many contexts. Studies have found, for example, high rates of PTSD in populations such as police, first-responders, and healthcare personnel.[14] More recently, researchers began to survey journalists and found this group to also be at risk of experiencing 'symptoms of post-traumatic stress disorder, major depression and general psychological distress'.[15]

Three of the authors of this chapter, Adam Brown, Sarah Knuckey, Margaret Satterthwaite, and their colleagues found in a 2015 survey that 19.4 per cent of human rights advocates who participated in their research met the criteria for PTSD and an additional 18.8 per cent for sub-threshold PTSD, a sub-clinical phenomenon in which a person reports symptoms of PTSD, but not enough to meet the DSM criteria.[16] These rates of PTSD are comparable, if not higher, than those found in studies examining PTSD in combat-war veterans.[17] The co-authors also found that many respondents either witnessed trauma directly or were 'indirectly exposed to trauma through work with clients, survivors and witnesses'.[18] The researchers found that greater secondary trauma exposure was correlated with greater PTSD symptom severity.[19] In a survey conducted by one of the authors, Sam Dubberley and his colleagues, 57 per cent of respondents working in human rights reported viewing distressing videos and photographs several times a week, but only 38 per cent would feel comfortable asking for support from their immediate hierarchy after viewing traumatic events.[20] More recently, in a 2017 study of security and protection issues among human rights defenders in Colombia, Mexico, Egypt, Kenya, and Indonesia by Alice Nah, 86 per cent of defenders studied said they were 'somewhat' or 'very' concerned about their mental well-being.[21] Nah found that defenders "tend to prioritize the necessity and importance of their work before thinking about their personal wellbeing', and felt that thinking about their own wellbeing was 'self-indulgent'.[22]

13 Gretchen Dworznik and Max Grubb, 'Preparing for the Worst: Making a Case for Trauma Training in the Journalism Classroom' (2007) 62 Journalism & Mass Communication Educator 190; Herman (n 9).

14 William Berger and others, 'Rescuers at Risk: A Systematic Review and Meta-Regression Analysis of the Worldwide Current Prevalence and Correlates of PTSD in Rescue Workers' (2012) 47 Social Psychiatry and Psychiatric Epidemiology 1001.

15 Anthony Feinstein, 'War, Journalists and Psychological Health: Guest Editorial' (2004) 7 African Journal of Psychiatry 1.

16 Amy Joscelyne and others, 'Mental Health Functioning in the Human Rights Field: Findings from an International Internet-Based Survey' (2015) 10 PLOS ONE e0145188.

17 George A Bonanno and others, 'Trajectories of Resilience, Depression, and Anxiety Following Spinal Cord Injury.' (2012) 57 Rehabilitation Psychology 236; Charles W Hoge and others, 'Combat Duty in Iraq and Afghanistan, Mental Health Problems, and Barriers to Care' (2004) 351 New England Journal of Medicine 13; Charles R Marmar and others, 'Course of Posttraumatic Stress Disorder 40 Years after the Vietnam War: Findings from the National Vietnam Veterans Longitudinal Study' (2015) 72 JAMA Psychiatry 875.

18 Joscelyne and others (n 16).

19 ibid.

20 Dubberley, Griffin, and Bal (n 8).

21 Alice Nah, 'Wellbeing, Risk, and Human Rights Practice, Human Rights Defender Policy Brief' Centre for Applied Human Rights, University of York (2017) https://securityofdefendersproject.org/s/HRD-Hub-Policy-Brief-1-EN.pdf accessed 20 June 2018.

22 ibid.

2.3 PTSD and Viewing Photos and Video

Although studies had shown that secondary exposure to traumatic material could lead to PTSD,[23] prior to 2013 such exposure was not explicitly labelled in the DSM as a potential source of trauma. For a diagnosis of PTSD, it had been necessary to have directly experienced or witnessed a traumatic event, or to have learned of a traumatic event happening to a close family member or friend. But in 2013, the American Psychiatric Association updated its DSM to include 'experiencing repeated or extreme exposure to aversive details of the traumatic events(s)', noting that '[t]his does not apply to exposure through electronic media, television, movies, or pictures, unless this exposure is work related.'[24] The work-related specification highlights the particular harm that can result from the kind of repeated and systematic exposure to distressing imagery inherent to some professions.[25] This recognition of vicarious trauma exposure in the DSM represents an important expansion of how the American Psychiatric Association defines traumatic stress, and an acknowledgment of the potential mental health consequences of working with traumatic materials.

Recognizing that working with open source content can be distressing does not mean that each open source investigator will develop PTSD or be traumatized. Generally, as Jonathan Bisson and colleagues note, '[p]eople do not develop a mental disorder after exposure to trauma.'[26] Much research indicates that people are generally resilient,[27] and have strong capacities to recover after exposure.[28] Brown, Knuckey, Satterthwaite and colleagues found that 43 per cent of the respondents in their study of human rights advocates reported no or only minimal symptoms of PTSD, despite the generally high levels of exposure to traumatic material in human rights advocacy.[29]

If a researcher views some distressing videos and feels upset about it, this does not mean that they will develop PTSD or another mental health disorder.[30] Many people can have some symptoms in the hours or days after viewing violent or otherwise distressing imagery. As Bruce Shapiro notes:

> Distress per se is not a sign of any kind of underlying emotional injury. Stories that involve human cruelty are likely to be upsetting ... Such periodic bouts of emotional 'bad weather' can be disruptive and annoying—and do require active self-care——but they are not signs in themselves that one needs to seek external help.[31]

[23] Sandro Galea and others, 'Psychological Sequelae of the September 11 Terrorist Attacks in New York City' (2002) 346 New England Journal of Medicine 982; Brian E Bride and others, 'Development and Validation of the Secondary Traumatic Stress Scale' (2004) 14 Research on Social Work Practice 27.

[24] American Psychiatric Association (n 12).

[25] Anushka Pai, Alina M Suris. and Carol S North, 'Posttraumatic Stress Disorder in the DSM-5: Controversy, Change, and Conceptual Considerations' (2017) 7 Behavioral Sciences 7.

[26] Jonathan I Bisson and others, 'Post-Traumatic Stress Disorder' (2015) 351 BMJ.

[27] George A Bonanno, 'Loss, Trauma, and Human Resilience: Have We Underestimated the Human Capacity to Thrive after Extremely Aversive Events?' (2004) 59 American Psychologist 20.

[28] Bisson and others (n 26).

[29] Joscelyne and others (n 16).

[30] Elana Newman, Roger Simpson, and David Handschuh, 'Trauma Exposure and Post-traumatic Stress Disorder among Photojournalists' (2003) 10 Visual Communication Quarterly 4.

[31] Bruce Shapiro, 'Managing Stress & Trauma on Investigative Projects' *Dart Center* (5 August 2015) https://dartcenter.org/content/staying-sane-managing-stress-and-trauma-on-investigative-projects accessed 4 May 2018.

These one-off views need, however, to be contrasted with researchers who are frequently and repeatedly exposed to distressing content. Such researchers do need to exercise particular care because of the heightened risks such repeat viewing over time can pose.[32] The human rights investigator verifying instances of police violence in Nicaragua, examining missile strikes by the US in Syria, studying videotaped cases of forced displacement in Myanmar, or tracking housing evictions in Brazil must often view and review videos or photos many times to find clues that can help in the research task. The human rights investigator needs to watch closely for signs that repeated exposure to graphic and/or upsetting material is creating accumulated stress, and beginning to take a harder and longer-term toll on the sense of personal well-being. Especially concerning are signs that work is leading to changes in social and occupational functioning or to thoughts of harming oneself or others. All of these changes are cause for concern, and thoughts of harm should prompt an investigator to seek immediate support.

2.4 General PTSD Risk and Protective Factors

Research has identified various factors which can make individuals more and less vulnerable to developing PTSD. Open source human rights researchers should know about these factors and how they relate to their work, so that they can develop an understanding of their own level of risk and take preventive steps or seek treatment if they notice symptoms of PTSD. Some of the most important factors are:

- *Having a prior history of trauma exposure and/or mental health issues increases current risk.* Prior history of trauma may increase reactivity to stress, thus representing a generalized vulnerability to mood and anxiety disorders as well as PTSD.[33]
- *Having a family history of mental health issues increases risk.* Studies have begun to identify factors that underlie the relation between family history and mental health issues. These include experiencing greater distress at the time of trauma exposure through the influence of genetic markers,[34] socio-contextual factors that support the development of adaptive emotion regulation skills, and maladaptive family dynamics.[35]
- *Having a higher education level mitigates risk.* Although the causal mechanisms are not fully understood, higher levels of education have often been associated with the

[32] Anthony Feinstein, Blair Audet, and Elizabeth Waknine, 'Witnessing Images of Extreme Violence: A Psychological Study of Journalists in the Newsroom' (2014) 5 JRSM Open 1 https://www.ncbi.nlm.nih.gov/pubmed/25289144 accessed 28 November 2018; E Alison Holman, Dana Rose Garfin, and Roxane Cohen Silver, 'Media's Role in Broadcasting Acute Stress Following the Boston Marathon Bombings' (2014) 111 Proceedings of the National Academy of Sciences 93; Keren Cohen and Paula Collens, 'The Impact of Trauma Work: A Meta-Synthesis on Vicarious Trauma and Vicarious Trauma Growth' (2013) 5 Psychological Trauma: Theory, Research, Practice, and Policy 570.

[33] Christine Heim and Charles B Nemeroff, 'The Role of Childhood Trauma in the Neurobiology of Mood and Anxiety Disorders: Preclinical and Clinical Studies' (2001) 49 Biological Psychiatry 1023.

[34] Karestan C Koenen and others, 'A Twin Registry Study of Familial And Individual Risk Factors for Trauma Exposure and Posttraumatic Stress Disorder' (2002) 190 Journal of Nervous and Mental Disease 209.

[35] Sabra S Inslicht and others, 'Family Psychiatric History, Peritraumatic Reactivity, and Posttraumatic Stress Symptoms: A Prospective Study of Police' (2010) 44 Journal of Psychiatric Research 22.

utilization of improved coping skills, facility in cognitive reframing of experience, and better prognosis following treatment.[36]

- *Having a good social support network can mitigate risk.* Social support may help to mitigate the negative impacts of stress and trauma by decreasing emotional disengagement and behavioural withdrawal, enhancing self-efficacy, decreasing stress-related physiological arousal, and facilitating greater community connectedness.[37]
- *Having significant non-trauma stress increases your risk.* Prolonged stress over time may lead to greater 'allostatic load' (greater physiologic 'wear and tear' on the body), which can lead to increased vulnerability, impair cognitive function, and affect regulatory processes.[38]
- *Some ways of thinking, such as perfectionism, increase risk.* Cognitive styles that are more flexible may facilitate positive adaptation following exposure to trauma, whose effects are often unpredictable and far-reaching, whereas more rigid styles of thinking, such as perfectionism, may represent a cognitive vulnerability to PTSD. Perfectionism has been conceptualized as the process in which a person consistently strives towards high personal standards and when those, often unrealistic, personal standards are not achieved, the individual then engages in persistent self-criticism.[39]
- *Human rights researchers who are members of marginalized communities may be at greater risk.* Discrimination is often a source of chronic stress, which may increase vulnerability to PTSD or may itself be a direct cause of PTSD symptoms.[40] In addition, several studies have now shown that members of marginalized communities are more likely to develop PTSD following exposure to a potentially traumatic event related to one's identity or traumatic events more generally owing to cumulative stress.[41]
- *Poor working conditions increase the chances of PTSD among trauma-exposed employees.* Among trauma-exposed employees, a lack of time to deal with a trauma, low job satisfaction, negative feelings towards work, poorly functioning equipment, lack of role clarity, negative interactions with colleagues, lack of support from supervisors,

[36] Richard J McNally, 'The Science and Folklore of Traumatic Amnesia' (2004) 11 Clinical Psychology: Science and Practice 29.

[37] Quyen Q Tiet and others, 'Coping, Symptoms, and Functioning Outcomes of Patients with Posttraumatic Stress Disorder' (2006) 19 Journal of Traumatic Stress 799; Anthony Charuvastra and Marylene Cloitre, 'Social Bonds and Posttraumatic Stress Disorder' (2007) 59 Annual Review of Psychology 301; Fatih Ozbay and others, 'Social Support and Resilience to Stress across the Life Span: A Neurobiologic Framework' (2008) 10 Current Psychiatry Reports 304.

[38] Bruce S Mcewen, 'Protection and Damage from Acute and Chronic Stress: Allostasis and Allostatic Overload and Relevance to the Pathophysiology of Psychiatric Disorders' (2004) 1032 Annals of the New York Academy of Sciences 1; Sonia J Lupien and others, 'Effects of Stress throughout the Lifespan on the Brain, Behaviour and Cognition' (2009) 10 Nature Reviews Neuroscience 434.

[39] Randy O Frost and others, 'The Dimensions of Perfectionism' (1990) 14 Cognitive Therapy and Research 449.

[40] Robert T Carter, 'Racism and Psychological and Emotional Injury: Recognizing and Assessing Race-Based Traumatic Stress' (2007) 35 The Counseling Psychologist 13.

[41] Hsiu-Lan Cheng and Brent Mallinckrodt, 'Racial/Ethnic Discrimination, Posttraumatic Stress Symptoms, and Alcohol Problems in a Longitudinal Study of Hispanic/Latino College Students' (2015) 62 Journal of Counseling Psychology 38; Sherry Lipsky and others, 'Traumatic Events Associated with Posttraumatic Stress Disorder: The Role of Race/Ethnicity and Depression' (2016) 22 Violence against Women 1055; Theresa Brockie and others, 'The Relationship of Adverse Childhood Experiences to PTSD, Depression, Poly-Drug Use and Suicide Attempt in Reservation-Based Native American Adolescents and Young Adults' (2015) 55 American Journal of Community Psychology.

long work hours, and workplace discrimination are all factors that have been associated with PTSD.[42] Of particular relevance to human rights investigators, research on war journalists indicates that inadequate training prior to potential trauma exposure and low levels of social support in a 'culture of silence' have been associated with PTSD.[43] A lack of workplace training about mental health and support services can also suggest a stigma is attached to mental health illnesses in that workplace, which in turn may impede a worker from accessing resources needed.

- *Human rights investigators often say that the adverse effects of trauma exposure that they experience pale in comparison to the effects of the actual events on the primary victims.* Activists often minimize their own experiences of harm. Minimizing the potential for secondary trauma can result in advocates taking no or inadequate steps to protect themselves or to respond to harm in themselves or their colleagues when it does occur. Individuals with PTSD symptoms may observe that others 'have had it worse' as a technique for tamping down the severity of their distress, but this may also become a further barrier to care.[44] Human rights advocates, research has found, often operate in a community that values selflessness, and it is common for advocates to deny 'their own needs in light of the gravity of human rights abuse', and to feel 'morally obliged to work to the point of physical and emotional exhaustion'.[45] Identifying these patterns may help human rights workers to break their hold over them, or at least mitigate their impact. Activists who become aware of their feelings of guilt and self-abnegation are in a better position to try to shift their frame of reference towards self-care.

3. Digital and Open Source Investigations and the Risk of PTSD

The mental health challenges inherent in human rights work can be magnified in certain ways and sometimes transformed into vectors of vulnerability in the context of digital or open source investigations.

In today's digital world, the speed and breadth of change in exposure to potentially traumatic content has been enormous. The rapid expansion of photographs and videos being published on social media networks has changed the world.[46] People now have access to cameras capable of recording, live-streaming, and sharing high-definition imagery instantly. People who witness atrocities can now rapidly report or show evidence of the abuse through social media platforms or social messaging apps. This volume, immediacy, and speed means that human rights and humanitarian organizations must frequently engage

[42] Cheryl Regehr and others, 'Social Support, Self-Efficacy and Trauma in New Recruits and Experienced Firefighters' (2003) 19 Stress and Health 189.

[43] Anthony Feinstein, John Owen, and Nancy Blair, 'A Hazardous Profession: War, Journalists, and Psychopathology' (2002) 159 American Journal of Psychiatry 1570.

[44] Institute of Medicine, *The Mental Health and Substance Use Workforce for Older Adults: In Whose Hands?* (The National Academies Press 2012).

[45] Kathleen Rodgers, '"Anger Is Why We're All Here": Mobilizing and Managing Emotions in a Professional Activist Organization' (2010) 9 Social Movement Studies 273.

[46] Zeynep Tufekci and Christopher Wilson, 'Social Media and the Decision to Participate in Political Protest: Observations from Tahrir Square' (2012) 62 Journal of Communication 363.

with deeply disturbing user-generated content sourced from clients, contacts, or social media as part of their efforts to respond quickly to global events.

Owing to the rapid development and adoption of social media and related internet platforms in recent years, many managers of human rights advocates have not worked significantly in a social media content environment themselves and are not necessarily aware of the workflows involved in discovery and verification and the distressing impact this secondary exposure to traumatic events can have. Such lack of awareness means there may also be a lack of preparedness when mental health challenges do appear in an organization. Training in resiliency and trauma awareness and mitigation for individuals and teams may be poor or non-existent, and no protocols may be in place when introducing new software tools for open source investigation. Some managers even dismiss vicarious or secondary trauma completely. As one investigator said: 'I heard a very senior manager say: "If I hear one more word about secondary trauma I will be sick. It does not exist and if people cannot deal with this stuff then they just need to get out.' "[47]

Minimal knowledge of how social media environments work, combined with the generally poor response of the human rights field to mental health risks, means that, currently, many human rights researchers using open source investigation techniques have seldom been trained in resiliency and how to cope in these environments. Seventy per cent of human rights advocates who participated in a survey conducted by some of the co-authors of this chapter reported they had received 'none' or 'minimal' training for, or education about, the potential impact of human rights work on their mental health,[48] and 74.7 per cent said that their employer or educational institution had offered or made available 'no' or 'minimal' psychological support.[49] In such contexts, researchers may feel unable to speak up about problems they are having with their managers, as they fear it may impact on their careers.[50]

These challenges come up against the mistaken assumptions of some managers and staff about the exposure to trauma involved in human rights investigations carried out from afar. The field's recognition of the risks human rights advocates face who work directly with witnesses and in high security risk areas is weak generally, though there has been some improvement in recent years.[51] For advocates working with digital materials, the situation can be particularly challenging. There is often little or no recognition of the risks. Indeed, there remains a stigma connected to recognizing the risks to mental health and well-being that come from exposure to distressing imagery. This stigma must be lifted within the managerial structures of organizations—large and small—so that digital human rights investigators can receive ready access to the support needed to do their work.

[47] Dubberley, Griffin, and Bal (n 8).

[48] Joscelyne and others (n 16).

[49] Sarah Knuckey, Margaret Satterthwaite, and Adam Brown, 'Trauma, Depression and Burnout in the Human Rights Field: Identifying Barriers and Pathways to Resilient Advocacy' (2018) 49 Columbia Human Rights Law Review 57.

[50] Dubberley, Griffin, and Bal (n 8).

[51] Ellen Connorton and others, 'Humanitarian Relief Workers and Trauma-Related Mental Illness' (2012) 34 Epidemiologic Reviews 145.

4. Strategies for Preventing, Mitigating, and Responding to PTSD

When researching or investigating an issue, country, or event using open source research, various factors in the discovery and verification process may increase the risk of exposure to PTSD triggers and distress. This section outlines steps that investigators can take to mitigate risk factors and offers general suggestions for human rights investigators who believe they may have been adversely affected personally by their work exposure. Human rights investigations of course come with inherent risks of exposure to traumatic material, and it is important for researchers to acknowledge openly the risks of secondary trauma, to be literate in the variety of those risks, and to put in place steps to mitigate them and alleviate the mental health impacts of the upsetting material to which investigators are exposed. Because everyone responds differently, it is important for each investigator to establish which techniques work best for them.

4.1 Awareness and Monitoring

An essential first step in preventing the development of PTSD is increasing awareness of how human rights work may be affecting one personally. It is crucial for each researcher to know and to be able to recognize what possible adverse mental health signs are—both in themselves and in their colleagues. Individuals can be affected psychologically, behaviourly, and relationally, and physically.[52]

The Dart Center for Journalism and Trauma[53] recommends that people be particularly alert for the following changes in themselves or in others:

- Marked changes in character.
- Unusual irritability, or explosive anger that fires up without apparent reason.
- Images or thoughts related to a project which intrude at unwanted times, are unusually persistent, and do not diminish with time—particularly if they involve situations in which you imagine yourself being followed or attacked.
- Unusual isolation or withdrawal.
- The sense that life has become meaningless or foreshortened.
- A persistent and general feeling of being numb or deadened inside.
- Increase in self-medication (alcohol, drugs, compulsive overworking, etc).

In their research, Dubberley and colleagues interviewed subjects who had noticed one or more of the effects listed above in themselves or in their colleagues. Changes in mood were particularly evident in the interview subjects, who reported being adversely affected by viewing distressing imagery sourced from social media. One human rights researcher

[52] Sam Dubberley and Michele Grant, 'Journalism and Vicarious Trauma: A Guide for Journalists, Editors and News Organisations' *First Draft News* (April 2017) https://firstdraftnews.org/wp-content/uploads/2017/04/vicarioustrauma.pdf accessed 4 April 2018.

[53] Gavin Rees, 'Handling Traumatic Imagery: Developing a Standard Operating Procedure' *Dart Center* (4 April 2017) https://dartcenter.org/resources/handling-traumatic-imagery-developing-standard-operating-procedure accessed 21 May 2018.

said: 'I'm very short tempered. Little things get to me, like silly things—I just snap.'[54] A legal analyst investigating a high intensity conflict noted: 'I do feel sad and depressed because of my work. I have not as yet taken up counselling and I know I should. I have had open conversations about needing time off.'[55]

Examining individual experiences for such changes can help identify potential problems before they become unmanageable, and can help human rights researchers know when and how to develop appropriate preventive and coping mechanisms, some of which are discussed below.

4.2 What to Do If You Think You Have Been Affected—General Suggestions

Dubberley and Grant outline the following tips for researchers who are feeling ill-effects from working with distressing imagery:

- Notice what is there and name it.
- Allow yourself time to process your experiences.
- Connect with others you trust (acknowledge and name the feelings and their symptoms).
- While 'gallows humour' is not uncommon in newsrooms (and, indeed, in human rights teams), if you notice a stronger cynicism setting in, take steps to restore meaning and hope by acknowledging and reaffirming with your values.
- Take time out for meditation or breathing-based calming techniques.
- Try some 'grounding' techniques (staying in the present), such as using your five senses to describe your environment, engaging in slow deep breathing, touching an object (pen, keys, clothes) to notice how they feel, stretching.
- Experiment with attention switching. This is not the same as trying to suppress or switch off a thought or emotion, but involves switching attention between alternatives.
- As soon as you recognize that your risk of developing PTSD has increased, talk to colleagues and ask them to watch for any escalation in visible signs.
- Let your managers know that you are at risk and talk to them if you need additional support.

In addition to these steps, research shows that certain types of therapy can be especially helpful following secondary trauma exposure. Cognitive-behavioural therapy (CBT), in which participants learn to reframe negative thoughts, has been found to be effective, as has eye-movement desensitization and reprocessing (EMDR), in which participants recall and speak about their trauma exposure while attending to small movements or sounds, as well as prolonged exposure (PE), through which participants are taught to achieve control over their negative feelings by safely confronting them.

[54] Dubberley, Griffin, and Bal (n 8) 34.
[55] ibid.

Research into untreated PTSD or PTSD-like symptoms indicates that lack of treatment leads to worse long-term outcomes for the sufferers.[56] Indeed, Hans Kapfhammer and Hans Rothenhäusler conclude that: 'If they are untreated, PTSD symptoms such as intrusive recollections, avoidance and hyperarousal may impair the patients' quality of life more' than the original exposure to upsetting material.[57]

4.3 Repeat Exposure: The Potential Personal Perils of the Verification Process

Repeatedly viewing distressing photos, videos, or distressing elements of videos can amplify our traumatic responses.[58] Unfortunately, repeat exposure is often inherent to the human rights investigator's task. Therefore, acknowledgement of the risks attendant to viewing graphic or violent content and ensuring self-care is thus key to undertaking investigations in a sustainable, healthy manner.

Some of the following tips may help mitigate the impact of repeatedly viewing distressing images or video:

- Take regular breaks. The duration of observing a traumatic event can increase its negative impact.[59] Breaking up exposure may therefore be beneficial, and it may in the long run help to reduce stress and burn-out.[60] Breaks can include short breaks during the day, as well as longer breaks after intense periods of work. Some people find it especially helpful to go outside or ensure an intake of fresh air and, if possible, to experience nature with, for instance, a short walk in a park. Some people also find that creating a schedule for working with potentially traumatic material can also be beneficial, with set times for starting and stopping the work.
- Maintain good sleep routines and regular exercise. Studies have shown that poor sleep may increase the risk of PTSD[61] and that exercise can support well-being.[62]

[56] Stefan Priebe and others, 'Consequences of Untreated Posttraumatic Stress Disorder Following War in Former Yugoslavia: Morbidity, Subjective Quality of Life, and Care Costs' (2009) 50 Croatian Medical Journal 465; Hans P Kapfhammer and others, 'Posttraumatic Stress Disorder and Health-Related Quality of Life in Long-Term Survivors of Acute Respiratory Distress Syndrome' (2004) 161 American Journal of Psychiatry 45 https://ajp.psychiatryonline.org/doi/abs/10.1176/appi.ajp.161.1.45 accessed 28 November 2018; Raymond B Flannery, 'The Employee Victim of Violence: Recognizing the Impect of Untreated Psychological Trauma' (2001) 16 American Journal of Alzheimer's Disease & Other Dementias 230.

[57] Rothenhäusler H-B and Kapfhammer H-P, 'Posttraumatische Belastungssymptome Als Folge Schwerer Körperlicher Erkrankungen—Eine Zunehmend Relevantere Konsiliarpsychiatrische Herausforderung' (2006) 2 Psychiatrie und Psychotherapie 15.

[58] Feinstein, Audet, and Waknine (n 32).

[59] Bruce P Dohrenwend and others, 'The Psychological Risks of Vietnam for U.S. Veterans: A Revisit with New Data and Methods' (2006) 313 Science 979.

[60] Christina Maslach and Michael P Leiter, 'Understanding the Burnout Experience: Recent Research and Its Implications for Psychiatry' (2016) 15 World Psychiatry 103.

[61] Ali A El-Solh, Usman Riaz, and Jasmine Roberts, 'Sleep Disorders in Patients With Posttraumatic Stress Disorder' (2018) 154 CHEST 427; Lauren M Oppizzi and Reba Umberger, 'The Effect of Physical Activity on PTSD' (2018) 39 Issues in Mental Health Nursing.

[62] Sammi R Chekroud and others, 'Association between Physical Exercise and Mental Health in 1.2 Million Individuals in the USA between 2011 and 2015: A Cross-Sectional Study' (2018) 5 The Lancet Psychiatry 739; Emily E Bernstein and Richard J McNally, 'Exercise as a Buffer against Difficulties with Emotion Regulation: A Pathway to Emotional Wellbeing' (2018) 109 Behaviour Research and Therapy 29.

- Cultivate cohesion in one's research team or organization. A lack of team cohesion is often associated with PTSD in occupations exposed to potentially traumatic events.[63]
- Take advantage of available peer-support systems within an organization—or build one if an appropriate one does not exist. Peer-support systems have been associated with reduced PTSD and greater motivation to engage in treatment.[64] Building strong personal support networks of family and friends is also beneficial.[65]
- Build different kinds of work into the day. This can be, for instance, a mix of research, administration, report writing, and verification. Vicarious trauma can build gradually; relentlessly viewing distressing material may eventually take its toll.
- Schedule periods of relaxation immediately after exposure to traumatic content can be helpful. This can include a yoga class, a walk, dinner with friends, watching a film, or any enjoyed activity.
- Special care should be taken in the hours and days following exposure to especially upsetting material. As a result of temporary changes in cognitive processes, sleep patterns, and arousal levels, people may be at increased risk for accidents and injuries following trauma exposure.
- It is good practice to 'give your best working hours to the worst material', the Dart Centre for Journalism and Trauma suggests. '[I]t is best to work with traumatic imagery during times in the day when you are at your freshest and most able to concentrate analytically. Our brains are less effective at processing traumatic material when we are tired.'[66]

Each human rights researcher can experiment with using different coping mechanisms to assess what is best for them as an individual. Some people will find certain methods for stress reduction more effective than others, and what is effective can change with time and context. It is important that individuals identify several types of coping strategies to be used in different circumstances. It can be helpful to start practising these coping skills when is not experiencing high levels of stress: people are more likely to implement protocols in high intensity contexts if they are well rehearsed.[67]

4.4 The Distress of Surprise

People who feel out of control during a traumatic event are at greater risk of developing PTSD, trauma researchers have found.[68] This may explain why human rights professionals have reported that being surprised by a violent or other distressing video can make it feel

[63] Kevin Brailey and others, 'PTSD Symptoms, Life Events, and Unit Cohesion in U.S. Soldiers: Baseline Findings from the Neurocognition Deployment Health Study' (2007) 20 Journal of Traumatic Stress 495; Jeeva Kanesarajah and others, 'Factors Associated with Low Unit Cohesion in Australian Defence Force Members Who Deployed to the Middle East (2001–2009)' (2016) 162 Journal of the Royal Army Medical Corps 366.

[64] Shaili Jain and others, 'Peer Support and Outcome for Veterans with Posttraumatic Stress Disorder (PTSD) in a Residential Rehabilitation Program' (2016) 52 Community Mental Health Journal 1089.

[65] Fatih Ozbay and others, 'Social Support and Resilience to Stress' (2007) 4 Psychiatry (Edgmont) 35.

[66] Rees (n 53).

[67] Tripp Driskell, Steve Sclafani, and James Driskell, 'Reducing the Effects of Game Day Pressures through Stress Exposure Training' (2014) 5 Journal of Sport Psychology in Action 28.

[68] Mary C Vance and others, 'Peritraumatic Distress: A Review and Synthesis of 15 Years of Research' (2018) 74 Journal of Clinical Psychology 1457.

more traumatic than it might otherwise be. For instance, one advocate said: 'Definitely unexpected things—it makes it harder. If you know what to expect, blood, killings, it's not easy to watch of course, but if you know what's coming it makes it a bit better. There were some torture videos ... from Nigeria, they used some hot liquid ... I wasn't expecting it and that made it rougher.'[69]

Researchers can mitigate surprise exposure through preparation. Before starting their work, investigators can consider the research task, any known background, and anticipate what they might see or read during the research process. In other words, a trauma exposure risk assessment can be conducted, just as researchers conducting site visits would conduct a security risk assessment before deployment. Similarly, when going through the process of discovering content on social media, a researcher can consider what a video or photo could contain or concern before opening and viewing it.

Researchers may also be responsible, however inadvertently, for cross-contaminating colleagues by sharing traumatic or distressing content without acknowledging the impact it may have.

> A senior editor at a news agency explained how they were traumatised by unexpectedly distressing content when walking into their newsroom early in the morning to be confronted by the picture of Alan Kurdi, a 3-year-old Syrian boy found drowned on a beach in Turkey in September 2015. They told us: 'The dead child on the beach. I walked into the office, a colleague rushed up to me saying 'look at this, look at this, it's really important', and you don't have time ... the guards haven't gone up, and I spent the entire evening in tears, I was really shaken by it. It is important to change your mental tack and put the bulletproof glass up before you deal with it.[70]

4.4.1 Tips for Avoiding Cross-contamination

- If researchers need assistance from a colleague in the verification process, colleagues should be informed that the content to be viewed could be distressing or traumatic and asked when would be best to share it.
- Each individual reacts to content in their own way, so the researchers should err on the side of caution—even if they do not personally find a video traumatic, they should consider that a colleague may and warn the person appropriately.
- Attention should be given to how content is shared with colleagues or across an organization. Emailing or instant messaging a URL of a video without a label to a colleague or co-researcher who is not expecting to view a distressing video may have a negative impact on that person.
- When preserving or archiving content steps should always be taken to avoid cross contaminating fellow researchers or colleagues or anyone who may see the distressing content in the future by making sure that distressing imagery is labelled as such.

[69] Dubberley, Griffin, and Bal (n 8).
[70] ibid.

4.5 The Special Impact of Audio Tracks of Human Suffering

'T]he value of [the] belliphonic [the sound of war] is ambiguous—that it can be received as simultaneously a rich source of tactical information and a profound source of trauma (in the form of hearing loss or post-traumatic distress, and other less-quantifiable injuries)—both complicates and magnifies its salience,; explains J Martin Daughtry.[71] Viewing videos that depict possible human rights abuses, war crimes, or breaches of international humanitarian law often requires us not only to watch but also to listen to distressing events. This can include the sounds of explosions and gunfire, people pleading for mercy before being executed, or the screams of parents as they carry their dead child. Listening to these sounds, as Daughtry[72] explains, can have a different impact on the researcher than viewing it does—and may increase the traumatic impact of imagery.[73]

When researchers are starting the verification process, they can watch a distressing video without audio or keep the volume low the first time to try and determine if it can be verified without listening to the audio track. If it cannot, researchers should exercise caution when reviewing and listening to the audio. If, after an initial review, the audio is useful but contains distressing elements, the following workflow is recommended:

- Time should be taken to isolate the audio sequences that assist in verification. Distressing sequences that do not assist can then be avoided.
- It may be useful to transcribe the audio to avoid repeatedly listening to the raw, distressing elements. Reading transcripts can also be distressing, but limiting emotive sounds may be helpful.
- If the verification process demands repeated listening to distressing audio, the researcher should build in regular breaks and time to decompress.
- If possible, work should be done in a space that avoids exposing others in a team to the audio unless completely necessary. Researchers should inform their colleagues why they are isolating themselves to work with the video.
- Consider working in pairs or teams. Having a partner in distressing work allows you to share your experience, process it through discussion, and hand over difficult work when you need a break.

4.6 The Risks of Personal Associations with Content

An investigator's personal association with an event or details of an event may exacerbate feelings of distress around it. Research has shown that therapists were more likely to experience secondary trauma when treating trauma victims with similar trauma histories to their own.[74] While it may not be possible (or desirable) for researchers to avoid working on issues

[71] J Martin Daughtry, *Listening to War: Sound, Music, Trauma, and Survival in Wartime Iraq* (Oxford University Press 2015).

[72] ibid.

[73] Søren R Staugaard and Dorthe Berntsen, 'Involuntary Memories of Emotional Scenes: The Effects of Cue Discriminability and Emotion over Time' (2014) 143 Journal of Experimental Psychology: General 1939.

[74] Sharon Rae Jenkins and Stephanie Baird, 'Secondary Traumatic Stress and Vicarious Trauma: A Validational Study' (2002) 15 Journal of Traumatic Stress 423.

that resonate with their experience, being aware of this dynamic is important. Researchers who are cognizant of the dynamic can better monitor their reactions, prepare for exposure to material that may have a personal connection, and take extra steps to mitigate impact by adopting some of the coping strategies set out in other sections of this chapter.

4.7 Coping with a Distressing Sense of Impotence in the Face of Human Rights Atrocities

Watching videos of abuse, but not being able to intervene directly or offer aid, may result in researcher feelings of helplessness, which in turn may exacerbate the risk of PTSD. A lack of agency, or self-efficacy, is strongly associated with PTSD across many trauma-exposed populations.[75] Conversely, Metin Başoğlu and colleagues[76] found that greater perceived control and psychological preparedness in tortured political activists appeared to mitigate some of the psychological consequences of torture. In a separate study with torture victims, loss of control was among the strongest predictors of PTSD and depression.[77] Building on the association between loss of control and negative mental health outcomes following mass-trauma and torture, Başoğlu developed a brief trauma-focused treatment that aims to reduce depression and PTSD by fostering hope and a sense of agency.[78] Finding activities that help enhance these feelings may be helpful for open source researchers.

In addition, experiments have shown that increased perceptions of self-efficacy lead to more adaptive cognitive functioning and emotion regulation following exposure to aversive stimuli, such as watching footage of a motor vehicle accident.[79] It is thus important for researchers to consider those factors that help to maintain a sense of self-efficacy,[80] experiences of mastery (the experience of successfully managing a stressful event), vicarious/social learning (learning from people who are similar to you in background or occupational role), social persuasion (receiving positive feedback and good mentorship), and states of physiology (the cultivation of strategies that support emotion regulation). Studies by one of this chapter's authors (Brown) are now underway to examine whether trainings centred around those four factors can prevent or reduce the severity of mental health issues such as PTSD in personnel routinely exposed to potentially traumatic events.

It is important for researchers to monitor themselves for any feelings of helplessness or impotence, and to work with their colleagues to ensure that the impact, meaning, and purposes of the work they are doing are clear, even if the time frame is a long one. Some steps researchers can take include: connecting with people involved in efforts to change the situations under investigation; seeking out and sharing good news or hopeful stories related

[75] Charles C Benight and Albert Bandura, 'Social Cognitive Theory of Posttraumatic Recovery: The Role of Perceived Self-Efficacy' (2004) 42 Behaviour Research and Therapy 1129.

[76] Metin Başoğlu and others, 'Psychological Preparedness for Trauma as a Protective Factor in Survivors of Torture' (1997) 27 Psychological Medicine 1421.

[77] Metin Başoğlu and others, 'Psychiatric and Cognitive Effects of War in Former Yugoslavia: Association of Lack of Redress for Trauma and Posttraumatic Stress Reactions' (2005) 294 JAMA 580.

[78] M Başoğlu and others, 'A Brief Behavioural Treatment of Chronic Post-Traumatic Stress Disorder in Earthquake Survivors: Results from an Open Clinical Trial' (2003) 33 Psychological Medicine 647.

[79] Adam D Brown and others, 'The Impact of Perceived Self-Efficacy on Memory for Aversive Experiences' (2012) 20 Memory 374.

[80] Albert Bandura, 'Self-Efficacy' in VS Ramachaudran (ed), *Encyclopedia of human behavior, vol 4* (Academic Press 1995).

to the situation under examination; and including elements under the researcher's control within definitions of success, such as truthful witnessing or careful evidence-gathering, not just things more or less outside of their control, such as ending a civil war or putting an end to gender-based violence.

5. What Human Rights Organizations Can Do to Promote Well-being among Researchers

The ethos of a human rights organization itself is key to mitigating the effects of primary and secondary trauma for those who work within its purview. Mental health is not only an individual issue—it can be harmed or enabled by organizational dynamics. Human rights organizations and their senior management should actively incorporate an awareness of trauma, vicarious trauma, and resilience into their human resource and management policies and practices and promote a structure for fostering well-being among staff, including researchers who monitor potential human rights violations. In addition, organizations should ensure that they carefully assess the impact on staff well-being of the strategies they implement.

The Antares Foundation, an organization which aims to enhance resilience in humanitarian workers by improving management practices, has produced guidelines to help practitioners and organizations improve their policies. The guidelines explain that 'managing stress is an important management priority in enabling the organization to fulfil its field objectives'.[81] An organization is as responsible for the well-being of its staff as individual team members are responsible for themselves. Indeed, many components of well-being and resilience can only be properly promoted at the organizational level.

Despite such efforts, well-being is being neglected in many human rights organizations, according to the findings of studies conducted by this chapter's authors.[82] The adoption of open source investigation methods on a large scale has especially challenged organizations' abilities to respond to staff who are viewing great quantities of open source audiovisual content sourced from the internet. Indeed, Dubberley and colleagues found that human rights researchers working with open source audiovisual content were particularly critical of their organizations when it came to assistance in mitigating trauma. This was attributed in interviews to a general culture summed up as: if 'you cannot handle the job then get out'.[83] One human rights lawyer noted that: 'There is a real stigma in our profession—you just cannot discuss [vicarious trauma]. You need to prove you can do the work and I would never talk about this at work to a manager or a colleague.'[84] In Dubberley and colleagues' survey of human rights workers involved in the verification of open source video and photographs, as noted in this chapter's opening pages, only 38 per cent of respondents felt that their workplace culture was such that they would feel comfortable in asking for help in handling traumatic content.[85]

[81] Antares Foundation, 'Managing Stress in Humanitarian Workers: Guidelines for Good Practice (3rd Edition)' (Antares Foundation 2012) 7 https://www.antaresfoundation.org/filestore/si/1164337/1/1167964/managing_stress_in_humanitarian_aid_workers_guidelines_for_good_practice.pdf accessed 4 May 2018.

[82] Knuckey, Satterthwaite, and Brown (n 49); Dubberley, Griffin, and Bal (n 8).

[83] Dubberley, Griffin, and Bal (n 8) 42.

[84] ibid.

[85] ibid 39.

The Antares Foundation[86] outlines the following eight principles that it suggests should govern a humanitarian organization's policies around the mental health of its staff. They are a useful starting point for any manager or organization looking to set up workflows aimed at mitigating vicarious trauma and establishing resiliency norms.

- The agency has a written and active policy to prevent or mitigate the effects of stress.
- The agency systematically screens and/or assesses the capacity of staff to respond to and cope with the anticipated stresses of a position or contract.
- The agency ensures that all staff have appropriate pre-assignment preparation and training in managing stress.
- The agency ensures that staff response to stress is monitored on an ongoing basis.
- The agency provides training and support on an ongoing basis to help its staff deal with their daily stresses.
- The agency provides staff with specific and culturally appropriate support in the wake of critical or traumatic incidents and other unusual and unexpected sources of severe stress.
- The agency provides practical, emotional, and culturally appropriate support for staff at the end of an assignment or contract.
- The agency has clear written policies with respect to the ongoing support it will offer to staff who have been adversely impacted by exposure to stress and trauma during their assignment.

The UK Psychological Trauma Society suggests similar guidelines for organizations that deal with trauma. It adds: 'Trauma-exposed organizations should ensure that staff who are recruited, or move, into [potentially stressful] roles have the opportunity to reflect on their suitability and preparedness for this work before they start the role" and that 'trauma-exposed organisations should incorporate trauma awareness into management, leadership and team training.'[87]

In their tips for human rights managers and supervisors, Sarah Knuckey and Su Anne Lee[88] stress the importance of creating pertinent organizational policies through participatory processes involving all staff. They also suggest that organizations grow peer-to-peer support networks, build an organizational culture that celebrates wins and shares positive experiences, encourage supervisors to check in with staff about their well-being, put in place mentorship from experienced advocates, ensure that mental health is part of any regular risk assessment process, and create organizational processes for accountability, reflection, and revising well-being policies and practices.

Dubberley and Grant[89] additionally recommend that senior managers:

- Ensure that psycho-education is part of standard training practices.
- Develop a culture in which mental health is considered as important as physical health.

[86] Antares Foundation (n 81).

[87] 'Traumatic Stress Management Guidance' UK Psychological Trauma Society (2014) 5.

[88] Sarah Knuckey and Su Anne Lee, 'Building the Foundations of Resilience: 11 Lessons for Human Rights Educators and Supervisors' *OpenGlobalRights* (7 March 2018) https://www.openglobalrights.org/building-the-foundations-of-resilience-11-lessons-for-human-rights-educators-and-supervisors/ accessed 28 June 2018.

[89] Dubberley and Grant (n 52).

- Spread this culture to middle managers.
- Ensure that all new hires are aware of the possible traumatic impact of viewing distressing imagery by, for example, raising the issue in job interviews and induction processes.
- Talk one-to-one and in groups to staff about how they feel after covering particularly harrowing events.

A 2007 study of World Trade Center disaster rescue and recovery workers concluded that workers and volunteers in occupations least likely to have had prior disaster training or experience were at greatest risk of PTSD.[90] This finding underscores the importance of awareness, prevention, and organizational training for human rights investigators who are exposed to potentially traumatizing content online.

As non-governmental organizations (NGOs) build their mental health programming, they should ensure that it is meaningful for staff and not a mere box-ticking exercise. Ann-Sophie Morrissette notes in 'Five Myths that Perpetuate Burnout Across Nonprofits'[91] that lip service to trauma management exacerbates burn-out or stress. Instead of lip service and a focus on external factors, she argues, organizations and management must actively help their colleagues and team members deal with stressful work: 'There is a pervasive fear among the field that focusing inwardly—on our staff, on our leadership, even on our own salaries—will take away from achieving our missions. We must, as leaders, be willing to take risks and challenge these myths. In not doing so, we are risking so much more—a highly talented, passionate, and committed workforce that cycles through rather than rises up.'[92]

A number of the suggestions set out above include establishing peer support systems within human rights organizations. Peer support programmes create structured opportunities for people who are experiencing the same mental health challenges to provide support to each other. A burgeoning body of research suggest that peer support is associated with better functioning and reduced mental health symptoms.[93] Peer-to-peer approaches may facilitate coping and self-management, increase engagement in other forms of treatment, and improve overall well-being. Although there is limited data specifically on the benefits of peer support for treating PTSD, interviews with veterans suggest that peer-to-peer programmes are associated with reducing loneliness, increased motivation to continue treatment, and greater ability to implement skills learned in therapy[94]. Peer support has also been shown to improve recovery and reduce relapse following acute crisis care[95].

[90] Megan A Perrin and others, 'Differences in PTSD Prevalence and Associated Risk Factors among World Trade Center Disaster Rescue and Recovery Workers' (2007) 164 American Journal of Psychiatry 1385.

[91] Ann-Sophie Morissette, 'Five Myths that Perpetuate Burnout across Nonprofits' *Stanford Social Innovation Review* (31 October 2016) https://ssir.org/articles/entry/five_myths_that_perpetuate_burnout_across_nonprofits accessed 21 May 2018.

[92] ibid.

[93] Darren Malone and others, 'Community Mental Health Teams for People with Severe Mental Illnesses and Disordered Personality' (2009) 35 Schizophrenia Bulletin 13; Matthew Chinman and others, 'A Cluster Randomized Trial of Adding Peer Specialists to Intensive Case Management Teams in the Veterans Health Administration' (2015) 42 The Journal of Behavioral Health Services & Research 109; Larry Davidson and others, 'Peer Support among Persons with Severe Mental Illnesses: A Review of Evidence and Experience' (2012) 11 World Psychiatry 123.

[94] Natalie E Hundt and others, 'Veterans' Perspectives on Benefits and Drawbacks of Peer Support for Posttraumatic Stress Disorder' (2015) 180 Military Medicine 851.

[95] Alyssa Milton and others, 'Development of a Peer-Supported, Self-Management Intervention for People Following Mental Health Crisis' (2017) 10 BMC Research Notes 588.

To ensure the well-being of advocates, changes are needed at all levels in the human rights field, including among funders. Individuals and organizations are embedded in structures of funding and evaluation that often exacerbate the stresses inherent in the work. As Gulika Reddy explains:

> Donors need to acknowledge the impact of demanding measurable results in a field that does not lend itself to immediate outcomes, especially when the work involves building trust and shifting values—both inherently difficult to measure. At an organizational level, donors and managers need to examine and address the effects of time and resource-strapped organizations trying to meet the urgent needs of as many people as possible. Managers also need to explore if there is enough trust within their organizations to have difficult discussions about personal challenges. At an individual level, staff need to confront their own barriers to setting boundaries including guilt and fear of appearing weak or uncommitted. And all actors involved need to examine how these factors reinforce each other and inhibit systemic change.[96]

5.1 Technology and Building Trauma-conscious Workflows

In addition to investigators and organizations implementing trauma-aware practices, it is important that tech developers and engineers—who are building or maintaining tools which assist in discovery, verification, or archiving processes—consider how the technology can be developed in trauma-aware and trauma-mitigating ways.

Some features of technology may exacerbate exposure to trauma, for example. In 2015, Vester Lee Flanagan shot and killed two journalists during a live broadcast on an American local news station. Flanagan posted the video to his Twitter account. A few months earlier, Twitter had introduced a feature it called 'autoplay', which automatically played videos on users' feeds, regardless of what the videos contained. Twitter users were therefore exposed to the video of the killings of two people without selecting to view it.[97] Similarly, on Periscope (Twitter's live-broadcast platform) users were exposed to the grisly aftermath of a terrorist attack in Bangkok, Thailand[98] and, on Facebook, a dashboard camera video of Philando Castile being shot by a police officer in the United States was played repeatedly on users' timelines.[99]

These examples illustrate why software developers and engineers working with or for human rights organizations or on any applications that have open source investigation in

[96] Gulika Reddy, 'Self-Care for Sustainable Movements: Difficult but Necessary' *OpenGlobalRights* (31 May 2018) https://www.openglobalrights.org/self-care-for-sustainable-movements-difficult-but-necessary/ accessed 30 June 2018.

[97] Alexis Sobel Fitts, 'The Reason You Saw the Virginia Shooting Video, Even If You Didn't Want to' *Huffington Post* (26 August 2015) https://www.huffingtonpost.com/entry/twitter-autoplay-virginia-shooting-video_us_55ddf6efe4b0a40aa3ad1a38 accessed 19 May 2018.

[98] Pete Brown, '"OMG I Can't Ever Unsee That": What Happened When the Aftermath of the Bangkok Bomb Blast Was ...' *First Draft News* (25 August 2015) https://medium.com/1st-draft/omg-i-can-t-ever-unsee-that-what-happened-when-the-aftermath-of-the-bangkok-bomb-blast-was-7a3f39ee2b0 accessed 19 May 2018.

[99] Stephanie Hepburn, 'How Facebook Autoplay Is Triggering Vicarious Trauma' *Huffington Post* (20 February 2017) https://www.huffingtonpost.com/entry/how-facebook-autoplay-is-triggering-vicarious-trauma_us_58ab6633e4b0417c4066c1b0 accessed 19 May 2018.

mind should, in the development process, consider any workflows which could minimize exposure to traumatic material or give users of technology more control over when and how they view online material. Developers and engineers could build tools to ensure that the risk of any surprise viewing of content is kept to a minimum—in near and long-term futures. This includes thinking about how content is verified (is it possible, for instance, to build software capable of automatically identifying and blurring videos or photographs and/or labelling them as depicting the aftermath of missile strikes or violence against children before a researcher sees them for the first time?), or how new features are designed (could developers build in features that provide the option to default to playing video without sound?). It also means that developers should think about how content is archived for future use in accountability or advocacy efforts (how to label effectively video or photographs as distressing or graphic in the archiving process, for instance). Or, for example, could apps created for recording and storing photos and video, especially those designed for citizen activists and researchers, come with prompts or information for users about the importance of adopting forms of self-care? Could databases designed to store and allow the viewing of large amounts of video include user-controlled suggestions to take a break after a certain amount of use?

The development of technological tools is, for the most part, not conducted with trauma mitigation in mind. However, building tools which can support researchers to mitigate the risk of viewing distressing content, or, if distressing content must be viewed, to ensure it is done in a manner controlled by the researcher, is an important part of building a holistic response to mental health risks and to promoting sustainable human rights practices.

6. Conclusion

Digital human rights researchers may be exposed to significant distressing or violent material, and it is important for investigators and organizations to consider how this work may affect researchers' mental health and well-being and to take steps to mitigate harm and build resilience. This chapter focused on PTSD as one of the most common types of adverse outcomes of direct or vicarious exposure to traumatic events, but it also underlined the importance of considering other negative psychological outcomes such as stress or burn-out. We outlined various tactics that researchers can use to mitigate the impact of viewing traumatic imagery, and introduced techniques that could be employed both to build individual resiliency and to shift work practices to avoid seeing the most distressing content when it is not strictly necessary to do so. Human rights organizations are lagging behind in responding to the risk of traumatization and PTSD among their staff, and it is critical for organizational leaders to understand the risks and implement measures and programmes for their researchers. Technical tools to assist in open source research should also be developed with the risk of traumatization—today and in the future—in mind. To be effective through the long term and to promote sustainable human rights advocacy, the human rights field must consider and take care of the mental well-being of those who investigate and expose abuse.

13

Open Source Investigations

Understanding Digital Threats, Risks, and Harms

*Joseph Guay with Lisa Rudnick**

1. Introduction

1.1 Overview

As other chapters in this volume have explored, open source investigations (OSI) hold tremendous potential for both advancing justice and accountability, and responding to humanitarian protection needs. The proliferation of information communications technologies (ICTs), digital platforms, and data-driven deployments have enabled innovative, timely, and cost-efficient ways of capturing a rich array of open source information and exploiting it as a political resource for actionable intelligence purposes, and as evidence in the pursuit of justice in the face of human rights violations.[1]

However, because they often focus on sensitive matters, involve vulnerable people, and operate in a domain that is hyperconnected, rapidly evolving, and only (s)lightly regulated, OSI practices can also exacerbate the harm faced by already-vulnerable populations, and introduce new dimensions of risk for investigators and those they serve.

In this chapter, we consider how emerging threats and risks can lead to digitally-derived harms that OSI practitioners working in the digital space need to be aware of. We do this by highlighting two kinds of digital threats that OSI practitioners must take into account: those that are malicious in nature (e.g. surveillance, monitoring, and intrusion, or the weaponization of information) and those that are incidental (e.g. the unintended harms that result from the accidental disclosure of sensitive information or that are associated with data experimentation).

By outlining threats posed by the operational context of digital investigations work (regardless of physical proximity to mass atrocity contexts) on the one hand, and unintended harm made possible from OSI practices themselves (and therefore engendered in our own

* This chapter is adapted from research conducted by Joseph Guay and Lisa Rudnick for the Human Rights Center at UC Berkeley, and was developed with assistance from Dr Alexa Koenig. Financial support for this research was awarded to the Human Rights Center by the Center for Long Term Cybersecurity and Stanford's Digital Impact Fund. The research conducted by Guay and Rudnick included: a review of the existing open source investigations literature; semi-structured and in-depth interviews with well-known scholars and practitioners on open source investigations across the fields of journalism, human rights, law enforcement, humanitarian action, and digital security; and in situ observations of digital practices involved in open source investigations. A portion of that research is available in the public report.

[1] Joseph Guay and Lisa Rudnick, 'Cybersecurity and Open Source Investigations' Human Rights Center (2019).

efforts to do good) on the other, we hope to build more practitioner awareness about some of the perils that accompany the promise of OSI for serving justice and responding to needs. We assert, along with a growing number of concerned voices, that such awareness is fundamental to ensuring the responsible, ethical, and safe use of open source data and digital technologies for human rights and humanitarian protection purposes.

1.2 (Re)Introducing *Dual Use*

From an operational standpoint, new ICT tools—and the data they generate in crisis environments—are enabling human rights researchers and practitioners 'to track events in real time, gain access to remote or inaccessible locations, connect with sources of information, and collect evidence they would otherwise not be able to access'.[2]

These tools, methods, and resources, mobilized through open source investigation approaches, have fundamentally augmented the capacity of human rights and humanitarian protection actors to do their work in service of crisis-affected populations and victims of human rights abuse. Moreover, alongside these new forms of action and data-driven interventions, an evolving landscape of relevant actors, roles, and relationships have emerged. This new terrain has opened up access to restricted environments to advocates, defenders, and humanitarian responders; diversified the sector and its practices; and empowered citizens and vulnerable populations to take action against injustice and protect themselves from harm.

However, the so-called 'digital revolution' through which this state-of-affairs unfolds also poses enormous challenges for crisis affected people and those who serve them. In particular, the exponential acceleration of openly-available digital crisis data has shifted the operational risk landscape in which OSI is conducted in ways that have not been anticipated by civil society actors and their technology partners who make use of—or are involved in—such practices. As OSI actors continue to experiment with new ways of generating, transmitting, storing, and disseminating highly granular, near real-time open source information in support of human rights advocacy work, operational protection efforts, and in criminal investigations, *they may in some cases—without the requisite skills, resources, and tools—do more harm than good.*

To illustrate this point directs our attention to two inter-related, yet distinct phenomena that characterize the context of contemporary open source investigations work in the digital age:

> *First, malicious threat actors* (such as repressive governments, criminal networks, armed groups, terrorist organizations, and hybrid non-state actor groups) *are exploiting our own information systems, communications networks, and digital platforms to gain actionable intelligence, and to cause harm.* Threat actors, for example, are leveraging novel surveillance and intrusion capabilities to acquire sensitive information created

[2] Robin Pierro, 'A Double-Edged Sword: Benefits and Recommendations for Using Information and Communication Technology to Monitor or Investigate Human Rights' Awarded Theses, European Inter-University Centre for Human Rights and Democratisation (2016) 7.

and gathered by open source investigators and their counterparts. They are also making innovative use of social media networks and online platforms to weaponize information against vulnerable populations and those who serve them, including OSI practitioners.

Secondly, unintended harms are resulting from the use of openly-available digital crisis data by OSI actors themselves, as victims of human rights abuse and violent conflict contend with the side-effects of digital data experimentation, violations of privacy and consent, and the mishandling of sensitive information that goes along with our own efforts to leverage the transformative potential of OSI efforts mobilized through remote-based, digital volunteer networks.

In short, increasingly sophisticated surveillance capabilities, new tools and forms of digital violence and exploitation, and the unintended negative externalities associated with our own efforts to do good creates a complex topology of risk, according to Stephanie Hankey and Daniel O'Clunaigh, that human rights defenders find 'increasingly difficult to navigate in an "artful" manner'.[3]

In this chapter, we unpack this landscape of digitally-derived threats, risks, and harms, in an effort to take stock of a rapidly shifting—and consequential—terrain, and its implications for open source investigators and the populations they serve.

We therefore situate the 'dual use' nature of information communication technologies—and the digital data generated and transmitted by them—back to the centre of discussion and debate among humanitarian and human rights technologists: While digital technologies and open-source data can be used for good, they can just as easily be *exploited to cause harm*; while such tools allow human rights defenders to target and profile alleged perpetrators of war crimes with increasing granularity, the reverse is also true.

This kind of orientation provides an important counterweight to the innovation-centric, techno-utopian worldview proliferating throughout much of today's human rights and technology community, particularly among digital volunteer communities of practice characterized by student-led investigations labs and related efforts. We believe that a more responsible, careful, and critical orientation can help support aspiring practitioners to maximize the transformative potential of OSI efforts while mitigating against the risk engendered by these practices, especially as the sector wrestles with the development of as of yet undefined minimum technical standards, operational protocols, and safeguards associated with this emerging, interdisciplinary—and exciting!—field of work.

We begin our discussion with matters of surveillance, monitoring, and intrusion, as well as the weaponization of information, and what these challenges mean for human rights defenders making use of OSI approaches. We then introduce a number of concerns around unintended digital harm and other negative externalities associated with the development and deployment of remote-based digital technologies and OSI workflows in use by social entrepreneurs, activists, student investigators, and the private sector for human rights advocacy and accountability purposes.

[3] Stephanie Hankey and Daniel O'Clunaigh, 'Rethinking Risk and Security of Human Rights Defenders in the Digital Age' (2013) 5 Journal of Human Rights Practice 31.

Our chapter ends with a brief discussion around emerging efforts to institute digital security, risk management, and data ethics back into the centre of this field, with considerations for digital volunteers and student investigators to think about as they explore this field.

2. Surveillance, Monitoring, and Intrusion

2.1 Digital Volunteer Networks as *Intelligence Assets*

Digital investigators analyze social media content to develop highly granular hierarchies of State military and armed actor groups in conflict zones. They geolocate citizen-generated media to forensically reconstruct alleged war crimes, such as unlawful executions of noncombatants. They use publicly available satellite imagery to identify military fortifications in remote environments, or mass civilian displacement patterns, which can be used to project front line defence outposts of armed groups or to identify vulnerable groups in transit. They use crowdsourcing APIs to aggregate reports of sexual and gender-based violence in conflict zones.

Consider for a moment, the information that a single university-based open source investigations team regularly generates, collects, stores, and transmits, throughout an investigation. This may include:

- Personally-identifiable information (PII) of victims (name, age, address, nature of harm/injury), family members, sources, eyewitnesses, informants, and other interested parties, including alleged perpetrators and their contacts and associates;
- Location-based data, such as the geo-coordinates of key incidents or the approximate placement of alleged crime scenes;
- Temporal data, such as a reconstructed timeline of key events, or patterns of behaviour between targets of an investigation, or between vulnerable demographic groups and armed actors;
- Primary data, in raw form, such as audio/video recordings, narrative transcriptions, photographic evidence, and the metadata (i.e. time stamps, information about recording device used to capture and store, etc) associated with such files;
- Internal information regarding how OSI projects are managed, for example, detailing how investigations activities are assigned and tasked, the confidential processes used for verification and triangulation, how analytical products are expected to be used for advocacy and accountability purposes, and information about how investigations teams are composed and function (meeting notes, etc).

This kind of information is highly valuable to repressive governments, criminal networks, armed actor groups, and terrorist organizations who are the targets of such work.

Simply by virtue of the information they gather, therefore, open source investigators—and the technologies and information systems they use to store and transmit sensitive data—have become valuable intelligence assets for a range of adversaries operating in cyberspace. Targets of human rights investigations work may already be going to great lengths to acquire this kind of intelligence from academic investigations labs, independent activist teams, and civil society consortia who make use of open source investigations approaches—to gain information about those organizations, the people those organizations are trying to help, and anything else that might be leveraged or exploited for nefarious purposes.

2.2 Means and Methods

Malicious actors would be likely to make use of both intrusion and non-intrusion based methods to monitor and keep civil society organizations under surveillance. Below, we briefly consider how these tactics might be deployed against remote-based, digital volunteer networks making use of OSI practices and workflows.

2.2.1 Intrusion-based Surveillance

John Scott-Railton and Bill Marczak from Citizen Lab have documented dozens of successful intrusion attacks against aid agencies, media outlets, human rights activists, and other groups acting to protect vulnerable populations in fragile contexts.[4] Their work shows how civil society organizations are targeted by carefully planned, politically-motivated spear phishing campaigns that make use of social engineering, lawfully-purchased spyware, and remote-access intrusion software to intercept communications, infiltrate systems, and exploit sensitive data.

Here's how it works: Attackers send malware-infected attachments to targets through e-mails or Skype communications channels that are carefully designed to appear to be from trusted colleagues, or members of a particular community or network. The moment the target opens the infected attachments, a remote-access trojan (RAT) payload is delivered, capable of recording all user activity on infected computers and sending the illicitly garnered information back to external servers controlled by the attackers. Unknown to the target, the spyware is in control of webcams and microphones (to record video and audio), keystroke loggers (to uncover passwords), file processing protocols (to view and extract documents and files containing sensitive data), and can track users' location, internet browsing history, and communications logs.

In situations of armed conflict, the exfiltration of this kind of information can be a matter of life and death.

Consider the following example. In 2015, FireEye came out with a Special Report entitled 'Behind the Conflict: Syria's Digital Front Lines'.[5] The report highlighted how armed opposition groups inside Syria were subject to a remote intrusion operation in which hackers gained access to 'a cache of critical documents and Skype conversations revealing the Syrian opposition's strategy, tactical battle plans, supply needs, and troves of personal information and chat sessions belonging to the men fighting against Syrian President Bashar al-Assad's forces'.[6]

[4] Citizen Lab, *Communities @ Risk: Targeted Digital Threats Against Civil Society* (Munk School of Global Affairs 2014); J Scott-Railton, 'Security for the High Risk User: Separate and Unequal' (2016) 14(2) *IEEE Security & Privacy* 79; Bill Marczak and others, 'Champing at the Cyberbit: Ethiopian Dissidents Targeted with New Commercial Spyware' *Citizen Lab* (5 December 2017).

[5] Daniel Regalado, Nart Villeneuve, and John Scott-Railton, 'Behind the Syrian Conflict's Digital Front Lines' *FireEye* (February 2015).

[6] ibid 4.

The operational intelligence gathered by attackers is telling. Compromised Skype accounts' stored chat history going back to 2012 included 'sensitive communications about strategy, logistical issues, supply routes … [and other] high-value artifacts that may have provided actionable military intelligence to the recipients'.[7] Moreover, the Skype logs revealed an incredible amount of information about interpersonal relationships (identities, shared contacts, relationships, personal information) between victims of this intrusion. Stolen files and documents revealed a range of military information, such as lists that identified hundreds of fighters (and other personally identifiable information such as names, blood types, phone numbers) and information about weapons and serial numbers that these fighters carried.

These files also contained 'correspondence, rosters, annotated satellite images, battle maps, orders of battle, geographic coordinates for attacks, and lists of weapons from a range of fighting groups'; as well as information regarding humanitarian activities in Syria such as material distributions, and personal information pertaining to refugees such as 'filled-out applications for assistance and education, and even the scanned ID cards of refugees and their CVs'.[8]

While this is not a case where a civil society group was directly targeted, the report illustrates the kinds of exposure CSOs are facing, given the interconnectedness of information systems and the kinds of sensitive information threat actors are able to gather through these digital attacks.

2.2.2 Non Intrusion-based Surveillance

Adversaries (be they governments, armed actor groups, or even private sector entities) are also adept at making use of publicly available information found on the web, or gleaned through third party platforms, to do their own tracking, profiling, and monitoring of activists, humanitarians, and human rights actors they perceive as hostile to them. No intrusion, spyware, or malicious code required.

The proliferation of internet-connected devices and the sharing of user-generated content through social media poses problems for human rights investigators and those they work with and serve when such technologies and platforms are used without due consideration to risks to privacy and anonymity. The use of these technologies and platforms by human rights researchers and activists can inadvertently expose sensitive personal information and/or create trackable and traceable digital data exhaust in the form of unique user signatures and inferential metadata that can be pieced together to create profiles on behaviour, transactions and interactions, movements, personal details and preferences, and personal relationships and networks of those that are the focus of such investigations.

For example, many students share personal information on Twitter, Instagram, LinkedIn, or Facebook that might expose them—or individuals within their networks—to profiling, tracking, and targeting through social media intelligence (SOCMINT) efforts. Without vigilance in ensuring anonymity and privacy online, investigators might inadvertently share audio/visual content or text-based information that could be weaponized against them or their loved ones, colleagues, and partners. A threat actor could access information posted

[7] ibid 7.
[8] ibid 8.

on social media as a non-user (without logging into the platform), authenticated user, by using fake profiles, and/or by requesting data from the social network itself.

These dynamics are relevant whether or not open source investigators have a physical presence in the environments they are investigating, although more often than not, local partners (CSOs, activist networks, local non-governmental organizations (NGOs)) are, in fact, directly implicated through their physical presence in such contexts. These individuals and groups especially vulnerable to this kind of tracking, monitoring, and surveillance that might be weaponized by threat actors and interested parties.

Take, for example, the case of detailed by Tactical Tech's Becky Kazansky,[9] which describes a concerted surveillance and weaponization campaign waged against LGBTQI rights activists in the global south, and carried out largely through social media platforms to both conduct surveillance as well as execute targeted attacks:

> Campaigns and threats of violence [against the LGBTQI activists] appeared to emerge from an organized collusion between nationalist groups and governmental actors, part of a larger effort to marginalize women's and LGBTQI rights ... The network of women's and LGBTQI rights activists heard from several sources that [a] neighboring country had sent *officials to train local media in how to wage these campaigns*, as part of a broader effort to exert their cultural influence. The network felt these campaigns were successful in changing public perceptions in a way that has impacted their ability to safely continue to push for women's rights.
>
> Amidst these developments, the network gained information that the neighboring country was also *tapping into phone lines and Internet Service Providers and tracking social interconnections visible through online social networking platforms*. Concern and anxiety over surveillance and intrusion were inflamed by stories of hacked websites and email accounts, strange sounds heard when using Skype, and the presence of clicking noises when using the landline telephone ...
>
> Before the violence and threats of violence began, the network felt a strong public presence, and thus a *visible online presence, was vital to the success of their activism*. The activists used their 'real', legal names in Facebook profiles, not just because Facebook's TOS states that users must do so, but because their profiles served as a public point of contact for those interested in joining their advocacy work. However, since the women's and LGTBQI rights network could now anticipate that a public presence and publicly organized actions might lead to more violence and harassment, they felt a need to use pseudonyms, and to generally be able to shape their identities as they saw fit. *Facebook's rigid 'real name' policy became a clear point of vulnerability*. They were thus forced to violate the policy in order to protect themselves.
>
> *Facebook's changing photo privacy settings also exposed the activist network to harm*. Despite vigilance over privacy settings, *personal photographs would find their way into new misinformation campaign videos*. Upon having time to sit down and pinpoint the source of the leak, the activists found that *the settings controlling the visibility of photographs had again been changed by Facebook. The harassers exploited this change to obtain new materials*

[9] Becky Kazansky, 'Privacy, Responsibility, and Human Rights Activism' (2016) 26 The Fibreculture Journal 189 http://twentysix.fibreculturejournal.org/fcj-195-privacy-responsibility-and-human-rights-activism/ accessed 3 January 2019.

> *for their campaigns.* After this incident, many activists simply deleted sensitive photos rather than risking further exposure. The activists learned to review their Facebook privacy and account settings on a regular basis due to this incident, but were still shocked to discover over the course of a workshop provided by Tactical Tech that once again, photographs previously visible only to friends had unexpectedly become 'public' without any actions taken on their part. Instead, this change could be attributed to Facebook itself.[10]

Our own work in the context of the Syrian conflict, east Africa, and in Myanmar suggests that alleged perpetrators of war crimes and human rights abuse are covertly infiltrating social media networks and platforms, posing as activists and community members, in order to gain valuable information such as the identities of activists and informants, and relational information about who is in their network, as well as being able to intercept communications (posts) that are assumed to be private. We have learned, for example, in Myanmar, Facebook is the preferred platform for organizing and sharing information publicly among and between socially-oriented groups (such as religious organizations, political movements, activists, etc) and even among the military, armed actor groups, police departments, and local authorities, and formal members of the humanitarian protection cluster.

Student investigators (as well as their team mates, partner organizations, and relevant contacts) may also leave behind digital data exhaust (i.e. signatures, traces, or metadata), simply through the use of information communications platforms and internet-enabled devices, *regardless of whether or not personal information is knowingly created and shared.* This can allow threat actors (or simply interested parties) to track and profile investigators, activists, and researchers over long periods of time.[11]

The Privacy Interaction report is sobering:

> More of our actions and interactions now generate data and metadata. *The act of communicating is no longer a prerequisite.* When we visit a website, a log is generated. If we read an article on that website, a further log is generated. When we see a 'like' button on a webpage, we know that metadata are being shared with a social media company. Our movements can be communicated by our mobile devices; our financial interactions, by the device we used, the bank accounts involved, or other intermediaries (e.g. the mobile application used). Even our phone's battery level can be traced and used to infer conduct and behavior.
>
> This phenomenon is linked to the rise in mobile applications that help people to engage with their world—book a hotel, pay for a service, travel, or track their athletic performance. These applications gather and monetize new kinds of data, many with little or no regard for people's privacy. Finally, *metadata surveillance no longer concerns itself with the individual.* Today's processing and storage capabilities mean that entire groups, populations, or

[10] Ibid.

[11] Metadata is information about a file (time and date it was created, information about the person, and device that created it) that is stored within the file itself, hidden from view. A recent joint publication between Privacy International the ICRC defines three types of metadata that warrant further discussion here: (1) *declared data* (information that is declared through a transaction or communication, such as sender and recipient); (2) *inferred data* (information that can be *deduced* about the nature of the information by combining declared data with other observations); and (3) *intent data* (information that can be discerned over time by looking at trends and patterns, such as transactional history, to deduce relationships). International Committee of the Red Cross (ICRC) and Privacy International, 'The Humanitarian Metadata Problem: "Doing No Harm" in the Digital Era' (October 2018) 34.

> regions can be placed under surveillance. Their movements, types and rates of interaction, use of services, and any other indicators of behavioral change can be invaluable sources of information for companies and intelligence agencies. To understand this, one must first look at how metadata are generated and processed and what information can be drawn or inferred from them.

Even internet-savvy activists have to navigate an ever-changing technical and regulatory environment. For example, according to Privacy International, new techniques are being developed and widely used that can counter anonymizing tools, such as device fingerprinting, which can cross-reference device properties (such as browser type and version) to match unique user signatures, even when conventional ad-blocking software is turned on. 'By cross-referencing data about specific users and/or devices across different services', the report notes that 'advertising networks are [still] able to infer a massive amount of personal information'.[12]

2.3 Implications

The implications of a successful spear-phishing attack against investigators, or the exploitation of digital traces to monitor and keep digital activist networks under surveillance can be paralysing to think about.

Consider an intrusion attack that successfully compromised an investigator's personal laptop and/or mobile device, when the appropriate security protocols are not in place. Many such teams work with information on the names and profiles of key targets of criminal investigations; eye-witness testimonies; contact information for key sources and informants; and information regarding humanitarian operations, military hierarchies, displacement patterns, and more. Attackers, armed with this kind of information, would be able to identify and target activists and sources involved OSI efforts, compromise the integrity of an investigation (i.e. by altering perpetrators, damaging, or destroying data, or intimidating witnesses) and/or covertly gain intelligence, over time, that allows perpetrators to anticipate and counter the actions human rights community.

Consider efforts to monitor and keep digital investigators under surveillance leveraging publicly-available means and non-intrusion-based methods. When student teams and digital volunteers engage in OSI work, and when they use their personal devices and accounts to do so, they may be inadvertently compromising sensitive information—either direct PII, or behavioural information that can be inferred—regarding an ongoing investigation. Uninformed OSI practitioners, for example, may be leaving digital traces, or signatures (data exhaust) behind when they conduct their work on line, and such information can be pieced together by threat actors. Such behaviour puts investigators, their local partners, and informants and victims at risk.

[12] PI 64–65. According to Privacy International, inferred data can be more reliable, accurate, and granular than declared data. 'The inferred data can be any given person's gender, sexuality, religion, location data, interpersonal relationships, and anticipated behavior (especially if several datasets are correlated, and predictive analytics used). Note that inferred data can be obtained, and deemed more reliable than declared data, even when a user has listed "false" data on their profile' (PI 90–91).

3. Weaponization of Information

3.1 Digital Volunteer Networks as *Political Targets*

Digital volunteer networks leverage open source information to promote and enforce human rights by publicizing information about abuses in real time in order to put pressure on duty-bearers to change their behaviour and to draw attention to violations for further investigation. Repressive governments, armed actor groups, violent extremists, and criminal networks, understandably, do not appreciate this. They may go to great lengths to exploit digital technologies, information systems, and online platforms to intimidate activists, erode trust in social institutions, and otherwise disrupt the activities of groups they perceive to be hostile to them, regardless of geographical proximity.

When digital volunteer networks engage in open source investigations, in other words, they must accept that they are now political actors and will be likely to be targeted as such.

3.2 Means and Methods

In addition to the monitoring, surveillance, and tracking for intelligence gathering purposes noted above, adversaries of human rights groups are making innovative use of big data-driven and digitally enabled tools and methods to spread disinformation through targeted defamation campaigns and tainted leaks, and to inflict physical, psychological, and social harm through the systematic deployment of cyber-hate speech, incendiary rhetoric, and online harassment.

In both cases, this results in the erosion of trust in public institutions through the manipulation of facts, and the degradation of OSI capabilities through loss of morale and/or social capital.

3.2.1 Disinformation Campaigns

As discussed in previous work,[13] ICTs can be leveraged to help promote and enforce human rights in fragile or politically repressive contexts by providing the press, public, and international community with information of abuses in real time. OSI approaches have augmented the role that images and eyewitness footage in particular play in raising public awareness around human rights violations, helping to put pressure on duty-bearers to change their behaviour, and provide the impetus for further investigation by drawing attention to violations of human rights.[14] In this context such information provides important evidentiary resources for human rights fact finders to 'independently, objectively and impartially collect relevant information, confirm its veracity, and analyze this information to

[13] Guay and Rudnick (n 1).

[14] Erica Frances Williams, 'Using Citizen Media and Open Source Investigations to Promote Human Rights: UC Berkeley's Human Rights Investigations Lab' Capstone Research Report, University San Francisco (Summer 2017). See also Ella McPherson, 'ICTs and Human Rights Practice: A Report Prepared for the UN Special Rapporteur on Extrajudicial, Summary, or Arbitrary Executions' Centre of Governance and Human Rights (2015) 2–4; and Molly Land, Patrick Meier, Mark Belinsky, and Emily Jacobi, '#ICT4HR: Information and Communication Technologies for Human Rights' World Bank Institute and others (November 2012) 13, who refer to this as 'naming and shaming' or 'the process of gathering information about a duty bearer's human rights record and publicizing that information in an effort to pressure or shame the duty-bearer into changing its conduct'.

produce credible evidence about violations, their causes and effects, and to identify their perpetrators'.[15]

Unfortunately, targeted disinformation campaigns are emerging as an effective attack against these efforts. These campaigns are waged to distort facts on the ground, coverup or obfuscate the actions of perpetrators, and cast doubt on investigations' findings in crisis environments where timely, credible, and accurate information is most needed. Digital volunteer networks, student investigators, and independent activists may indeed be caught in the middle of this hybrid form of information warfare.

For example, research from Graphika, the University of Washington and the Signal Program at HHI, and Oxford's Computational Propaganda programme, have detailed how Russia's Internet Research Agency (IRA) has made systematic use of troll farms, botnets, and fake accounts to amplify manufactured claims and false accusations against the White Helmets in the context of armed conflict in Syria. These coordinated and deliberate online defamation campaigns attempt to delegitimize the White Helmets status as a neutral and impartial humanitarian actor (in an attempt to make them a legitimate targets for kinetic attacks), and censor the voices of affected communities reporting attacks by the Syrian government on civilian populations.

As a consequence, the operational capabilities of the White Helmets and their human rights and humanitarian partners are eroded, as they navigate a sustained defamation campaign that erodes morale, diverts attention away from life-saving activities, and intimidates affiliates of the organization. OSI initiatives that partner with local organizations that are caught up in such attacks may risk becoming targeted, regardless of whether or not they are based in open source investigation units thousands of miles away.

For example, Citizen Lab has uncovered the practice of 'tainted leaks' the Russian government has used against journalists and human rights activists abroad. Their report shows how 'documents stolen from a prominent journalist and critic of Russia were tampered with and then leaked to achieve specific propaganda aims'.[16] This tactic illustrates an integration of traditional phishing attacks with engineered disinformation campaigns 'used in combination to infiltrate civil society targets, and to seed mistrust and disinformation'.[17]

3.2.2 Online Harassment, Social Cyber-attacks, and Incendiary Rhetoric

Threat actors have also shown to be particularly adept at weaponizing incendiary information (such as rumours, cyber-hate speech, and dangerous rhetoric) to undermine community acceptance, erode social cohesion, or to incite panic and/or violence (interview with digital security experts).

Many of these operations are meant to manipulate social interactions on the ground in conflict environments. In what have been termed 'social cyber-attacks', EISF notes,

> people use social media or other communication systems to spread malicious rumors or incite panic. In Assam, India, in 2011, false social media messages, including doctored

[15] Christoph Koettl, 'Citizen Media Research and Verification: An Analytical Framework for Human Rights Practitioners' CGHR Practitioner Paper No 1 (2016) (quoting Navi Pillay). See also Williams (n 14) 3.

[16] Adam Hulcoop and others, 'Tainted Leaks: Disinformation and Phishing with a Russian Nexus' *Citizen Lab* (25 May 2017).

[17] ibid.

photos of violence from other situations, were used to convince people that riots and violence were happening in their neighborhoods, leading to mass exodus' (EISF at 9)[18].

As a prominent example, misinformationmisinformation, including both organic rumorsrumours (i.e. arising from people speculating based on limited information without malicious intent) and deliberate disinformation, has played a significant role in fomenting intercommunal violence in Myanmar's Rakhine State, especially helping to drive anti-Muslim sentiment through social media. The large-scale violence against the Rohingya minority (a Muslim ethnic group) and subsequent refugee crisis in recent years has highlighted the role that rumorsrumours and disinformation can play in exacerbating conflict and hindering diplomatic and humanitarian responses.[19]

But organized violence, exploitation, and attack is not limited to conflict zones. Open source investigative organizations like Bellingcat and Digital Forensic Research Lab (DFRL) have been subject to repeat online harassment campaigns carried out by pro-Russian botnets in an attempt to discredit or intimidate their researchers and investigators. These adversary groups have exposed the personal information of investigators such as home addresses and names of family members (a technique known as 'doxxing'), and have mobilized online networks to verbally abuse targets on their personal social media accounts ('trolling') (interview on file with the authors).

3.3 Implications

The risks of these attacks against open source investigators or their local partners are both serious and increasingly likely. University-based OSI teams have already published reports on the plight of the Rohingya in Rakhine State, or the chemical attacks in Syria, which implicate both the Burmese government as well as the Syrian government and its allies (both governments known to be making use of information warfare). It is not far-fetched to imagine that as such reports gain media attention (for example through local or national news media that profiles the work of such teams) individual investigators might be targeted in online defamation campaigns, or implicated by coordinated disinformation operations.

Governments that are the subject of open source investigations might publish slanderous information about an investigations team. Doctored reports might be leaked to social media via fake accounts with findings deliberately altered or inconsistent with previous analysis or messaging. The personal information of investigators and their partners might be disclosed on various online forums, and they might begin to receive threatening messages via Facebook and Twitter.

This situation is concerning for investigators making use of remote-based digital volunteer networks, as it raises questions around practitioners' ability to navigate an increasingly hostile digital terrain, whereby repressive regimes and other threat actors are weaponizing

[18] See Daniel Gilman, Cyber-Warfare and Humanitarian Space," in Vazquez Llorente R. and Wall, I. (eds.) (2014) *Communications technology and humanitarian delivery: challenges and opportunities for security risk management*. European Interagency Security Forum (EISF)., page 8-9 https://www.eisf.eu/library/communications-technology-and-security-risk-management/

[19] E-mail correspondence with Christopher Tuckwood, The Sentinel Project (On file with the author, November 2018).

incendiary information. By generating impressions of politically-aligned motives and aspirations, threat actors can jeopardize the safety and security of human rights activists and their partners. Doxxing and trolling can intimidate researchers and investigators, erode moral, and damage the reputation of organizations that host such initiatives.

This invites discussion on the responsibility of organizations to ensure the safety, security, and well-being of investigators in this context, and consideration of the extent to which such situations can both erode credibility and confidence in OSI work more broadly in the human rights field, and expose organizations to legal action by victimized parties.

4. Unintended Harm

4.1 Digital Volunteer Networks as *Threat Vectors*

Finally, the human rights and humanitarian sectors must also contend with the actual, unintended harms that might result from the generation, use, and dissemination of their data by remote-based, volunteer networks carrying out open source investigations work.

Researchers have raised concerns about the disclosure of personal data, security challenges for those collecting and handling data in volatile contexts, difficulties around ensuring participant anonymity, over-reliance on third party platforms, information overload, and revictimization, among others.[20] Such concerns are, of course, amplified in complex human rights and humanitarian emergency situations, where, in the words of Rahel Dette, 'the consequences of implementing technology-based projects poorly or overseeing unintended consequences can be detrimental and sometimes lethal'.[21]

And yet, civil society is only just now beginning to grapple with the negative externalities that result from the unintended consequences of digital data activities deployed in already fragile operational environments.

Raymond and Sandvik believe this to be the result of a deeply flawed logic embedded in common understandings of the relationship between information communication technologies and protection outcomes for affected populations—that is, that more information about mass atrocity situations leads intrinsically to better outcomes for affected people. They make the case that not only is there 'no extant base of scientific evidence that in any way suggests, let alone proves, the existence of what in our conceptualization can be referred to as a causal protective or preventative effect (PPE) from the use of information and communication technologies in mass atrocity producing environments',[22] but that, in reality, the opposite may be the case: digital technologies may be, in many cases, a causal vector for harm.[23]

[20] Nathaniel Raymond and others, 'Building Data Responsibility into Humanitarian Action' OCHA Policy and Studies Series (1 May 2016); Land and others (n 14); 'Cameras Everywhere: Current Challenges and Opportunities at the Intersection of Human Rights, Video, and Technology' *WITNESS* (2011) 10; McPherson, 'ICTs and Human Rights Practice' (n 14) 2.

[21] Rahel Dette, 'Do No Digital Harm: Mitigating Technology Risks in Humanitarian Contexts' in Silvia Hostettler, Samira Najih Besson, and Jean-Claude Bolay (eds), *Technologies for Development* (Springer 2016) 4–6.

[22] Kristin Bergtora Sandvik and Nathaniel A Raymond, 'Beyond the Protective Effect: Towards a Theory of Harm for Information Communication' (2017) 11 Genocide Studies and Prevention: An International Journal 9.

[23] ibid 9.

We find Sandvik and Raymond's 'Myth of the Ambient Protective Effect (APE)' to be a useful starting point for reflecting on the unintended digital dangers that open source investigations may present to affected populations.

4.2 Means and Methods

In our interviews and literature review, we identified three especially urgent and consequential ways in which open source investigations may lead to unintentional harm. They include: (1) the inadvertent disclosure of sensitive information through negligent data management practices; (2) violations of privacy expectations; and (3) harmful effects of data experimentation.

4.2.1 Inadvertent Disclosure

Near-real time, publicly available crisis data can be used by a digital attacker to target affected populations, compromise the integrity of human rights investigations, and gain actionable intelligence about humanitarian logistics.[24] Repressive governments and armed actors have already learned to make use of the wealth of readily available open-source crisis data provided by humanitarian NGOs, human rights groups, and traditional news media. For example, publishing real-time data on the conditions, routes, and profiles of asylum seekers in the Horn of Africa region can inadvertently provide smugglers and human traffickers valuable information they can use for exploitative practices (research in Kenya, on file with the author).

Indeed, the Sudanese, Syrian, Pakistani, Egyptian, and Burmese governments have all leveraged such information to target vulnerable communities, activists, journalists, humanitarian organizations and other civil society groups.[25] New research even sheds light on how Amnesty International's Eyes on Darfur project may have led to increased violence against civilian populations as retribution against Amnesty's advocacy efforts.[26] Recent research also raises concerns around the dissemination of user-generated audiovisual information that might expose the identities of witnesses[27] or the coordinates of an area of interest. Such phenomena could lead to re-victimization and targeting of populations of concern.[28]

Such scenarios are made possible by the failure of digital volunteer networks—and their humanitarian, human rights, and private sector counterparts—to adequately calibrate the sensitive nature of the information they release to the public or share with third parties.[29] Human rights and humanitarian practitioners must therefore make thoughtful judgment calls about the specificity of information they share with the public in the course of their advocacy and accountability work.

However, protecting the privacy of people and places is getting harder and harder to accomplish due largely to something called the 'mosaic effect'. The mosaic effect can be loosely defined as the ability to generate highly granular information—even personally identifiable

[24] Dette (n 21) 6; McPherson, 'ICTs and Human Rights Practice' (n 14) 3; Koettl (n 15) 49.
[25] Raymond and others (n 20) 2.
[26] Sandvik and Raymond (n 22) 14–15.
[27] McPherson, 'ICTs and Human Rights Practice' (n 14) 3; Koettl (n 15) 49.
[28] Pierro (n 2) 51.
[29] Sandvik and Raymond (n 22) 18.

information[30]—from the aggregation and layering of multiple data sets and seemingly disparate or isolated units of information.[31] The implications of the mosaic effect are alarming for human rights, humanitarian protection, and human security in the digital age as it makes traditional conversations about PII both technically and theoretically redundant, raising questions about the adequacy of anonymization practices (the removal, or scrubbing, of specific identifiers) to prevent re-identification.[32]

Ultimately, it may be demographically identifiable information, and not personally identifiable information, that poses the biggest human security threat for vulnerable populations caught up in open source investigations work. Demographically identifiable information is defined by Raymond as 'either individual and/or aggregated data points that allow inferences to be drawn that enable the classification, identification and/or tracking of both named and/or unnamed individuals, groups of individuals, and/or multiple groups of individuals according to ethnicity, economic class, religion, gender, age, health conditions, location, occupation and/or other demographically defining factors'.[33]

Demographically identifiable information 'can result from the transformation of seemingly disparate, unrelated data sets into an amalgamated data product that can be easily weaponized into a means for doing harm'.[34] Approximated, category-based information is thus under some circumstances enough to engender harm. As George Chamales and Rob Baker note, 'hostile organizations such as oppressive governments do not necessarily need a reason to target a specific individual or group'.[35] Rather than simply relying on individually identifiable information alone, potential perpetrators of abuses can now make use of anonymized, community- and category-based information generated and shared through publicly available open source investigations work.[36]

These possibilities all raise questions about the conceptualization of 'sensitive data' for matters of human rights and humanitarian protection work in the digital age. First, unlike personally identifiable information, demographically identifiable information's ethical implications are not categorically determined. 'Demographically identifiable information's harm, and thus its ethical implications', write Sandvik and Raymond, 'emanates from simply whether the possibility exists that it can be even created'.[37]

Second, data sensitivity is not confined to understandings around what is public versus what is private. An expert on digital security and open source intelligence put it this way:

[30] Personally identifiable information is defined as 'any representation of information that permits the identity of an individual to whom the information applies to be reasonably inferred by either direct or indirect means'.

[31] Daniel Gilman, 'Cyber-Warfare and Humanitarian Space' in R Vazquez Llorente and I Wall (eds) 'Communications Technology and Humanitarian Delivery: Challenges and Opportunities for Security Risk Management (European Interagency Security Forum (EISF) 2014) 15; Sandvik and Raymond (n 22) 19; Nathaniel Raymond, 'Beyond Do No Harm and Individual Consent: Reckoning with the Emerging Ethical Challenges of Civil Society's Use of Data' in Linnet Taylor and others (eds), *Group Privacy: New Challenges of Data Technologies* (Springer International Publishing 2017) 75.

[32] Gilman (n 31) 15.

[33] Raymond (n 31) 76.

[34] Sandvik and Raymond (n 22) 19.

[35] George Chalames and Rob Baker, 'Securing Crisis Maps in Conflict Zones' IEEE Global Humanitarian Technology Conference (October 2011) https://www.researchgate.net/publication/221567927_Securing_Crisis_Maps_in_Conflict_Zones

[36] Raymond, 'Beyond Do No Harm' (n 31) 74.

[37] Sandvik and Raymond (n 22) 19.

While the information I start with is not sensitive, per se, the analysis certainly is. Having disparate pieces of information from satellite imagery isn't sensitive. But if someone takes that and cross-references it with social media and other historical information to identify troop type, capabilities of assault, and contextualizes that information into a narrative timeline, it is that additional context and framing that is the sensitive part, even though each piece is open source and publicly available. The contextualization, the analysis telling you something you didn't know before, that is sensitive intelligence that can be used to drive decision-making.[38]

4.2.2 Privacy Violations and the 'Consent Paradox'

Another acute concern of open source investigators is privacy. Because social media blurs lines between what is public and private, the use of information posted to social media platforms introduces a host of ethical concerns around matters of consent. 'While journalists might imagine that their words are cited and used in different contexts', write Bittner, Bors, and Turk, 'the use of tweeted information or other sources from the ground without the author's consent raises ethical questions and issues of privacy—especially if the information can be connected to a discrete geolocation'.[39]

A central challenge, therefore, in dealing with social media communications is how open source investigators should ethically and responsibly deal with information in the public domain (Pierro at 66–67).[40] Individuals are often not aware of the digital information embedded in the content they create and share online (Land and Meier at 24). Further, people have different expectations regarding what is public and what is private. In the view of UNGP, 'Humanitarian and development practitioners should...take into account that not every piece of information shared freely and publicly on social media or radio, for example, has been shared with a proper understanding of what 'public' means. Expectations of privacy can vary from one community to another'.[41]

Additionally, the contemporary, multi-stream digital environment is rapidly changing in how quickly and how far something might be shared. 'Information, once shared, is easily shared again and remixed, and it may not be possible to guarantee to a participant that his or her information will not be used for other purposes,'.[42] 'Thus', argues Raymond,

> even if some of the data was originally obtained through consent, some initially consented single source streams of data are likely being used to develop cross-corroborated insights that may significantly transcend the initial stated purposes for which one or more stream

[38] Interview on file with the authors.

[39] Christian Bittner, Michel Bors, and Cate Turk, 'Turning the Spotlight on the Crowd: Examining the Participatory Ethics and Practices of Crises Mapping' (2016) 15 ACME: An International E-Journal for Critical Geographies 207.

[40] Pierro Robin, 'A Double-Edged Sword: Benefits and Recommendations for Using Information and Communication Technology to Monitor or Investigate Human Rights.' Awarded Theses, European Inter-University Centre for Human Rights and Democratisation (2016) 66–67

[41] UN Global Pulse, "Improving Data Privacy & Security in ICT4D" A Workshop on Principle 8 of the Digital Development Principles (May 8, 2015
UN Headquarters, New York) Available here - https://digitalprinciples.org/privacy-security-workshop-principle-8-digital-development-principles-report/.

[42] Land and others (n 14) 24.

of data was first collected. This act of fusion invalidates any previously informed consent specific to a single stream's collection if the terms of the consent did not cover its integration with other streams of data.[43]

This situation is all the more complicated when considering the remote-based nature of much open source investigations work. As civil society organizations increasingly rely on remote-based information and communication technology-based interventions for collecting digital information from inaccessible environments, trying to obtain informed consent becomes near impossible. Researchers therefore face significant challenges in any attempt to gain informed consent from uploaders in conflict-affected, or repressive, or otherwise inaccessible environments.[44]

These concerns are amplified if, by using their material in advocacy reports, investigators place unwitting sources in danger.[45] Human rights investigators therefore face ethical dilemmas when it comes to unwanted attention drawn to the citizen activists whom they rely on for open source investigations.

4.2.3 Harmful Effects of Data Experimentation

Inspired by new partnerships and business models and empowered by emerging technologies and agile project management practices, human rights organizations and humanitarian agencies are understandably seeking to harness the transformative potential of innovation for rights-based protection in the digital age. Ultimately, however, innovation is premised on experimentation: the action or process of trying out new ideas, methods, or activities. And yet, the concept of experimentation is seldom associated with what is happening in humanitarian and human rights innovation labs all over the world. Instead, experimentation is replaced by more palatable language and concepts (and the behavioural norms that accompany those concepts) such as employing 'agile design', engaging in 'rapid prototyping', and 'failing fast'.

Data experimentation using call-detail records for contact-tracing purposes during the Ebola outbreak in West Africa is a prime example (Sandvik et al 2017, at 16). In that instance, There [were] strong indications that the humanitarian community asked for access to data that was illegal for it to have, under false pretenses, without a strong rationale or proof of value,' writes McDonald. 'This wasted significant resources, complicated coordination, and broke a wide range of laws,' exposing the organizations involved to significant legal liabilities.[46] Such instances raise important ethical questions around human-subjects research, responsible data practices, and proportionality, as the technologists involved are considered to have violated international legal standards and infringed on the privacy protections of civilian populations.

By uncritically adopting innovation-centric terminology, practitioners are failing to acknowledge the experimental nature that characterizes contemporary technology

43 Raymond, 'Beyond Do No Harm' (n 31) 74.

44 ibid 78.

45 Pierro (n 2) 66–67.

46 Kristin Sandvik, Katja Lindskov Jacobsen, and Sean Martin McDonal, 'Do No Harm: A Taxonomy of the Challenges of Humanitarian Experimentation' (2017) 99(904) International Review of the Red Cross 323.

development for humanitarian and human rights purposes, thereby ignoring or under-valuing the risks posed to vulnerable populations—the human subjects, end users, and recipients of this experimentation.[47] What does it mean to fail fast when lives are at stake? What does iteration look like in highly insecure environments?

Unfortunately, these questions go largely unasked, as principled, reasoned, and evidence-based approaches towards programme design are crowded out by a tidal wave of hackathons, makeathons, accelerators, hubs, networks, incubators, and labs. In other words, today's generation of techno-activists, investigators, and digital humanitarians are embracing significant risk without the requisite capacities to mitigate a range of increasingly adverse effects.

The situation is amplified in situations of remote-based volunteerism, as the geographical distance between subjects and innovators may lead to social distancing between activists and the populations they serve. As this remoteness grows, it becomes more difficult to effectively monitor and ensure the quality of experimental programmes and services, or to understand and mitigate the security threats to stakeholders involved, knowingly or unknowingly, in a project's 'pilot' phase.

If innovation is to achieve its transformative potential towards more relevant, effective, and accountable rights-based protection work, practitioners must come to grips with the harmful effects of data experimentation. New research presents a strong case for moving beyond 'treating highly vulnerable populations affected by extreme crisis events as experimental subjects of largely untested, non-consented and remotely applied technological interventions'.[48]

4.3 Implications

Civil society is only just now beginning to grapple with the negative externalities that result from the unintended consequences of digital data activities in already fragile operational environments. Even seemingly successful digital interventions raise questions around the potentially harmful effects of experimentation, violations of privacy, and disclosure of sensitive data that might expose vulnerable populations to new threats to their security, safety, and well-being. As humanitarian and human rights practitioners, we must learn how to identify and mitigate these risks and continuously reflect on our own practices.

If we do not address our own failure to account for a shifting operational landscape and the emerging negative externalities associated with data-driven interventions, at best our efforts will be ineffective, or divert needed resources away from more effective interventions. At worst, we risk turning ourselves into threat actors. The longer these practices continue to be carried out without adequate reflection, analysis and mitigation, the more we risk failing to protect vulnerable populations from harm and eroding the very principles that provide the foundation for our work.

[47] ibid 5.

[48] Sandvik and Raymond (n 22) 16–17.

5. Conclusion

5.1 Common Vulnerabilities

In our work with university-based OSI labs and with remote-based digital volunteer networks, we have identified the following vulnerabilities that practitioners should be aware of. Each area intersects with matters of (a) surveillance, monitoring, and intrusion; (b) weaponization of information; and (c) unintended digital harm, and exposes investigators (and their partners) to risk in different but consequential ways.

5.1.1 Leveraging Students and Volunteers for This Work Poses Unique Challenges

When volunteers are the primary human resource in investigations work (in contrast to paid employees), responsibilities and obligations are difficult to enforce. There are limited incentives, obligations, or enforcement mechanisms that organizations can impose on a volunteer corps to ensure that investigators follow procedures, deliver on tasks, or meet even the most baseline competencies (digital security or otherwise) or performance indicators. Student investigators also tend to be highly mobile in terms of lateral mobility (between projects and teams), temporal mobility (as students cycle in and out of academic calendars and matriculation), and geographic mobility (i.e. travelling abroad and/or sometimes returning to their countries of origin, which in some cases are governed by authoritarian or repressive regimes). This mobility puts them at risk.

5.1.2 Unsafe Data Practices

Data practices are of course at the very heart of open source investigation work. It is through such practices that investigators enter into the operational space of the cybersphere, and through which their choices and actions can have real world consequences. Therefore, the ways in which data practices are understood and carried out by student investigators, volunteer network leads, and OSI lab management can represent key weaknesses (from the point of view of threats) that leaves such initiatives open to exploitation. In our observation, weaknesses in data practices generate a significant number of vulnerabilities, most of which we felt could be attributed to three key issues: basic awareness, workflow, and personal-professional integration.

5.1.2.1 Limited Awareness and Skills for Safe and Secure Data Practices

We observe limited awareness among digital volunteers around crucial matters of *basic digital hygiene*,[49] *data sensitivity*,[50] *data harm*, the principles of *data minimization*,[51] or why such matters are central to their ability to conduct investigations safely, for themselves and

[49] Digital hygiene can be defined as practices associated with the purposeful and sustainable usage of digital devices. This includes account management (2FA, password manager), communications (encryption), storage (encryption, back-up, usage of third party platforms, etc), navigating online space (VPN, https secure, digital traces, social media, default settings).

[50] Investigators should not view matters of privacy or confidentiality as the *sole* criteria for discerning the sensitivity of an investigation. Investigators should also pay attention to granularity, timeliness, passive versus proactive solicitation, operational environment, focus area (gravity of abuse) and purpose (application of data) when it comes to the features that might make data more or less sensitive.

[51] Defined as the effort to collect or generate only the minimum required information necessary to achieve programmatic outcomes, data minimization requires that investigators identify—at the outset—the information needed to fulfill advocacy, operational, and evidentiary requirements, *and collect nothing more than what is needed.*

especially for others. Individual awareness is just one aspect of the weakness represented by data practices in open-source investigations, but in the hyperconnected context of the digital space where the weakest link can introduce the greatest harm, awareness is a key component of the ability to realize the values and principles of responsible digital citizenship (especially in the context of human rights work).

5.1.2.2 Variation in Workflows

Second, we have observed significant variance with regard to the workflows, processes, techniques, and tools in use by practitioners. This variation appears to stem less from an assessment of operational security considerations, or a strategic or analytic assessment of the data needs for responding to a brief, and more from an individualized, ad-hoc approach to organizing work and project design. Overall, the more variation there is at each stage of workflow (i.e. data acquisition and storage, organization and tasking, analysis and interpretation, and the generation and dissemination of information products) the greater the attack surface is for any investigations team.

5.1.2.3 Reliance on Personal and Shared Devices and Accounts

We are concerned with the extent to which volunteer investigators rely on personal equipment to attend to their investigations work, the degree to which they maintain separation between digital accounts, and between personal and professional activities in online accounts and activities as well. For example, in terms of equipment, students and volunteers tend to rely on their personal computers and mobile phones to conduct their OSI work. But reliance on personal machines significantly compounds known vulnerabilities by increasing the attack surface of users (i.e. outdated software or variance in tools, apps, plug ins) and complicates diagnostics and recovery work in the event of a successful intrusion or attack (i.e. loss of standardization and control). The way open source investigators conduct their behaviour online matters: authorities are able to observe patterns of online behaviour (data exhaust, digital fingerprints), which can be used to reveal information about the student's research and/or possibly compromise the identities of teammates, informants, clients, or other witnesses and victims.

5.1.3 Forced Reliance on Third Party Platforms

Many OSI practitioners use and rely on unsecured third party digital tools, networks and systems for their communications, and for the gathering, storing and sharing of sensitive data related to incident reporting and response activities. Reliance on popular third-party communications platforms (Facebook, YouTube, Google, etc) for work is problematic because these platforms don't offer default settings that would naturally protect the data of higher-risk users (such as 2FA, or limits to sharing and tagging).

Users of these platforms will always find approaches to protect their privacy (and that of their partners and sources) insufficient because the systems do not belong to them. Kazansky writes at length about the problem of opaque, commercial platforms offering little protection and no control:

> We call this a forced reliance because Facebook, as a networking platform, facilitates the maintenance of existing social ties and serves as a popular and dominant channel through which new relationships are created and sustained, and because there is no comparable

replacement available. Baumer et al (2013) describe this forced reliance as a form of 'lagging resistance' wherein users express high levels of dissatisfaction with a tool but ultimately continue to use it for lack of viable alternatives. The phenomenon of lagging resistance demonstrates a systematic failure to provide users with adequate choices, protections, or controls over their privacy.

This issue is further complicated by the ever-changing nature of social media providers' privacy and data protection policies. Users often have little or no say in accepting these updates (i.e. they must either accept the update or deactivate/delete the account). Meanwhile, it is very difficult for users to know which data are being generated and processed by the platforms they use; which actors have access to these data (each social media platform has its own policy on transparency reporting); and what the regulatory environment is.

> Like all users, protecting their privacy requires that they understand the properties and extent of 'data traces' left behind when using online consumer services and software; that they know the complex legal rights they have through commercial platforms' Terms of Service (TOS); that they be able to manage the technological options available to change default user settings; and that they are able to apply additional technological remedies to compensate for the lack of protection or control such platforms provide. (Kazansky 190-192)

5.1.4 Tensions between Visibility and Anonymity

Finally, there is an engrained tension between visibility (being 'seen' and 'heard') and anonymity:

> that while digital technologies—primarily social media and mobile phones—can help amplify and create visibility for marginalized activists' issues, at the same time they make the activists themselves visible in ways that they often find they are unable to control. This inability to control their own visibility as activists presents risks to their work, particularly if their work deals with sensitive issues that directly challenge institutional power or corruption.[52]

This is particularly problematic when visibility can lead to exposure to digital threats, risks, and harms. For example, Ganesh writes that 'increased online visibility for the issues faced by marginalized communities has the side effect of making individuals visible too—often to their detriment, because they are working in hostile local political contexts'.[53] She continues: 'For marginal and invisible communities, visibility is an important aspect of claims to rights and advocacy, and technology is a way of achieving this. But top-down bureaucracies that function to organise and manage society tend to make marginal communities visible and vulnerable.'[54]

[52] Maya Indira Ganesh, Jeff Deutch, and Jennifer Schulte, 'Privacy, Anonymity, Visibility: Dilemmas in Tech Use by Marginalized Communities' Tactical Technology Collective (2016) 6.

[53] ibid 5.

[54] ibid 10.

5.2 Closing Remarks

In this chapter, we unpacked this topology of digitally-derived threats, risks, and harms in an effort to take stock of a rapidly shifting—and consequential—landscape, and its implications, for open source investigators and the populations they serve.

We have argued that the diversification and digitalization of human rights practice—including the emergence of open source investigations as a methodological approach—pose enormous challenges for crisis-affected people and those who serve them. As established above, civil society organizations and their partners have become valuable targets of repressive governments, criminal networks, armed groups, terrorist organizations, and hybrid non-state actor groups simply by virtue of the data they now generate.

While advances in digital communications have made open source investigatory work possible on the one hand, they also make it harder to curb disinformation and control security incidents on the other. They have, in the words of McPherson, 'created new platforms for making threats, and new ways in which aid agencies' information can be accessed and stolen'.[55] This state of affairs raises important questions about the dilemmas that human rights and humanitarian actors face in the digital age: their very reliance on digital technologies to collect, transmit, and store enormous quantities of sensitive, mission critical information may be exposing vulnerable populations, and those who serve them, to new threats.

Digital technologies have therefore created new points of weakness for civil society groups, Hankey and O'Clunaigh note, 'exposing human rights defenders' whereabouts, activities and networks, and creating evidence against them through data leakages, digital traces, and direct surveillance and interception'.[56] 'The speed and scale at which this is happening,' write Hankey and O'Clunaigh, coupled with 'the relatively limited resources required to stay on top of this . . . is unprecedented'.[57] Human rights defenders, in other words, are thus facing an unprecedented range of vulnerabilities.

OSI practitioners, however, are not alone.

Many open source investigations teams are taking a leadership position on tackling very real and grave threats to their investigators and the people they serve.

Such efforts represent initial but significant first steps towards improved understanding and effective positioning to mitigate a range of evolving threats to human rights actors and the populations they serve. To counter the very real risk of inadvertent harm, open source investigations teams must continue to invest resources to (1) build awareness and core competencies around a baseline of digital security and data protection for all stakeholders, (2) integrate security concepts, methods, and resources into their daily processes, (3) and acquire in-house capacity to diagnose, respond to and recover from adverse events. This work, we hope, will help build awareness around key security issues that characterize the contemporary human rights and humanitarian landscape in the digital age.

[55] Vazquez Llorente and Wall (n 31) 4; McPherson, 'ICTs and Human Rights Practice' (n 14) 3.
[56] Hankey and O'Clunaigh (n 3) 536; Pierro (n 2) 64.
[57] Hankey and O'Clunaigh (n 3) 538.

PART IV

14
Open Source Information
Part of the Puzzle

*Fred Abrahams and Daragh Murray**

The foundation of most human rights investigations has traditionally been and will likely remain research on the ground: getting as close as possible to the people affected and the places where the violations occurred. Today, however, a host of other methods exist to document, expose, and help end abuses. The use of satellite imagery and drones, online investigations, video forensics, data analysis and, most recently, artificial intelligence, all form part of the modern investigator's toolkit.

This chapter focuses on one of the most significant of these new tools, and the main subject of this book—the use of open source material. The revolution in information publicly available online, especially on social media, has changed the landscape for those who investigate human rights violations perpetrated by governments, armed groups, corporations, and others.

We focus here on how investigators can use open source material to great effect, not only where physical access is limited or denied, and while considering security, ethics and verification. This material can produce compelling information on its own and can facilitate powerful documentation, especially when used in conjunction with the traditional field-based approach and other investigative techniques.

1. The Investigator's Toolbox

A rigorous and professional human rights investigation requires using a wide range of techniques and tools to identify, obtain, and analyse information from different sources. A failure to utilize all available options can lead to biased or incomplete findings. As the Siracusa Guidelines for International, Regional and National Fact-Finding Bodies note, a fact-finding body should 'adopt and implement a methodology that allows it to gather facts and draw conclusions in an objective manner'.[1]

1.1 On-the-ground Investigations

For many years, a human rights investigator's first instinct has been to travel to the place where a violation took place, in order to speak with those affected. A host of reasons

* The authors would like to thank Josh Lyons and Brian Root for their valuable insight, and Jonathan Cobb for editing assistance.

[1] Guideline 1—Independence and Impartiality. M Cherif Bassiouni and Christina Abraham (eds), *Siracusa Guidelines for International, Regional and National Fact-Finding Bodies* (Intersentia 2013).

continue to justify this approach. First, field work allows investigators to collect information first-hand, meaning physical evidence, relevant documentation when available, and what one gleans from personal observations. Investigator observation and on-the-ground experiences can give insight into the nuances of political, social, and economic dynamics that aid human rights fact-finding, such as the power structure within a community or the relations between armed groups. Secondly, on-the-ground investigations bring the victims and witnesses of abuse to the fore. Directly affected individuals can relay the detailed facts about cases and patterns of abuse—of course subject to corroboration. They can explain in their own voices what happened, how the event changed their lives, and what steps they want taken next. By presenting the personal side of human rights violations, investigators more effectively elevate victims' and witnesses' voices, and better engage audiences to the plight of others. In short, personal testimony establishes human rights as grounded in the experiences of the people the reporting is intended to support.

On-the-ground investigations also lend legitimacy to fact-finding endeavours because the investigator(s) and relevant organizations can speak from a position of increased authority about what they saw and heard. The lack of a field visit, conversely, may open the findings to criticisms of a partial or superficial approach to the issue.

At the same time, field research can present challenges and has its limitations. First, access to the areas in question might be limited or controlled, which can affect the quality of information one obtains. When access to some areas is blocked, for instance, the overall investigation can be skewed by what does not get heard. Likewise, some individuals may be kept away from investigators on purpose by those seeking to control access to information or on account of their status within a community. This may affect access to women, children, youth, older people, minorities, or people with disabilities.

The challenges related to access increase as the scope of the investigation expands. While it may be possible to speak directly with victims and witnesses to a specific incident, that can become more difficult as investigators seek to document patterns of violations across different locations and times.

Second, individuals that investigators do meet may try to hide or distort facts for one or another reason. Perhaps they have an agenda, have been coached or coerced, or are simply worried about how an outside investigator may perceive the information they provide. The impact of trauma on memory can also play a role. Research shows, for instance, that 'individuals who witness (or are victims of) violent events are more likely to misperceive than individuals who witness nonviolent events because the ability to perceive declines when an individual is experiencing stress'.[2] To overcome these challenges, professional investigators regularly cross-check information and rely on multiple sources. However, critics and detractors may attempt to dismiss human rights findings by claiming that the investigators were duped.

Third, physical and digital security may play an important role in limiting an investigation. Investigators who dutifully consider the safety of themselves, their partners, and their interlocutors may limit where they go and with whom they speak.

[2] Nancy A Combs, *Fact-Finding Without Facts: The Uncertain Evidentiary Foundations of International Criminal Convictions* (Cambridge University Press 2010) 15.

Fourth, on a more practical level, research trips can be expensive; some organizations lack the finances to conduct a proper field investigation that allows for the collection of accurate information in a safe and secure manner.

To address these concerns, fact-finding projects are increasingly utilizing other angles of approach, gathering information from diverse sources. This is true not only when physical access is blocked: open source information should also be used in conjunction with material gathered on the ground. Failing to explore such options could needlessly limit the amount, diversity and quality of information received.

1.2 Remote Sensing

One increasingly accessible source of information is aerial imagery from satellites or drones that can provide a 'bird's eye' view of the location under investigation. Access to this imagery has dramatically increased in recent years as the number of commercially operated satellites grows. The challenge is no longer limited data but rather the capacity to take advantage of the explosion in earth observation data over the past eight years.

The most obvious advantage to using aerial imagery is that it does not require researchers to have physical access to the locations in question—particularly useful for hostile environments. In places where access is possible, the imagery can be collected with no security implications for people on the ground. The exception comes with the use of drones, which requires a presence in or near the area, and can raise a number of legal, security and privacy concerns.

Aerial imagery also offers a powerful form of evidence that critics find difficult to refute. While authorities under investigation can argue that witnesses manipulated investigators, they cannot so easily dismiss imagery that shows signs of abuse—although some governments do try.[3]

Often these images stand as compelling evidence on their own. They are strengthened further when combined with other sources of information, most effectively with testimony from the ground. Aerial imagery may demonstrate that a patch of field has been freshly worked, for instance, and testimony from area residents can explain whether the field was recently ploughed or contains a mass grave. Equally, aerial imagery may show the destruction of a village, but witness testimony will can fill in other pieces of information, such as who carried out the attack, why, and when.

Satellite and drone imagery also offers powerful ways to visualize human rights violations with maps, before/after sliders and other graphics. This is important because human rights reporting increasingly includes multimedia elements, web features and distribution on social media. Images of impact craters from heavy artillery in densely populated areas can drive home the violation of indiscriminate attacks in a visceral way that testimony alone finds difficult to match.

[3] Government refutes rights group on Rakhine' *Global New Light of Myanmar* (17 November 2016) http://www.globalnewlightofmyanmar.com/government-refutes-rights-group-report-on-rakhine/ accessed 17 December 2018.

Such visuals can also present violations over time, such as the steady shrinking of Lake Turkana in Kenya owing to dams in Ethiopia, which impacts the rights to water, food, and life.[4] Together with testimony and open source photos or videos, aerial imagery allows for the geolocation of incidents—pinpointing on a map where a violation took place. This can enable the creation of 3D models to assist analysis and presentation of violations, such as the unlawful use of force,[5] or airstrikes that unlawfully killed civilians.[6]

Going forward, the development of machine learning offers the possibility to detect the physical signatures of potential human rights abuses automatically, such as land clearance, burn scars, or demolished homes. Instead of an analyst having to scan images, a programme could automatically identify relevant changes on the ground, and serve as an early alert system, radically altering the way some human rights abuses are discovered.

Remote sensing has its drawbacks, too. Most obviously, one must obtain the imagery itself, and while this has become significantly easier and more affordable in recent years it is often not without cost, especially if an investigation seeks imagery of a certain area at a specific time. Cloud cover can also limit what satellite sensors are able to record, although drones offer an alternative, should resources allow. The more serious limitation, however, is access to analytical expertise.[7] Some objects might be obvious to the untrained eye, but many others require specialized training to identify and understand. Aerial imagery requires interpretation and analysis.

Ultimately, while remote sensing can provide powerful evidence for some types of violations, the images usually tell only part of the story, and proper documentation requires additional work—ideally testimony from those who were affected, but also documents, official statements, and open source photos or videos. Taken together, this material can effectively link an event (such as village burning) to a violation (arson, or property destruction) and a perpetrator.

1.3 Data Analysis

Another significant source of information is statistical analysis –one of the fastest growing areas in human rights research, thanks to rapidly increasing digitization and the availability of data.[8] In contrast to qualitative information, such as what is gleaned from narrative interviews, quantitative data can expose otherwise unseen patterns and trends, such as violations over time or space, and can offer a sense of the overall scope of potential violations.

[4] Human Rights Watch, 'Ethiopia: Dams, Plantations a Threat to Kenyans' (2017).

[5] See eg Forensic Architecture, 'Nakba Day Killings' https://www.forensic-architecture.org/case/nakba-day-killngs/ accessed 8 December 2018.

[6] See eg Forensic Architecture, 'Al-Jinah Mosque' https://www.forensic-architecture.org/case/al-jinah-mosque/ accessed 8 December 2018.

[7] Joshua Lyons, 'Documenting Violations of International Humanitarian Law from Space: A Critical Review of Geospatial Analysis of Satellite Imagery During Armed Conflicts in Gaza (2009), Georgia (2008) and Sri Lanka (2009)' (2012) 94(886) International Review of the Red Cross 739 https://www.icrc.org/en/international-review/article/documenting-violations-international-humanitarian-law-space-critical/ accessed 17 December 2018.

[8] Ann Marie Clark and Kathryn Sikkink, 'Information Effects and Human Rights Data: Is the Good News about Increased Human Rights Information Bad News for Human Rights Measures?' (2013) 35(3) Human Rights Quarterly 539, 541.

One powerful example was showcased in the 2002 trial of former Yugoslav President Slobodan Milosevic at the International Criminal Tribunal for the Former Yugoslavia in The Hague when one of the world's leading human rights statisticians, Patrick Ball, presented his findings on killings and forced expulsions. Using data gathered from Kosovo-Albania border posts, as well as coded testimony, Ball showed how most of the killings in Kosovo were likely not to be related to NATO air strikes or action by the ethnic Albanian insurgent group. Rather, his findings were 'consistent with the hypothesis that Yugoslav forces forced people from their homes, forced Albanian Kosovars from their homes, and killed people'.[9]

Data analysis can also provide a powerful tool to document violations of economic, social and cultural rights. A 2018 Human Rights Watch report on the inappropriate use of antipsychotic medication on older patients in US nursing homes, for instance, analysed data to estimate the number of people affected.[10] The analysis allowed for mapping of geographic data to display where the right to health was most at risk.

As with satellite imagery, professionally done data analysis can offer compelling evidence of abuse, be it in a court of law or the court of public opinion. It also offers the potential for compelling visuals, such as graphs, charts, or interactive designs. However, it takes resources and expertise to obtain and analyse data properly and attempts to do so without the necessary specialists are likely to produce unreliable and easily discredited results. A key element is considering what data are not being obtained, and why. For instance, if reports of human rights violations are decreasing in an area, are those violations really decreasing or are journalists, human rights organizations and others who monitor those violations being silenced or repressed?[11]

As with the aerial imagery, evidence of violations gleaned from data analysis becomes stronger when combined with testimony and other types of information. For instance, Ball's findings on refugee flows from Kosovo had added impact when considered together with harrowing statements from refugees who fled killings, rapes and other abuse that were consistent with his findings.[12]

1.4 Open Source Information

A fourth source of human rights information comes from the vast amount of information available in the public domain, most commonly online—what we have been terming open source material. As explained in this and other chapters, open source investigations have become an essential feature of a human rights investigator's toolbox.

1.4.1 Opportunities Offered by Open Source Information

Open source information constitutes a rich, and in many respects unique, source of information relevant to human rights investigations that should be considered both at the outset

[9] Tina Rosenberg, 'The Body Counter' *Foreign Policy* (27 February 2012) https://foreignpolicy.com/2012/02/27/the-body-counter/ accessed 8 December 2018.

[10] Human Rights Watch, '"They Want Docile": How Nursing Homes in the United States Overmedicate People with Dementia' (2018).

[11] Clark and Sikkink (n 8) 550.

[12] Human Rights Watch, 'Under Orders: War Crimes in Kosovo' (2001).

of, and throughout, the investigative process. In some cases, a photo or video posted to social media may provide the first indication that a violation has occurred, or is occurring, which in turn may allow for a faster human rights response.

A significant amount of open source information relevant to human rights investigations is now publicly available. Approximately 400 hours of video are uploaded to YouTube every minute. The digital preservation and analysis organization the Syrian Archive has amassed approximately 1,500,000 videos and images potentially relevant to human rights abuses committed in the Syrian conflict.[13] Indeed, the extent of open source information is so great that one of the main challenges researchers now face is filtering the content, verifying its authenticity, and identifying what is of relevance to a particular investigation. Automated techniques are now being developed to assist in this task, addressing various stages of the process, from discovery to verification.[14]

The contribution of open source information to human rights cases is clearly demonstrated by the 2018 indictment that the International Criminal Court issued for the Libyan Mahmoud Al-Werfalli. Charged with killing or ordering the killing of thirty-three people in seven incidents, the indictment relies heavily on videos of the killings that were posted on Facebook.[15]

This section will address the benefits of using open source material in human rights investigations, looking at the evidence and compelling visuals that this material can provide, as well as the opportunity to do research in restricted areas, to present additional voices, and to conduct collaborative investigations.

1.4.2 Varied Sources of Information

During traditional investigations, human rights investigators respond to an allegation or incident by conducting an investigation after the fact. Evidence is typically gathered through victim and witness testimony, medical records, or site analysis. While these remain essential sources of information, advances in modern technology—in particular smartphones with cameras—allow incidents to be recorded as they occur, and then distributed on social media. This was the case with the Al-Werfalli killings in Libya and with many other violations around the world, from individual incidents of discrimination to large scale war crimes. In Angola, for example, observers with a phone recorded the police using violence against people in wheelchairs demonstrating for disability rights.[16] In Cameroon, videos on social media showed security force members committing torture and extrajudicial executions.[17]

[13] See Syrian Archive, 'About' https://syrianarchive.org/en/about/ accessed 13 June 2018.

[14] Two projects relevant in this regard include the Human Rights, Big Data and Technology project based at the University of Essex Human Rights Centre http://www.hrbdt.ac.uk and the Open Source Research for Rights project based at the University of Swansea https://osr4rights.org.

[15] *Prosecutor v Mahmoud Mustafa Busyf Al-Werfalli* (Case Information Sheet) ICC-PIOS-CIS-LIB-03-002/18 (2018) https://www.icc-cpi.int/CaseInformationSheets/al-werfalliEng.pdf accessed 4 June 2018 and *Prosecutor v Mahmoud Mustafa Busyf Al-Werfalli* (Warrant of Arrest) ICC-01/11-01/17 (15 August 2017). See also Emma Irving, 'And So It Begins ... Social Media Evidence in an ICC Arrest Warrant', *OpinioJuris* (17 August 2017) http://opiniojuris.org/2017/08/17/and-so-it-begins-social-media-evidence-in-an-icc-arrest-warrant/ accessed 30 December 2018.

[16] Human Rights Watch, 'Angolan Police Attack Protesters in Wheelchairs' (2017).

[17] See Amnesty International, 'Cameroon's Secret Torture Chambers: Human Rights Violations and War Crimes in the Fight against Boko Haram' (2017) 13.

In Syria, photos and videos have been used to document the Assad government's use of chemical weapons.[18]

The use of this material presents a number of distinct advantages. First, images or recordings of an event can allow a scene-by-scene analysis of the event as it unfolded. Footage can offer the strongest possible source of information, as investigators do not have to reconstruct the event based on testimony or other sources. This may allow for more robust engagement with the underlying facts, as opposed to relying on recollections or perceptions of those facts.[19] This is particularly important because demonstrating some human rights and humanitarian law violations requires knowledge of the circumstances prevailing at the time. In a law enforcement context, for example, the killing of an individual by a state agent is not, of itself, determinative of a violation: the circumstances must be evaluated to determine whether the deceased posed a real and immediate danger to life or limb, and whether the use of lethal force was required.[20] This is often difficult to assess after the fact as claims and counter-claims emerge, but a video of the incident might shed light on whether a state agent used unlawful force. Examples here include the 2018 killing of Stephon Clark by police in Sacramento[21] and the 2014 killing of protestors in Ukraine's Maidan Square.[22]

Open source materials can also be used to counter official narratives of an event in a manner that would otherwise be difficult, if not impossible. For example, on 15 May 2014, two children were killed at a protest in Beitunia, in the West Bank. An initial investigation by the Israeli military concluded that its soldiers had used rubber-coated bullets rather than live fire.[23] Open source materials, including video from CNN and a local business' security camera, however, showed that the children were unarmed when they were shot, and that they did not pose a threat. Video and sound analysis showed that at least one soldier did indeed fire live ammunition. Furthermore, only one soldier appeared to have line-of-sight view of one of the children who was shot, thereby identifying the responsible soldier.[24]

Chemical weapons attacks in Syria offer another compelling case. Through the use of open source materials, organisations such as the Syrian Archive were able to document more than 200 such attacks, some of them attributed to the Syrian government.[25] Significantly, this research also strongly suggested that one attack, previously identified by the French Foreign Ministry as a chemical weapons attack, was in fact conducted using conventional weapons.[26]

[18] See Syrian Archive, 'Database of Chemical Weapons Attacks' https://syrianarchive.org/en/collections/chemical-weapons/database accessed 8 December 2018.

[19] Frédéric Mégret, 'Do Facts Exist, Can They Be "Found," and Does It Matter?' in Philip Alson and Sarah Knuckey (eds), *The Transformation of Human Rights Fact-Finding* (OUP 2016) 30.

[20] *Nachova and Others v Bulgaria* Application nos 43577/98 and 43579/98, Judgment (6 July 2005) para 107; *Nadege Sorzema and Others v Dominican Republic*, Judgment, IACtHR (24 October 2012) para 85.

[21] See Barbara Marcolini, Chris Cirillo, and Christoph Koettl, 'How Stephon Clark Was Killed by Police in His Backyard' *The New York Times* (23 March 2018) https://www.nytimes.com/video/us/100000005813009/stephon-clark-killed-police-sacramento.html accessed 30 December 2018.

[22] See Mattathias Schwartz, 'Who Killed the Kiev Protestors? A 3-D Model Holds the Clues' *The New York Times* (30 May 2018) https://www.nytimes.com/2018/05/30/magazine/ukraine-protest-video.html accessed 30 December 2018.

[23] See Peter Beaumont, 'Video Footage Indicates Killed Palestinian Youths Posed No Threat' *The Guardian* (20 May 2014).

[24] The investigation is discussed in detail in Forensic Architecture, 'The Killing of Nadeem Nawara and Mohammad Mahmoud Odeh Abu Daher in Nakba Day Protest outside of Beitunia on May 15th, 2014' http://beitunia.forensic-architecture.org accessed 4 June 2018.

[25] See Syrian Archive, 'Database of Chemical Weapons Attacks' (n 18).

[26] ibid.

A second advantage of open source information is that it allows human rights investigators to paint a more complete picture of an event. For instance, open source information may include recordings of an event taken from multiple vantage points or from before and after an incident, which would illuminate the prevailing circumstances surrounding the event and add layers of contextual knowledge.

Open source information may also have been recorded by members of the different parties involved in an incident—victims, witnesses, and perpetrators—allowing a deeper understanding of the incident. This facilitates compliance with the London-Lund International Human Rights Fact-Finding Guidelines, which states: 'Wherever possible the delegation should interview all parties relevant to the situation under consideration in order to achieve a balanced, comprehensive picture.'[27]

This is not to suggest that investigators should rely exclusively on open source information. When possible, interviews and other components from the 'traditional' toolbox remain essential, but the greater the variety and quantity of sources, the better the quality of the research. For instance, when conducting investigations, human rights researchers often rely on local contacts or 'fixers' to identify, and provide introductions to victims, witnesses, and experts. Although techniques and best practices exist to overcome intermediary bias, and to identify bias in victims and witnesses, open source information provides an additional means to achieve that end.

The more complete picture facilitated by open source information can also help to counter the harmonized accounts that sometimes develop in communities, whereby one version of a story gets regarded as 'the truth'. The emergence of a so-called 'village narrative' may be deliberate, in that it is intended to obscure potentially relevant facts—such as the presence of an armed group at the time of a government attack—but it may also develop naturally. Research has shown that 'a witness's memory of an event can be substantially altered by information that person later learns about the event. In some studies, subjects who were merely asked about a particular item inaccurately incorporated that item into their memory of the events'.[28]

This possibility was addressed by the Appeals Chamber of the International Criminal Tribunal for the former Yugoslavia, which noted: '[T]he frailties of human perceptions and the very serious risk that a miscarriage of justice might result from reliance upon even the most confident witnesses who purport to identify an accused without an adequate opportunity to verify their observations'.[29] Open source information and footage recorded at the time and place of a violation can help to pierce both intentional and unintentional narratives, presenting a more detailed picture of the events, helping to overcome bias—or allegations of bias[30]—and facilitating more accurate analysis. While perpetrators of human rights violations may try to discredit findings based primarily on victim and witness testimony, it is much more difficult to discount properly verified images that depict the abuse, especially when those images corroborate what the victims and witnesses have said.

[27] London-Lund International Human Rights Fact-Finding Guidelines, 2009. Produced by the International Bar Association and the Raoul Wallenberg Institute https://www.ibanet.org/Fact_Finding_Guidelines.aspx accessed 30 December 2018.

[28] Nancy A Combs, *Fact-Finding without Facts: The Uncertain Evidentiary Foundations of International Criminal Convictions* (Cambridge University Press 2010) 16.

[29] *Prosecutor v Kupreskic* (Judgment) ICTY IT-96-16-A (23 October 2001) para 34.

[30] For instance, if a claim is made against a state based on testimony from individuals associated with, or sympathetic to, an opposition group, the state may argue that the claim itself is biased.

1.4.3 Communicating with Victims and Witnesses: Voice, Access, and Retraumatization

During the course of human rights investigations, particular categories of victims or witnesses may be inaccessible to investigators. In some cases, the culture or community dynamics may mean that a representative speaks on behalf of a group, that women or children cannot be interviewed, or that victims may be unwilling to provide testimony because of the nature of the crime, particularly if this relates to sexual exploitation or abuse. It is worth noting, for example, that only 13 per cent of witnesses appearing before the International Criminal Tribunal for the former Yugoslavia were women, and a similar imbalance is reflected in other international tribunals, though that might also reflect the bias of investigators and prosecutors.[31] The availability of open source information may allow for easier investigation of some crimes in this respect, and may allow witnesses to communicate their experiences directly through social media or other forms of messaging. New technologies and the use of open source information have the potential to strengthen traditional human rights fact-finding models—by allowing for greater participation in the documentation process, and allowing insight on previously inaccessible topics, issues or crimes.[32] However, as noted in Chapter 4, access to and familiarity with the internet and social media varies widely around the world; in this sense, technology also has the potential to exclude.

Another advantage of open source material is that it avoids the risk of retraumatizing victims and witnesses with interviews that cover harrowing events. Especially after high-profile atrocities, the same victims and witnesses can be subject to repeat interviews by local and international human rights investigators, as well as the media. Of course, such repeat interviews should be avoided where possible, even in the absence of open source information, as they raise clear ethical and legal concerns.

1.4.4 Safety and Access

The use of open source information provides straightforward benefits in maintaining the safety of researchers and in getting information from otherwise inaccessible areas. The process of conducting an 'on the ground' human rights investigation can expose researchers and their interlocutors to physical harm, either from ongoing conflict or hostility from a government, armed groups, or local populations. The ability to conduct remote but effective investigations clearly may alleviate many of these safety concerns.

Equally important, the availability of open source information can allow for human rights investigations in areas that would otherwise be impossible. Situations in some parts of Syria or Yemen are too dangerous for most on-the-ground inquiries, while in other situations access is denied by those who control the area. Myanmar's decision to keep humanitarians, human rights investigators and journalists out of Rakhine State during military operations in 2017 stands out as a case in point. Restricted access to so-called closed countries that are not experiencing armed conflict but are also known for rampant human rights abuses is also noteworthy, such as North Korea, Ethiopia, and Iran.

[31] United Nations International Criminal Tribunal for the former Yugoslavia, 'Witness Statistics' http://www.icty.org/en/about/registry/witnesses/statistics accessed 14 December 2018.

[32] See in this regard Molly K Land, 'Democratizing Human Rights Fact-Finding' in Philip Alston and Sarah Knuckey (eds), *The Transformation of Human Rights Fact-Finding* (OUP 2016) 402.

1.4.5 Collaborative Methods

The nature of open source information makes it suitable for collaborations in ways that traditional human rights investigations typically are not. For instance, digital volunteers may be tasked with conducting an initial analysis of data and preparing it for more in-depth study (crowd tasking). Amnesty International's 'Digital Decoders' project, discussed in Chapter 1, is one example of this approach. A diverse range of collaborators may also be engaged to verify specific pieces of open source information, actively contributing to the research and analysis. The work of weapons identification offers one example, with a network of military experts working together to identify a munition or other piece of military equipment that has been shared online. Another example is Amnesty International's ground-breaking Digital Verification Corps, which brings together students from different universities to work with satellite imagery, online content and other open source material (see Chapter 1). Such models have the potential to boost engagement among a broader human rights community and to increase the resources available to an organisation.

The nature of open source verification also helps to avoid a problem often associated with collaborative human rights research; namely, that those initiating collaboration depend on the quality and reliability of their partners, lest they suffer reputational harm. As open source information must be verified, and the verification process can be clearly evaluated, this risk is reduced.

1.4.6 Presenting the Case

The verification of open source information is based on a logical, rational, and repeatable process.[33] For instance, reverse image searching is used to verify that an image has not been posted online prior to the event in question or does not portray a different event. Clues in a video are used to assist with geolocation, and distinctive features can be highlighted and cross-referenced against maps or other imagery. Analysis of shadows can indicate the approximate time of day at which a video or image was recorded. Similarly, the ability to view the events surrounding an incident or to conduct frame-by-frame analysis means that researchers can in some instances methodically step through the evidence, identifying and analysing elements of interest.

These possibilities also assist with the presentation of research findings. Instead of relying exclusively on information from witness testimony or site analysis, researchers can use images to guide the audience through the event, visually highlighting elements of interest. Specific clues can be emphasised, allowing the researcher to explain their relevance. For instance, if video footage emerges of police shootings resulting in the death or injury of protestors, researchers may be able to show the context of the shooting, whether the protesters used weapons, whether police officers tried to use non-lethal methods, and perhaps the trajectory and timing of the lethal shots. Such analysis and presentation can provide greater clarity for the audience than was typically available in the past and, as noted above, also helps to counter any claims of bias.

These factors make open source information particularly amenable to modern forms of communication, such as interactive features for websites or hand-held devices,[34] and

[33] This is discussed further elsewhere in this volume. See chs 5–10.

[34] See Amnesty International and Forensic Architecture, 'Black Friday: Carnage in Rafah during 2014 Israel/Gaza Conflict' https://blackfriday.amnesty.org accessed 8 December 2018.

for distribution via social media. More advanced options might include the use of virtual reality to guide an audience through the scene of an abuse.[35] Information presented in these formats can be viewed quickly, shared easily, and can form a valuable means of public engagement and advocacy.

2. Potential Challenges with Open Source Information

Open source information can contribute significantly to a human rights investigation, but its use does give rise to a number of concerns that should be taken into account, as we have seen in Chapter 11 in particular.

2.1 Maintaining Perspective on the Value of Open Source Information

As a new method that presents significant advantages for human rights investigations, open source information could become the principal, or even exclusive, focus of some investigations. In most cases, this would be inappropriate. As discussed above, open source information forms part of the overall investigative toolbox, and each of the other 'tools' has value in its own right. An over-reliance on open source information can lead to biased results for various reasons.

First, open source information might only provide partial information. A video posted to social media, for example, might show the aftermath of an airstrike that killed individuals who appear to be civilians but miss the armed fighters who passed by on a motorbike immediately prior to the strike, or may not reveal that some of those killed were in fact active members of an armed group not in uniform.

Second, it might limit or prevent an examination of abuses that tend not to get recorded and posted on social media, such as sexual abuse or domestic violence. Documenting crimes like these often require the careful and nuanced approach of an experienced researcher on the ground.

Third, an over-reliance on social media posts can create false impressions about the scope and severity of abuses, victim and perpetrator profiles, and timing. Disaster alert tools that rely on social media posts to find people in need offer a case in point: the people who urgently require assistance may have the least access or time to announce this on Facebook or Twitter.

Fourth, interest from human rights investigators and others could skew the information that gets posted online—the so-called Hawthorne or observer effect. For example, a high level of interest in cluster munitions and barrel bombs in Syria might have influenced which photos and videos Syrians posted online, giving an inaccurate impression about the use of these weapons in relation to others.

Lastly, the contextual analysis so critical to human rights investigations can be difficult to conduct with an over-reliance on open source information. For instance, modern armed conflicts—such as in Cameroon, Afghanistan, Syria, and Yemen—are typically dynamic

[35] See 'Nazi VR' https://vimeo.com/246967410 accessed 18 June 2018.

and fast changing. Alliances between armed groups are established and dissolved; new actors emerge while others fade; control over territory changes hands. To understand these environments, first hand corroborated information is typically required, whether through on-the-ground investigation, or, if this is not possible, through remote contact with people on the ground.

The use of other tools adds rigor to investigations and can assist legal analysis. For instance, remote sensing can provide an overview of a conflict area, indicating the extent of destruction and possibly the time at which it occurred. This can reveal the scale and patterns of violations and potentially address counterclaims of military necessity as a rationale for attack. Equally, data analysis can reveal the scale of violations and show how patterns of shootings relate to the applicable rules of engagement. Both remote sensing and data analysis can help to demonstrate whether attacks on a civilian population was carried out in a widespread or systematic manner, and thus whether crimes against humanity took place.

Finally, victim and witness testimony should continue to play a central role in human rights reporting. It is important that victims and witnesses are heard, in order to give voice to their experiences and to humanize the often devastating impact of violations.

There are, of course, certain situations where only open source information is available. Sole reliance on this information may be sufficient to prove a violation of an absolute prohibition, such as of torture or summary execution. In general, however, open source information should be used in conjunction with other tools.

2.2 The Future of Fakes

As the use of open source information for human rights investigations increases, so do the attempts to manipulate and obfuscate this information for nefarious ends. Investigators must reckon with a steady dose of doctored or misidentified images, fake documents, and other purposeful attempts to hide or distort facts. User generated content should never be taken at face value, and as discussed in Chapter 9, investigators must take specific measures to verify content. The same is true of other potential sources of information, such as statistics, documents, or government records, which must be verified to ensure that they are genuine, and that they pertain to the issue under investigation.[36]

Going forward, technological advances will likely complicate the verification process further. Key in this regard is the application of artificial intelligence techniques in order to create fake, but seemingly authentic, videos. Synthetic videos, commonly known as 'deepfakes,' can be created to modify content, and to place the image of someone seamlessly into an existing video.[37] Other artificial intelligence techniques can be used to create entirely new content. Researchers at the University of Washington, for instance, created a speech by former US President Barack Obama entirely from scratch.[38] Countering these

[36] See *Citizen Lab*, 'Tainted Leaks: Disinformation and Phishing with a Russian Nexus' (25 May 2017) https://citizenlab.ca/2017/05/tainted-leaks-disinformation-phish/ accessed 17 December 2018.

[37] Sven Charleer, 'Family Fun with Deepfakes: Or How I Got My Wife onto the Tonight Show' *Medium* (2 February 2018) https://towardsdatascience.com/family-fun-with-deepfakes-or-how-i-got-my-wife-onto-the-tonight-show-a4454775c011 accessed 18 June 2018.

[38] Jennifer Langston, 'Lip-syncing Obama: New Tools Turn Audio Clips into Realistic Video' *University of Washington News* (11 July 2017) https://www.washington.edu/news/2017/07/11/lip-syncing-obama-new-tools-turn-audio-clips-into-realistic-video/ accessed 18 June 2018.

new forms of faked material will add complexity to investigator's tasks, including expertise in video forensics.

2.3 Security Risks

As with field research, the use of open source material can entail security risks, physical and digital, especially for those who disseminate or are depicted in the material (see Chapter 13).

The most formidable challenge is obtaining informed consent from individuals to distribute images in which they are portrayed—this means making certain the person understands how the images will be used and the risks involved and agrees without coercion or offer of benefits to the images' use. During field research, that consent is typically obtained in person, when the details of the situation can be evaluated and discussed. During open source investigations, contacting that person, or the person who originally recorded the material, might not be possible. If contact is possible, the remote nature of the conversation (and potential digital security threat it entails) might prevent a thorough examination of the attendant risks.

Whenever possible, human rights investigators have an obligation to try to contact a person to get informed consent to distribute their image publicly. When this is not possible, as is often the case, serious deliberation is required to determine whether the material should be disseminated. The questions to ask include: (1) Did the subjects of the photo/video know they were being recorded and consent to that? (2) Did the subjects understand the material would be widely disseminated? (3) Do the subjects face any potential risks from further dissemination of the material or its use in a human rights investigation? and (4) If so, what are those risks and how might they be mitigated (such as by blurring faces, distorting voices, or altering background visuals)?

If human rights investigators believe that the distribution of open source material will likely place a person at risk—and they are not able to get informed consent from that person—then the material should *not be distributed*. To do so would violate the principle of 'do no harm'.

The threshold for disseminating potentially risky material is lower for vulnerable groups, such as minorities, children and people with disabilities, who in many contexts can less effectively defend themselves by speaking out against abuse, generating media coverage, getting political protection, or seeking legal redress.

Another type of risk is faced by the investigators themselves and their colleagues: potential secondary trauma from looking at disturbing material. Numerous studies show that exposure to such violent and disturbing material can, especially over time, have a serious impact on a person's well-being, and in some cases cause secondary trauma, with symptoms including sleeplessness, anxiety, and even PTSD. Those who will be viewing such material should receive proper training and support on how to minimize the risks and how to handle stress if it arises.[39] This includes not just investigators but others on the team who will view the material.

[39] For further discussion on this area see ch 12.

3. Conclusion

The use of open source material does not offer a magic pill. It does not solve many of the complex challenges that investigations may face, and it entails certain risks. But human rights organizations and other investigators would be remiss if they failed fully to explore the information that open source material can provide. At times this material might be the sole source of information. In best case scenarios it is combined with field research and other methods to help reconstruct a full and accurate account of violations that convince the public, policymakers and, if relevant, judicial bodies tasked with holding perpetrators to account.

15

Open Source Investigations for Legal Accountability

Challenges and Best Practices

*Alexa Koenig and Lindsay Freeman**

A milestone in the practice of international criminal law was marked on 15 August 2017. That day, the International Criminal Court issued a warrant of arrest for a person of interest—Mahmoud Mustafa Busayf Al-Werfalli of Libya[1]—that relied primarily on information derived from social media as the basis for the warrant. Legal scholars lauded this milestone as an important step in strengthening the use of digital content to secure accountability for human rights abuses and grave international crimes.[2]

Using publicly accessible online resources to support criminal and civil human rights cases is a relatively new practice, but as the chapters in this book show, one that is advancing quickly. Various international and national courts are beginning to recognize the potential value of cooperating with 'first responders', who frequently reach crime scenes long before international criminal investigators, the latter of whom may face diplomatic, legal, and/or pragmatic barriers to accessing such sites.[3] Civil society actors—journalists, grass roots activists, and others—may also be the first to locate and acquire relevant content in *digital* space. This suggests there may be significant value in facilitating cooperation between legal actors and civil society actors to maximize the quality of digital information used as evidence. Increasingly, civil society organizations are using social media and user-generated content in their documentation of human rights violations—experimenting with online research methods to identify relevant material, preserve information that may become critical evidence in future prosecutions and is at risk of being removed, or identifying potential witnesses to events.[4]

* This chapter is based on research that the authors conducted with Eric Stover at the Human Rights Center at the University of California, Berkeley School of Law to support publication of an International Protocol on Open Source Investigations, which is being considered for co-publication with the United Nations Office of the High Commissioner for Human Rights in 2020.

[1] International Criminal Court (ICC), *Situation in Libya: In the case of Prosecutor v Mahmoud Mustafa Busayf Al-Werfalli* (Warrant of Arrest) ICC-01/11-01/17 (15 August 2017) https://www.icc-cpi.int/CourtRecords/CR2017_05031.PDF.

[2] See eg Lindsay Freeman, 'Digital Evidence and War Crimes Prosecutions: The Impact of Digital Technologies on International Criminal Investigations and Trials' (2018) 41 Fordham International Law Journal 282; Emma Irving, 'And So It Begins . . . Social Media Evidence in an Arrest Warrant' *Opinio Juris* (17 August 2018).

[3] Silviana Cocan, Joseph Rikhof, and Érick Sullivan, 'Prosecuting International Crime Series: Defining Legal Concepts and Frameworks' (2018) 2 PKI Global Justice Journal 16; Andrea Lampros, Alexa Koenig, Stephen Smith Cody, and Julia Raynor, *First Responders: An International Workshop on Collecting and Analyzing Evidence of International Crimes* (Human Rights Center 2014).

[4] Cocan, Rikhof, and Sullivan (n 3).

However, such cooperation faces several barriers, including lack of training and guidance about how to identify what digital content might have evidentiary value in legal proceedings, how to collect and preserve digital content to a forensic standard, and how to maintain data in an archive that perserves its authenticity and makes it easily accessible to the appropriate end user (in this case, legal investigators).[5]

Interest in such cooperation has motivated the development of diverse guidance designed to help mature open source investigations as a branch of respeted legal practice.[6] The guides that have been developed so far have been organized to help ensure admissibility in court as well as maximize the judicial weight accorded to verified content. They also serve as a basis for training lawyers, investigators, judges, and first responders who document atrocities; strengthen due process (for example, by supporting thorough verification and peer review to help ensure accuracy); and encourage best practices around everything from data generation to data handling to presentation in court.

While this area of practice is still relatively new, the past couple of years have seen its critical growth. For example, in October 2017 a number of experts in international criminal law and open source investigations met in Bellagio, Italy to discuss the need to develop a common lexicon, set of principles and other guidance to standardize open source investigations to generate lead, linkage and crime-based evidence for courts. The goal was to bring clarity to open source investigations as a set of practices and ultimately enhance recognition of both their limitations and their utility as a tool for supporting victims and ensuring justice. In spring 2018, a team of experts (the authors of this chapter among them) drew from the definitions and principles identified at Bellagio to begin developing a manual to support the effective use of open source information for the investigation and prosecution of human rights violations and atrocity crimes, a manual that could be globally disseminated in the form of an international protocol.

2. Big Picture Considerations

Legal investigators ideally gather three types of information when building cases: (1) physical evidence (such as the murder weapon, or soil samples), (2) testimonial evidence (witnesses' stories, expert testimony), and (3) documentary evidence (contracts, written orders, photographs, videos, etc). As an increasing amount of communications use digital channels, lawyers have begun to recognize the extraordinary value of web-based information for corroborating other evidence and filling holes in their evidentiary records. As noted by Lindsay Freeman in Chapter 3, such digital information usually (but not always) falls into the category of documentary information. Such online data can be a critical source of lead information (that which 'leads' a lawyer or legal investigator to additional sources), linkage evidence (that which 'links' low-level perpetrators, such as 'trigger pullers' to commanding generals, or presidents of countries), and contextual information that helps to paint the 'who, what, when, where, why and how' of the incidents underlying case. The objective of

[5] See chs 6, 7, and 9 in this volume.

[6] See eg Kelly Matheson, *Video as Evidence Field Guide WITNESS, 2016*; *International Protocol on Open Source Investigations: A Manual on the Use of Online Open Source Information for the Investigation and Prosecution of Human Rights Violations and International Crimes* (Human Rights Center 2019).

any legal investigation is to get sufficient corroborating information—ideally from each of these three information buckets—to establish each element of a crime so that in a criminal proceeding any alleged wrongdoing by the accused can be proven beyond a reasonable doubt, and in a civil case, so it can be established through a preponderance of the evidence.

2.1 Underlying Principles of Using Open Sources in Legal Investigations

The emerging practice of conducting online open source investigations for legal accountability is founded on—and ideally reflects—several principles. Some of these are common to all online open source investigations, while others are tied to some of the heightened considerations that arise when using online open source content in a legal context.[7] At a minimum, these principles include security, impartiality, independence, accountability, legality, preservation, and equality, as summarized below.

2.1.1 Security

One of the first considerations when gathering online open source information to support legal accountability is security.[8] Before designing an evidence collection plan that includes online open source content, an investigator should think through the potential physical, digital and psycho-social security risks that may result from accessing, viewing and handling open source information. For example, how can investigators best protect their identity—and thus the physical or digital security of their colleagues, anyone identified in the materials, the uploader(s), and themselves—when combing social media platforms for information related to a person of interest? Will they potentially reveal information that endangers the confidentiality of the investigation or the identity of possible witnesses? If members of the team have to comb through large volumes of graphic content, is there a plan in place, as Chapter 12 suggests, to strengthen resiliency and mitigate the likelihood of trauma? Once information is captured from the internet, how should it be stored so that investigators (1) can locate the needed information later, (2) preserve chain of custody (by logging who acquired the information, from where, and when), and (3) maximize data security?

2.1.2 Impartiality

Any strong legal investigation includes a plan for mitigating—and ideally eliminating—bias. This may mean employing multiple working hypotheses (developing multiple theories of the case) to avoid biased data collection and analysis; trying to prove the null hypothesis (for example, that the accused was innocent as opposed to guilty); and collecting both incriminating and exonerating data without favour. Search terms should be designed to maximize the likelihood of finding relevant and probative information without a preference

[7] The following overview of principles and practices was derived from two sources: Alexa Koenig, *The New Forensics: Using Open Source Information to Investigate Grave Crimes* (Human Rights Center 2018) and *International Protocol on Open Source Investigations: A Manual on the Use of Online Open Source Information for the Investigation and Prosecution of Human Rights Violations and International Crimes* (draft protocol on file with the authors).

[8] See ch 13 in this volume.

to benefiting either the prosecution or defense—as should the choice of which platforms to search. Impartiality can be further strengthened by having team mates primed to check for bias and/or conducting some form of internal or external peer review. While rarely feasible, the gold standard from a research perspective would be to conduct some form of double blind review, where neither the original investigators' identity nor that of the reviewers is known to each other.

2.1.3 Independence

Legal investigations must be independent of the personal or professional interests of any particular individual or institution and safeguarded from the actual or perceived appearance of outside influence. For non-governmental organizations, this may mean limiting or rejecting funding from governments or individuals that may have an interest in the outcome of one or more cases under investigation. This principle helps safeguard the perceived legitimacy of the investigation and the court in which the materials are eventually used.

2.1.4 Accountability

The principle of accountability is related to the potential replicability of the underlying analysis. Replicability is the basis for most scientific information and thus a critical factor for introducing information as scientific evidence in court. This principle is closely tied to transparency, specifically the transparency of the underlying methods that were used to access content and reach particular conclusions. Such transparency is intended to empower outside observers to analyse the potential validity of the results and the appropriateness of the methods used. To maximize potential acceptance as evidence for court purposes, investigators should log every step in their discovery and verification process and maintain the chain of custody of captured materials. At a minimum, this can be done by noting who handled the materials, when, and what they did with them.

2.1.5 Legality

The legality of the investigation (and any consequences for illegality) depends on the specific jurisdiction in which one is practicing and/or in which the open source materials may be submitted as evidence. To further maximize the likelihood that the findings of their research will be accepted in court, investigators and lawyers should review and understand the rules of evidence for the jurisdiction in which they are practicing and/or to which they will be submitting the information they collect.[9]

Many open source investigators violate the terms of service of the platforms they search by establishing a dummy account to protect their identity, even though that platform requires that individuals be transparent about who they are. Investigators should note whether such practices, or whether any laws that might be transgressed (such as violation of privacy regulations), could result in the exclusion of critical information. While international courts such as the ICC often have fairly lenient admissibility rules, even there, materials can be excluded if the collection process threatens the collected materials' reliability or inflicts 'serious damage on the integrity of the proceedings'.[10] For example, information

[9] See eg Louise Arbour, 'In Our Name and on Our Behalf' (2006) 55 International and Comparative Law Quarterly 511.

[10] Rome Statute, arts 55, 69.

that the court believes was obtained in violation of human rights is supposed to be excluded, and privacy violations may well fall within the ambit of human rights. Under Article 68 of the Rome Statute—the body of laws that underlies the ICC—the investigator and lawyer are also mandated to protect victims and witnesses, court staff, and the public.

2.1.6 Preservation of Evidence

Preservation of open source evidence raises a number of critical issues for investigators and lawyers. First, *how* should information be stored? Increasingly, social media sites are being scraped or information from the internet is being crowdsourced, resulting in large data sets. How that information is tagged and coded will have concrete ethical and pragmatic ramifications, ranging from whether relevant and probative information can be located when needed, to the amount of time that must be expended to review potentially relevant materials. There are also chain-of-custody considerations (who has had access to the information and whether that information has been subsequently manipulated). The investigator should also note any information that is critical to authentication (for example, time and date stamps, as well as the identity of the machine on which the information was captured and the relevant URLs). Ideally, investigators will capture and preserve the source code underlying the online content. Such careful documentation may provide a certain degree of self-authentication of the evidence and thus may minimize the need for the investigator to testify about a particular piece of content in court.

2.1.7 Equality

Another consideration for human rights investigators and lawyers is the extent to which an open source investigation may influence which crimes are charged and which are virtually ignored because less visible and accessible. Will a heavy reliance on online open source investigations strengthen certain charges (such as chemical weapons attacks) to the exclusion of others (such as sexual violence) that may be less likely to be captured on film or discussed on chat sites? Will crimes or other harms perpetrated against certain demographics (for example, men, or people in technologically sophisticated countries) drown out equally important and perhaps even more pervasive crimes that target less advantaged groups? Investigators and lawyers should consider as well whether their familiarity with certain platforms (for example, Facebook, or YouTube) means that they will give scant attention to less common sources of information where relevant content may be located (such as WeChat or Sina Weibo in China, or Orkut in Brazil).

2.1.8 Ethics

A final note on ethics: As discussed in Chapter 11, ethical considerations are relevant not only to open source information collection for human rights generally, but also to human rights cases. There are, in addition, ethical considerations at each stage of the investigative and prosecution process, which differ based on jurisdiction and other content. Both investigators and lawyers should be aware of those considerations and how they affect public and legal acceptance of open source investigations practices.[11]

[11] For more information on an ethical framework relevant to open source investigations, please see the International Protocol on Open Source Investigations.

2.2 Investigative Processes

There are a number of process considerations that should also be incorporated into designing an online open source investigation that may feed into legal cases. These range from preparation for the investigation, through discovery, to acquisition and preservation of content, to analysis and presentation in court—and of course on through the full data life cycle. Common practices around each of these stages are nascent, dynamic, and evolving. Thus, the considerations touched on below are a starting place for practice but are not comprehensive.

2.2.1 Preparation

As with any legal process, investigators should develop a plan of attack in order to maximize the efficiency and efficacy of their work.

Investigators should distinguish between background, exploratory research intended to provide general information about a situation, and formal investigatory work aimed at identifying, collecting, and analysing information that's relevant to a particular legal situation or case and may serve as evidence. Formal investigatory work raises documentation and disclosure requirements from which exploratory research is generally exempt.

Plan objectives include (1) defining the investigation's scope; (2) articulating objectives; (3) defining the universe of potentially helpful sources; and (4) designing digital, psychosocial and physical security protocols. In terms of substance, the plan should incorporate a search strategy designed around a relevant research question,[12] which helps focus and guide the investigation. This research question should incorporate multiple working hypotheses in order to limit the potential for biasing the investigation from the outset—confirmation bias (the non-objective interpretation of information in a manner that confirms one's pre-existing beliefs) is a risk in all investigations, but a particularly acute one in online investigations.

The plan should also document initial search queries that include specific terms (with keywords charted in all relevant languages), locations, coordinates, individuals, hashtags, platforms, and the like. The plan should also incorporate some thinking about the various crimes that may be relevant to the situation under investigation—and the elements of those crimes—as well as the various types of evidence that may be helpful to proving each element (physical, documentary and testimonial evidence being the 'big three'). For example, if a case includes a charge of genocide—which often hinges on whether a prosecutor can prove the accused had an intent to 'destroy in whole or in part an ethnic, national, racial or religious group'—is there online material that suggests that the accused had such genocidal intent, such as tweets or Facebook posts calling for the destruction of particular populations?

The individuals designing the plan should be aware that platform use may vary dramatically between geographic locations and between populations within geographic locations (for example, based on age or gender, with populations varying in their access to and comfort level with various digital resources). Thus, investigators should map the technological landscape of the conflict or issues under investigation, including an overview of the demographics of those who use each of the technologies, and incorporate those insights into their

[12] Anthony Olcott, *Open Source Intelligence in a Networked World* (Continuum 2012).

investigations plan. Many open source investigators have particular facility with certain platforms over others; conducting a technology mapping exercise before commencing research will mitigate the risk of discovery blind spots and biasing the discovery of relevant data to favour content on one platform over others.

Finally, the plan should outline the processes, including any tools, that the investigator or investigative team will use to locate, preserve, and analyse captured data. For example, investigators will ideally incorporate mechanisms for anonymous internet browsing and even the manual or automated collection of websites that are visited during the course of the formal investigation. If the investigation is being conducted by a team, there needs to be a plan for the safe sharing of relevant data and rapid communication as new leads and information are uncovered.

2.2.2 Discovery

Legal investigators often engage in three types of discovery: (1) monitoring (e.g. following a topic, conflict, or set of variables over time); (2) exploring (conducting research to better understand a conflict or topic); and (3) systematically gathering information (the formal stage of an investigation).

Monitoring refers to keeping on top of what is coming out over social media related to a particular situation as it is unfolding and as a means to help ensure critical information about people and incidents is not overlooked.

Exploring is a scoping exercise that often takes place prior to commencing formal fact-finding activities. This will often occur as part of a preliminary examination or when deciding if an open source investigation may be helpful to an incident under investigation. It consists of determining which platforms might be relevant and/or helpful, and what kinds of information may be available.

With *planned information gathering,* investigators may choose to start from a very narrow inquiry that broadens with the accumulation of information or start broadly and narrow down. Which is most helpful or appropriate will vary based on the information already in hand and the particulars of a case. Especially important is that investigators isolate the task from their personal browsing activities and record every step of the investigative process so that any member of the investigative team can testify to the process if needed. In addition to making the investigation easier to track and record, this will ensure a clean search history if that is ultimately reviewed as part of the disclosure process.

2.2.3 Acquisition and Preservation

Acquisition consists of identification of relevant online material; preliminary review of that content; and collection. Acquisition is followed by preservation.

Identification consists of finding and accessing relevant content. The potential evidentiary value of some content will be immediately apparent, while others may not be as clear cut. As online, digital content is ephemeral—and is at risk of removal if graphic or otherwise violative of platform community standards or terms of service—it is especially important to capture and preserve such information if it may conceivably be critical to later legal processes. If content is relevant on its face and at high risk of deletion, the information should be captured using the best method that time constraints allow. This may mean simply screenshotting the information and/or dropping the URL into a website (such as Internet Archive), or using a tool to capture the information in an evidentiarily-sound manner (such as Hunchly and Digital Evidence Vault). If the relevance and probative value are not immediately obvious, then the investigator may want to note the content but delay acquisition. While some investigators collect everything that may be relevant and analyse that content later, that method often results in over collection (bogging down the analysis and documentation process at later stages) and may violate data minimisation principles.

Best practices for capturing web pages vary and are evolving quickly. Once a digital asset has been located, investigators should connect to a time server to ensure their computer clock is accurate and document that accuracy; log their IP address (which will help establish that they were connected to the internet at a particular date and time through a particular computer); and download, screenshot, PDF, scrape or otherwise 'capture' the data that they want to collect. Collection is the moment when the investigator takes custody of the content. Collection may be mass and automatic (using specialized programs designed for online capture), itemized and semi-automatic (relying on custom or commercial scripts), or itemized and manual. Investigators should be aware that the method employed at this stage may have a later bearing on both admissibility and the weight accorded the content in court.

A forensic capture of the information will include metadata, content, and context. Best practices potentially include hashing or blockchain registration to preserve the original and demonstrate that the item—as presented in court—has not been modified from the original.[13]

Finally, if information is at risk of take down, the investigator may want to work with law enforcement or other official authorities to issue a subpoena or preservation order for that content. When not affiliated with a legal authority, it may still be worth reaching out to the platform to encourage preservation.

Once acquired, the content should be added to a secure online server with redundant offline back-ups (see Chapter 7). At this point, standard digital forensic methods should be employed to preserve the integrity of the digital evidence and document the chain of custody.

Some basic principles to keep in mind during the collection and preservation process:

(1) Locate and preserve the original or 'first post' of a particular item if possible.
(2) Collect information in as close to real time as possible.
(3) Preserve, if possible, all relevant metadata, links, networks, content and comments, manually or via scraping (although in the latter case, make sure that scraping will not destroy the data's admissibility since scraping often violates terms of service).
(4) Preserve chain of custody, manually or automatically.
(5) Preserve the 'original' content and work on a copy.
(6) Organize, store, and code the data so that it can be located when needed.

When organizing archived data, it is often best not to organize the data around potential charges unless those charges are known. More helpful is tagging for the location depicted in the content (whether with geo-coordinates or the name of the city, town, etc) and the date of capture and/or of the events or people depicted in the content (when known, so that the content can be tied to a particular incident), and briefly describing what the contents include.[14]

[13] See ch 7 in this volume.

[14] For a more detailed overview of basic archiving principles, see chapter 7 in this volume.

One final note on acquisition and preservation: it is important to avoid overcollection, for a number of reasons. First, in legal contexts, much of what is gathered may be subject to discovery by the opposing side. Therefore, data collection should be thoughtful—over-collecting can be strategically and logistically problematic, as well as costly, when that information has to be disclosed. Second, as noted above, over-collection creates a 'volume' problem, draining data storage capacities and potentially obscuring critical evidence in relatively valueless content.

2.2.4 Analysis

Analysis refers to 'the process of reviewing, evaluating and interpreting factual information or evidence to develop substantive findings relevant to the investigation, and reporting those findings to support strategic, operational and legal decision-making' (International Protocol). Assessments should include the following questions:

- How is this content relevant? (How does this content relate to any dispute at issue in an investigation or trial?) Note that relevancy may shift over the course of a legal investigation.
- Is this item authentic? (Is it what it purports to be? Has this item been faked, forged, staged, manipulated or misrepresented?) This step may include a review of both content and the content's provenance.
- Is this item complete? (Have you captured the entire video, full web page, etc?) Partial documents may be excluded at trial for lack of completeness.
- If this is not the original, can you explain why not and establish an acceptable reason for using a copy?
- Is this information reliable? In addition to analysing the content, you may want to check the reliability of the poster by reviewing their posting history, related accounts, apparent proximity to the events at the time in question, online networks, and any other corroborating information they may have posted.
- Can you identify the original source of the information and is that source credible? (Has the source lied in the past? Does the source have any apparent biases or affiliations that create an appearance of bias?)
- What is this content's probative value? This requires developing inferences from the data. The content may, for example, be helpful to establish basic facts including the geographic location of a particular incident, to identify social networks, to determine patterns of criminality (that may, for example, speak to legal issues such as whether a particular act was 'systematic and widespread' and thus potentially a crime against humanity), to establish intent or other state of mind, and so on.

2.2.5 Presentation

One of the greatest areas of experimentation with this new type of evidence is the way in which it may be presented—from analytical reports introduced through an expert witness to more creative demonstrative displays. Another milestone in international criminal law that precedes the ICC's *Al-Werfalli* arrest warrant was the open source investigations report developed in support of the *Al-Mahdi* case from Mali, as discussed in Chapter 2. In *Prosecutor v. Al-Mahdi*, the Senior Trial Lawyer for the prosecution used an interactive digital platform created by SITU Research in his opening statement (see Chapter 2). The platform combined satellite imagery, ground-level images, and 360-degree panoramic photography on a map to show the relationship between various mausoleiums that had been damaged or destroyed.[15] Al-Mahdi's guilty plea meant that this platform and accompanying expert reports supporting the geolocation of the imagery was never tested as a form of evidence, disappointing those who were eagerly waiting to see how the chambers would respond.

When presenting an open source investigation report in court, there are two dominant risks. One is that the relevant finders of fact (whether judge or jury) may be so dazzled by the interplay of technologies (such as the use of satellite imagery to corroborate the location of events depicted in several videos, further supported by social media posts that confirm the likely presence of the purported source, for example) that they overvalue the investigation report. They may not know how to interrogate the underlying materials or analysis and thus over-credit the report as depicting the 'truth' (much as has been seen with DNA analysis, which is now known to be fallible in certain circumstances but has historically been portrayed as a conclusive 'silver bullet'). The second risk is that fact-finders who are not familiar with the underlying technologies or methodologies will be concerned about their ability to evaluate the report and therefore will discard or otherwise undervalue the report in their decision-making. Thus, it is critical that the presentation of the results of an open source investigation be as clearly and carefully explained as possible. From a due process perspective, it is important that both prosecution and defense (or claimant and respondent), as well as the judge or jury, have the basic skills to adequately evaluate the relevant information.

Beyond how the report is compiled, a second issue is who is best situated to serve as a witness. Open source investigative reports may reflect the work of multiple parties. Issues include whether an expert needs to speak to particular parts of the report, or whether individuals could be certified as generalized 'open source investigators' who can speak not only to the individual methodologies but the overall analysis.

Several prosecutors have suggested that there should be one individual who is designated as the potential expert who could be called to speak to the report. That person should be informed about every stage of the investigation and analysis so that they can answer any concerns about the authenticity of the report and the validity of its findings. As with any expert witness, an individual may be called to provide expert testimony if an expert with the necessary 'knowledge, skill, experience, training, or education', in which case, in the words of US Rule of Evidence 702, the individual

> may testify in the form of an opinion or otherwise if a) the expert's scientific, technical or other specialized knowledge will help the trier of fact to understand the evidence or to determine a fact in issue; b) the testimony is based on sufficient facts or data; c) the testimony is the product of reliable principles and methods; and d) the expert has reliably applied the principles and methods to the facts of the case.[16]

[15] Freeman, Digital Evidence and War Crimes Prosecutions, p. 312, 316: "When the testimony is this specialized and technical, judges are put in the difficult position of either rejecting it because they do not understand it or accepting the conclusions without qualification—both dangerous propositions for the interests of justice."

[16] United States Federal Rule of Evidence 702.

The significance of qualifying a witness as an expert is two-fold—it allows that witness to testify beyond the scope of his or her first-hand account and to give opinions, which witnesses are normally not allowed to provide to the Court.

A third issue is the *form* that presentation takes. Depending on the technical capacities of the courtroom, the report may range from a text-based report to a multi-source video or an interactive platform. One option is to compile the content derived from open source material, along with any corroborating data and relevant information derived from closed resources, into an expert report that may be submitted as evidence at trial. Such reports should include, at a minimum, an executive summary, a methodology section that identifies all steps taken to collect and analyse the information, and the information itself. The report should not include conclusions unless written by a qualified expert witness who can testify as to how those conclusions were reached. The report should be written for a layperson so that it can be understood by a judge, attorneys, or defendants without specialized expertise.

3. The Future—What Comes Next

Much as DNA and satellite imagery analysis had to evolve as fields of practice and gain legitimacy recognition by courts,[17] open source investigations have to be standardized and a community of peers established before they will be deemed similarly reliable by judges. That evolution is still in its early stages but holds tremendous promise for diversifying the kinds of content that can be relied upon to hold war crimes perpetrators, human rights violators, and others who commit grave international crimes to account. Perhaps one of the biggest risks is that an increasing amount of communication will move behind 'closed doors' (for example, onto encrypted private messaging apps like Signal or WhatsApp instead of on publicly accessible sites) and thus an increasing amount of critical evidence that might have once been in the public domain will be inaccessible to human rights investigators. However, as long as perpetrators brag about their exploits, or reach out broadly for recruitment purposes, their work will leak into the open. It is up to the international community to develop the necessary standards and advance the methodologies that make up open source investigations if such work will reach its potential to produce critical evidence for courts.

4. Conclusion

While open sources have long played an important role in information gathering for evidentiary purposes, digital technologies are emerging and changing so rapidly that it is difficult to stay on top of all of the ways that open sources can support case development. Formalizing and disseminating open source methods as a means to contribute to the successful adjudication of human rights cases is vital. As more and more communication moves online, it will be increasingly important for lawyers and legal investigators to understand

[17] Jonathan Drake and Theresa Harris, *Geospatial Evidence in International Human Rights Litigation: Technical and Legal Considerations* (AAAS 2018).

the diverse online locations in which relevant information sharing is happening. Justice depends on the international community, including legal actors, knowing how to find, preserve, analyse, and present that key information to support witness testimony in ways that meet evidentiary standards and thus have weight in court. Soon, open source investigations may no longer be optional and/or supplementary to the ethical practice of law, but central to and required for achieving justice.

Select Bibliography

Aahsberg F and others, 'Introductory Guide to Open Source Intelligence and Digital Verification' (University of Essex Human Rights Centre Clinic 2017).

Allcott H and Gentzkow M, 'Social Media and Fake News in the 2016 Election' (2017) 31 Journal of Economic Perspectives 211.

Alston P, 'Introduction: Third Generation Human Rights Fact-Finding' Proceedings of the Annual Meeting (American Society of International Law) (2013).

Alston P and Knuckey S, 'The Transformation of Human Rights Fact-Finding: Challenges and Opportunities' in P Alston and S Knuckey (eds), *The Transformation of Human Rights Fact-Finding* (Oxford University Press 2016).

Amnesty International, 'Cameroon's Secret Torture Chambers: Human Rights Violations and War Crimes in the Fight against Boko Haram' (2017) 13.

Amnesty International, 'We Leave or We Die: Forced Displacement under Syria's 'Reconciliation' Agreements' (2017).

Amnesty International and Forensic Architecture, 'Black Friday: Carnage in Rafah during 2014 Israel/Gaza Conflict' https://blackfriday.amnesty.org accessed 8 December 2018.

Anderson C, 'Syrian Rebel Gets Life Sentence for Mass Killing Caught on Video' *The New York Times* (22 December 2017) https://www.nytimes.com/2017/02/16/world/europe/syrian-rebel-haisam-omar-sakhanh-sentenced.html accessed 11 December 2018.

Arnstein SR, 'A Ladder of Citizen Participation' (1969) 35 Journal of the American Planning Association 216.

Aronson JD, 'Computer Vision and Machine Learning for Human Rights Video Analysis: Case Studies, Possibilities, Concerns, and Limitations' (2018) 43 Law and Social Inquiry 1188.

Asher-Schapiro A, 'YouTube and Facebook Are Removing Evidence of Atrocities, Jeopardizing Cases against War Criminals' *The Intercept* (2 November 2017) https://theintercept.com/2017/11/02/war-crimes-youtube-facebook-syria-rohingya/ accessed 21 October 2019.

Barry A, 'Political Situations: Knowledge Controversies in Transnational Governance' (2012) 6 Critical Policy Studies 324.

Bassiouni MC and Abraham C (eds), *Siracusa Guidelines for International, Regional and National Fact-Finding Bodies* (Intersentia 2013).

Beach B, 'How Long Do Disk Drives Last?' *Backblaze Blog* (12 November 2013) https://www.backblaze.com/blog/how-long-do-disk-drives-last/ accessed 29 December 2018.

Bean H, 'Is Open Source Intelligence an Ethical Issue?' in Susan Maret (ed), *Government Secrecy (Research in Social Problems and Public Policy, Volume 19)* (Emerald Group Publishing Limited 2011) 394.

Beaumont P, 'Video Footage Indicates Killed Palestinian Youths Posed No Threat' *The Guardian* (20 May 2014).

Bellingcat, 'How a Werfalli Execution Site Was Geolocated' (10 March 2017) https://www.bellingcat.com/news/mena/2017/10/03/how-an-execution-site-was-geolocated/ accessed 20 December 2018.

Bentham J, 'An Introduction to the Principles of Morals and Legislation', first published in 1789, http://www.koeblergerhard.de/Fontes/BenthamJeremyMoralsandLegislation1789.pdf accessed 21 October 2019.

Berger S, 'The Evolving Ethics of Preservation: Redefining Practices and Responsibilities in the 21st Century' in RJ Black (ed), The Voices of the Future (Routledge 2009) 67.

Blackwell A and others, 'Computer Says "Don't Know": Interacting Visually with Incomplete AI Models' (2018) https://digital.lib.washington.edu/researchworks/bitstream/handle/1773/42857/DTSHPS18-Proceedings-final%20v2.pdf?sequence=8&isAllowed=y accessed 2 January 2019.

Bois WEB du and Anderson E, *The Philadelphia Negro: A Social Study* (Reprint edn, University of Pennsylvania Press 1995).

Bourdieu P, 'Cultural Reproduction and Social Reproduction' in J Karabel and AH Halsey (eds), *Power and Ideology in Education* (Oxford University Press 1977) 487–511.

boyd d and Marwick A, 'Social Privacy in Networked Publics: Teens' Attitudes, Practices, and Strategies,' paper given at Oxford Internet Institute 'Decade in Time' Conference (2011).

Brachman JM, '*High-Tech Terror: Al-Qaeda's Use of New Technology*' (2006) 30(2) Fletcher Forum of World Affairs 149.

Bridle J, Citizen Ex [Website] (2016) http://citizen-ex.com/stories/io accessed 3 September 2018.

Brown University, 'Making Choices: A Framework for Making Ethical Decisions' Brown.Edu (2013) 1 https://www.brown.edu/academics/science-and-technology-studies/framework-making-ethical-decision accessed 11 May 2018.

Bruno I, Didier E, and Vitale T, 'Statactivism: Forms of Action between Disclosure and Affirmation: Partecipazione e Conflitto' (2014) 7(2) The Open Journal of Sociopolitical Studies 198.

Bruns A, 'Facebook Shuts the Gate after the Horse Has Bolted, and Hurts Real Research in the Process' *Internet Policy Review* (2018) https://policyreview.info/articles/news/facebook-shuts-gate-after-horse-has-bolted-and-hurts-real-research-process/786 accessed 9 May 2018.

Burgis T, 'Chile's Torture Victims to Get Life Pensions' *The Guardian* (30 November 2004) https://www.theguardian.com/world/2004/nov/30/chile accessed 11 December 2018.

de Busser E, 'Open Source Data and Criminal Investigations: Anything You Publish Can and Will Be Used against You' (2014) 2 Groningen Journal of International Law 90.

Cadwalladr C and Graham-Harrison E, 'Revealed: 50 million Facebook Profiles Harvested for Cambridge Analytica in Major Data Breach' *The Guardian* (17 March 2008) https://www.theguardian.com/news/2018/mar/17/cambridge-analytica-facebook-influence-us-election accessed 29 August 2018.

Cairo A, 'Emotional Data Visualization: Periscopic's "U.S. Gun Deaths" and the Challenge of Uncertainty' *Peachpit* (3 April 2013) http://www.peachpit.com/articles/article.aspx?p=2036558 accessed 16 December 2018.

Chadwick P, 'Don't Let Data Protection Undermine Journalism' *The Guardian* (10 June 2018) https://www.theguardian.com/commentisfree/2018/jun/10/data-protection-press-freedom accessed 10 August 2018.

Charleer S, 'Family Fun with Deepfakes: Or How I Got My Wife onto the Tonight Show' *Medium* (2 February 2018) https://towardsdatascience.com/family-fun-with-deepfakes-or-how-i-got-my-wife-onto-the-tonight-show-a4454775c011 accessed 18 June 2018.

Chen J, 'What Is an API and Why Does It Matter?' *Sprout Social* (31 January 2018) https://sproutsocial.com/insights/what-is-an-api/ accessed 11 December 2018.

Chesney R and Citron DK, 'Deep Fakes: A Looming Challenge for Privacy, Democracy, and National Security' (2018) 107 California Law Review https://papers.ssrn.com/sol3/papers.cfm?abstract_id=3213954.

Clark AM and Sikkink K, 'Information Effects and Human Rights Data: Is the Good News about Increased Human Rights Information Bad News for Human Rights Measures?' (2013) 35(3) Human Rights Quarterly 539, 541.

Cole A, 'Technology for Truth: The Next Generation of Evidence' *International Justice Monitor* (18 March 2015) https://www.ijmonitor.org/2015/03/technology-for-truth-the-next-generation-of-evidence/ accessed 29 December 2018.

Combs NA, *Fact-Finding without Facts: The Uncertain Evidentiary Foundations of International Criminal* Convictions (Cambridge University Press 2010) 16.

Consultative Committee for Space Data Systems, Reference Model for an Open Archival Information System (OAIS) Recommended Practice CCSDS 650.0-M-2 Magenta Book, (June 2012) https://public.ccsds.org/pubs/650x0m2.pdf.

Cox J, 'Dodgy "Hackers" Target Bellingcat Investigators Who Call BS on Moscow' The Daily Beast (17 November 2017) https://www.thedailybeast.com/polish-hackers-target-investigators-who-call-bs-on-moscow accessed 9 May 2018.

CrossTrax, 'Preparing Open Source Intelligence (OSINT) for Litigation' (November 2016).

Cryer R and others, *An Introduction to International Criminal Law and Procedure* (3rd edn, Cambridge University Press 2014).

Day M, 'The Long-Term Preservation of Web Content' in Julien Masanès (ed), *Web Archiving* (2006 edn, Springer 2006).

Desrosières A, *The Politics of Large Numbers: A History of Statistical Reasoning* (Camille Naish tr, Harvard University Press 2002).

D'Ignazio C and Klein LF, 'Feminist Data Visualization' *VIS4DH: 2016 Workshop on Visualization for the Digital Humanities* (2016) 3.

van Dijck J, *The Culture of Connectivity: A Critical History of Social Media* (Oxford University Press 2013).

Dougherty R, 'Documenting Revolution in the Middle East' (2011) 31 FOCUS on Global Resources https://www.crl.edu/focus/article/7435.

Douglas L, 'Film as Witness: Screening Nazi Concentration Camps before the Nuremberg Tribunal' (1995) 105 Yale Law Journal 449 https://digitalcommons.law.yale.edu/ylj/vol105/iss2/3.

Drake J and Harris T, *Geospatial Evidence in International Human Rights Litigation: Technical and Legal Considerations* (AAAS 2018).

Dubberley S 'In the Firing Line: How Amnesty's Digital Verification Corps Changed Official Narratives through Open Source Investigation' (18 May 2017) https://citizenevidence.org/category/verification-corps/ accessed 16 August 2018.

Dubberley S and Grant M, 'Journalism and Vicarious Trauma' *First Draft News* (2017) https://firstdraftnews.org/wp-content/uploads/2017/04/vicarioustrauma.pdf accessed 10 August 2018.

Duggan M, 'Online Harassment 2017' Pew Research Center: Internet, Science & Tech (11 July 2017) http://www.pewinternet.org/2017/07/11/online-harassment-2017/ accessed 11 May 2018.

Dunn A and Miller R, 'Responsible Data Leaks and Whistleblowing' *The Engine Room* (26 October 2016) https://www.theengineroom.org/responsible-data-leaks-and-whistleblowing/ accessed 12 May 2018.

Eghbal N, 'Roads and Bridges: The Unseen Labor behind Our Digital Infrastructure' (2016) 2–5 https://www.fordfoundation.org/media/2976/roads-and-bridges-the-unseen-labor-behind-our-digital-infrastructure.pdf accessed 10 May 2018.

Electronic Frontier Foundation, 'Threat Model' https://ssd.eff.org/en/glossary/threat-model accessed 24 August 2018.

Elish MC, '(Dis)Placed Workers: A Study in the Disruptive Potential of Robotics and AI' *WeRobot* (2018).

Engle Merry S, *The Seductions of Quantification: Measuring Human Rights, Gender Violence and Sex Trafficking* (University of Chicago Press 2016).

Eubanks V, *Automating Inequality: How High-Tech Tools Profile, Police, and Punish the Poor* (St Martin's Press 2017).

European Commission 'European Case Law Identifier (ECLI)' European e-justice Portal (19 July 2017) https://e-justice.europa.eu/content_european_case_law_identifier_ecli-175-en.do.

Forensic Architecture, 'Al-Jinah Mosque' https://www.forensic-architecture.org/case/al-jinah-mosque/ accessed 8 December 2018.

Forensic Architecture, 'The Killing of Nadeem Nawara and Mohammad Mahmoud Odeh Abu Daher in Nakba Day Protest outside of Beitunia on May 15th, 2014' http://beitunia.forensic-architecture.org accessed 4 June 2018.

Forensic Architecture, 'Nakba Day Killings' https://www.forensic-architecture.org/case/nakba-day-killngs/ accessed 8 December 2018.

'Foreword', Report of the Chilean National Commission on Truth and Reconciliation, vol I/II (University of Notre Dame Press 1993).

Frankenberg G, 'Human Rights and the Belief in a Just World' (2014) 12 International Journal of Constitutional Law 35

Franklin S, *Biological Relatives: IVF, Stem Cells, and the future of Kinship* (Duke University Press 2013)

Freelon D, McIlwain CD, and Clark MD, 'Beyond the Hashtags: #Ferguson, #Blacklivesmatter, and the Online Struggle for Offline Justice' Center for Media and Social Impact (2016) http://cmsimpact.org/resource/beyond-hashtags-ferguson-blacklivesmatter-online-struggle-offline-justice accessed 12 May 2018.

Gagne M and Deci EL, 'Self-determination Theory and Work Motivation' (2005) 26(4) Journal of Organizational Behavior 331.

Ghost Boat, 'How 30 Seconds of Your Time Could Help Find the Ghost Boat' *Medium* (2015) https://medium.com/ghostboat/how-30-seconds-of-your-time-could-help-find-the-ghost-boat-33bcbd7a0219 accessed 14 May 2018.

GitHub, Open Source Survey (2017) http://opensourcesurvey.org/2017/ accessed 9 May 2018, https://securityintelligence.com/tough-challenges-cybersecurity-ethics/ accessed 9 May 2018.

Guardian Research Department, '19 June 1901: The South African Concentration Camps' *The Guardian* (19 May 2011) https://www.theguardian.com/theguardian/from-the-archive-blog/2011/may/19/guardian190-south-africa-concentration-camps accessed 31 December 2018.

Guarino N, Oberle D, and Staab S, 'What Is an Ontology' in *Handbook on Ontologies* (Springer-Verlag 2009).

Guberek T and Silva E, 'Human Rights and Technology: Mapping the Landscape to Support Grantmaking' *Partners for Human Rights Information, Methodology and Analysis* (2014) https://www.fordfoundation.org/media/2541/prima-hr-tech-report.pdf accessed 3 January 2018.

Guenette Thornton I, McPherson E, and Mahmoudi M, 'No Tech, Low Tech, Slow Tech: Human Rights Practitioners' Resistance to ICT4D' [Forthcoming] International Journal of Human Rights.

Gürses S, Kundnani A, and Van Hoboken J, 'Crypto and Empire: The Contradictions of Counter-Surveillance Advocacy' (2016) 38 Media, Culture & Society 576.

Hamilton RJ, 'User-Generated Evidence' (2018) Columbia Journal of Transnational Law.

Hanus MD and Fox J, 'Assessing the Effects of Gamification In The Classroom: A Longitudinal Study on Intrinsic Motivation, Social Comparison, Satisfaction, Effort, and Academic Performance' (2015) 80 Computers & Education 152.

Harding S, 'Feminism, Science, and the Anti-Enlightenment Critiques' in Linda J Nicholson (ed), *Feminism/Postmodernism (Thinking Gender)* (Routledge 1990).

Hartmann T and Klimmt C, 'Gender and Computer Games: Exploring Females' Dislikes' (2006) 11(4) Journal of Computer-Mediated Communication 910.

Harvey C, 'Big Data Challenges' *Datamation* (5 June 2017) https://www.datamation.com/big-data/big-data-challenges.html accessed 11 December 2018.

Helliwell J, 'Open Source Intelligence: Sharing the Future of Investigations' (2016).

Hewlett Packard Enterprise, IBM and Quantum, 'What is LTO Technology?' Ultrium LTO https://www.lto.org/technology/what-is-lto-technology/.

Hill E, 'Opinion: Silicon Valley Can't Be Trusted with Our History' *Buzzfeed* (2018) https://www.buzzfeed.com/evanhill/silicon-valley-cant-be-trusted-with-our-history?utm_term=.sxJ9wjkwz#.iv1PzEez3 accessed 12 May 2018.

Hopgood S, *Keepers of the Flame: Understanding Amnesty International* (Cornell University Press 2006).

Howard A, 'Open Government Experts Raise Concerns about "Mosaic Effect" in Open Data Policy' *E Pluribus Unum* (20 May 2013) http://epluribusunum.org/2013/05/20/open-data-mosaic-effect/ accessed 23 May 2018.

Howe J, 'The Rise of Crowdsourcing' *Wired* (2006) www.wired.com/wired/archive/14.06/crowds.html accessed 20 July 2018.

Human Rights Watch, 'Under Orders: War Crimes in Kosovo' (2001).

Human Rights Watch, '"They Want Docile": How Nursing Homes in the United States Overmedicate People with Dementia' (2018).

Information Systems Security Association, 'Code of Ethics' *Issa.Org* http://www.issa.org/?page=CodeofEthics accessed 9 May 2018.

International Committee of the Red Cross, 'Documenting Violations of International Humanitarian Law from Space: A Critical Review of Geospatial Analysis of Satellite Imagery during Armed Conflicts in Gaza (2009), Georgia (2008) and Sri Lanka (2009)' (30 June 2012) https://www.icrc.org/en/international-review/article/documenting-violations-international-humanitarian-law-space-critical/ accessed 17 December 2018.

International Criminal Court Office of the Prosecutor, Strategic Plan June 2012-2015 (11 October 2013).

International Criminal Court Office of the Prosecutor, Strategic Plan June 2016-2018 (16 November 2015).

International Criminal Court, 'Public redacted version of the "Prosecution's Fifth Request for the Admission of Evidence from the Bar Table", ICC-01/05-01/13-1498-Conf' (27 November 2015) https://www.icc-cpi.int/CourtRecords/CR2015_23087.PDF.

International Criminal Court, 'Public Redacted Version of Defence Response to Prosecution's Third Request for the Admission of Evidence from the Bar Table (ICC-01/05-01/13-1170)' (30 November 2015) https://www.icc-cpi.int/CourtRecords/CR2015_19327.PDF.

International Criminal Court 'Warrant of Arrest' (15 August 2017) https://www.icc-cpi.int/CourtRecords/CR2017_05031.PDF.

International Criminal Court, *Prosecutor v Ahmad Al-Faqi Al-Mahdi* Case Information Sheet, ICC-PIDS-CIS-MAL-01-08/16_Eng (20 March 2018).

International Criminal Tribunal for Rwanda, 'The Audio-Visual Digitization and Redaction Project of the ICTR' *ICTR Newsletter* (February 2010) 7–8 http://wwww.unictr.org/sites/unictr.org/files/news/newsletters/feb10.pdf.

Interview by the author with Kelly Matheson (23 October 23 2018) Berkeley, California.

Interview by the author with Brad Samuels (8 November 2018) Skype.

Ireland K and Bava J, 'The American Servicemembers' Protection Act: Pathways to, and Constraints on, U.S. Cooperation with the International Criminal Court' (Stanford Law School: Law and Policy Lab 2016) https://law.stanford.edu/publications/the-american-servicemembers-protection-act-pathways-to-and-constraints-on-u-s-cooperation-with-the-international-criminal-court/ accessed 29 December 2018.

Irving E, 'And So It Begins ... Social Media Evidence in an ICC Arrest Warrant' *Opinio Juris* (17 August 2017) http://opiniojuris.org/2017/08/17/and-so-it-begins-social-media-evidence-in-an-icc-arrest-warrant/ accessed 30 December 2018.

Isc2, 'Code of Ethics | Complaint Procedures | Committee Members' *Isc2.Org* https://www.isc2.org/Ethics# accessed 9 May 2018.

ISO/TC 46/SC 11 Archives/records management, 'Building a Metadata Schema: Where to Start', National Information Standards Organization (12 September 2008) https://committee.iso.org/files/live/sites/tc46sc11/files/documents/N800R1%20Where%20to%20start-advice%20on%20creating%20a%20metadata%20schema.pdf.

Johnson K, 'Why Bellingcat Wants to Teach Normal People to Be Investigative Journalists' *Throughcracks.Com* (31 March 2017) http://throughcracks.com/why-bellingcat-wants-to-teach-normal-people-to-be-investigative-journalists/ accessed 9 May 2018.

Kahng M and others, 'GAN Lab: Understanding Complex Deep Generative Models Using Interactive Visual Experimentation' *NoiseLab* (2018).

Kalliatakis G and others, 'Detection of Human Rights Violations in Images: Can Convolutional Neural Networks Help?' [2017] arXiv:1703.04103 [cs] http://arxiv.org/abs/1703.04103 accessed 11 December 2018.

Kayyali D and Althaibani R, 'Vital Human Rights Evidence in Syria Is Disappearing from YouTube' *WITNESS* (30 August 2017) https://blog.witness.org/2017/08/vital-human-rights-evidence-syria-disappearing-youtube/ accessed 29 December 2018.

Keck ME and Sikkink K, 'Transnational Advocacy Networks in International and Regional Politics' (1999) 51 International Social Science Journal 89

Kennedy D, 'International Human Rights Movement: Part of the Problem?' (2002) 15 Harvard Human Rights Journal 101

Kenyans for Peace with Truth and Justice, 'All Bark, No Bite? State Cooperation and the International Criminal Court' (December 2014).

Khan KAA, C Buisman, and C Gosnell, *Principles of Evidence in International Criminal Justice* (Oxford University Press 2010) https://global.oup.com/academic/product/principles-of-evidence-in-international-criminal-justice-9780199588923?cc=tr&lang=en& accessed 29 December 2018.

Knight G, 'Framework for the Definition of Significant Properties' *InSPECT Project* (5 February 2008) https://www.kdl.kcl.ac.uk/fileadmin/documents/digifutures/materials/preservation/DF09_prsrv_knight-definingSigProperties.pdf.

Knowles A, 'Tough Challenges in Cybersecurity Ethics' *Security Intelligence* (12 October 2016) https://securityintelligence.com/tough-challenges-cybersecurity-ethics/ accessed 9 May 2018.

Koenig A, 'The International Criminal Court at RightsCon: Upping Its Cyber Game' *HuffPost* (5 November 2014) https://www.huffingtonpost.com/alexa-koenig-/the-international-crimina_1_b_4936346.html accessed 29 December 2018.

Koenig A, 'The New Forensics: Using Open Source Information to Investigate Grave Crimes' (The Human Rights Center at the University of California, Berkeley, School of Law 2018) https://www.law.berkeley.edu/research/human-rights-center/publications/reports/new-forensics-using-open-source-information-investigate-grave-crimes/ accessed 29 December 2018.

Koenig A, '"Half the Truth Is Often a Great Lie": Deep Fakes, Open Source Information, and International Criminal Law' (2019) 113 American Journal of International Law 250.

Koenig A, Cody S, Crittenden C, and Stover E, 'Digital Fingerprints: Using Electronic Evidence to Advance Prosecutions at the International Criminal Court' (The Human Rights Center at the University of California, Berkeley, School of Law 2014).

Koenig A, Hiatt K, and Alrabe K, 'Access Denied? The International Criminal Court, Transnational Discovery, and The American Servicemembers Protection Act' (2018) 36(1) Berkeley Journal of International Law 1 http://www.berkeleyjournalofinternationallaw.com/vol-36-iss-1/access-denied-the-international-criminal-court-transnational-discovery-and-the-american-servicemembers-protection-act/ accessed 29 December 2018.

Koettl C, 'Citizen Media Research and Verification: An Analytical Framework for Human Rights Practitioners' (University of Cambridge Centre of Governance and Human Rights 2016)

Konopatzky S, 'Zentrale Personendatenbank' in R Engelmann (ed), *Das MfS-Lexikon. Begriffe, Personen und Strukturen der Staatssicherheit der DDR* (2011).

Krogh G von and Spaeth S, 'The Open Source Software Phenomenon: Characteristics that Promote Research' (2007) 16 Journal of Strategic Information Systems 236.

Kroker P, 'Emerging Issues Facing the Use of Remote Sensing Evidence for International Criminal Justice' Harvard Humanitarian Initiative (2014).

Lampros A, Rayner J, Cody S, and Koenig A, 'First Responders: An International Workshop on Collecting and Analyzing Evidence of International Crimes' (Human Rights Center 2014).

Land M, 'Democratizing Human Rights Fact-Finding' in P Alston and S Knuckey (eds), *The Transformation of Human Rights Fact-Finding* (Oxford University Press 2016)

Langston J, 'Lip-syncing Obama: New Tools Turn Audio Clips into Realistic Video' *University of Washington News* (11 July 2017) https://www.washington.edu/news/2017/07/11/lip-syncing-obama-new-tools-turn-audio-clips-into-realistic-video/ accessed 18 June 2018.

Lee TB, 'Open User Interfaces Suck' *Bottom-up* (15 November 2010) http://timothyblee.com/2010/11/15/open-user-interfaces-suck/ accessed 11 December 2018.

Legal Information Institute, Cornell Law School, https://www.law.cornell.edu/wex/adhesion_contract_%28contract_of_adhesion%29, accessed 14 May 2018.

Library of Congress, 'Sustainability Factors' Sustainability of Digital Formats: Planning for Library of Congress Collections https://www.loc.gov/preservation/digital/formats/index.html.

'"Link Rot" and Legal Resources on the Web: A 2014 Analysis' The Chesapeake Digital Preservation Group (2014) http://cdm16064.contentdm.oclc.org/cdm/linkrot2014 accessed 29 December 2018.

London-Lund International Human Rights Fact-Finding Guidelines, 2009. Produced by the International Bar Association and the Raoul Wallenberg Institute https://www.ibanet.org/Fact_Finding_Guidelines.aspx accessed 30 December 2018.

'Lubanga Judgment: The Prosecution's Investigation and Use of Intermediaries' *International Justice Monitor* (20 August 2012) https://www.ijmonitor.org/2012/08/lubanga-judgment-the-prosecutions-investigation-and-use-of-intermediaries/ accessed 29 December 2018.

Lunden I, 'News Corp Pays $25M for Storyful, Which Digs Up and Verifies News from Social Sites Like Twitter and Instagram' *TechCrunch* (20 December 2013) http://social.techcrunch.com/2013/12/20/news-corp-buys-storyful-for-25m-to-dig-up-verified-news-from-social-media-sites-like-twitter-and-instagram/ accessed 29 December 2018.

Makau M and Anghie A, 'What Is TWAIL?' Proceedings of the Annual Meeting (2000) 94 American Society of International Law 31.

Marcolini B, Cirillo C, and Koettl C, 'How Stephon Clark Was Killed by Police in His Backyard' *The New York Times* (23 March 2018) https://www.nytimes.com/video/us/100000005813009/stephon-clark-killed-police-sacramento.html accessed 30 December 2018.

Marr B, 'How Much Data Do We Create Every Day? The Mind-Blowing Stats Everyone Should Read' *Forbes* (21 May 2018) https://www.forbes.com/sites/bernardmarr/2018/05/21/how-much-data-do-we-create-every-day-the-mind-blowing-stats-everyone-should-read/ accessed 3 September 2018.

Martin B and Richards E, 'Scientific Knowledge, Controversy, and Public Decision-Making' in Sheila Jasanoff and others (eds), *Handbook of Science and Technology Studies* (Sage 1995).

Marwick AE and Caplan R, 'Drinking Male Tears: Language, the Manosphere, and Networked Harassment' *Feminist Media Studies* (26 March 2018) 1.

Matheson K, 'Video as Evidence Field Guide' *WITNESS* (2016) https://vae.witness.org/video-as-evidence-field-guide/ accessed 29 December 2018.

S McDonald, '"Racists Getting Fired" Exposes Weaknesses of Internet Vigilantism, No Matter How Well-Intentioned' *Washington Post* (2 December 2014) https://www.washingtonpost.com/news/morning-mix/wp/2014/12/02/racists-getting-fired-exposes-weaknesses-of-internet-vigilantism-no-matter-how-well-intentioned/ accessed 9 May 2018.

McPherson E, 'Technologies for Human Rights Witnessing: Humans, Machines and Ethics' 2019 (Working Paper).

McPherson E, 'Advocacy Organizations' Evaluation of Social Media Information for NGO Journalism: The Evidence and Engagement Models' (2015) 59 American Behavioral Scientist 124.

McPherson E, 'Digital Human Rights Reporting by Civilian Witnesses: Surmounting the Verification Barrier' in R Ann Lind (ed), *Produsing Theory in a Digital World 2.0: The Intersection of Audiences and Production in Contemporary Theory*, vol 2 (Peter Lang Publishing 2015).

McPherson R, Shokri R, and Shmatikov V, 'Defeating Image Obfuscation with Deep Learning' *ArXiv* (2016) https://arxiv.org/pdf/1609.00408v2.pdf accessed 20 August 2018.

Medina E, *Cybernetic Revolutionaries: Technology and Politics in Allende's Chile* (The MIT Press 2011).

Mégret F, 'Do Facts Exist, Can They Be "Found," and Does It Matter?' in P Alson and S Knuckey (eds), *The Transformation of Human Rights Fact-Finding* (OUP 2016) 30.

Miguel C, 'Visual Intimacy on Social Media: From Selfies to the Co-Construction of Intimacies Through Shared Pictures' (2016) 2 Social Media + Society 1.

Mihailidis P and Viotty S, 'Spreadable Spectacle in Digital Culture: Civic Expression, Fake News, and the Role of Media Literacies in "Post-Fact" Society' (2017) 61(4) American Behavioral Scientist 441.

Moyn S, *The Last Utopia: Human Rights in History* (Belknap Press 2012).

Museum of Obsolete Media, 'Video Format Timeline' http://www.obsoletemedia.org/digital-betacam/.

Myers, P. 2019. 'How to conduct discovery using open source methods' [Book details]

O'Donnell P, Crittenden C, Koenig A, and Stover E, 'Beyond Reasonable Doubt: Using Scientific Evidence to Advance Prosecutions at the International Criminal Court' (Human Rights Center 2012).

O'Flaherty K, 'YouTube Keeps Deleting Evidence of Syrian Chemical Weapon Attacks' *Wired UK* (26 June 2018) https://www.wired.co.uk/article/chemical-weapons-in-syria-youtube-algorithm-delete-video accessed 11 December 2018.

Okafor O, 'International Human Rights Fact-Finding Praxis: A TWAIL Perspective' in P Alston and S Knuckey (eds), *The Transformation of Human Rights Fact-Finding* (Oxford University Press 2016).

Olcott A, *Open Source Intelligence in a Networked World* (Bloomsbury 2012) https://www.bloomsbury.com/us/open-source-intelligence-in-a-networked-world-9781441166081/ accessed 29 December 2018.

Oluo I, 'Taking Down Bigots with their Own Weapons Is Sweet, Satisfying—and Very, Very Wrong' *Medium* (6 April 2015) https://medium.com/matter/actually-it-s-about-ethics-in-doxxing-1651b3deac77 accessed 9 May 2018.

Orentlicher D, 'International Norms in Human Rights Fact-Finding' in P Alston and S Knuckey (eds), *The Transformation of Human Rights Fact-Finding* (Oxford University Press 2016).

Orlavsky K and Roche-Mair A, *Evidence Matters in ICC Trials* (International Bar Association 2016).

Patrikarakos D, *War in 140 Characters: How Social Media is Reshaping Conflict in the Twenty-First Century* (Basic Books 2017) 3.

PBS News Hour, 'Internet History Is Fragile. This Archive Is Making Sure It Doesn't Disappear' (2 January 2017) https://www.pbs.org/newshour/show/internet-history-fragile-archive-making-sure-doesnt-disappear.

Perez S, 'Twitter Is Opening up Its Full Archive to the Broader Developer Community' *TechCrunch* (2 January 2018) https://techcrunch.com/2018/02/01/twitter-is-opening-up-its-full-archive-to-the-broader-developer-community/ accessed 29 December 2018.

Periscopic, 'U.S. Gun Deaths' (2013) https://guns.periscopic.com/ accessed 15 December 2018.

Phillips M and others, 'The NDSA Levels of Digital Preservation: An Explanation and Uses' [2013] National Digital Stewardship Alliance 7 http://www.digitalpreservation.gov/documents/NDSA_Levels_Archiving_2013.pdf.

Piracés E, 'The Future of Human Rights Technology' in M Land and J Aronson (eds), *New Technologies for Human Rights Law and Practice* (Cambridge University Press 2018).

President and the Prosecutor of the International Criminal Tribunal for Rwanda, 'Report on the Completion Strategy of the International Criminal Tribunal for Rwanda as at 5 November 2014' http://unictr.unmict.org/sites/unictr.org/files/legal-library/141119-completion-strategy-en.pdf.

President and the Prosecutor of the International Criminal Tribunal for Rwanda, 'Report on the Completion Strategy of the International Criminal Tribunal for Rwanda as at 5 May 2015' http://unictr.unmict.org/sites/unictr.org/files/legal-library/150515-completion-strategy-en.pdf.

'Prosecuting War Crimes of Outrage upon Personal Dignity Based on Evidence from Open Sources: Legal Framework and Recent Developments in the Member States of the European Union' Eurojust Genocide Network (2018) http://www.eurojust.europa.eu/doclibrary/genocide-network/KnowledgeSharing/Prosecuting%20war%20crimes%20of%20outrage%20upon%20personal%20dignity%20based%20on%20evidence%20from%20open%20sources%20(February%202018)/2018-02_Prosecuting-war-crimes-based-on-evidence-from-open-sources_EN.pdf.

Rainie SC, Rodriguez-Lonebear D, and Martinez A, 'Policy Brief: Data Governance for Native Nation Rebuilding' (2017) Native Nations Institute http://usindigenousdata.arizona.edu/sites/usindigenousdata/files/spotlight/files/policy_brief_data_governance_for_native_nation_rebuilding_version_2.pdf accessed 29 August 2018.

Ramcharan BG, 'Introduction', *International Law and Fact-Finding in the Field of Human Rights* (Martinus Nijhoff Publishers 1982).

rDisorder, 'Building a Data Pipeline from Scratch' *rDisorder* (9 August 2016) https://www.rdisorder.eu/2016/08/09/building-a-data-pipeline-from-scratch/ accessed 11 December 2018.

Report of the Chilean National Commission on Truth and Reconciliation (Notre Dame 2000).

Revolutionary Echoes from Syria (Hourriya 2016).

Riley J, *Understanding Metadata: What Is Metadata, and What Is It For? A Primer* (National Information Standards Organization 2017).

Robinson D, 'The Controversy over Territorial State Referrals and Reflections on ICL Discourse' (2011) 9 Journal of International Criminal Justice 355.

Rosen A, 'Erasing History: YouTube's Deletion of Syria War Videos Concerns Human Rights Groups' *Fast Company* (7 March 2018) https://www.fastcompany.com/40540411/erasing-history-youtubes-deletion-of-syria-war-videos-concerns-human-rights-groups accessed 29 December 2018.

Roth K, 'Defending Economic, Social and Cultural Rights: Practical Issues Faced by an International Human Rights Organization' (2004) 26 Human Rights Quarterly 63.

SalahEldeen HM and Nelson ML, 'Losing My Revolution: How Many Resources Shared on Social Media Have Been Lost?' in P Zaphiris, G Buchanan, E Rasmussen, and F Loizides (eds), *Theory and Practice of Digital Libraries, vol 7489* (Springer 2012) http://arxiv.org/abs/1209.3026 accessed 29 December 2018.

Schuppli S, 'Entering Evidence: Cross-Examining the Court Records of the ICTY' in Forensic Architecture (ed), *Forensis: The Architecture of Public Truth* (Sternberg Press 2014) http://susanschuppli.com/writing/entering-evidence/ accessed 29 December 2018.

Schwartz M, 'Who Killed the Kiev Protestors? A 3-D Model Holds the Clues' *The New York Times* (30 May 2018) https://www.nytimes.com/2018/05/30/magazine/ukraine-protest-video.html accessed 30 December 2018.

Seko Y, 'Internet Research Ethics: New Contexts, New Challenges—New (Re)Solutions?' *Spir.Aoir.Org* (2015) https://spir.aoir.org/index.php/spir/article/view/1069 accessed 12 May 2018.

Sharp DN, 'Human Rights Fact-Finding and the Reproduction of Hierarchies' in P Alston and S Knuckey (eds), *The Transformation of Human Rights Fact-Finding* (Oxford University Press 2016).

Shen T and others, '"Deep Fakes" Using Generative Adversarial Networks (GAN)' *NoiseLab* (2017).

'Shutdown Announcement' *Bambuser* (2017) https://go.bambuser.com/shutdown-announcement accessed 29 December 2018.

Silverman C, 'Journalists Are Criticizing Facebook for Its Data Collection. At the Same Time, They Often Use It to their Advantage' *BuzzFeed News* (11 April 2018) https://www.buzzfeednews.com/article/craigsilverman/facebook-cambridge-analytica-journalism-data-criticism-osint accessed 11 December 2018.

Smith S, 'The End of the Beginning for Storyful' *Irish Central* (4 February 2014) http://www.irishcentral.com/business/startups/The-End-of-the-Beginning-for-Storyful.html accessed 29 December 2018.

Stamboliyska R, 'Women in OSINT: Diversifying the Field, Part 1' *Bellingcat* (8 December 2015) https://www.bellingcat.com/resources/articles/2015/12/08/women-in-osint-diversifying-the-field/ accessed 18 August 2018.

Star SL, 'The Ethnography of Infrastructure' (1999) 43 American Behavioral Scientist 377.

Sterling J, 'For Syrian Activists, YouTube Is a Sword and Shield' *CNN* (15 March 2012) https://edition.cnn.com/2012/03/14/world/meast/syria-youtube-uprising/index.html accessed 4 June 2018.

Suarez-Villa L, *Globalization and Technocapitalism: The Political Economy of Corporate Power and Technological Domination by Luis Suarez-Villa* (Routledge 2012).

Syrian Archive, 'Database of Chemical Weapons Attacks' https://syrianarchive.org/en/collections/chemical-weapons/database.

Taylor A, *The People's Platform: Taking Back Power and Culture in the Digital Age* (Picador 2014) 220.

Townend J, 'Freedom of Expression and the Chilling Effect' in H Tumber and S Waisbord (eds), *The Routledge Companion to Media and Human Rights* (Routledge 2017).

The Cleaners (dir Hans Block and Moritz Riesewieck, Gebrueder Beetz Filmproduktion 2018).

Tufekci Z, 'Google Buzz: The Corporatization of Social Commons' *Technosociology* (2010) http://technosociology.org/?p=102 accessed 11 May 2018.

UN General Assembly, 'Universal Declaration of Human Rights' UN 217 (III) A (1948) https://www.un.org/en/universal-declaration-human-rights/ accessed 9 May 2018.

United Nations International Criminal Tribunal for the former Yugoslavia, 'Witness Statistics' http://www.icty.org/en/about/registry/witnesses/statistics accessed 14 December 2018.

United Nations Office on Drugs and Crime 'The Use of the Internet for Terrorist Purposes' (2012) https://www.unodc.org/documents/terrorism/Publications/Use_of_Internet_for_Terrorist_Purposes/ebook_use_of_the_internet_for_terrorist_purposes.pdf.

United States Office of the Director of National Intelligence, Intelligence Community Direction No 301, National Open Source Enterprise (11 July 2006).

University of Essex Human Rights Centre Clinic, *Introductory Guide to Open Source Intelligence and Digital Verification* (2017).

Vermaaten S, Lavoie B, and Caplan P, 'Identifying Threats to Successful Digital Preservation: The SPOT Model for Risk Assessment' (2012) 18 D-Lib Magazine http://www.dlib.org/dlib/september12/vermaaten/09vermaaten.html accessed 29 December 2018.

Wakabi W, 'Judges Admit NGO Reports into Evidence against Bemba' *International Justice Monitor* (8 July 2013).

Wattenberg M, 'GAN Lab: Understanding Complex Deep Generative Models using Interactive Visual Experimentation' *NoiseLab* (2018).

Weinberger S, 'Defence Research: Still in the Lead?' (2008) 451 Nature 390.

Werbach K and Hunter D, *For the Win* (Wharton Digital Press 2012).

Wexler R, 'Life, Liberty, and Trade Secrets: Intellectual Property in the Criminal Justice System' (2018) 70 Stanford Law Review 1343.

Whatmore SJ, 'Mapping Knowledge Controversies : Science, Democracy and the Redistribution of Expertise' (2009) 33(5) Progress in Human Geography 587

Whiting A, 'Dynamic Investigative Practice at the International Criminal Court' (2014) 76 Law and Contemporary Problems 163.

Wiener N, *Cybernetics, or Control and Communication in the Animal and the Machine* (MIT Press 1961).

Williams B, 'A Critique of Utilitarianism' in JJC Smart and B Williams, *Utilitarianism: For and Against* (Cambridge University Press 1973).

Wilson RA, 'Representing Human Rights Violations: Social Contexts and Subjectivities' in RA Wilson (ed), *Human Rights, Culture & Context: Anthropological Perspectives* (Pluto Press 1997).

Winner L, 'Do Artifacts Have Politics' (1980) 109 Daedalus 121.

YouTube, 'An Update on Our Commitment to Fight Terror Content Online' *YouTube Official Blog* (8 January 2017) https://youtube.googleblog.com/2017/08/an-update-on-our-commitment-to-fight.html accessed 29 December 2018.

YouTube, 'The Importance of Context' *YouTube Help* https://support.google.com/youtube/answer/6345162?hl=en.

Zheng H, Li D, and Hou W, 'Task Design, Motivation, and Participation in Crowdsourcing Contests' (2001) 15(4) International Journal of Electronic Commerce 57.

Zittrain JL, Albert K, and Lessig L, 'Perma: Scoping and Addressing the Problem of Link and Reference Rot in Legal Citations' *Social Science Research Network* (2013) SSRN Scholarly Paper ID 2329161 https://papers.ssrn.com/abstract=2329161 accessed 29 December 2018.

Index

Note: *For the benefit of digital users, indexed terms that span two pages (e.g., 52–53) may, on occasion, appear on only one of those pages.*
Figures and boxes are indicated by *f* and *b* following the page number